Studying Contemporary Western Society
Method and Theory

Margaret Mead

with an introduction to this edition by
William O. Beeman

Berghahn Books
New York • Oxford

Published in 2004 by

Berghahn Books

www.berghahnbooks.com

© 2004 The Institute for Intercultural Studies

Library of Congress Cataloging-in-Publication Data

A catalog record for this book is available
from the Library of Congress.

British Library Cataloguing in Publication Data

A catalogue record for this book is available
from the British Library.

Printed in the United States on acid-free paper.

CONTENTS

CONTENTS

Part Three
PERSPECTIVES ON CONTEMPORARY SOCIETY

SERIES PREFACE

To celebrate the one-hundredth anniversary of the birth of Margaret Mead, Berghahn Books and the Institute for Intercultural Studies are proud to reissue a series of classic works. Written or inspired by Dr. Mead, the materials in these seven volumes investigate the study of contemporary Western cultures.

Most of the world today knows Margaret Mead through her earliest publications, *Coming of Age in Samoa, Growing Up in New Guinea, Sex and Temperament,* and numerous others that examine the peoples of the South Pacific, New Guinea, and Indonesia. Two decades after these pioneering works appeared, Dr. Mead had significantly turned to the study of the contemporary societies of Europe and the United States. Through this later work she gained her widest public audience and arguably became the best-known cultural anthropologist who has ever lived. All of these works on contemporary culture, a number of which were originally issued in limited editions, have long been out of print.

The volumes in this series are being issued under the general title Margaret Mead: The Study of Contemporary Western Cultures. It is thought that this will provide a clear identification for the series. However, a more accurate title for the series might be Margaret Mead and Friends. Mead was a great collaborator; in the seven volumes that compose the series, dozens of her contemporaries are represented. One volume, *Themes in French Culture:A Preface to a Study of French Culture* for example, has as its primary author Mead's close collaborator, the eminent anthropologist Rhoda Métraux, with Mead as second author. Another volume combines Mead's study *Soviet Attitudes toward Authority* with Geoffrey Gorer and John Rickman's *The People of Great Russia,* upon which Mead's study heavily draws.

Mead as solo author is represented in her pioneering critique of American life, *And Keep Your Powder Dry*. The last three volumes in the series, likewise compilations of Mead's solo writings, examine the methodology of studying contemporary cultures, the study of the future, and visual culture—all of which have lasting relevance for today's researchers.

The first volume, *The Study of Culture at a Distance*, is in many ways a key to the entire series. This book, edited by Mead and Metraux, is a "manual" showing the research methodologies of the group of scholars that surrounded them in New York during the 1940s and 1950s. It could be argued that Mead—along with Metraux, Ruth Benedict, Gregory Bateson, and Geoffrey Gorer, among others— was instrumental in founding a true school of anthropological research at that time. More than 120 scholars were associated with this group during its five-year formal existence from 1947-52 as the Columbia University Research in Contemporary Cultures (RCC) project. The number is even larger when one considers that the impetus for the research began in a more informal manner in 1940. Organized by Ruth Benedict, efforts were made to contribute to cultural under- standing in order to meet the crisis of World War II. The Institute for Intercultural Studies was founded in 1944 to serve as a home for this research. Aside from Mead, Bateson, Benedict, Métraux, and Gorer, those whose names will be most familiar to anthropologists today are Conrad Arensberg, Alex Bavelas, Jane Belo, Ruth Bunzel, Erik Erikson, Paul Garvin, Ruth Landes, Eleanor Leacock, Vera Schwarz, Y. C. Wang, Eric Wolf, Martha Wolfenstein, and Mark Zborowski. Volumes two through seven of this series all derive in one way or another from the work of this research group. Had the McCarthy era not intervened in the 1950s to spread suspicion and doubt about the virtues of trying to understand foreign cultures on their own terms, this group might still be active today.

One of the most exciting aspects of bringing these works to life again has been to realize the remarkably modern quality of the methodologies developed by Mead and her associates during and immediately following World War II. This group was the first to adopt many of the now commonplace analytic tools of scholars who today identify themselves with cultural studies and media studies. The analysis of film, literature, and public imagery in particular was thor- oughly and exhaustively explored in this early research. Although the theoretical goals of Mead and her contemporaries often differed from those of many current students of culture, their methodologies and clear analytic vision could be emulated with much profit by today's researchers.

In fact, their contributions have inspired three generations of intellectuals, though often those who have been influenced by their work are unaware of the source of that influence. Whereas Mead and her colleagues are recognized as public celebrities of the past, among anthropologists today there is a vaguely patronizing attitude toward their work. In short, their intellectual achievements do not receive the attention they richly deserve. Why this is so is a poignant question. It is hoped that the reissue of these important works will help to remedy this oversight.

Acknowledgments and Dedication

I am pleased to acknowledge the help of the following people in making this series possible: Matilde Andrade, Mary Catherine Bateson, Shannon Carson, Wilton Dillon, Frank Farris, Shirley Gordon, Richard Gould, Katherine Grimaldi, Karen Iny, Philip Leis, Anne Brownell Sloane, and Mary Wolfskill and the staff of the Library of Congress Documents Division where the Margaret Mead Archives are currently housed. I would like to dedicate this series to my mother, Florence Lucille O'Kieffe Beeman, who, as a highly successful professional sociologist and social worker, led me to the works of Margaret Mead and her contemporaries, and ultimately to my own profession as an anthropologist.

William O. Beeman

INTRODUCTION
Margaret Mead: America's Premier Analyst
William O. Beeman

The United States has never needed the insights of Margaret Mead as much as in today's world. Born in 1901, Mead saw the outbreak and ending of two world wars, and more limited conflicts in Korea and Vietnam before her death in 1978. She also witnessed the McCarthy purges of the 1950s, the Cold War and the growing influence of American culture throughout the world, as well as the civil rights movement, the growth of women's rights, the sexual revolution and the burgeoning culture of youth in the West.

Throughout all of this century of change, she had one driving impulse in her work and her life. This was to bring cultural understanding to the people of the United States—understanding of the people of the world, but also understanding of America's own developing culture.

Few anthropologists today realize the pioneering role Margaret Mead played in the investigation of contemporary cultures. Although her professional reputation within anthropology rests on her work in Oceania, more than half of her professional life was devoted to the study of contemporary Western society—primarily the society of the United States.

Mead was clear about the need to bring the lessons of the field home to our own society. In her autobiography, *Blackberry Winter*, she makes this abundantly clear, even in her description of the writing of her first mass circulation book, *Coming of Age in Samoa*. Whereas she reported on her Samoan research in a number of professional venues, *Coming of Age* was designed to send a message to Americans—to get readers in the United States to consider their own society by contrasting it with that of the people of Samoa.

The same impetus prompted her other great works: *Growing Up in New Guinea, Male and Female, Sex and Temperament in Three Primitive Societies* and so many others. Always there was a clear message for the contemporary American reader, who was invited to make the contrast between American life and that of the varied societies Mead studied both alone and with her husbands and colleagues.

The World War II Watershed

World War II gave a new direction to Mead's work. She and her then husband, Gregory Bateson, were actively involved in the War effort. Before the United States became involved, they wrote a number of works early in the conflict dealing with American society—with the morale of troops, with family relations in times of violence and increasingly with matters that had an impact on American relations with other nations.

During the war, Mead seemed intent on serving as a kind of national morale officer. She wrote on nutrition, on the status of women during the war, on evolving family life, and on a host of topics that anticipated the end of the war. Her insights on rebuilding community after conflict seem to prefigure the Marshall plan in Europe and Japan. In this effort, she joined her friend and mentor, Ruth Benedict, who was keen to help the United States win the war effectively in any way she could. Benedict founded Columbia University Research in Contemporary Cultures—the precursor of modern think tanks, in New York. Active during and after the War, the RCC group tried to generate insights on the contemporary cultures of Europe and Asia that Americans needed desperately to know more about. Upon Benedict's untimely death in 1948, the leadership of the effort was assumed by Mead and Rhoda Métraux. Their methodology, which is outlined in a 'manual,' *The Study of Culture at a Distance* (reissued by Berghahn Books in 2000) shows how a group of seasoned researchers can study cultures if necessary, even without doing *in situ* fieldwork by using literature, film, interviews, child training manuals and a host of other secondary materials.

Having written the introduction to the reissued *Study of Culture at a Distance*, I will refer readers to that volume for much more detailed information on the effort. The RCC group later became the Institute for Intercultural Studies, which is still functioning today to carry out scholarly and public work in the spirit of the original group.

This volume collects and presents a variety of her essays on research methodology relating to contemporary cultures. Many of these essays were printed originally in limited circulation journals, research reports and books edited by others. They reflect Mead's continuing commitment to searching out methods for studying and extending the anthropologist's tools of investigation for use in complex societies. Essays on American and European societies, intergenerational relations, architecture and social space, industrialization, and interracial relations are included in this varied and exciting collection.

A Return to Roots

Although I have suggested above that Mead had taken a new direction in her work during and after World War II by turning to contemporary American society, in an important way, she was actually returning to her earliest work.

Occasionally when I have students studying the history of anthropology, I ask them to seek out the earliest published work by the greats of the field. Usually in a scholar's first article are contained the seeds of their life's work. Mead's first published paper, included in this volume, was "The Methodology of Racial Testing: Its Significance for Sociology" from the *American Journal of Sociology* in 1926. At Columbia Mead was involved with a number of research efforts, and in this paper she skewers the notion that racial groups can be differentiated on the basis of intelligence. This is not only a methodologically sound piece of work, but it makes a bold political statement at an early stage of American consciousness about racial attitudes. Perhaps we should expect nothing less from a student of Franz Boas, but Mead was off and running in her insistence that Americans needed to learn from anthropologists about the cultural limitations of their own understandings about humanity.[1]

Anthropologists often do not know that Mead received an M.A. degree in Psychology before turning to anthropology. She also was a teaching assistant in sociology, and had been exposed to this discipline through her mother, who was an advanced graduate student in that discipline. These influences may have informed both her interest in helping Americans understand their own society, and her rigorous methodological training. In a way, Mead brought data collection and analytic methods from the psychologist and sociologist's tool kit to her anthropological enterprise. In her pre-World War II work, she always revealed her analytic process with detailed profiles of her interviews, copious catalogs of her photographic materials, and thousands of file cards and documents, all meticulously cataloged. She wanted to make certain that future generations would be able to work from her data, and build on it.

She wanted both for the public to learn from her experience, and for future generations of anthropologists to learn how to educate the public. Because her lifelong career position was at the American

Museum of Natural History, she never had a primary university appointment. She did teach, of course. She taught at least one course a year at different institutions, pioneering the explicit teaching of field methods.[2] She worked occasionally with graduate students from Columbia University, but never sustained an ongoing program of graduate education. Therefore, her own personal 'craft' was conveyed primarily through her writings, and for ten years or so, through the workings of the RCC group.

She also provided advice to anyone who had the sense to ask her for it. An apocryphal story has an exasperated Senator asking her during a hearing, "Dr. Mead, is there anything on which you do not have an opinion?" There may well not have been. However, her boldness in addressing both the mighty of the earth, and the middle class American readers of *Redbook* magazine, stemmed from the same desire to bring cultural understanding to as many people as possible, for their own benefit.

Mead's Purpose

Mead captured the public's attention, I believe, because she was so obviously carrying out her work with their best interests in mind. She was in her earliest fieldwork, America's precocious little sister, then its older sister, then worldly aunt, and finally wise grandmother, sharing her experience, always staying one step ahead of Americans trying to grope their way through a changing world.

She believed profoundly that one's own experience was never adequate to develop a proper perspective on the world. In order to be an informed citizen, prepared for whatever might come, it was necessary to find a way to adopt the perspective of multiple 'others.'

These might be the 'others' of distant societies with profoundly different ways of living. They might be the 'others' of a different generation than one's own, or of a different race. This was an effective strategy for life, she believed, because she felt that people were capable of learning from each other. Interdependence was never seen as a weakness, but rather a great strength that allowed dissimilar people to combine strengths for the greater good of all of humanity.

Mead had an abiding optimism in the ability of members of any given society to solve their own problems, provided they can gain sufficient perspective on those problems. This assurance was a manifestation of her basic belief in human plasticity, an extension of the training she received at the hands of her mentor Franz Boas. The key to this process is engagement with the 'whole.' Human societies may solve problems by engaging with the whole of humanity. Human learning is facilitated by understanding that it is not just the mind that is trained, but the whole body. Problems in the natural world are best approached by understanding the relationship of human beings with their environment. Put all together, Mead believed that interrelationships between nations could be revised through a change in perspective. This question was of primary importance to her. As Mead pointed out, in speaking about human conflict:

> Various modifications of our present conceptions of the nation state are possible. The present definition predicates the state upon its absolute right and continuing ability to make war on other states. This definition, supported by properly developed sanctions and accepted definitions, could be changed to an emphasis on nationhood, in which the identity and power of each state was a function of the identity and power of all other nations. ... The definition of nations as owing their status to the existence and prosperity of other nations, their security to the security of other nations, and emphasis upon interdependence rather than independence, could result in concepts of nationhood replacing concepts of nationalism. (1968: 223)

She was fond of pointing out during the cold war that the Soviet Union was the most important guarantor of the safety of American children, and the United States government the most important guarantor of Soviet children.

Methodological Insights

When Mead began her career, anthropology was still very young as a discipline. Anthropologists were continually working to define the nature of anthropological praxis. In the first selection of articles for this volume, we have presented a selection of Mead's views of the discipline at various stages of her career. In fact, she wrote extensively on this topic, having produced not only a textbook, but also a reader. "Anthropology as a Discipline" is an article-length treatment of the subject, in which the familiar canons of cultural relativity, fieldwork, and anthropological praxis are systematically laid out. It is a conventional summary that would be comfortable in many classrooms today.

"Toward a Human Science" was a version of her presidential address for the American Association for the Advancement of Science, late in her life, published just two years before her death in 1976. Her teacher, Franz Boas, was the last anthropologist before her to hold the AAAS presidency, and it was undoubtedly a great honor for her to be elected to that office. In the address, she both situates anthropology firmly within the realm of the sciences, and extends the range of anthropology. She makes it clear that a truly human science should be addressing matters of contemporary importance. She cites Brown vs. the Board of Education, the launching of Sputnik, and a range of other highly contemporary issues. The purpose of the essay is to try to forge a new philosophical statement about a fusion of the *methods* of science with their *application* for the good of humanity. She additionally points out the essential importance of understanding how humans function in conjunction with each other as essential for developing an understanding of the universe. Science in her view, therefore, cannot take place outside of a closely examined human framework.

> As a first step in this direction I suggest that it is necessary to recognize that our knowledge of ourselves and of the universe within which we live comes not from a single source, but from two sources—from our capacity to explore human responses to events in which we and others participate through introspection and empathy, as well as from our capacity to make objective observations on physical and animate nature. (1976: 905)

She goes on to insist that these two areas of learning are complementary and supportive of each other, rather than antagonistic, and that just as the understanding of human processes is not easily incorporated into the science laboratory, the methods of the physical sciences can become "stultifying and dangerous" when applied to the investigation of human behavior.

In an effort to bring the anthropologist's methodologies closer to that of the laboratory scientist, she promoted a series of methodological advances in recording and documentation. At the beginning of the article, she notes that the presidential address was a multimedia presentation, and regrets that this cannot be reproduced in the printed version.

Two other papers in this initial section, "What is a Culture? What is a Civilization?" from Charles Madden's collection, *Talks with Social Scientists*, and "Anthropologist and Historian: Their Common Problems" grapple with the most fundamental concepts of anthropology, applied to complex contemporary societies. In sorting out the notion of culture and society, in this post World War II discussion, she grapples with the difference between those concepts and 'nation,' which in the context of the German state had gained an unpleasant overtone. Mead modulated the concept of 'nationhood' to emphasize the interdependency of nations as contingent cultural unit. Overall she champions the treatment of "each nation as a unit of dignity of its own," and makes the interesting observation that civilizations no

cle, "The Swaddling Hypothesis: Its Reception," she also is able to make a convincing case for looking at child-rearing practices such as this as important formative elements in the analysis of adult behavior and patterns of thought. She points out that in no case can a single custom be determinant of the cultural traits of a society, but taken in conjunction with a multiplicity of other factors, a complex of dominant factors can be seen as highly significant indicators of dominant cultural attitudes and practices.

Mead was deeply concerned with communication and communication processes, and two papers are included here that show how anthropologists consider these processes in complex modern societies.

In "Some Cultural Approaches to Communication Problems," Mead defines communication, explaining its different purposes in different cultures. She explores various methods of communicating, the diverse intentions and ensuing responses, such as prompting emotional response, getting attention, and formulating propaganda. Often in the United States, she claims, irresponsible people exploit communicative symbols for their own ends—showing how the image of Florence Nightingale was used in World War II and the post-war period. In "A Case History in Cross-National Communication," Mead applies her observation to the analysis of British and American opinions of each other around the period of World War II. Many of the difficulties experienced by the two cultures: perceptions of American 'boasting' and British 'arrogance' can be seen as differences in communication styles. A famous case study outlining differences in expectations regarding romantic relationships between British girls and American soldiers is one of the features of this article.

The final three papers in this section deal with the topic that Mead is perhaps best noted for, namely the study of children and youth. Robert Levine, in a lecture given at Brown University in honor of Mead's Centennial, credits her with the founding of a sub-field, "the anthropology of children and adolescence." This is certainly not hyperbole. Mead was deeply concerned that Americans learn about their own youth through contrast with other systems. In this manner, Americans could see the value in their own systems, but likewise the weaknesses, though having a point of contrast. For example, emphasis on independence in youth yields self-reliance, but at the price of uncertainty, rebelliousness and anxiety.

In "Adolescence in Primitive and Modern Society: The New Generation," Mead extends the main finding of her immensely popular book, *Coming of Age in Samoa*. The distinction between 'primitive' and modern society vanishes when we consider the period surrounding puberty as "the growth period of personality," the form and nature of which will vary from culture to culture. Seen this way, 'adolescence' becomes a specific Western cultural category—a function of complex society, not merely of the human life cycle. She points out in "Our Educational Emphasis in Primitive Perspective," that our educational system, emphasizing novelty and innovation, contrasts with the traditional emphasis in less technologically advanced societies on the need to learn that which is fixed and traditional.

> Today, owing to the meeting and mingling of peoples among whom superiority was claimed by one as over against another, our concepts of education have been shaped by the will to teach, convert, colonize or assimilate adults. From the observation of this process in the next generation, we have come also to believe in the power of education to create something new, not merely perpetuate something old. But not until the dogma of superiority of race over race, nation over nation, class over class is obliterated can we hope to combine the primitive idea of the need to learn something old and the modern idea of the possibility of making something new. (1943:633)

In "Early Childhood Experience and Later Education in Complex Cultures," she again returns to the underlying theme of Gorer's swaddling hypothesis. Underscoring the basic tenets of psychology and psychiatry, Mead once again points out the interplay of cultural practice and character formation through a careful examination of childrearing practices. Here she reminds readers that the ways that members of Western cultures rear their children are distinct cultural practices, reflective of the cultures in which they occur.

Perspectives on American Life

In the final section of this volume, I collect a few of the best of the papers Mead wrote about American life and its cultural dynamics. Mead published more than a hundred studies of every aspect of life in the United States following World War II, from food habits to children's playground equipment. The range of her interests was astonishing. In every case she provides some cultural insight which informs the reader of some twist or wrinkle in a commonplace aspect of daily life that is generally unanticipated.

In "From Plight to Power: Youth as a Political and Economic Force," Mead virtually defines the baby-boom generation. She anticipates the effect this segment of the population will have on American society in the following decades. In "Religion in the Melting Pot: Religion and our Racial Tensions," she anticipates the tension between organized religious groups and progress in racial equality. Her sketch of the American family in "The Contemporary American Family as an Anthropologist Sees it," prefigures the complex move away from the basic nuclear family, and the range of activities and forces pulling the members of the modern family apart. Two prescient papers on sexuality in the United States could have been written by Foucault. "Sex and Censorship in Contemporary Society," explains why Americans feel compelled to enforce moral standards over literature, film and other artistic products. "Sexual Behavior: An Anthropologist Looks at the Kinsey Report," is a brilliant attack on the report itself, much in the same way that Mead attacked standardized intelligence testing for racial groups and others that might have varying cultural standards as minority communities within the majority. Finally, in "Jealousy: Primitive and Civilized," Mead shows that feelings of jealousy, far from being personal emotional expressions, are in fact conditioned by social and cultural institutions. Just as earlier in her career, she debunked the idea that adolescence necessarily leads to trauma, so in this discussion does she demonstrate that jealousy, as we understand it, is by no means universal for humankind.

Compiling these papers for modern readers was a pleasure, but it was also difficult because there were so many others that might have been included. Many of the very best papers appeared in surprising places. Mead felt she had a mission and a message. She was eager to speak to many audiences and could not wait for the tedious process of professional peer review for everything she wrote. There is no question of her excellence as a scholar, or the professional respect with which her work was regarded. Although there is hardly a year of her life when she did not publish in the standard peer-reviewed professional journals of anthropology, she was as likely to publish something about which she cared in the *School Lunch Journal* , *The Futurist, The Saturday Review,* or through her monthly column in *Redbook* magazine, written with her friend and colleague Rhoda Métraux.

Never boring, she spoke to her contemporaries in a way that would help them, but she also spoke to a whole generation of anthropologists, psychologists, social scientists and others who needed to understand contemporary complex societies as intensely as they needed to understand less-developed societies.

Mead's kind of understanding is as vital as ever—perhaps more so. Suddenly the United States is the world's sole superpower. It no longer faces the rivalries it did as an underdog fighter earlier in the 20th Century. Now the opposite problem exists—becoming a bully. As a result, the U.S. is undergoing an identity crisis on the same scale as at the beginning of World War II when Mead turned her primary attention to the study of contemporary western cultures. It is my hope that rereading her vibrant work will rekindle the spirit that brought so much wise understanding to the American People.

The United States bears a special responsibility in the quest for world peace and well being. With an understanding of how cultural predilections shape behavior, it may eventually find itself fit to operate in the world in a worthy manner. As Mead said at the end of *And Keep Your Powder Dry*, first published in 1942:[3]

> As a people it has taken us almost four centuries to weld ourselves into what is now 'almost' a united nation. Much of what we have accomplished has come about through the pressures of the outside world. Strong, wealthy, and powerful, we must now turn toward the rest of the world ready to accept a responsibility that is bound not to the duties, the loyalties, and hopes of earlier years, but to the whole world, the only world in which we can act today and carry out our highest hopes for the future. We have no other. (2000: 197).

Notes

1. Mead continued her interest in disproving racial inequality all of her professional life. She served on an the AAAS Committee on Science in the Promotion of Human Welfare, which issued a report entitled "Science and the race problem" which denounced the use of questionable data to 'prove' racial inequality in the United States. Her committee was attacked for their report, but they defended themselves admirably in the journal Science in 1963 (Commoner, et. al. 1963).
2. Her syllabi are on file at the Library of Congress along with her other documents.
3. The book was reissued in 1965 and again in 2000, in each case with new introductions.

Reference

Commoner, Barry; Brode, Robert B., Byaerly, T.C.; Coale, Ansley J.; Edsall, John T.; Frank, Lawrence K.; Mead, Margaret; Roberts, Walter Orr; and Wolfle, Dael 1964 Science and the Race Problem (reply to Henry E. Garrett and Wesley C. George) Science, New Series 143: 3609 (February 28) p. 915.

TOWARDS A HUMAN SCIENCE*

The ceremonial character of the annual address by the president of the American Association for the Advancement of Science makes it impossible for me to disassociate myself as a person, a woman, and a cultural anthropologist from the office. However deeply I may feel as an individual, I must be wary because inevitably whatever I say will reflect in some manner, for better or worse, not only on the 116,000 members of our organization but also on the far greater number of American scientists who do not yet feel sufficiently strongly about the objectives of the Association to become members (1).

The principal topic to which I shall devote myself is the significance of multisensory experience and the value of specific kinds of instrumentation in the development of a fully human science. My spoken address was a multimedia presentation in which I used still photographs, films, and tapes to illuminate the discussion. It was accompanied by a translation into the sign language of the deaf as a way of expressing the concern of the AAAS for the handicapped and my own wish to demonstrate the necessity of always taking into account the multisensory nature of human functioning. In this written version of my address, I can include only a small number of illustrative photographs, which will cross-reference to the oral presentation, but in addition I have asked to abandon tradition and include references to provide background for the points I wish to make.

The ceremonial aspect of the occasion also has advantages. It has long been customary for presidents to draw on the thinking of their predecessors in office as a most felicitous way of linking past and present and also significant themes in different disciplines. In deference to this custom I have chosen two of my predecessors whose addresses show a progression in the definition of the role of the Association as each of them looked to a future we are still in the process of attaining.

As the first I have chosen Franz Boas, the last anthropologist to hold this office, in 1931, and my professor. Franz Boas was the founder

*Originally published on March 5, 1976 in *Science Magazine*, volume 191, issue 4230.

of American anthropology as a scientific discipline and also one of the first social scientists to address himself fearlessly to the problem of race as an issue on which anthropologists must take the central responsibility. Characteristically, in his address, "The Aims of Anthropological Research" (2), Boas confined his remarks to the role of anthropology and he concluded that "by a study of the universality and variety of cultures anthropology may help us to shape the future course of mankind."

As my second predecessor I have chosen Warren Weaver whose presidential address, "Science and People" (3), was given in 1955 in Atlanta, only a few months after the Supreme Court, in Brown *vs.* the Board of Education of Topeka, ruled that all segregation in public schools is "inherently unequal" and denies black pupils in segregated schools equal protection of the law as guaranteed by the Fourteenth Amendment. At that moment of transition to a new era for Americans, Warren Weaver declared that "science belongs to all the public opinion," and William Faulkner, a great artist, on the need for "the scientist and the humanitarian" to save our dream of our civilization. It was at that same Atlanta meeting that a committee on Science and Society was established which later was commissioned to pursue the goal of "science in the promotion of human welfare"—a goal that has become increasingly salient in the work of the Association over the past 20 years.

Weaver discussed the dangers that arise when the public attitude toward science combines "mistrust, fear, and overestimation" and scientists are regarded "one-third of the time as amusing but beneficial eccentrics, one-third of the time as sorcerers, and one-third of the time as irresponsible rascals" and "careless dabblers with danger." He attributed this negative attitude principally to the belief, shared by many scientists and the public alike, that the ideas of science are too difficult for the ordinary citizen to grasp. The pervasiveness of such beliefs about science and scientists among Americans, particularly young, school-age Americans, was abundantly documented in a study which Rhoda Métraux and I carried out on behalf of the AAAS and reported in 1957 (4). The findings showed not only what the public response to science and scientists was then but also predictively how Americans, in spite of (perhaps also because of) intensified exposure to formal science education, would continue to respond in years to come. And in 1957, when the Soviet Union launched Sputnik, outspoken black Americans bitterly attributed the American failure to be first to the waste of talent resulting from segregated education (5). Science, politics, and ethics were merging in a civil rights movement.

ceptively. The limiting case, then, is the human neonate who cannot yet communicate except through expressive sounds and movements. Nathan Kleitman once accused me of anthropomorphism when I ventured an interpretation of the behavior of human infants.

I wish to emphasize in the midstream of my argument that I am here concerned with the form of knowing that we call science—that is, with knowledge that can be arrived at and communicated in such a way that it can be shared with other human beings, is subject to their independent verification, and is open to further exploration by investigation in accordance with agreed-upon rules. True, Warren Weaver pleaded for a recognition that every man, to the extent that he makes a correct analysis of some physical situation, is "a good scientist." In this sense Weaver said "even primitive men were scientists, and in certain aspects of accurate and subtle observation it would probably be hard to beat the ancient skilled hunter." In this view modern science involves mainly an increasing refinement of procedures rather than the emergence of new procedures, different in kind. However, I am not including in this discussion the accumulation of knowledge, either of the natural world, animate and inanimate, or of human behavior which is not a conscious, purposefully directed activity. We may well speak admiringly of the knowledge that a primitive people has of the stars or of the animals they hunt or of the therapeutic properties of plants, but the mere acquisition of this knowledge, valuable as it is, and its transmission from members of one generation to the next, is not the practice of science in the sense I am using the term (7). There are, I believe, contextual differences between the proto-scientific activities of the ancient hunter—as well as those of the ancient plant gatherer—and the scientist's systematic, organized pursuit of knowledge.

The capacity of human beings to observe and understand and systematize their knowledge of the behavior of other human beings has proceeded discontinuously, as Boas pointed out, but progressively as human beings have organized themselves into larger, more complex social units and have included a larger portion of humankind within their definition of humanity. But as long as the understanding of human behavior was not arrived at by methods that included systematic recording in ways that can be shared and tested, I would not speak of a human science. In the past, each great integrator of knowledge had to rely chiefly on his own capacity as a whole human being to observe the behavior and speculate about the past of members of his own species in ways that were—and are—unique to the human mind and dependent on the development of human culture. In more complex cultures, sharing the same traditions and education opened

them as straw men to be knocked down. On the contrary, I want to emphasize how very difficult it was to achieve such clarity about the relationships between theory and existing methods. Both the methods of science and the conflict of views about their more general applicability were developed within Euro-American culture and it is never easy to break out of such deeply felt but culturally bound conceptions. But because of the clarity which has been achieved I believe we can move from conflict toward a new kind of integration.

As a first step in this direction I suggest that it is necessary to recognize that our knowledge of ourselves and of the universe within which we live comes not from a single source but, instead, from two sources—from our capacity to explore human responses to events in which we and others participate through introspection and empathy, as well as from our capacity to make objective observations on physical and animate nature.

It is also necessary to recognize that the inappropriate extension into the physical world of human beings' understanding of themselves harms rather than enhances the development of the kind of objective understanding that we call science. Equally we must now come to realize that the extension into the human world of the methods of the physical sciences can be stultifying and dangerous. It is only when we do recognize that there are two distinct complementary—rather than antagonistic—sources of knowledge that we can fully develop methods appropriate to each and consider how such methods can serve to support and reinforce each other.

Within this wider context, introspection which becomes anthropomorphism is a vice when the problem has to do with the nature of the relationship between the sun and the moon, and is decreasingly useful in studies of the behavior of other primates, mammals, invertebrates, and finally, viruses. But disciplined introspection and empathy are essential to the study of the unique characteristics of humankind. The wonder and curiosity of early human beings began to produce two kinds of knowledge. Observation of relatively stable physical phenomena, such as the tides, the seasons, and the movements of heavenly bodies, allowed men to build up knowledge of the natural world. But human beings also have the capacity to understand their fellows because they are sufficiently like themselves so that attention to their own internal states provides information about the internal states of others. Obviously, such understanding is enhanced by language and the development of appropriate and accurate vocabularies through which people can communicate to one another what they feel, how they perceive others and themselves, and how they conceptualize internal and external events proprioceptively and extero-

help to a real understanding." He also considered that "moral behav-ior, *except in so far as it is checked by increased understanding of social needs* [emphasis added], does not seem to fall into any order."

He spoke with the greatest certainty when he discussed race and the indispensability of founding "the study of the race as a whole on that of the component genetic lines and of their variants, and on inquiries into the influence of the environment and selection upon bodily form and function. The race must be studied not as a whole but in its genotypical lines as developing under varying conditions" (6).

Boas, in 1931, and Weaver, in 1955, selected the biological field as the human domain within which the methods of science can be applied—but only within limits. And both men placed the study of man in a context which to a degree is outside the domain of science in its more usual sense as a pursuit in which the aim is to establish regularities. Boas denied the possibility of arriving at any generalized conclusions "that will reduce the data of anthropology to a formula which may be applied to every case, explaining its past and predict-ing its future. ... The phenomena of our science are so individualized, so exposed to outer accident that no set of laws could explain them. It is as in any other science dealing with the actual world surrounding us. For each individual case we can arrive at an understanding of its relation to inner and outer forces, but we cannot explain its individ-uality in the form of laws."

In addition, both men placed those human activities which are least dependent on the universals of physical functioning and geo-graphical limitation—art and the humanities—essentially in another realm, one which Weaver feels that science "must thoroughly respect and perhaps should envy."

Both men—as scientists speaking a generation apart and repre-senting quite different fields of science—visualize scientific method as it originated in the attempt "to understand and control the forces of physical nature" and both emphasize its limited usefulness in the search for a fuller understanding of human beings. Boas points to the discontinuities inherent in the historical process through which vari-eties of culture have developed, whether in contact with other cul-tures or in isolation; Weaver refers to confusing instabilities and the consequences of small causes. And, finally, both men advocate humil-ity. Weaver castigates the arrogance of the physical scientist who is convinced that the methods of science can be applied to all problems and Boas expressly describes limits to the usefulness of these methods in informing us about the nature of man.

My intention in discussing in some detail the comparable posi-tions taken by my two illustrious predecessors has not been to treat

In his address Weaver asked what had been "man's major successes" and grouped what "men have really done well" in two pairs:
the understanding of physical and organic nature; and the development of ethical principles and the enrichment of life through the
arts. "Probably the most conspicuous, the most universally recognized, and the most widely applied success," he said, "lies in the
understanding and control of the forces of physical nature. Coupled
with this, I would place the progress that has been made—even
though it is but a start—in the understanding of organic nature."

He listed certain characteristics of physical nature which had
made possible the success of the physical sciences as loose coupling,
the possibility of studying it "bit by bit, two or three variables at a
time, and treating these bits as isolated." In contrast, what makes
progress in studying animate nature so difficult, he suggested, is that
it "presents highly complex and highly coupled systems. ... It takes a
lot of variables to describe a man, or for that matter a virus; and you
cannot often usefully study these variables two at a time. Animate
nature also exhibits very confusing instabilities, as students of history,
the stock market, or genetics are well aware."

Franz Boas in his presidential address 25 years earlier stated what
he believed to be the limitations of the study of man in terms of the
methods of that day. Like Warren Weaver, Boas differentiated between
those activities of humankind which are broadly cumulative in
nature—that is, knowledge and invention—and other activities
which he regarded as essentially noncumulative.

Boas had concluded that both human biology and human culture must be studied historically. But he recognized that there is "one
fundamental difference between biological and cultural data which
makes it impossible to transfer the methods of the one science to the
other. Animal forms develop in divergent directions, and an intermingling of species that have once become distinct is negligible in
the whole developmental history. It is otherwise in the domain of culture. Human thoughts, institutions, activities may spread from one
social unit to another. ... Undoubtedly there are dynamic conditions
that mould in similar forms certain aspects of the morphology of
social units. Still we may expect that these will be overlaid by extraneous elements that have no organic relation to the dynamics of
inner change. This makes the re-construction of cultural history easier than that of biological history, but it puts the most serious obsta-
cles in the way of discovering the inner dynamics of change."

Boas expressed his feeling that because of the extreme complexity of cultural phenomena, such general laws as can be established
"will be necessarily vague and ... so self-evident that they are of little

the way to an understanding of the insights of a philosopher, a historian, or an ethical leader who reported his observations in a shared language or demonstrated his ideas through artifacts or great works of art familiar to everyone involved. But just as in communication among physical scientists, more than a shared natural language is essential.

Human speech itself was the first condition for shared understanding, and the recognition that languages can be learned and are not intrinsic to any specific bodily form, skin color, or geographical location made possible the first objective understanding of the nature of culture (8). It is significant that Boas and his early students made extensive use of written records of oral communications—that is, chunks of organized speech, folktales, descriptions of procedure such as cooking recipes or the formulas of love and hunting magic, and other complexly organized materials. Once phonetic transcription had been invented and interlinear translations had been made, all these materials became accessible and, even without a knowledge of the particular language, intelligible to other students. Even today, Claude Lévi- Strauss, working with essentially impoverished records—interlinear texts at best—has captured the fascinated attention of anthropologists and lay persons alike (9).

As long as we lacked photographic and acoustical techniques of recording, we were dependent for a scientific approach to the whole domain of human behavior on fragmenting methods of quantification of evoked behavior (evoked, for example, by questionnaires) or of records of partial observations coded in ways that give the results an illusory appearance of science. In some types of studies human individuals were—and still are—treated like parts of an aggregate and in others like entities that can be understood only through culture-bound tests of isolated traits like speed or accuracy of response.

Today, certain of the most important concepts of the human sciences have failed to enter constructively into the thinking of many scientists and lay persons principally because full understanding depends on the completion of an apprenticeship training of a peculiarly intense kind, such as the experience of a tedious and time-consuming procedure like psychoanalysis *(10)* or the experience of prolonged actual immersion in the life of more than one unfamiliar culture *(11)*. Formerly, anthropologists were trained in techniques of what was rather vaguely known as "participant observation." For, unlike the data of the physical sciences which are required to be of a kind that can be replicated and reexamined, the data of the human sciences are in great part derived from time-consuming shared experiences that cannot be replicated.

True, many of the findings of physical science are accepted uncritically by those who do not have any real comprehension of the nature of the scientific enterprise. But there is still a tremendous difference between the very precise techniques of communication—and of sharing experience—which have been developed in the physical sciences and the inevitably imprecise communication by the human scientist who has been dependent on words alone for communicating his observations. While he is studying an individual or the members of a culture, the human scientist observes thousands—or more likely hundreds of thousands—of items of behavior; the greatest difficulty comes when he must condense his observations into words alone— words that may very well convey meanings alien to the experience described. He may make what he considers to be a bare verbal statement, for example: "the men put on their masks and their ornaments … and thence sally forth to dance and perform before the women" (12). Yet such a statement inevitably evokes discrepant and irrelevant images in the mind of the reader who is unfamiliar with the Iatmul or any other Papua New Guinea culture.

There is the added difficulty that pencil-and-paper recording was at best selective and depended not only on the trained awareness of the observer but also on the speed with which he could record what he experienced and, to a large extent, on his having highly developed verbal skills, including the ability to translate from the various types of linguistic and nonverbal communications of one culture into the accepted literary language of another.

In the conscious pursuit of knowledge about the natural world on the one hand, and of knowledge about human beings on the other, progress has depended on the development of more refined techniques of collecting and analyzing data, that is, on the development of instruments that extend our human capacities to observe, record, and reproduce data and to carry out the various functions of analysis (13). In the physical sciences, great advances have come about through the development of reliable instruments that permit observations of the very small and the very distant, instruments that can record in accurate codes various forms of sensory experience and instruments that make possible various kinds of measurement that are independent of the human observer. In the human sciences the principal emphasis in training has been on teaching the human scientist how to function as a very complex instrument, to use his body's own sensory equipment as a multifaceted recording device. The next advances have come as we have acquired forms of instrumentation that record and later allow for the replication of the observation without the intervention of verbal description. Instrumentation which makes possible the recording in full detail of auditory (14) and visual (15) aspects of events by means of tapes, still photographs, and films can provide us with records of nonrecurrent phenomena (16) so that we can juxtapose events separated in time and space and provide material for later comparison and analysis by others who did not share in making the original observations.

In effect, the basic techniques of observation and recording in the physical and the human sciences are complementary. The human scientist has had to learn how to relate self-knowledge of him- or herself as a multisensory being with a unique personal history as a member of a specific culture at a specific period to ongoing experience and how to *include* as far as possible this disciplined self-awareness in observations on other lives and in other cultures (17). In contrast, the physical scientist has had to learn how to *exclude* as far as possible the effects of temperament, individual life experience, and culture on his observations and interpretations of data (18). Without appropriate instrumentation neither can go beyond certain limits or communicate to others what has been observed.

It is in the sciences of living things that we find the greatest confusion but also the clearest demonstrations of the ways in which the two kinds of observation—the observation of human beings by human beings and of physical nature by human beings—meet. One group of students of living beings have attempted to adopt as far as possible the methods of the physical sciences through the use of controlled experiments, the deliberate limitation of the number of variables to be considered, and the construction of theories based on the findings arrived at by these means. The other group, taking their cues from our human capacity to understand through the observation of natural situations, have developed their methods from a natural history approach in which the principal reliance is on the integrative powers of the observer of a complex, nonreplicable event and on the experiments that are provided by history and by animals living in a particular ecological setting.

Students of human behavior who derive their methods of obtaining data from the physical sciences have constructed ingenious puzzle boxes and mazes and artificial stimulus situations. In research carried out by means of these techniques, the behavior of experimental animals and, even more, the behavior of human subjects has been fragmented in increasingly refined ways in order that aspects of behavior may be studied "bit by bit, two or three variables at a time, and treating these bits as isolated"—that is, by using in their investigations methods which, as Weaver pointed out, were eminently successful in studies of physical nature.

In research carried out by the other group of human scientists, the basic methods of observing whole events as whole human beings have now been supplemented by vastly improved techniques of recording and preserving recordings of whole events (19), techniques of keeping intact whole archeological sites or the full record of elicited materials—first in the form of verbatim linguistic and folklore texts and finally within the last quarter-century through the use of actual visual and sound recordings.

I would argue that it is not by rejecting one or another but by appropriately combining the several methods evolved from these different types of search for knowledge that we are most likely in the long run to achieve a kind of scientific activity that is dominated neither by the arrogance of physical scientists nor by the arrogance of humanists who claim that the activities which concerned them cannot meaningfully be subjected to scientific inquiry.

New forms of cooperation among scientists are already prefigured in the new field of ethology which draws on methods of research with many different origins. Two sets of interdisciplinary conferences for which ethology provided the central focus—the four annual conferences on child development, 1953-1956 (20) and the five annual conferences on group processes, 1954-1958 (21)—illustrate the fruitfulness of using methods originally developed far apart and for very diverse purposes. For example, Konrad Lorenz was persuaded to apply the case history method of psychological study to the behavior of individual geese (22) and Helen Blauvelt used her experience with observing newborn kids and lambs to discover that newborn human infants have the capacity to propel themselves up the human body (23). Discussions of ritual were illuminated by comparisons between species-typical ritual behavior in birds and culturally transmitted rituals in human societies (22). Electroencephalographic explorations of the brain threw light on discussions of the relationship between imagery and human creativity (24). The experimental use of models was complementary to studies of color preferences and imprinting processes among birds (25). I believe that ethology will continue to be in the forefront of innovation and interplay in new kinds of scientific creativity (26).

In conclusion I wish to touch briefly on certain more general social implications of our advances in the human sciences.

There are, I believe, important implications for education, which today oscillates uneasily between emphasizing mastery and freedom from restraint discipline and spontaneity, conformity and originality of the kind usually associated with the arts and religious inspiration. These dichotomies are expressions of older culturally limited conceptions of the human person. What we need now is to develop systems of education that are consonant with human development—in which precision is cultivated in relation to spontaneous multisensory involvement and the disciplined use both of the mind in the usual sense and of the whole body in the light of our new knowledge about the participation of the whole body in thinking as well as in overt action (27) and in fostering the growing child's undistorted sense of its own body (28).

The advances in the human sciences also make possible far more integrated picture of evolutionary and historical human development and of our place in the cosmos (29). C.H. Waddington and Julian Huxley have discussed the evolutionary significance of an ethical sense (30). A cosmic sense has been identified as the biological root of human curiosity about the universe (31). Niels Bohr has pointed out the relevance of complementarity in the fields of psychology and physics (32). And finally, the necessity of including the whole of humankind in planetary socioeconomic arrangements is underwritten by our definitive knowledge that all branches of the human race have comparable capacities for cultural growth (33).

The recently recognized need to shift away from a concentration on land and water boundaries that must be jealously maintained and defended at all costs toward a concern for the earth's atmosphere that must be protected has created a situation in which it is very desirable—and, indeed, very urgent—to invent new, more appropriate political forms (34). We shall have to draw on the resources of all the sciences in order to deal constructively with the chaotic but irreversibly interdependent planetary community. And we shall need still newer kinds of instrumentation—macroscopes that can simply without distorting the complexity of our knowledge of the biosphere and the cosmos within which a recognition of all disciplined human endeavor must now take place (35).

MARGARET MEAD
1976

Notes

1. The objectives of the American Association for the Advancement of Science are to further the work of scientists, to facilitate cooperation among them, to improve the effectiveness of science in the promotion of human welfare, and to increase public understanding and appreciation of the importance and promise of the methods of science in human progress.
2. F. Boas, *Science* 76, 605 (1932).
3. W. Weaver, *ibid.* 121, 1255 (1955).
4. M. Mead and R. Métraux, *ibid.* 126, 384 (1957).
5. R. Metraux, unpublished research on first responses to Sputnik (1957).
6. This principle is one which many contemporary human scientists are far from understanding or taking into account in research on questions of race. It is common practice in such studies to compare, for example, a hybrid group of Americans of known or imputed part African ancestry with some other mixed group of Americans of no known African ancestry and then to attribute differences in the abilities of the two groups to race. This kind of confusion is not limited to physical scientists but is shared by some biologists and psychologists and even some anthropologists (33) [A. R. Jensen, *Harvard Educ. Rev.* 39, 1 (1969)].
7. J. Brown, *Science* 189, 38 (1975).
8. M. Mead, *Continuities in Cultural Evolution* (Yale Univ. Press, New Haven, Conn., 1964).
9. C. Levi-Strauss, *Mythologique.* (Plon, Paris, 1964-1971). vols. 1-4.
10. I. Ramzy, *Int. J. Pychoanal.* 55, 543 (1974).
11. R. Naroll and R. Cohen, Eds., *A Handbook of Method in Cultural Anthropology* (Natural History Press, Garden City, N. Y., 1970).
12. G. Bateson, *Naven* (Cambridge Univ. Press, Cambridge, 1936; ed. 2, Stanford Univ. Press, Stanford, 1958).
13. R. L. Birdwhistell, in *International Encyclopedia of the Social Science.*, D. L. Sills, Ed. (Macmillan and Free Press, New York, 1968). vol. 8, pp. 379- 385.
14. A. Lomax, Ed., *Folk Song Style and Culture* (AAAS, Washington, D.C.. 1968); *Science* 177, 228(1972).
15. P. Hockings, Ed., *Principles of Visual Anthropology* (Mouton, The Hague, Netherlands, 1975).
16. E. R. Sorenson, *Science* 186, 1079 (1974).
17. M. Mead, *Semiotica* 1, 13 (1969); T. A. Sebeok, A. S. Hayes, M. C. Bateson, Eds.. *Approaches to Semiotics* (Mouton, The Hague, Netherlands, 1964).
18. E. Schrodinger, *Science and the Human Temperament* (Norton, New York, 1935).
19. G. Bateson and M. Mead. *Balinese Character* (New York Acad. of Sciences, New York, 1942).
20. J. M. Tanner and B. Inhelder, Eds., *Discussions on Child Development* (International Universities Press, New York, 1957-1960), vol. 4.
21. B. Schaffner, Ed.. *Group Processes* (Josiah Macy, Jr. Foundation, New York, 1955-1960), vols. 1-5.

22. K. Lorenz, in *ibid.*.vol.4, pp.181-252.
23. H. Blauvelt, in *ibid.* vol. 2, pp. 94-140.
24. G. Walter, in *Discussions on Child Development,* J. M. Tanner and B. Inhelder, Eds. (International Universities Press, New York, 1956). vol. 1, pp. 132-160.
25. E. H. Hess and W. C. Gogel, *J. Ornithol* 38.483 (1954).
26. C. H. Waddington, Ed. *Biology and the History of the Future* (Aldine-Atherton, Chicago, 1972).
27. M. C. Bateson, *Ann. N.Y. A cad. Sci.* 263, 101 (1975); M. Feldenkrais, *Awareness Through Movement* (Harper & Row, New York, 1972); V. V. Hunt. *Neuromuscular Structuring of Human Energy* (University of Wisconsin, Madison, 1970); P. D. Maclean, *Ann. N.Y. Acad. Sci* 193, 137 (1972); K. H. Pribram, *Languages of the Brain* (Prentice-Hall, Englewood Cliffs, N.J.. 1971); R. Spitz, *Grief—A Peril in Infancy* (New York University Film Library, New York, 1953). 16-mm, 30 minutes, black-and-white, silent.
28. M. Mead, *Science* 126, 957 (1957).
29. G. Bateson. *Steps to an Ecology of Mind* (Chandler, San Francisco, 1972).
30. T. H. Huxley and J. S. Huxley, *Touchstone for Ethics* (Harper, New York, 1947); C. H. Waddington, *The Ethical Animal* (Atheneum, New York, 1961).
31. E. Cobb. *Daedalus* (summer 1959), *p.* 537; M. Mead, In *Behavior and Evolution,* A. Roe and C. G. Simpson, Eds. (Yale Univ. Press, New Haven, Conn.. 1958); in *Expression of the Emotions in Man,* P. H. Knapp, Ed. (International Universities Press, New York, 1963), p. 326.
32. N. Bohr, *Nature (London) 143,268 (1939).*
33. M. Mead, Th. Dobzhansky, E. Tobach, E. R. Light. Eds. *Science and the Concept of Race* (Columbia Univ. Press, New York, 1968).
34. B. Fuller, *Utopia or Oblivion* (Bantam, New York, 1969); M. Mead, *J. World Hist.* 13, 765 (1971).
35. M. Mead and K. Heyman, *World Enough: Rethinking the Future* (Little, Brown, Boston, 1976).

TALKS WITH SOCIAL SCIENTISTS: Margaret Mead on what is a culture? what is a civilization?*

DR. MEAD: Today we are supposed to be dealing with the difference between culture, or cultures, and civilization or what we mean by civilization. In the first place, it is important to clarify the difference between culture, which is the system of transmitted and learned behavior of all human beings everywhere on this planet, and what we mean when we say *a* culture. When we say a culture, we mean the particular forms of behavior that belong to a particular group of people. We might talk about French culture or Japanese culture. We might talk about the culture of a tiny little island out in the Pacific like the island of Tikopia. We might even talk about the culture of the people on the south coast of the Admiralty Islands that I wrote about in *Growing up in New Guinea* where there were only about two thousand people. Or, we can find even smaller cultures. I once worked on the island of New Guinea with a group of people where there were only six hundred who spoke the language and shared the customs that they had learned from their ancestors. When we use the term a culture we refer to a particular society—a society that has developed through history. Some of them may be thousands of years old; some of them may be only a few generations old. But, we have to realize that, however different these various cultures may be, they are all equally to be considered as cultures and part of culture itself. Culture itself is the peculiar way in which human beings have learned to pass on to their children things they, themselves, have learned. This is what distinguishes human beings from creatures like insects who have to pass on their behavior in very stereotyped ways because they don't have any way of storing information, of putting it away in any form, and of teaching it to future generations. So insect behavior has to be built in—genetically.

Now another important thing about culture is that it is shared by the human beings everywhere on this planet. All human beings are

*Originally published in *Talks with Social Scientists*. Edited by Charles F. Madden. Southern Illinois University Press, 1968.

members of one species. This is something that we didn't know until a few years ago because we didn't know what other kinds of human beings we might find somewhere in the depths of the jungle, or on a high mountain peak, or on a tiny island. It was possible that there might be some earlier forms of man—some really primitive or archaic forms of man who differed physically in significant ways from modern man. However, we have now explored this whole planet. There seems to be no possibility that there are any survivals from earlier forms of man anywhere on this planet. We now know that all human beings, wherever found—in Asia, Africa, Australia, Europe, the Americas, or the islands of the seas—are all members of one species with the same potentiality for learning, for inventing, and for transmitting their cultures. This is quite new information. We couldn't say this for certain until we had explored the whole planet and many people have not yet fully absorbed this information and think of different races as representing earlier or later forms of man. But we have to say that we are all members of the same species, all dependent upon human culture to adjust in the world.

One of the striking ways of thinking about human culture is to realize that a single infant left alone would die at once. But this is equally true of a lamb, or a kid, or an infant monkey. An infant whose parents have not prepared some way to care for it and shelter it will die. But this is true of birds who need nests. However, to be a full human being a person has to grow up in a society with more than one family to care for him, to learn relationships to old and young, to both sexes, to people that are close and to people that are far away. It's only by growing up in such a society that we become fully human.

We can also say, in thinking about human cultures all over the planet, that there are certain universals. People in every culture have families; they all educate their children to behave as the adults have behaved; they have tools; they have language, they have some form of religion; and they have some form of relating people which is larger than the small family.

When we start to distinguish between cultures and civilization we come up against a quite different problem. Over the last ten thousand years and possibly longer—we don't know yet—there have periodically appeared in different parts of the world dense populations, a tremendous increase in the number of people and a corresponding increase in the ability to grow food and to store it. Under the impetus of people living with far greater density, we have developed—this has been developed several different times in different parts of the world—our capacity to manage such large groups of people. This means keeping accounts, keeping records. It means some kind of taxation and revenue. It means a great deal of division of labor so that large groups of people can divide among themselves all the skills and tasks and knowledge that are necessary to manage a large civilization—like ancient China, like the civilization of the Incas in South America, or the civilization of the Maya and Aztecs in Mexico, like ancient Greece or Rome, and like our own complex civilization today.

One of the important things about civilizations in the past is that they have developed up to a peak and then have fallen, either because they were conquered by other people or because they disintegrated—they could no longer maintain the high pitch of activity that was true in their heyday and their days of glory. One of the very important questions that people are asking today is: What will happen to particular modern civilizations today? In the later forties many people were predicting that Europe was finished, that Europe was a dying civilization and would never again reach any kind of height. In 1964 we know that this is not true. Europe today is a thriving economic community moving toward a Common Market and, far from being a dying society, it is one that is perfectly strong and capable of challenging the United States on an exporting or industrial level and certainly on a cultural level. Then there are those who compare the United States to the Roman Empire. I always suspect we are rather like the Romans in our capacity for getting together a great network of peoples over a very large territory, building roads, managing the problems of plumbing and sanitation, and organizing life. But it is important to realize that when these other civilizations fell they were like solitary mountain peaks. Around them, for a great distance, people with much lower orders of organization and technology lived. Today, for the first time, this whole planet is in intercommunication. Every inch of this earth's surface is claimed—in different ways, of course, but claimed—by some group of people. We're now so interrelated that no group can be allowed to fall. We're past the time of empires that topple over, where the people around about would pick up the pieces, learn whatever interesting techniques had been developed, take a little of the art, and in due time develop a civilization of their own. Today we have instant communication between high civilization and lower civilization, very simple cultures where people are living as they have lived for thousands of years. All this communication means that what's available in a high civilization today can be made immediately available to people in very simple cultures. It means a good many other things too. It means that people who, when they are discovered by Europeans, are living in very small groups (as fishermen, food gatherers, hunters), knowing only how to scratch the ground with a digging stick—without even a hand-driven plow—

need not go through all the stages that men went through in developing civilizations in the past. We can give them immediate entrée into the best that we know of technology and knowledge, and they can skip all the intervening periods and pick up exactly where we are instead of going laboriously through all the stages.

We are now reaching a stage in human history where, if we can accurately estimate what any society knows that would be useful to any other society, this knowledge can be put in a form that can be made available to all. This is particularly important because many people in Europe and North America are worried about the capacity of people who have lived a much simpler life, technologically, to manage in the modern world. We see new nations struggling with problems of power and government and feel that they are not able to manage their society in the way that we manage ours. It is particularly difficult for us Americans, who are convinced that our method of political organization is better than any other, to realize that our kind of democracy is terribly old and is especially suited to our kinds of character structure, but is not a very exportable form. We have been attempting to export our kind of democracy to other countries for a long time, and we see in South American countries examples of the difficulty they have in using a form of democracy which is particularly suited to the English-speaking peoples but may not be as suited to the particular conditions of Latin American countries, or Asian countries, or African countries.

If we are going to deal with planetary problems in such a way that we have an orderly world—a world which will not, blow itself up in a thermonuclear war or destroy itself by other kinds of scientific warfare—we're going to have to use this network of interchange among advancing civilizations and newly emerging people as fully as possible. We are going to have to realize that our relationship to newly emerging peoples is not like the relationship of Greece or Rome, the Incas or the Aztecs, or the Babylonians, or the ancient Chinese empire to surrounding barbarians. Our relationship is quite a new one because of the invention of nations, of treating each nation as a unit with dignity of its own, as a member of the United Nations. We have made an invention which, from one point of view, puts us all on a par so we can have give and take in both directions—we can begin to learn from people very far away from us and very different just as they can begin to learn from us. We must realize that, if we start exporting some of our ideas, our items of manufacture, for instance, electronic devices, we can expect other people to take these, readapt them, change them around, and fit them into their particular form of society.

For example, in the United States we have mental institutions where we crowd people in by the thousands and then try very hard to get anyone to care for them. Millions of dollars are being spent to understand the relationships of the mentally ill to other people, and to include the families in some kind of therapy. We find in Nigeria an open hospital is being developed by a Western-educated Nigerian psychiatrist. Members of the family come with the patient and learn how to take care of him. They are developing an old African style of caring for the sick, combined with the most modern psychiatric insights that can be found in London or New York.

It is from this sort of interplay between ancient wisdom and ancient style of other societies and scientific and technical advances of our own that we can expect to build a quite different kind of world society. A society in which the great nations happen to be the largest and wealthiest can make one kind of contribution; middle-sized nations can make another, very small nations can make quite a different one because no one will be jealous of them in the same way that they may be of larger groups. We can begin to work on the problem of spreading the advantages of civilization over the face of the globe and at the same time attempt to keep the individual style of each particular culture. It would be most unfortunate if in the course of giving people the benefit of new forms of medicine, for example, or new forms of transportation and communication, we leveled them all out so there was no individuality left and wherever one went in the world one found identical types of people. This would be dull. It would cut off the possibilities of innovation and change. It might throw us all into a single system which had very few alternatives.

At the same time it is important to realize that there are some things in Western civilization that the people of the world crave very much. They crave modern medicine, which will keep their children from dying. They crave the tools that will keep people from back-breaking labor. They crave sufficient food so that their people will be well nourished. They also crave ways of balancing their population against their food supply, the size of their country, and the aspirations that they have for everyone who is in their country. We can draw upon both the willingness and the self-interest of the great powers to make their technical achievements available to other people, to give some of the results of their stored-up capital to other countries, and we have a corresponding desire on the part of the receiving countries for some of these things.

But, unless there is enough recognition of the individuality, strength, and pride of each group, there is danger that this interchange will not proceed in a way that will distribute the advantages of civilization, and still keep the unique historical heritage of each group. When we used to think of nations and talk about nationalism, we spoke of nationalism as an almost unmitigated evil. It was opposed to internationalism and it was spoken of as something that was wrong and inevitably brought conflict and war. But today we have a new phrase, and that is the phrase nationhood, which means that each nation has a part in a whole. Instead of each nation working for self-advantages, instead of each nation seeking to aggrandize itself at the expense of all other nations, today each nation is part of a whole. Each nation has an investment in maintaining the safety and welfare of each other nation. We do not dare to let any other nation sink below a certain level of health, of order, because this threatens the whole of the world. So, as we long ago spoke of things like statehood and learned in this country that each state had both a tradition of its own and an obligation to the whole, on a quite different level we are beginning to build a planetary society where each country can be proud of the contribution that it makes. Members of each race can be proud of themselves and glad of their own physique without downgrading the racial characteristics of different races. Membership in a whole—a variegated and diverse whole—can be substituted for an arrogant membership in any one group, nation, race, or ideology that thinks of themselves as superior to all others. With this new type of sharing the gains of civilization, on the one hand, and the recognition of the rights of each group, on the other, we recognize that one other new thing has happened; and that is, that each country has now become the keeper of the children of all other countries, whether they are friends, allies, or apparent enemies. The safety of each group is dependent on the safety of all.

Looking back on the whole history of civilization, we can show our indebtedness to ancient Egypt, to ancient China. There has been one long, cumulative rise of human invention in the world. And now this long, steady stream of invention is going to be put into a state where it can be made available to all the peoples of the world, including people in the center of New Guinea who have been isolated from all contacts with civilization for thousands and thousands of years so that when we find them they, who belong to the same species we do, are living under conditions that some of our ancestors lived under a hundred years ago, some a thousand, and some ten thousand years ago. I am now ready to receive questions.

Wilberforce: I recently read an article that you wrote called "Culture and Social Changes." You seemed to indicate that in Manus too much emphasis was placed on early childhood experiences. I wondered if you would expand on that?

DR. MEAD: I don't think there's too much emphasis placed on early childhood experiences, but early childhood experiences do not cause political or social institutions. That is, Americans don't have representative government and a balance of power and a Supreme Court because they were bad or slapped in a particular way as children. But slapping and beating them and being gentle with them and playing with them are ways in which people who live in the United States under our institutions teach children to be the kind of people who can live under those institutions. So then, it is not that early childhood is not very important, but the early childhood alone is not responsible for the whole of our behavior. It is simply a very important time in which children learn to be like their parents and share in their whole society.

Wilberforce: When does a culture become a civilization?

DR. MEAD: Well, this is a matter of definition. Looking at the past we have called societies civilizations when they have had great cities, elaborate division of labor, some form of keeping records. These are the things that have made civilization. Some form of script, not necessarily our kind of script, but some form of script or record keeping; ability to build great, densely populated cities and to divide up labor so that they could be maintained. Civilization, in other words, is not simply a word of approval, as one would say "he is uncivilized," but it is technical description of a particular kind of social system that makes a particular kind of culture possible.

Southern: Is our concern today for foreign lands and people mainly a reaction to conditions created by World War II, or simply the manifestation of fear?

DR. MEAD: No, I think that World War II helped because so many Americans went all over the world. It is primarily our recognition that we live in one world today. If a plague breaks out in the center of Tibet it affects us here. In a matter of hours we can get from one side of the world to the other side of the world. We know that foreign lands are now part of the world we live in. This is, of course, greatly helped by television. People see programs based in many parts of the world.

Southern: As an anthropologist, do you always evaluate foreign civilization in terms of our own?

DR. MEAD: No. Anthropologists are trained not to evaluate other civilizations in terms of our own. The categories that we have built up, which we use in describing other cultures, have been built gradually from the study of other cultures. So, for example, we found in the South Seas that people had something called taboo. A large part of their behavior was related to things that were forbidden. The word taboo was added to our language. We look at other societies to see if they too have taboos and what kind of taboos. We build up an outline through which we can look at any society in terms of our knowledge of all other society. We are very carefully trained not to say that something is good or bad simply because we have it. At the same time, we can make the distinction between a society that is technologically complicated or technologically simple; a society that is rich or a society that is poor; a society that emphasized the arts or one that does not. But this does not mean that we are not treating each society as a whole.

Le Moyne: What are some specific effects that the introduction of a Western culture has on a primitive culture?

DR. MEAD: You must first consider that we have been having introductions from a high culture to a lower culture, in the sense of technical differences, for thousands and thousands of years. The Roman Empire, when it came to the islands of Britain, was bringing a high culture to a simple, or primitive, culture. It was bringing things like writing and road building and government and things of this sort. So this has been going on for a very long time. Not until the mid-twentieth century was there a complete clash or a complete meeting of the most advanced technical things that had ever happened in the world, like an airplane, with the simplest people still alive on earth. The contrast today is more dramatic than it has ever been before. The effects differ depending on who brings them. Sometimes they are brought by missionaries, sometimes by government, sometimes by traders. If the people are more interested in getting material things than anything else, their old culture may break up; if the government is interested in taxing them so they will work for plantations or something of the sort, this may wreck their old culture. On the other hand, if they are given a sense of dignity, if they are allowed to move rapidly under their own power, they may be able to retain a large amount of their old style, but express it in new ways—new forms of tools, new ways of working with things, and new relationships with each other.

Le Moyne: Concerning the societies that you studied, what was it about them that made you decide to refer to them as cultures instead of civilizations?

DR. MEAD: Well, because they haven't any large population, they haven't any cities, they haven't any script, they haven't any complicated technology or complicated organization. Culture is the word that we apply to a little group of Eskimos or to the people of France. Every human group has a culture. We use the word civilization for these special, complex developments that have occurred at different times in history, such as in ancient Egypt. For a very long time afterward Egypt was barely a civilization at all. People became very poor, and there was very little concentration of organization in large cities. The people of Yucatan once had a great civilization, but the temples crumbled away, the cities fell apart, and the people today are quite simple peasants who are beginning to participate in a new kind of civilization that comes to them from the modern Western world.

Le Moyne: In our biographical information the statement is made that "Dr. Mead observed primitive people." Because of the differences in culture, were you able to be other than an observer? In what areas of their life did you feel that you were one with the people just because you were a human being? In what areas of life did you cease to be an observer?

DR. MEAD: When one enters the life of a group of people in New Guinea, although I *can* eat their food, I *don't* eat it most of the time, partly because they have very little food and adding three or four new people to a village may be more than the food supply can stand and partly because I have grown up in a different society and I might get sick, although they don't, from eating the same thing. So I cook their food somewhat differently or I may add more greens to it than they do and things of this sort. I wear more clothes than they do. They are usually interested in acquiring clothes, and, furthermore, I represent a community where the standards of modesty are different from theirs. I try to wear clothes they'll enjoy. I wear clothes, which are made from material with pictures on it and things of that sort that the children there will enjoy. I, of course, belong to another society, and I maintain the kind of social distance from people that one maintains toward people that one doesn't expect to marry, so I am very often given a very large supply of relatives. For instance, when I arrived in Manus with my husband, the natives immediately said, "You can't live here all alone with a husband. This would be very dangerous. No woman can live alone with her husband, she needs a brother to run away to if her husband beats her." And so one of our friends in the village said, "I will be your brother." And, although I never had to run away to him, his wife, when I went back twenty-five years later, still called me sister-in-law. It is far easier for the anthropologist to participate in the life of the people he has studied, or she has studied, than for those people to understand the anthropologist's world. I learn their language; I hold their babies in my arms; I taste their food; I sit on the ground as they sit. They, on the other hand, have no clear picture of the world from which I come. I am far stranger to them than they are to me. But I found in going back after twenty-five years to the Manus that they have become part of the modern world. Now we talk to each other far more as people who understand each other. They now understand why I was studying them and so we talk much more as people who share a common understanding of what is going on in the world.

Kansas Wesleyan: What are the minimum conditions, in terms of culture for the establishment of a nation?

DR. MEAD: Today it is primarily accidental because it has been, unfortunately, in the interests of power politics to take old lines that were drawn by colonial powers in different parts of the world and treat these groups as nations. Sometimes they have been well prepared to be nations in that they have been bound together by sharing some language like French or English or Spanish; sometimes, on the other hand, they were merely accidental aggregations of people who felt themselves to be very separate. In this case it has been very difficult, and is going to be very difficult, for many leaders of countries in Africa, as it was in the past for South America, to hold these groups of people together. The minimum requirements for a nation are a shared language, a shared set of political institutions to which everybody gives allegiance and which they can place above their allegiance to their regions or their tribe or their religious group. When it is possible to do this, then the new nation has a long, difficult, struggling time.

Kansas Wesleyan: In *Age and Sex in the Social Structure* the author says, "The age of youth in our society is one of considerable strain and insecurity." Do you find this to be true in the various countries you have studied?

DR. MEAD: No. There is great variation. In some societies youth is hard and middle age is easy, in other societies youth is easy and age is hard. In old Manus the children had a lovely time and once they entered late adolescence they never had a good time again. On the other hand, in France children are very rigorously disciplined, made to study very hard, and are allowed very few pleasures until they've grown up. So societies differ enormously which period in life they make easy and which period they make difficult. Some societies make all periods difficult, and others make all periods relatively easy.

Grambling: During the early part of your lecture you made the statement that all human beings are limited to one species and have the same capacity for learning. Does the environment of your community have any effect on the mental capacity of an individual?

DR. MEAD: The environment has no effect on the inherent, or innate, capacity. But if you took a pair of identical twins, Eskimo twins for example, and put one of them among the Eskimos and the other among the French, when they grew up they would be enormously different. One child would have learned to read and write, to understand ancient civilization, to play the piano, to understand modern economics and things of this sort. The other child would have learned how to stalk a seal, how to build a snow house, but would have known very little of the civilization of the modern world. So as adults they would be enormously different although originally they started with absolutely identical inheritance.

Grambling: Since we are knowledgeable of the cultural differences of many countries, the density of the population, the need for expanding the resources, skills, and knowledge of other countries, what is causing the rejection by some countries of domestic aid from other countries? Are these political problems or cultural problems?

DR. MEAD: I think these are mainly political, although sometimes this occurs in very old countries where a new part of the population is rising to power, peasants, members of backward groups, other castes as in India. Sometimes the old holders of power want to reject aid from other countries because they are afraid that it will undermine their power. Sometimes they want to take it in order to keep their power. But I would say these are more questions of power and of relative allegiance to one political block or another, or playing one block against the other, than they are questions of culture as such.

DR. CARPENTER: Thank you, Dr. Mead. We have gained a great deal from this conversation. It has been quite up to our expectations and beyond. It was lots of fun having you with us.

DR. MEAD: Good-bye.

ANTHROPOLOGIST AND HISTORIAN:
Their Common Problems*

The idea that periods of contact between hitherto isolated human societies have been periods of fruitful development is so old, so well accepted, that it is astonishing how often we have failed to use it as an analogy in discussing cooperation among different fields of human endeavor.* Whether the advocates of "inter-disciplinary" research have felt it necessary to cast their arguments into a sterner pattern to match the self-conscious "purity" of those who wish to keep each discipline pure and uncorrupted by intellectual contact, only a specific inquiry could tell us. But it is evident, even to the casual ear, that "breaking down the barriers between disciplines" has usually been presented as a very arduous and, consequently, moral and exacting form of intellectual activity. From those who have attempted inter-disciplinary research, we hear report after report of hard going—how each group has held on to their own concepts and resisted the concepts of the others.

Even a summer holiday in Italy might be described in such unrewarding terms by a traveler who spoke only English—who, eyes to the ground, refused to eat fresh almonds unless they were pronounced in English, and by the Italian vendor who insisted that he would eat his own almonds himself unless they were designated in the exact lilt of the local dialect. But this is not the way lovers of foreign travel speak in describing how every cell in one's body feels different when one wakes in a strange land and eats a new kind of breakfast served with the accompanying excitement of a strange tongue in which the word for almond blends with the taste of almonds and with the quality of the sunlight on the Mediterranean.

Perhaps in a cooperative venture in which both "social sciences"—history and anthropology—are also often grouped together as "humanities," it may be possible to preserve enough of the concrete pleasures of the new and strange, that some of the grimmer

*Originally published in *American Quarterly*.

aspects of inter-disciplinary cooperation—including the training table overtones of the phrase "team work"—may be avoided in favor of the adventure of exploring each other's methods and delighting in each other's insights.[1]

Historians and anthropologists—in contrast to social scientists in other fields—have a special relationship to their concrete materials, to the particular document or to the sequence of rites performed at a particular ceremony. For these concrete materials—whether they be the single copy of an obscure document from a remote historical period, or the single record of the only initiation ceremony ever witnessed and recorded in a tribe which has since given up initiation, or whether they be one of a set of documents which differ among themselves or one of twenty records of initiation from the same tribe—are nevertheless irreplaceable, unique events from the details of which new insights may be drawn by succeeding, more sophisticated generations. Both historians and anthropologists are dependent upon that which occurs *in the natural course of human social life* for their materials, every facet of which becomes precious. This loving preservation of the actual detail contrasts with the single-minded emphasis upon abstractions and generalizations of the scientist who works with experiments that can be repeated and from whom it is required not that he "surrender to the material," but that he set up his hypotheses and so construct his experiments that they will provide him with data to prove or disprove them. The little phrase "the data shows" suggests a proper humility in the historian and anthropologist—and a state of incompetence in the experimenter.

From the necessities of their methods, both historians and anthropologists place a special value on the unique event in all its uniqueness. They know that it is the fine web of specific relationships, when something was done in relation to the occurrence of some other small act—a conversation, a letter, a resignation, a quarrel—which makes it possible for later historians, for other anthropologists, to ask, and to get answers to, new questions from old materials. The footnotes and interpolations and misspellings, which would be lost in reediting and rearranging materials, become invaluable sources. Similarly, the anthropologist may find that faces in the background of a photograph or moving picture provide a way of testing a hypothesis not fully developed in the field. So in the Balinese material,[2] psychiatrists who looked at the pictures were inclined to question the difference in the tone of voice of the mother who—lightheartedly—teased her child, and of the child who—heavyhearted—reacted against the same teasing by sulky withdrawal. A reëxamination of films of the crowd scenes of two rituals—one of which embodied the parents' attitudes towards children (the *Sangijang Dance*) and the other the children's attitudes towards parents (the *Tjalonarang)*— showed a marked contrast in the faces of the children in the two crowds: relaxed, gay, and unanxious in the former; anxious and tense in the latter. If the abstractions had been drawn from the material and the "data" had then been thrown away, no such further exploration would have been possible.

This preoccupation with the actual data, which serves to unite historians and anthropologists, is less intelligible to those scientists who create their data by experiments as they need it, as critics they always seem to be asking why one didn't go somewhere else or study a different period, insensitive to the importance of learning what a particular culture or a particular period can provide—better than any other. It is only when historians and anthropologists become interested not only in what did happen and what does exist but also in the nature of social processes and in the regularities which may be found in them, that this gap between historical fidelity and experimental freedom can be bridged.

Traditionally, historians and anthropologists have been distinguished from one another by the materials which they have studied: the historian dealing with past periods and the anthropologist with primitive peoples. This distinction is fast becoming obsolete as both are turning their attention to contemporary problems of the great civilizations of the world—including our own. There has also been a difference in the degree to which members of each discipline have been able to take the *whole* of a society into account. The early anthropologist dealt with part of the culture of a society, usually with a society which was already in process of rapid change; he attempted to reconstruct from the accounts of elderly informants such parts of the formal pattern as could be worked out without a detailed study of any living interacting group of human beings. The historian was limited by the nature of the documents which were available and by the current conventions of historiography which dictated the kind of constructs one could make from such documents. The units of both these traditional types of research were *items of behavior,* performed at an identified time and in an identified place by identified individuals; from them, patterns of "feudalism" or of "age societies" could be derived. In neither procedure was it possible to study living societies in which the units for analysis are not items of behavior, but instead *individuals* [and] *groups of individuals.*[3] The study of whole societies waited for field work in which the anthropologist would stop digging into the memories of old men and women and instead learn to speak the native language and record the living, changing, particular primitive community of his own time,[4] and research in which the historian would regard as part of his task the study of living institutions against the time depth provided both by the memory of older men and by available documentation.[5]

The discussions at the 1939 meetings of the American Historical Association suggested the growing preoccupation with groups which had been neglected by historians—the illiterate, the socially obscure, the peasant, the worker, the immigrant, and with sources, such as oral tradition, which had been overlooked in the past. The anthropologist was paralleling this new inclusiveness by adding observations of actual behavior to his former principal reliance on descriptive words. At the same time, both historian and anthropologist were looking for new types of connections which could be recognized when old sources were examined from a new point of view.[6]

So, both in anthropology and in history, we have been working steadily from a consideration of those parts of the society or those aspects of the culture, which our traditional methods made accessible, toward methods through which more of the whole could be included. For both disciplines this search has led to unorthodox uses of sources. The search has led also into the areas of the inarticulate, the unrecognized, the unformulated. Penetration of these new areas has been very much facilitated in anthropological studies, less so in historical studies proper, by the inclusion of findings from studies of human growth and learning and from clinical explorations of the unconscious.[7]

Anthropologists have begun to work toward theories of social change and so to compensate for their previous concentration on synchronic studies of single societies at one moment of time, and historians have begun to lay more emphasis upon the total social complex at a given period. In the past, anthropologists have compensated for the lack of a time dimension in their studies by spatial studies of the distribution of traits. The definition of the place of a given culture in a known "culture area"—the traits of which were also described—was, in effect, a way of holding "history constant,"[8] a way of saying that, as a member of a given culture area, the particular society may be assumed to have had access at some unspecified period to such a trait as the dog sled or pottery making. The enforced necessity of working without documents on the primitive level was carried over to some extent into early applications of anthropological methods to our society, notably in the Yankee City Series.[9]

Criticism of the lack of a complete time perspective in these earlier studies has sometimes been carried over into uncritical attacks on studies of contemporary American life which are not also historical treatises. It would be useful for anthropologists and historians together to clarify how cross-sectional studies, on the one hand, and, studies of single developments through time, on the other, can be made so as not to violate their combined standards for the proper allowance for time-space dimensions. The present level of criticism both within and between the two disciplines tends to be either pejorative or meaningless, as studies are pronounced "too narrow" or "too broad," "too limited" or "too ambitious" without reference to criteria that have been agreed upon or are even identifiable. The more we try to work with *wholes*—with whole societies, with members of those societies seen as whole persons, and with whole periods—the more important it will be to find some way of deciding what whole should be taken into account in considering a given problem.

Within both disciplines, attempts to handle wholes—synchronically by historians and diachronically by anthropologists—and to relate structure, function and change, have been given impetus by concepts of equilibrium and balance: in anthropology by the new approach of cybernetics; in economic history by Schumpeter's theory of "moving equilibrium."[10] This is perhaps the area where the use of models drawn from the natural sciences may be expected to provide the basis for coöperation among anthropologists and historians who are interested in systematizing problems of social change.

Another area where anthropologists' and historians' problems meet is that area, once known as "personality and culture," and currently referred to as "national character," because of the emphasis in such studies upon the contemporary cultures of great nation states. These present studies have little in common with earlier methods for the delineation of national character by reference to race or climate; instead they are ways of relating anthropological studies of culture, historical studies of consistencies within the same group of people over time, Freud's work on the formation of the individual character, and modern studies of child development and learning. In the Romanes lecture which he gave fifty years after Thomas H. Huxley's famous lecture on "Science and Ethics," Julian Huxley has pointed out that recent studies of the way learning takes place in childhood have provided us with the necessary links between man's biological nature and social ethics, so that man's highest aspirations as well as his most undisciplined and anti-social impulses can now be included within the natural order—rooted in the way human beings learn the patterns of their cultures.[11]

Briefly, these modern studies of national character are concomitant analyses of the character structure of individuals of different ages who embody a culture and of the child rearing, educational, and initiatory practices of the culture within which these individuals have been reared. By cross-checking these observations, we arrive at a diagrammatic statement of the particular process of character formation by which human beings—at birth capable of learning any human language and the rest of any human culture—come to learn a particular language and to embody their particular culture. In such a study, areas of experience are explored which are unverbalized or which are publicly disallowed, as well as those areas which are made explicit. We are thus carried one step further toward considering the whole, toward placing man-in-society with a long social history and man-as-a-mammal with a long biological history in one frame of reference.

National character studies, as these were developed during World War II, were wartime efforts to obtain rapid information about the expected behavior of enemies and allies. They were partial studies in that only a few adult informants were available, so that the behavior of a few adults, in interview situations, had to be analyzed in the light of reported, rather than observed, methods of infant care and education. This emergency method has now been developed, under the continued stress of need to understand peoples whose societies are inaccessible to direct observation, into a method that can be used to bridge the gap between the procedures of the historian and the cultural anthropologist. By working together on the understanding of the culture of societies which have greatly changed, so that there are only individual survivors and the culture can no longer be perpetuated (for example, the culture of Great Russia previous to the 1917 Revolution), or the members of which have dispersed into new environments in groups which still can be studied (for example, the culture of the Eastern European Jewish *shtetl* or small town), the special contribution of each discipline can actually become apparent to the other.

The crux of the methodological differences between historians and anthropologists can be summed up in the two words "document" and "informant." The historian uses written materials which have been created within the ordinary ongoing social process without reference to his inquiring intent, and he distrusts material as probably biased, when it has been written for the purpose for which he, himself uses it. In contrast, the anthropologist finds informants, whose place in their society he learns very carefully so that from these living human beings he can elicit materials on the culture, which traditionally he writes down, on the spot.

This contrast in method was summed up vividly by an experience in Bali with a visiting Dutch student of native law who had expressed an interest in the recent spread of a new dance form, called the *djanger,* which had recognizable European elements. We asked him whether he would like to see some *djanger texts*—meaning running observations in Balinese and in English and verbatim reports of conversations which had taken place at the meetings of the local *djanger* club. He was eager to do so, but then exclaimed in dismay: "These aren't texts! These are something that just happened."

Further light is thrown on the problem by the ill fate which met my attempt to regularize group research in contemporary cultures by having all the interviews with informants processed for group use, numbered and filed. When one of the group wrote an article in which he referred to this unpublished material by number, it was turned down by an anthropological editor on the ground that the article was based "only on unpublished material"—although it is acceptable anthropological practice to base published work on a statement of the order: "This material was collected during ten months' field work on the island of Borabora in 1910." Conversely, an historical editor asked me very severely on how many interviews with informants a certain statement was based. When I asked how many published documents would have been needed to authenticate it, he agreed that he would accept a minimum of one, providing there were no contradictory evidence. Finally, a young historian recently advised us to call our recorded interviews with carefully identified informants "unpublished memoirs."

In the course of cooperative work such as I shall suggest, most of these misunderstandings will disappear, if it is possible to push behind, these disciplinary blind spots, so that an anthropologist can watch an historian criticize the usefulness of a *document,* weigh it, test it, compare it with "other evidence," and if an historian can watch an anthropologist record a series of interviews with an informant and weigh them, test them, and compare them with "other evidence." And they will disappear, I believe, in the exploration of what is meant by the term "other evidence"—which, aside from other documents, has remained largely inexplicit among historians as each one trusted to his growing "feeling for the period." This is an area in which anthropologists have become steadily more self-conscious; in their case, the "other evidence" can be handled systematically by reference to successive steps in the learning process or to the formal characteristics of some other facet of the culture.

For example, during the early days of our Balinese field work, we continually received accounts of "marriage by capture." This was definitely not in accord with such "other evidence" in Balinese culture as the almost complete absence of any physical fighting among children, the handling of quarrels by silence, and a break in all communication between the disputants, etc. Here historians, distrusting a document, and anthropologists, distrusting informants' reports, are still on the same ground—the item of information does not fit. We were able to solve this apparent incongruity when we found that "marriage by capture" was a carefully planned elopement in which it was necessary to simulate capture as a gesture of courtesy to the culturally preferred marriage which was being evaded, and that this was done with conscious theatricality. The theatricality of the Balinese could further be referred to in the way in which the climatic expression of emotional sequences was broken in childhood by a mother whose only fully enacted sequences are of theatrical or simulated emotion.[12]

I would suggest that the most practical way for historians and anthropologists to learn from each other is in a situation in which they can really experience each other's methods. Such a situation would be provided by work on a common problem located in a period for which both living persons—as informants—and well-ordered documents were available, a problem so conceived that each facet would be systematically referable to larger structural wholes.

Such a group working together might, for example, investigate a small New England city between 1900-1914, studying its economic and social development with particular reference to changes in job opportunity, shifts in ownership and decision-making, and in the way in which the small city was integrated with the social and economic life of the region, the nation, and the world. Older men and women could be used as informants, actual changes in residence and communication within the community could be mapped, the history of economic and social change could be followed through local records. The pictures of the past obtained by the different methods could be systematically compared, and materials obtained by members of both disciplines could be referred to the series of widening circles or wholes within which the study was made.

In such a joint venture, historians would be responsible for maintaining the sense of trend, of movement over time, and for making it clear to the anthropologists why they regarded it necessary to go back to the Civil War in examining one sequence, back only to 1890 in examining another, and why they were willing to label a sequence as new, or beginning in a certain year. At present it is exceedingly difficult for anthropologists to discover how the historian makes such selections, what in fact are the criteria by which the historian decides that certain periods provide the most relevant sequential or diachronic setting for his investigations. Instead of the young historian learning from his seniors until he got a "feel" for the necessary data, he would be challenged by a "why" from his contemporaries trained in a different discipline.

Meanwhile, the anthropologist, who would be responsible for the adequacy and inclusiveness of the working model of the "whole community" and the "whole culture," would be equally and relevantly pressed. Instead of carrying over in bits and pieces his knowledge that kinship or ceremonials of crisis are something one ought to investigate, he would have to show the relationship between the biological requirements of a human society (in which men and women with defined biological needs and potentialities must reproduce and nourish and train the young) and the culture and specific social structure of that society.

Working together, historians and anthropologists would also become more sharply aware of the problems involved in surrendering their traditional devices for maintaining detachment—the historian by working with periods which are in the past,[13] the anthropologist by working with primitive peoples whose value systems are far removed from his own. Neither type of detachment is feasible for those working on contemporary societies.

Historians, after trying to obtain perspective on their material by permitting a sufficient amount of time to elapse, have often been much franker than other social scientists in recognizing that they belong to their own period and are writing for it. The interpretation itself has been treated as normative with a hope that it is tempered by a longer time perspective and the seasoned wisdom which comes from the knowledge of the follies men have committed, the depths to which men have fallen, and the heights to which they have risen again.

Anthropologists have taken a somewhat different course. We have explicitly demarcated an area of "applied anthropology" in which we are using our disciplined knowledge to affect the lives of identified people or groups. (A comparable area in the discipline of history would be the rule of historians in policy formation, in international organizations, in the revision of textbooks for occupied countries, etc.) For this particular area we have adopted a code of professional ethics,[14] in which we assume responsibility for the foreseeable effects of our acts.

Studying and publishing upon our own civilization falls inevitably under the heading of applied science, because each pronouncement upon contemporary culture by historian, anthropologist, or any other student of society, will change that culture. One way of meeting this challenge is purposely to include the cultural membership of research workers in the research, orchestrating the research team by the inclusion of members of the culture being studied and members of at least two other cultures. It should be anticipated that in cooperative research on recently past periods, in which historians and anthropologists might work together for the express purpose of exploring each other's methods, this same procedure might be followed. In a study of American civilization of a given region between 1900-1914, a working team would include individuals who had matured in that city and at that period, younger students, and, in addition to American anthropologists and American historians, social scientists from at least one European society.

I myself have found the mere attempt to outline some of the possibilities of such collaboration so stimulating that it would seem reasonable that the experience of working on a common problem might prove rewarding to members of both disciplines.

MARGARET MEAD

Notes

*This paper was originally presented in part at the "Conference on American Civilization" held at Brown University, November 3 and 4, 1950, under the chairmanship of Dr. Edmund S. Morgan, at which I was asked to discuss the contribution of cultural anthropology to historical studies.

1. Eleven years ago the American Historical Association devoted several sessions to a consideration of the cultural approach to history, which was later issued in a volume edited by Caroline Ware, *The Cultural Approach to History* (New York: Columbia University Press, 1940). The volume included an excellent summary by Geoffrey Gorer of existing theory in cultural anthropology. In my discussion I have relied on this volume as a kind of bench mark, taking its suggestions into account and attempting to add to it in the light of growth in anthropological theory over the last decade, experience in working in inter-disciplinary teams which did not include historians, and experience (especially in Columbia University Research in Contemporary Cultures and in the American Museum of Natural History project "Studies in Soviet Culture") in working closely with historians and with members of the culture being studied, who had been well-grounded in the history of some aspect of their own culture. These last two experiences are distinct and differently rewarding—at least for the anthropologist.
2. G. Bateson and M. Mead, *Balinese Character: A Photographic Analysis* (New York: 'New York Academy of Sciences, 1942).
3. For systematic discussions of these distinctions, cf. Gregory Bateson, *Naven* (Cambridge University Press, 1936); *Cooperation and Competition*

Among Primitive Peoples, edited by Margaret Mead (New York: McGraw-Hill Book Co., 1937); Ralph Linton, *The Study of Man* (New York: D. Appleton-Century Co., 1936); A. R. Ratcliffe-Brown, "On Social Structure," *Journal of Royal Institute of Anthropology*, LXX (1940), 1-12.

4. The work of Bronislav Malinowski in the Trobriands, my work in Samoa, Ruth Bunzel's work in Zuni, and the series of studies carried on under Radcliffe-Brown at the University of Sydney, are examples of this shift of emphasis from attempts to reconstruct the culture of a bygone period to work with whole communities as they exist.

5. Philip Mosely's studies of the Zadruga are pioneer studies in this combination of the historical approach with the case studies of actual communal joint families. Cf. 'The Zadruga: or Communal Joint Family in the Balkans and its Recent Evolution," in Ware, *op. cit.* pp. 95-108.

6. For example, Ruth Benedict's treatment of the material on the Kwakiutl Indians in *Patterns of Culture* (Boston: Houghton Mifflin, 1934) and R. K. Lamb's work in which hitherto unemphasized connections through family and clique membership among statesmen and landed and merchant families are providing a new basis for the analysis of early American entrepreneural history. See "Entrepreneurship in the Community" in *Explorations in Entrepreneural History*, Vol. 11, No.3, 114-127.

7. Cf. Arnold Gesell and Frances L. Ilg, *Infant and Child in the Culture of Today* (New York: Harper and Bros., 1943); David Riesman, *The Lonely Crowd* (New Haven: Yale University Press, 1950); E. H. Erikson, *Childhood and Society* (New York : W. W. Norton, 1950); M. Mead, "On the Implications for Anthropology of the Gesell-Ilg Approach to Maturation," *American Anthropologist* (Jan.-Mar. 1947), Vol. 49, No.1, 69-77; Gregory Bateson, "Social Planning and the Concept of Deutero Learning," part of Chap. iv, *Second Symposium on Science, Philosophy and Religion* (New York 1942); John Dollard, *Criteria for the Life History* (New Haven: Yale University Press, 1935).

8. Gregory Bateson, "Cultural Determinants of Personality," in McVeigh Hunt, *Personality and the Behavior Disorders* (New York: Ronald Press, 1944), 714-735.

9. W. L. Warner and others, *Yankee City Series*, I-IV (New Haven: Yale University Press, 1941, 1942, 1945, 1947).

10. Gregory Bateson, "Bali: The Value System of a Steady State" in *Social Structure: Studies Presented to A. R. Radcliffe-Brown*. ed. by Meyer Fortes (Oxford: Clarendon Press, 1949), 35-3; Jurgen Ruesch and Gregory Bateson, "Structure and Process in Social Relations" in *Psychiatry* (May 1949), Vol. XII, No.2, 105-124; Eliot D. Chapple and Carleton S. Coon, *Principles of Anthropology* (New York: Henry Holt and Co., 1942); L. F. Richardson, "Generalized Foreign Politics," *British Journal of Psychology* Monograph Supplement XXIII (1939); J. A. Schumpeter, *The Theory of Economic Development* (Cambridge: Harvard University Press, 1934); Frank Tannenbaum, "The Balance of Power in Society" in *Political Science Quarterly* (December 1946), Vol. LXI, No.4, 481-504.

11. T. H. Huxley and Julian Huxley, *Touchstone for Ethics* (New York: Harper and Bros., 1947).

12. G. Bateson and M. Mead, *Balinese Character: A Photographic Analysis*, *op. cit.*

13. How dangerous it can be to surrender the detachment provided by a lapse of time without replacing it with some new ethic, is only too vividly demonstrated in Dorothy Thomas and Richard Nishimoto: *The Spoilage* (Berkeley and Los Angeles: University of California Press, 1946). Overtly the study lacks value judgments, but a covert bias is displayed in the choice—as subject matter—of the 10 per cent of the interned Japanese for whom the experience was disastrous.

14. Report of the Committee on Ethics, *Human Organization* (Spring 1949), Vol. 8, No. 2, 20-21. For a history of some of the thinking in this field, cf. Margaret Mead, "The Comparative Study of Cultures and the Purposive Cultivation of Democratic Values, 1941-1949," in *Perspectives on a Troubled Decade: Science, Philosophy, and Religion*, 1939-1949, *Tenth Symposium*, ed. by Lyman Bryson, Louis Finkelstein, R. M. MacIver (New York: Harper and Bros., 1950); 87-108.

CHANGING STYLES OF
ANTHROPOLOGICAL WORK*

The last 20 years have seen an enormous growth of institutions devoted to anthropological enterprises, membership within the discipline, and students, textbooks, and paraphernalia. From a tiny scholarly group that could easily be fitted into a couple of buses, and most of whom knew each other, we have grown into a group of tremendous, anonymous milling crowds, meeting at large hotels where there are so many sessions that people do well to find those of their colleagues who are interested in the same specialty. Today we look something like the other social science disciplines, suffering some of the same malaise, and becoming cynical about slave markets and worried when grants and jobs seem to be declining.

It has been a period of excessive growth; it is astonishing, looking back, to recount how many large enterprises have been undertaken. The year 1953 marked the end of the Korean War and the final exodus from Washington of almost all the remaining anthropologists who had lingered on to make the kind of contribution to national affairs that had developed in wartime. Most of the ventures that had been specifically influenced by the immediate post-World War II world drew to a close: Columbia University Research in Contemporary Cultures, Studies in Soviet Culture, American Museum of Natural History Research in Contemporary Cultures A and B, (189, 213), the Coordinated Investigations of Micronesian Anthropology, the period of affluence in the Foreign Service Institute, the intensive exploitation of the Human Relations Area Files, and the preparation of manuals and directives for participation in technical assistance and foreign aid (13, 191,269). A few anthropologists stayed on for several more years, but activities of the House Un-American Activities Committee had disillusioned anthropologists with government, and as their participation in government shrank, so did the receptiveness of government agencies to anthropological contribu-

*Originally published in *Annual Review of Anthropology* Oct. 1973, vol. 2, p. 1-27.

tions because there was no one to inaugurate them, receive them, or interpret them.

Anthropologists came out of the war years with several important new orientations. They had learned that their skills could be applied fruitfully to problems affecting modern societies and the deliberations of national governments and nation states. They had learned to apply themselves to problems they had not themselves chosen, and to work with members of other disciplines. While this was most conspicuously true in the United States, the English style of operational research involved anthropologists in many unfamiliar fields, and some of the theoretical approaches of the French underground also meant a novel use of anthropology. A rationale for the kind of contribution that anthropologists could make to problems of national and worldwide scope was developed (171). But, at the same time, the experience of anthropologists during the war was summed up in the dictum, "you can't advise an adviser." If anthropologists were to participate in public activities, it meant some of them had to accept positions within various parts of the establishment, and this they became increasingly unwilling to do. The contradiction between a willingness during World War II to become involved and a disinclination to become involved later has not yet been resolved. This, in addition to the rejection of the Vietnam war, may account for the rather meager participation of anthropologists in the last 20 years in problems involving technical assistance, modernization, arms control, the prevention of nuclear warfare, peaceful uses of atomic energy, population control, and the environmental crisis (122).

In the earlier years, anthropology was so slightly established that the usual academic punishment for unorthodoxy was confined to excluding from it those who expressed very large heresies, such as the racist approach or an overemphasis on the dependence of American Indian culture on importations from Asia. After the war, although such major unorthodoxies persisted to a certain extent, the scene shifted to rewarding those who took part in currently popular minor theoretical discussions. Students were advised to concentrate on very recent polemics, and small, specific discussions of kinship, or variations in response to Lévi-Strauss (144, 160), became the road to academic advancement.

This exodus from any situation connected with national policy coincided with a tremendous growth in research opportunities and academic appointments. The National Institutes of Mental Health and National Science Foundation programs, and in the 1960s the development of programs vaguely conceived as foreign aid that would be relevant to political purposes abroad, such as the Ford

Foundation Area Studies programs, all provided funding for academically phrased research. There were not enough funds for the tasks that needed doing, but there were more than enough for the strength and capabilities of those who were mature enough to lead and direct these programs.

An enormous number of new possibilities opened up in the United States through the establishment of new departments in old universities, transformation by upgrading old institutions, and a proliferation of new institutions. The establishment of new universities in the United Kingdom, new forms of cooperation in Paris (through coordination provided by the Sixieme Section de L 'Ecole Pratique des Hautes Etudes and the Maison de la Science de l'Homme), and the new universities in Australia, India, and the new countries of Africa and Oceania also widened the field.

Movement from academic post to project to a different academic post was very rapid, and in the scramble for projects and posts there was little time for writing up the large amount of field work that was being funded. A great many young men and women wrote their dissertations, their three short papers, did a few reviews, presented a paper or so, and went on to a tenured appointment with very little opportunity to show their mettle. As the period of educational expansion slows down, it may well be that one legacy from those years will be a layer of middle management, the members of which reached their positions by a kind of gamesmanship that is no longer as relevant to a world where stringency, frugality, and specific capacities critically appraised are again in vogue.

Internationally, there have been a series of large enterprises: the Wenner-Gren Conference of 1952, which held us together for another decade (150,280); *Current Anthropology,* with its network of associates and commentators; the big University of Chicago symposium on evolution (279); the Wenner-Gren Conferences at Burg Wartenstein and in the United States, the International Congresses of Anthropology and Ethnology, and a strong anthropological presence at the Pacific Science Congresses; the development of the Center for the Study of Man at the Smithsonian; the Laboratoire d' Anthropologie Sociale in Paris; the New Guinea Research Unit of the Australian National University; and the present (culminating) effort for the Ninth Congress of Anthropological and Ethnological Sciences to be held in Chicago in September 1973. These clusters of impressive activities owe a great deal to the imagination and energy of three people: Sol Tax, Editor of *Current Anthropology;* Lita Osmundsen, Director of the Wenner-Gren Foundation; and Clemens Heller of the Ecole Pratique des Hautes Etudes, in Paris. As available openings for research, personnel, and funds have been identified and deployed around the world, these people have enlisted the cooperation of many institutions and seized opportunities for amplifying organizational efforts.

This has also been a period of large research programs, varying from the Caribbean program of the Institute for the Study of Man, the continuing area-based projects, like the Chiapas project (296), Watson's New Guinea project (297), Goldschmidt's African project (114), the associated sets of fellowships and activities of the East-West Center in Hawaii, the New Guinea Research Unit of the Australian National University, the Arctic Institute of North America, Vayda's ecology project on the New Guinea Rainforest, the widespread studies emanating from the University of Manchester, the cluster of studies in French West Africa and French Oceania, integration of studies on political and social organization in the Netherlands at the Hague, and the Australian Institute of Aboriginal Studies. And there are many, many more programs in which there has been an attempt to bring together groups interested in an area with various related anthropological specialties. The large scale long term projects have had, I think, no higher rate of failure—failure to complete work, write it up, or integrate results—than other social science projects which had less complicated logistical problems (177).

The catholicity of anthropology, with its ideological insistence on the psychic unity of man, and its traditional disregard of race, ethnicity, age, and sex as criteria for academic posts or research capabilities, combined with the political instabilities of the post-World War II world, has resulted in another form of international cooperation and interpenetration of different nationally based anthropological traditions. When I was a graduate student, Jochelson, a refugee from the new Russia, was writing the last of his volumes on the Koryak (148) in the tower of the American Museum of Natural History, and an Ansa African student from the Gold Coast (187) was giving us lessons on how Africans viewed their own kinship systems. During these early years, a Nez Perce American Indian left Columbia to be welcomed in the Soviet Union as a member of a persecuted minority, and Boas and Manuel Gamio were planning joint studies in the United States and Mexico. In the early 1930s Radcliffe-Brown was teaching at the University of Chicago and—to the great disapproval of his American colleagues—was being considered for the directorship of a large international effort. Since World War II, the mix of students, students as informants, and faculty members drawn from allover the world, partly due to political upheavals, partly due to the great number of foreign fellowships available, has increased enormously. Americans teach in Japan. Frenchmen in India, Indians in the United States,

Ceylonese in Australia and the number of anthropologists from the new African, Asian, and Oceanic countries has increased. The vociferous group making political demands for more representation of Third World points of view has almost completely ignored this movement of scholars, between countries, which has also included Third World political leaders who have studied anthropology in some Euro-American country. It is true that anthropology was born among the Euro-American metropolitan powers and flourished most vigorously among countries with colonial interests or identifiable minorities within their gates. But it is also true that this very anthropological emphasis has brought with it an insistence upon the comparable capacities for political and social development of all the members of *Homo sapiens,* and so has made a substantial intellectual contribution to the process of political democratization in different parts of the world. The current emphasis upon the symbolic processes found in primitive man (166), while it stems (at least within the French tradition) from Lévy-Bruhl, nevertheless reflects just as much interest in the existence of primary process thinking in modern man and the importance of symbolism and ritual in modern life as it does an emphasis on the more vivid and bizarre elements of the culture of preliterate peoples (28, 49-51, 73 74, 101. 236, 288, 289). One of the belated effects of criticism of Freud's *Totem and Taboo* (88, 195) has been to establish that primitive man could think in ways as rational as modern man, as Boas maintained, and that primitive children might be more rational than primitive adults, and that civilized adults might display the kind of egocentric thinking of civilized children (190, 278). With this it has been established that it is necessary to rethink our whole overevaluation of rational linear thinking, with its dependence upon script and script-like processes (24, 28, 47, 178, 260). There has also been a new interest in cross-cultural studies of cognition and perception (61, 261, 290) and a return to a study of multimedia contexts.

At the same time, there are ways in which anthropologists have remained almost incredibly ethnocentric. Forty years ago Radcliffe-Brown suggested a system of kinship nomenclature that was not only cross-cultural but also a way in which kinship relationships could be read back as reciprocal (242). (I put this system on my typewriter in 1931.) Yet in 1972 Conrad Arensberg (12) can call for real "scientific models" and still express beautifully generated kinship relations as abbreviations of English terms *fa si da* or *mo br da*. We do little better in archeology, or physical anthropology, and only slightly better in linguistics. It is true that we need an agreed-upon terminology, but it is equally true that we need terminology that is not ethnocentric, favoring members of one linguistic group or world religion over another.

The last 25 years has also been a period of massive individual enterprises. These have included: Murdock's progressive exploitation of the Human Relations Area Files, first in *Social Organization* (218) and later in his *Ethnographic Atlas* (219); Lévi-Strauss' enormous and detailed study of the myths of the world (166); Yehudi Cohen's intensive use of cross-cultural comparisons and systematic attempts to grapple with the complexities of large areas (58-60), combining field work and integration of the literature; the Whitings' continued cross-cultural studies (304); Mandelbaum on India (182); Goldman's *Ancient Polynesian Society* (112); Leach's *Social Systems of Highland Bunna* (159); and the Geertz's work on Indonesia and Morocco (97,99, 102). These activities are comparable to the syntheses of an earlier day in which art, folklore, and material culture were organized within theoretical frameworks for the benefit of other students. They are notable for the way in which the individual integrating intelligence, handling vast amounts of material collected by hand, is still the prevalent style, only slightly helped by IBM cards or computers.

Traditionally, the sciences have advanced with the help of complementary interrelations between theory, instrumentation, and the stimulating or diverting effects of the climate of opinion within which their practitioners were working. There has been an increasing amount of critical and historical work on anthropological theory, such as Stocking's very distinguished work on Boas (273) combined with a series of trivial father-killing attacks (251, 302), reassessments of Malinowski to the point of boredom of all those participating, Marvin Harris's portenteous evaluation of everyone else (130), and the interesting experiment of using biography as a method of assessment of periods and national schools of anthropology in the *International Encyclopedia of the Social Sciences* (201). Encyclopedias have become one of the ways that the anthropological ideas which originated in the West have been incorporated into the thinking of other parts of the world, e.g. the *Educational Encyclopedia* published in Hebrew (77) and the Japanese version of the Encyclopedia Britannica. But the Wenner-Gren conference on The Nature and Function of Anthropological Tradition, held in 1968, which attempted to delineate the various national streams in anthropology failed both to draw together a sufficiently representative group and to integrate the results (162).

Biography, in a more personal sense than the theoretical evaluations, has also flourished: *Alfred Kroeber* by Theodora Kroeber (151), *Franz Boas* by Herskovits (135), the new series edited by Charles Wagley on Columbia anthropologists (173, 222), *An Anthropologist at*

Work, Writings of Ruth Benedict (192) are examples. Autobiographies of various sorts include (166, 185,271), *High Valley* (244), *Return to Laughter* (42), *Women in the Field* (111), and *Blackberry Winter* (206). There have also been passionate ethnologies like Jules Henry's *Culture Against Man* (132), and Colin Turnbull's *The Mountain People* (287). The furor over the publication of Malinowski's *Diary* (181) represents a low point in the discipline's degree of sophistication. In the inflamed political atmosphere of the 1960s, Malinowski was attacked because of his private diary, which records his tribulations and miseries as he did his magnificent field work. A Polish word, which he used for the Trobrianders when he was most emphatically fed up with them, was translated as "nigger." The increase in self-evaluation and puzzled, troubled exposure of difficulties in the field has not been accompanied, as it might have been, with greater charity or detachment. Anthropologists have continued to be highly personal, unskilled in separating their own affects from their material, polemic, given to *ad hominen* arguments and, as if they were all members of one giant extended family, personal rather than relevant nit-picking.

The question of whether anthropology should be regarded as a self-sufficient science, and as such be required to generate its own propositions and hypotheses without the use either of concepts or the findings of other human or social sciences, remains a subject of controversy (220). At the Wenner-Gren Conference in 1952, David Mandelbaum demanded that the field of culture and personality should make its own contributions and validate its own premises (280), and this same demand has been made by psychoanalysts, because they objected to the importation of physiological data into the validation of their discoveries, as in the famous study of Benedek & Rubenstein (35) in which the findings of the analysts are juxtaposed and validated by records of endocrinological occurrences. Importations from other sciences, whether social and human or biological, are treated by Arensberg (12) as analogies, and yet what he wished to identify as anthropology is "interaction theory," with a heavy dependence on physiological theory and measurement (55).

The argument has several facets. Should there be more than one science concerned with the behavior of human beings, as individuals, in groups, as carriers of culture? Are we not enormously hindered when sociologists, social psychologists, clinical psychologists, psychiatrists, or ethologists attack the same problems as anthropologists, and develop their own set of terminologies, methods, and literature? Shouldn't we all be branches of one human science, which would include human biology, evolution, history and prehistory, distinguished by our methods rather than by the areas or fields that we study? How can we compensate for the damage done by attempts to synthesize a science of human behavior that relies on secondary sources, as Freud did in *Totem and Taboo* (188, 195), as George Land is doing in *Transformation* (157), or on a smaller scale as Barkun (18) is doing in his study of millenarian movements? As long as each sub-discipline of the human sciences persists in its myopic, academically bounded contemplation of its own navel, we will have over-reliance on secondary sources, because access to all the small self-contained subdisciplines will be impossible for the synthesizer.

In addition to the objections that can be raised equally to any of the discussions within the human sciences, there are special conditions in anthropology which complicate the matter even further. One of these is the circumstance that we are dealing with vanishing materials; primitive cultures are swallowed up, remote, isolated human populations interbreed, rare languages vanish when the last two old women who speak them die, archeological remains are destroyed by road-building and dam construction. The data can never be recollected in the light of later paradigms. Thomas Kuhn's illuminating discussion of the way paradigms are finally replaced in the natural sciences (153) simply does not apply to any branch of anthropology, and only to a limited degree to some of the other human sciences. True, a Bavelas experiment may be repeated on a later group of MIT students (30) or Bell Telephone employees, but won't the difference in period contaminate the experiment, as the later subjects have been reared in a different social milieu, eaten different food, breathed different air? The explicit demand of the natural sciences that an experiment be replicable is simply impossible in anthropology. The nearest approach we can make to it is to preserve observations in as complete a form as possible. Sound-synch film today is the closest we can come to the preservation of a complex event which will be subject to later analysis in the light of new hypotheses. With a *360°* sound-synch camera we will come even closer. But replicability we cannot produce. The anthropologist must take earlier data into account; he cannot simply wipe the slate clean and begin allover again as the physical scientist can, and he must therefore continue to use the kind of tools and understandings that will enable him to work with data collected under very different conditions in the past (16).

Furthermore, anthropology shares with other field sciences, with ethology and geology, an extraordinary degree of interpenetration between particular sets of data and theory. Anthropology continues to have such special and peculiar characteristics which on the one hand provide the cement that holds us together as a discipline and on the other hand limit and define our work by the conditions under which it is done. In the laboratory sciences, one laboratory is very like another, better or worse equipped and endowed, but nevertheless laboratory scientists in Japan, Africa, Germany, and the Americas are linked by common methodologies, and scientists can move easily from one country to another. But in the field sciences, the actual conditions of work, bound in as they are with the geography, cultural areal style, politics, logistics, and state of equipment, are so intimately related to the discipline that while the processes of dealing with them provides a basic bond of sympathy between ethnologists a world apart in theory and national origin, they also preserve the extraordinarily idiosyncratic, apprentice style of the discipline.

But this close relationship between the nature of a particular area and the temperament, capabilities, and theoretical orientation of individual field workers has certain other consequences. As anthropology has expanded, the literature has proliferated to such an extent that it is almost impossible to keep up with publications in one's own area, so that an area of specialization shrinks accordingly from the Pacific, to Melanesia, to the Solomon Islands, for example; from New Guinea, South America to jungle dwellers only. We do not, on the whole, relinquish our close relationship to our own field materials, and most theoretical work that matters is tightly bound, although sometimes rather remotely, as in the case of Lévi-Strauss, or Radcliffe-Brown in his later years, to the individual's own field work. But the sense of scope which it was possible for Boas, or Kroeber, or Lowie, or Haddon to have is becoming lost under the torrent of publications, many of them unpredictably trivial or unidentifiably magnificent. It is not, I believe, the kind of loss that we anticipated a generation ago, when the 1952 Wenner-Gren conference (150) was designed to hold together the diverging classical fields of archeology, linguistics, ethnology, and physical anthropology. Instead of a split into these larger fields, as we feared, there has been a kind of fragmentation, by areas, by schools, by instruments used, by approaches preferred, by style of work, into sub fields which are as complex as whole cultures seen in their complete ecological settings. This fragmentation may perhaps reflect the greater sense of holistic imperatives just as much as it does the sort of narrowing of approaches that one finds in biology—the development of embryology, the merging effect found in biochemistry, or the development of experimental ethology.

There has been an increased but still rather limited response to general systems theory, as variously reflected in the work of Bateson (24), Yayda (293), Rappaport (243), Adams (3), and an interest in the use of computers, programming, matrices, etc (105). But the interaction between general systems theory [as represented, for example, by

the theoretical work of Von Bertalanffy (33, 39)] has been compromised, partly by the state of field data, extraordinarily incomparable
as it inevitably is, as well as historical anthropological methods of
dealing with wholes. General systems theory has taken its impetus
from the excitement of discovering larger and larger contexts (163),
on the one hand, and a kind of microprobing into fine detail within
a system, on the other (41, 258). Both of these activities are intrinsic
to anthropology to the extent that field work in living societies has
been the basic disciplinary method. It is no revelation to any field-
experienced anthropologist that everything is related to everything
else, or that whether the entire sociocultural setting can be studied in
detail or not, it has to be known in general outline. General systems
theory, in a sense, is no news at all, as Von Foerster found out when
he attempted to organize a conference of general systems people and
anthropologists (162). In a sense, the situation is comparable to that
found by the Committee for the Study of Mankind, in which a committee that included Robert Redfield tried to get each discipline to
consider its relationship to the concept of Mankind. Anthropologists
replied, "we are related already," and so they were. Something similar
may be said of attempts to date in mathematical anthropology (107,
149). The kind of information that a computer program can finally
provide, on a level of a particular culture, is simply a reflection of how
detailed field work has been done, and to the careful field worker, on
kinship, for example, it provides no illumination. This is, however, in
strong contrast to the uses to which computer programming can be
put, as in the work of Alan Lomax (174, 175), where it has been possible to map world styles in song and dance, combining Murdock's
technologically defined areas (219) with analysis of films, records,
and tapes made by many field workers in many parts of the world.

Without the kind of unification that might be provided by a
recourse to some sort of agreed-upon complex mathematical analysis,
which would include information retrieval, prediction, and genuine
standardization of data collection, the discipline fragments in the way
in which Bali, for example, has been studied. Anthropologists have
taken samples of one village in detail and studied trance in selected
spots. Orchestral music has been recorded and defined for the whole
island. Temple ceremonial has been studied at different levels of complexity, and there have been restudies of specific spots. The construction of one ceremonial object found in many ceremonies has been
detailed, photographic records of various aspects of the culture have
been made, along with cinematographic studies of artistic behavior,
etc. Such methods of unsystematically interrelated probes, some tax-
onomic, some following older categories of analysis, some searching

for large chunks of unanalyzed materials, relate each field worker to a different network of interdisciplinary fellow scholars and scientists. One has only to mention the names of Bateson & Mead (25, 26), Kunst (154), Jane Belo (33,34), Colin McPhee (179), H. J. Franken (86), C. Holt (142), C. and H. Geertz (96, 100, 103), to illustrate this.

So we have had such incomparable, cross-cutting developments as the Society for the Study of Oceania and the Society for Visual Anthropology, Urban Anthropology, and Structural Anthropology. There are those who have developed *festschrifts* for Boas, Herskovits, Radin, Bateson, and the group in applied anthropology who worked on interaction theory (12). And there are those archeologists who combine archeology and ethnology; those who combine primatology and the study of hunters and gatherers; anthropologists who are using video tape; those who are interested in the study of child development, or millenary movements, or ethnohistory, or blood types, ethnoscience, latent structures, and somatotyping. Any given anthropologist of any experience today will be found to have his interests anchored and flourishing in half a dozen fields. So, for example, the late Oscar Lewis was interested in: Mexico (163, 169, 170), Puerto Rico (171), and Cuba; restudies (168), poverty (172), urbanism; the use of tape, multiple familial interviewing, collection, transcription, translation, and integration by one field worker (169), integration of interviews collected and transcribed by many field workers (171) relationship of recorded ethnographic materials and those whose lives are recorded; photography, projective tests, child-rearing, and effects of social revolution. Journals read and articles written span such a variety of fields that it is not surprising that when I asked 80 colleagues, variously selected from many areas and lines of association, to name the five most important books of the last 5 years, only four books were mentioned more than twice. Each respondent revealed his deep involvement in one or more sets of overlapping fields. The interpretation that one informant placed on it, that nothing of very much importance has really happened in the last 5 years, is simply inaccurate. A great deal has happened, but no consensus can be reached, because of the extraordinary diversity within the subject.

This diversity is somewhat paralleled by the increasingly rapid oscillation between the search for universals and the emphasis on diversity. Kluckhohn signaled the search for universals, and the whole series of value studies, eagerly grasped at by other disciplines, represents attempts to find cross-cultural units of analysis which I lose the depth of the cultures from which they come. The earlier period of *etic* research, in which etic or cross-culturally viable units that disregarded the specific cultural unities of the cultures within which they were found, has given place to a much more sophisticated use of comparisons. We contrast, for example, the earlier correlation studies from the Human Relations Area Files, their criticism by Norbeck (228), and Mead & Newton (215), and Cohen (58), the substitution of very detailed studies of clusters of cultures, Vizedom (295), and Textor's type of "more" or "less" associations (281). This trend is beautifully summed up in Lévi-Strauss' Gildersleeve Lecture (167) in 1972, in which he says:

> Should we insist on sticking to the "etic" /"emic" distinction, this can only be done by reversing the acceptances currently given to those terms. It is the "etic" level, too long taken for granted by mechanistic materialism and sensualist philosophy, which we should consider as an artefact. On the contrary, the "emic" level is the one where the material operation of the senses and the more intellectual activities of the mind can meet, and altogether match with the inner nature of reality itself. Structural arrangements are not a mere product of mental operations; the sense organs also function structurally, and outside us, there are structures in atoms, molecules, cells, and organisms. When the mind processes the empirical data which it receives previously processed by the sense organs, it goes on working out structurally what at the outset was already structural. And it can only do so inasmuch as the mind, the body to which the mind belongs, and the things which body and mind perceive, are part and parcel of one and the same reality.

At the same time, anthropological interest in diversity has been given a boost by the worldwide responses to such homogenizing trends as the green revolution, which sums up both tendencies. At the same time that there is a drawing together of a huge genetic pool of human experiments in the domestication of a particular grain and, the development of synthetic types appropriate for the assumed average growing conditions, there is the rediscovery of the dangers of monocrops and a return to the previous uses of diversity in the horticulture of such areas of poor soil as East Africa (46) and the ecologically varied slopes of the mountainsides of Peru or Guatemala. This renewed enthusiasm for diversity—which is after all our particular concern and heritage—was demonstrated by the symposium held at Brown in the spring of 1971 (240).

Today there is a growing movement towards ecological synthesis and systematization of world materials (8, 284). This is evidenced by the considerations of the planetary environment, the simulations of the Club of Rome (217), the search for an Index for the Quality of Life, the development of a Law of the Seas, the search for appropriate regulation and provision of cross-culturally usable soft-ware in the satellite program, the design of new towns and regions, the development of new energy sources, the invention of new life styles, the revision of education to fit a world of rapid cultural change, and the extreme divergence that exists at present between the experience of the generation in power and the young people under 30 (204).

The more that anthropologists respond to these movements, the more they are almost inevitably forced into narrower specializations, as they try to keep up with the specialized vocabulary of the area of worldwide problems with which they are dealing, the places within anthropological literature where the particular area is being tackled, and those anthropologists—who may be at the moment anywhere in the world—who are concentrating on one aspect of the whole. Who would have expected one of the most brilliant pieces of research relevant to planetary political organization to be developed by a field worker in the Congo (307) and published initially in an African newsletter, or that we would be able to tie it in easily with Morton Fried's paper at the NYAS on tribalism (89) and Adams' discussion (3) of Central American national political structures? Would we have expected that in the field of urbanization it would be difficult for a student of social integration in the city, who follows work at the Athens Ekistical Institute with graduate work in Sydney, to be at once conversant with legislative proposals for utility corridors and attempts to think about the present status of unemployed youth; or that in the field of child development, it is equally difficult to integrate Lawrence Malcolm's studies of protein deficiencies in New Guinea (180) to the Society for Social Anthropology's gingerly approach to problems of childhood by way of studies of socialization (186)?

There is another set of these clusters which centers about the use of specific instruments, either psychological or technical, and still another of those who are interested in particular theoretical approaches. One of the great advances of recent decades has come in the whole field of semiotics, ushered in by the conference at Indiana University (260). We now have the well-developed fields of Kinesics (41), Proxemics (126-128), Choreometrics and Cantometrics (174), and Paralinguistics (260), all dependent upon a fine scale analysis based on film and tape, and more recently on video tape. These specialities overlap with the interaction studies of Arensberg (12), Bateson (23, 26), Oliver (231), and the interaction chronograph of Eliot Chapple (55), which in turn overlap with cybernetically oriented field studies like Rappaport's (243), studies in Psychiatry (24) and Primatology (71), and studies of conference techniques and reporting (203, 208).

Other groups are formed around the use of psychological instruments, a sophisticated use of Human Relations Area Files (172, 219, 224, 281), the Whitings' continued studies of judgments of selected anecdotes (156, 304), use of questionnaires on mother-child behavior

(5), Rorschachs, Raven Matrices, Mosaics, etc. Each user has to have at least a working knowledge of what is being done by others using the same instruments, and these uses are likely to cross every other subdivision, geographical or subdisciplinary.

Another consequence of the proliferation of data is that each theorist became so tied in with the particular field experience within which his theoretical stance became clarified for him—but not for others—that there has developed a complementary tendency to ignore other people's work and start from scratch. It is perhaps not accidental that in *The Nature of Cultural Things* (129), Marvin Harris only uses the work of a social psychologist, Roger Barker (17), who himself insisted on starting from scratch, ignoring all previous work that had been done in the same field. So we have insights, some of them developed decades ago, which prove periodically illuminating to a new generation, such as Dateson's *Naven* (23) or Chapple's *Interaction* chronograph (12). And finally we have books about books "I about books, like Murphy's *The Dialectics of Social Life* (221), and those by Barnes .(19) and Jarvie (147). However, one distinctive feature of the present day set of attack and counterattack is the willingness to discuss, analyze, dissect, propound, and expound the findings of Lévi-Strauss during the course of his work, where in previous periods, except for book reviews, very little of this was done until a master was dead (160).

It is not surprising that there has been such a proliferation of field manuals and field work reports, and quasi-autobiographical discussion of field problems, such as *In the Company of Man* (48), *Crossing Cultural Boundaries* (298), Hilger's story of an Araucanian (138), Golde's *Women in the Field* (III), Williams' *Field Methods in the Study of Culture* (305), Freilich's *Marginal Natives* (87), and including the mammoth and outrageously delayed handbook by Naroll & Cohen (225). But the writers of most of these manuals have to rely on methods that are not very much of an improvement over those of the 1920s and 1930s. They expose a student to intimate and detailed accounts of the troubles and struggles that other anthropologists have had, just as we expose a student to exercises in a variety of languages and accounts of a variety of kinship systems, with the hope that somehow they will be able to incorporate a sense of how to do their field work with different equipment and under quite different conditions. The traditional tendency to avoid teaching concrete methods of field research has been exacerbated by the extremely rapid changes in technology of taping, filming, photographing, preserving, developing, viewing, retrieving, and preparing materials for suitable forms of publication and exposition. When to this is added the complexity of preparing for a field trip, in terms of selecting and testing equipment, and the length of time it takes to process grant applications, it is perhaps not surprising that efforts to do any systematic teaching in the use of both kinds of instruments break down. But when we add to this a lack of training, and the requirement that predoctoral students elect a narrow problem that often precludes their making the absolutely essential study of the culture first, it is not surprising that a great deal of incomplete work has come out of the areas which have been popular for predoctoral study. It is even possible that the present financial stringency may keep a certain number of graduate students at home, doing book theses and learning how to organize materials before they plunge prematurely into an area which they may only learn to dislike.

There have been curious discrepancies in the application of anthropology also. Ecology became fashionable over a decade ago, and a whole school has grown around the meticulous reporting of terrain, crop, land ownership, ethnobotanical knowledge, soil fertility, and relative shares of food allotted to families of men of different rank. One might have expected that as the environmental crisis deepened there would be contributions from the field of anthropological ecology. Equally, it might have been expected that a field so deeply concerned with the study of kinship and related problems might have contributed to the whole question of population control. In fact, there are only a handful of workers in either field.

It also might have been expected that those who had clamored most loudly for a scientific and objective approach would have eagerly availed themselves of the new exactness of recording provided by film and tape (1, 2, 14, 16, 26, 94, 189). Actually, it was not until video tape appeared that this kind of instrumentation received much approval, and this, I believe, is because video tape will permit the anthropologist to join the sociologist and social psychologist in distancing himself from his data. Someone else, several someone elses, can code the hours and hours of video tape, and the traditional close tie between observation and recording is broken. Those who demand that anthropology be objective and scientific for the most part have been uninterested in improving upon the pencil as a recorder of anecdotes, subsequently given a rank order by three trained observers. So, in spite of the very greatly increased number of anthropologists, both the funds and the personnel needed to make records of existing primitive peoples are missing, and those who emphasize the use of film are likely to be told they aren't doing real anthropology.

The post-World War II period has been characterized by two kinds of turning towards high cultures: intensive work in countries like India and Japan; and attention to subgroups within our own society, such as transvestites, drug addicts, those living in communes, and ethnic minorities. However, work on the white majority is still somewhat suspect; the demand that anthropology should be comparative seems often to be translated into the demand that there must be something strange and other worldly about the people whom the anthropologist studies. This provision was originally not only a way of fulfilling our responsibility to record vanishing cultures, but was also believed by Boas to be a way of attaining a limited degree of objectivity. Boas did not believe that objectivity was possible or even desirable within one's own culture, where the responsible anthropologist, like any responsible citizen, had to take sides on matters of social justice. He believed it was possible to learn that a member of another culture, far away physically and in technological level, might smack his lips aloud as a sign that he had eaten well, and that this was good manners, and still be critical of the manners of ill-bred persons in our midst. But we would, he used to tell his students, be a little more tolerant as we came to understand that manners were learned cultural behavior and not matters of absolute right and wrong.

However, this achievement of a scientific objectivity, and even the achievement of the ethically desirable stance of tolerance, looks very different today from the way it did 50 years ago. Those who are studied, whether they be members of other races, other ethnic groups, the poor, the oppressed, the imprisoned, feel that to use their lives to obtain a kind of objectivity is to treat them as objects, not as subjects (65, 292). And all over the world the previously dispossessed and ignored are actively demanding an identity which the rest of mankind must respect. For many anthropologists, the recognition of these new demands has coincided with new situations which they welcomed, such as the greater ability of previously non literate people to participate in research, to write about their own cultures (20), to become ethnologists themselves, and to engage in a mutual interchange, instead of an exchange in which one side was at least partially ignorant of the motivations of the other (234). But such recognition has not by any means been universal; in many divisions of the human sciences, human beings are spoken of as digits, as middle-aged white ethnic males, or black unemployed females; nameless, faceless, they appear as statistics, or as individuals described in terms that the reporter has taken no pains to make bearable. The protests of English-speaking "objects of study" became merged with various forms of political protest and partisanship for the oppressed (291). The possessive "my people" or "my village" appears arrogant where once it appeared affectionate and personal. In fact, the application of anthropological methods to our own society, especially when they are

applied to groups other than our own, contaminates the study of
other peoples, who become, not the primitive peoples whom we fully
respected as representatives of whole cultures, but instead members of
disadvantaged groups contending for a place in the sun (291, 292).
And the anthropologist, who has developed the idea of culture, in the
name of which they are pleading their case, is simultaneously
attacked for having somehow been responsible for their primitive
state, which they now wish to redefine or repudiate (64). When this
is combined with the identification of applied anthropology in fields
like technical assistance or community development, as colonial,
neocolonial, or imperialistic maneuvers, the whole ethic of research
and applied research becomes ambiguous (123, 124).

Another of the current ambiguities in anthropology is the question of the new feminism. Anthropology has traditionally been very
receptive to the participation of women. In England, in France, in the
United States, and more recently in Japan, women students have been
given opportunities to do research, in spite of the objections of introducing women into parts of the world where there are many physical
dangers. Yet today there is a lively movement among young women
anthropologists against their own departments, against the paucity
of data on the primitive societies that have been studied on matters
of interest to women: pregnancy, childbirth, women's health, the
menopause, etc. There is also a movement against theories of the
early division of labor between men and women, which they assert
neglect the contributions that prehistoric women made to the development of culture. Too often none of these claims and accusations are
analyzed with the degree of cultural sophistication which anthropology should provide. Scarcity of data on women in primitive cultures
is due primarily to the fact that most women anthropologists were
more interested in doing the same kind of work that men did, rather
than studying women and children. Early theories of the consequences of the division of labor, which assigned disproportionate
roles to man the hunter, had to wait for correction until studies made
on hunters and gatherers provided data on the relative contributions
of each sex to subsistence, now estimated at something like 80 percent produced by women. (There is, it is true, one major discovery
which had to have been made by women, and that is the discovery of
the role of paternity; only women were in a position to make it.) But
the revival of discredited speculations about previous matriarchies
does no credit to historical perspective and threatens to cloud discussions which should proceed on a different level. University establishments do discriminate against women in all departments. We have
been short of data on the female contribution to food supply, and we

know far less than we would like to about the many aspects of women's lives in primitive societies. "Male" speculations about matri-archies may make attractive daydreams, just as the widely spread myth of the island of women—a male nightmare fear that women could get along without them—is at present being turned into a fem-inine daydream by some feminist extremists. But as in the question of race, it is a great mistake to let contemporary partisan politics distort a disciplined look at the facts as we now know them.

I wish to return again to the subject of applied anthropology. Applied anthropology involves working with interdisciplinary teams and administrators and politicians. This field, so highly and promis-ingly developed during and immediately after World War II, has lan-guished during the last two decades (214). A number of conditions have contributed to this decline: loss of interest in psychoanalysis—which mediated between the field of mental health and anthropology (66, 68, 193, 267, 268); disillusionment with government where many such projects originated; easily found, well-paying jobs in acad-emia and the realization that anthropology is becoming an academic-based discipline with rather rigid hierarchical relationships, from the prestigious universities, through a series of lower echelons, all acade-mic, and the awareness that the ambitious young anthropologist is likely to be penalized for working outside these frozen hierarchies. Anthropology was a vocation until World War II; when it became a field that men and women entered instead with high sensitivity to their career hopes and problems and posts which would fulfill their professional ambitions, something was lost. It may be that the con-trast between the relations of pre-World War II field workers and the people they studied or attempted to help in a variety of ways, and the postwar inflation of the field by those who thought of it as just one way of making a living, may also be somewhat responsible for some of the extravagant political accusations of the last decade.

Anthropology, like all the social sciences, has been subjected to intentional politicizing, by the demands of minorities, including students and women, by a questioning about the relationship of sci-entific work to the state of the world, the inequities of the establish-ment, the hope of revolution, the mysticism about the people themselves. For anthropology, the intense polarization about these issues has been intensified by a number of special problems: (a) almost all of our field work has been done on the cultures of those who are now subsumed under the term Third World; (b) almost all of our field work involves complicated relationships with some form of official-dom—foreign offices, district officers, Indian agents, or customs offi-cers—and we are also likely to encounter movements and activities

which are illegal, from methods of burying the dead, the illegal cultivation of opium, and militant nativistic cults, to politicized rebellions
and conspiracies. Furthermore, we have been the discipline concerned
with race, with the comparable abilities of all members of the human
species, with records of past glory or past primitiveness, with problems of language—dialects, developments of national languages, new
orthographies. In a world that is teeming with the rising expectations
of minorities, with new nations, and revolutionized or modernized
old nations, almost every anthropologist stands somewhere in a cross-
fire position, knowing too much about the renascence of old customs,
or providing information that may be used by some agency of modernization, suppression, or militarization, etc.

The original response to anthropologists participating in national
activities during World War II culminated in the code of ethics developed by the Society for Applied Anthropology in 1953 (209), with its
insistence on anthropologists taking responsibility for all foreseeable
effects. Since then, there have been a succession of crises. There were
objections to participation in secret research which was to be guarded
against by open publication as represented in the Heals report (31).
This was followed by the seemingly contradictory demand that information be hidden from government agencies that might misuse it,
which resulted in the Thailand investigation in 1971 (10a, 10b, 11a,
11b) and the recognition that anthropologists not only had to protect
their informants and the cultures they studied, but also identifiable
communities which might become targets. They are also called upon
to become more active protectors of threatened minority primitive
peoples around the world, such as the aboriginal peoples in the Ama-
zon valley who are being threatened at present.

The question of the participation by a people in studies of their
culture has been raised in many ways: in demands that the Indians
receive a percentage of research grants, on the grounds that someone,
anthropologist or society, was exploiting them for gain; the assertion
that only an ethnic group was equipped to study itself; and proposals,
notably by Alan Lomax, that the material collected by anthropologists—especially on music and dance and folklore—be fed back to the
people themselves as an element in their cultural renewal. These
demands parallel the discussions in medicine which ranged through
a suggestion of giving experimental subjects the status of coinvesti-
gator in a relationship of collegiality (123), to a recognition that the
aims of the investigator and experimental subject might be so different that only organization on the part of the proposed subjects would
meet the situation. The classical position of trust and cooperation
between an anthropologist and his informants, no matter how dis-

parate their education, in which both were devoted to recording a vanishing culture and assuring the safety of its artifacts, has now been replaced by a relationship in which the anthropologist must sometimes either espouse the cause of some ethnic group within a revolutionary formula, or be forced to acknowledge that there are no longer such shared values.

It has been a period of minimal detachment and capacity for cultural self-consciousness and loyalty. We could pride ourselves that no anthropologist denounced a fellow anthropologist in the various anticommunist witch hunts of the late 1930s and early 1950s. But the 1960s have involved us in a mass of denunciations and counter-denunciations, in the failure of seniors to recognize the implications of the generation gap, or in a refusal to consider any discussions whatsoever of racial differences, some of which, like the campaign against Carleton Coon's book (62) and the extreme views expressed in the symposium on Science and Race (210), do us little credit.

Intellectual ferment has taken as many and as diverse forms as the formation of clusters of co-workers and recognition of subgoals. Evolution, formerly a battle cry which assumed lines drawn up on both sides, has become a respectable central object of discussion (6, 196, 230, 264, 303), illuminated by studies of the behavior of primates in the wild (115) and attempts at teaching chimpanzees to communicate (238), studies of the brain (43, 239, 241, 300), and by the claims of the various types of structuralists for a basic brain-based grammar (56, 164) and dialectics of opposites (166). While the study of evolution has been enriched by the new kinds of archeology—which united thousands of years of selective adjustment to the same terrain, or by the combinations of studies of living hunters and gatherers and associated primates and ungulates—it has also been given extra urgency by considerations of the present technological crisis. A serious consideration of man-made crises, and the need for a middle technology has revived interest in material culture, for example, and the role of museums, and attempts to understand earlier artifacts by making them. It also brings into focus the role of conscious purpose in our increasingly man-made, interdependent world (28).

Ethology has seriously entered into the theoretical considerations of anthropologists only during the last two decades (255), and comparative studies of man and other creatures, the arguments over aggression and war (91, 119, 176, 203, 264) and a reconsideration of the degree of patterning of instinctive behavior have proceeded in parallel with discussions of the structure of the brain and its products (248). Here again, political ideology has clouded the issue and the clarity of the arguments; new findings (235) call for drastic revisions in over-elaborate schemata of human development. The specter of behavior modification, of the loss of autonomy and freedom, not only haunts any discussion of biological engineering, but also hinders investigation into the functioning of the brain, the effects of psyche-delic drugs, and the interpretation of insights provided by natural and laboratory experiments with animals (165). There seems little doubt that cross-disciplinary research in the wild, taking in wider and wider considerations of the total environment (78, 238), is a more promising field for anthropological cooperation with other sciences than patching together results of isolated laboratory procedures. The very circumstance that recent studies of the brain involve the whole brain (300) reinforces the traditional anthropological preference for the study of whole cultures and whole societies, with the integrative capacity of our major scientific resource, single human minds (197).

The peculiar history of anthropological field work has introduced a new dimension into the discipline, as field workers have been able to make restudies of earlier work, especially their own. The limitations of purely synchronic records of a people at a given moment in time, and subjects who had the same speed of movement and life-span as the investigator, has been mitigated by the rapidity of culture change. When people studied at 20 or 30-year intervals are changing within a world scene where everything else is changing as well, new opportu-nities for research have been automatically introduced, as new tools, new concepts, and new conditions enable the field worker to study quite new problems. Boas inaugurated this kind of thing when he took recording and film equipment to the Kwakiutl when he was in his sixties (192), and since then we have had along series of restudies: by Oscar Lewis (170), Redfield (246, 247), Firth (81), Mead (199), to mention only a few. The possibility of studying fully identified groups over a long period has enormously increased the capacity of anthro-pology to include individual differences and continuities of personal-ity within statements of cultural regularities. This in turn has made it possible to distinguish levels of analysis more sharply. Taking Lévi-Strauss' categories into the field may illuminate field research, but importing far more detailed studies of myth-making or myth-telling into Lévi-Strauss' work would only be disruptive.

Anthropology is entering a new era, the flesh pots are emptier, the difficulties of doing field work increase geometrically as the equip-ment grows more elaborate and the political situation in many parts of the world becomes more unsettled. In such meager times as these, anthropology can take several directions: an increased interest in pro-fessional careers that involve professional competence in related fields, like town planning, health, nutrition, and political organization; an intensive reexamination of existing materials (where Lévi-Strauss has erected such a challenging theoretical structure); concentration on audio-visual recordings in an attempt to obtain the new kind of records of still living cultures with film and tape (14, 16, 94, 95); a renewed dedication to the preservation of cultural diversity; and a greater involvement in an increasingly endangered planet. The problem remains of how to keep so many extraordinarily diverse and discrepant foci of interest and competence in active interrelationship. The very peculiarity of the task may be what will make it possible.

Literature Cited

The following kinds of references are included: *(a)* literature cited in text; *(b)* publications which were suggested by one or more of the author's colleagues (starred); *(c)* books the author considers especially interesting; (d) references to the author's own work, particularly articles which have extensive bibliographies.

1. Adair, J., Worth, S. 1967. The Navajo as filmmaker: A brief report of research in the cross-cultural aspects of film communication. *Am. Anthropol.* 69: 76-78
2. Adair, P ., Boyd, B. 1967. *Holy Ghost People.* 16 mm black & white film, sound (60 min). New York: McGraw- Hill
3. Adams, R. N. 1970. *Crucifixion by Power: Essays on Guatemalan National Social Structure, 1944-1966:* Austin: Univ. Texas Press
4. Adams, R. N., Preiss, J. J., Eds. 1960. *Human Organization Research.* Homewood: Dorsey
5. Ainsworth, M. D. 1967. *Infancy in Uganda.* Baltimore: Johns Hopkins Univ. Press
6. Alland, A.1967. *Evolution and Human Behavior.* New York: Natural History Press
7. Alland, A. 1971. *Human Diversity.* New York: Columbia Univ. Press
8.* Albertson, P., Barnett, M., Eds. 1971. *Environment and Society in Transition.,* NY Acad. Sci.
9.* Albisetti, C., Venturelli, A. J. 1968-1969. *Enciclopedia Bororo.* Compo Grande, Mato Grasso, Brasil: Museu Regional Dom Bosco (first volume publ. 1962)
10a. Am. Anthropol. Assoc., M. Mead, chairman, 1971. Charge to the ad hoc committee to evaluate the controversy concerning anthropological activities in relation to Thailand. *Newsletter Am. Anthropol. Assoc.* 12, No.3
10b. Am. Anthropol. Assoc. 1971. Report of the ad hoc committee to evaluate the controversy concerning anthropological activities in relation to Thai-

land, Sept. 27, 1971. Part I: Anthropological Activities in Thailand; Part II: Guidelines on Future Policy

11a. Am. Antrhopol. Assoc. 1972. Council rejects Thai controversy committee's report. *Newsletter Am. Anthropol. As- soc.* 13, No.1:1,9

11b. Am. Anthropol. Assoc., M. Mead, 1972. Thailand controversy response to the board's response to the discussion. *Newsletter Am. Anthropol. Assoc.* 13, No.2:1,6

12. Arensberg, C. M. 1972. Culture as behavior: Structure and emergence. *Ann. Rev. Anthropol.* 1:1-26

13. Arensberg, C. M., Niehoff, A. H. 1964. *Introducing Social Change: A Manual for Americans Overseas.* Chicago: Aldine.

14. Asch, T., Chagnon, N., Neel, J. V. 1971. *Yanomama.* 16 mm color film sound (43 min). Center for Documentary Anthropology, Brandeis Univ.

15.* Balandier, G. 1971. *Political Anthropology.* New York: Pantheon

16. Balikci, A. 1969. *Netsilik Eskimos of the Pelly Bay Region of Canada.* 9 films, 16 mm color, sound (approx. 30 min each). New York: Universal Education and Visual Arts

17. Barker, R. G., Wright, H. F. 1971. *Midwest and Its Children.* Hamden: Shoe String Press (first publ. 1954)

18. Barkun, M. *Disaster and the Millenium.*

19.* Barnes, J. A. 1971. *Three Styles—The Study of Kinship.* Berkeley: Univ. California Press

20.* Barnett, D. L., Mjama, K. 1966. *Mau Mau from Within.* New York: Monthly Review Press

21.* Barth, F., Ed. 1969. *Ethnic Groups and Boundaries.* Boston: Little, Brown

22. Bateson, G. 1956. The message "this is play." In *Group Processes,* ed. B. Schalfner, 2:145-242. New York: Macy Found.

23. Bateson, G. 1958. *Naven.* Stanford Univ. Press. 2nd ed.

24. Bateson, G. 1972. *Steps to an Ecology of Mind.* San Francisco: Chandler

25. Bateson, G., Mead, M. 1962. *Balinese Character: A Photographic Analysis.* N. Y. Acad. Sci. (first publ. 1942)

26. Bateson, B., Mead, M. 1952. *Character Formation in Different Cultures* series. 6 films, 16 mm, black & white, sound. New York Univ. Film Library
    a. *A Balinese Family* (17 min)
    b. *Bathing Babies in Three Cultures* (9 min)
    c. *Childhood Rivalry in Bali and New Guinea* (20 min)
    d. *First Days in the Life of a New Guinea Baby* (19 min)
    e. *Karba's First Years* (20 min)
    f. *Trance and Dance in Bali* (20 min)

27. Bateson, M. C. 1970. *Structural continuity in poetry.* PhD thesis. Harvard , Univ., Cambridge

28. Bateson, M. C. 1972. *Our Own Metaphor.* New York: Knopf

29. Bateson, M. C. 1973. Ritualization: A study in texture and texture change. In *Pragmatic Religions,* ed. I. Zaretsky, M. Leone. Princeton Univ. Press

30. Bavelas, A. 1951. Communication patterns in task-oriented groups. In *The Policy Sciences,* ed. H. D. Laswell, D. Lerner, 193-202. Stanford Univ. Press

31. Beals, R. L. 1969. *Politics of Social Research: An Inquiry into the Ethics and Responsibilities of Social Scientists.* Chicago: Addine-Atherton
32. *Behavioral Science* 1956 to date. Mental Health Res. Inst. Univ. Michigan, Ann Arbor
33. Belo, J. 1960. *Trance in Ball* New York: Columbia Univ. Press
34. Belo, J. 1970. *Traditional Balinese Culture.* New York: Columbia Univ. Press
35. Benedek, T., Rubenstein, B. 1939. Correlations between ovarian activity and psychodynamic processes: I. The ovulative phase; II. The menstrual phase. *Psychosom. Med.* I :245 ff., 461 ff.
36.* Bennett, J. W. 1969. *The Northern Plainsmen.* Chicago: Aldine
37.* Berger, P., Luckmann, T. 1966. *Social Construction of Reality.* Garden City: Doubleday
38.* Berlin, B. 1970. A universalist-evolutionary approach in ethnographic semantics. In *Current Directions in Anthropology,* ed. A. Fischer. *Bull. Am. Anthropol. Assoc.* 3:3-18
39. Bertalanffy, L. von 1969. *General System Theory: Essays on Its Foundation and Development.* New York: Braziller
40. Binford, L. R., Binford, S. R., Eds. 1968. *New Perspectives in Archeology.* Chicago: Aldine-Atherton
41. Birdwhistell, R. L. 1970. *Kinesics and Context.* Philadelphia: Univ. Pennsylvania Press
42. Bowen, E. S. 1964. *Return to Laughter.* Natural History Library 36. Garden City: Doubleday (first publ. 1954)
43. Braud, L. W., Braud, W. G. 1972. Biochemical transfer of relational responding (transposition). *Science* 176:942-44
44. Brown, D. 1971. *Bury My Heart at Wounded Knee.* New York: Holt, Rinehart & Winston
45.* Butzer, K. 1971. *Environment and Archeology.* Chicago: Aldine-Atherton
46. Campbell, J. 1971. *Agricultural development in East Africa: A problem in cultural ecology.* PhD thesis. Columbia Univ., New York
47. Carpenter, E. 1970. *They Became What They Beheld.* New York: Outerbridge & Dienstfrey
48. Casagrande, J. B., Ed. 1960. *In the Company of Man.* New York: Harper
49. Castaneda, C. 1968. *Teaching of Don Juan: Yaki Way of Knowledge.* Berkeley: Univ. California Press
50. Castaneda, C. 1971. *Separate Reality.* New York: Simon & Schuster
51. Castaneda, C. 1972. *Journey to Ixtlan: The Lessons of Don Juan.* New York: Simon & Schuster
52. Caudill, W., Lin, Tsung-Yi Eds..1969. *Mental Health Research In Asia and the Pacific.* Honolulu: Univ. Hawaii Press
53. Caudill, W., Weinstein, H. 1969. Maternal care and infant behavior in Japan and America. *Psychiatry* 32: 12-43
54. Chagnon, N. A. 1968. *Yanomamo: The Fierce People.* New York: Holt, Rinehart & Winston
55. Chapple, E. D. 1970. *Cultural and Biological Man: Explorations in Behavioral Anthropology.* New York: Holt, Rinehart & Winston

56. Chomsky, N. 1972. *Language and Mind*, enl. ed. New York: Harcourt, Brace, Jovanovich .

57.* Clastres, P. 1972. *Chronique des Indiens Guayaki*. Paris: Plon

58. Cohen, Y. A. 1964. *The Transition from Childhood to Adolescence: Cross-Cultural Studies of Initiation Ceremonies, Legal Systems, and Incest Taboos*. Chicago: Aldine

59. Cohen, Y. A. 1968. *Man in Adaptation: The Cultural Present*. Chicago: Aldine

60. Cohen, Y. A. 1971. *Man in Adaptation: The Institutional Framework*. *Chicago: Aldine*

61. Cole, M., Gay, J., Glick, J. A., Sharp, D. W. 1971. *The Cultural Contexts of Learning and Thinking: An Exploration of Experimental Anthropology*. New York: Basic Books

62. Coon, C. S. 1962. *The Origin of Races*. New York: Knopf

63.* De Laguna, F. 1960. *The Story of a Tlingit Community: A Problem in the Relationship Between Archeological, Ethnological, and Historical Methods*. Washington, D.C.: GPO

64. Deloria, V. Jr. 1969. *Custer Died for Your Sins*. New York: Macmillan

65. Deloria, V. Jr. 1970. *We Talk, You Listen*. New York: Macmillan

66. De Reuck, A. V. S., Porter, R., Eds. 1965. *Transcultural Psychiatry: A Ciba Foundation Symposium*. London: Churchill

67. Deutsch, K. W. 1966. *Nationalism and Social Communication*. Cambridge: MIT. 2nd ed.

68. Devereux, G. 1967. *From Anxiety to Method in the Behavioral Sciences*. The Hague: Mouton

69. Devereux, G. 1968. *Reality and Dream. New York: Doubleday (first publ 1951.) 2nd ed.*

70. Devereux, G. *Dreams in Greek Tragedy*. Oxford: Blackwell.

71. DeVere, I., Ed. 1965. *Primate Behavior*. New York: Holt, Rinehart & Winston

72. Dillon, W. S. 1968. *Gifts and Nations: The Obligation to Give, Receive and Repay*. New York: Humanities Press

73. Douglas, M. 1966. *Purity and Danger*. New York: Praeger

74. Douglas, M. 1970. *Natural Symbols*. New York: Pantheon

75.* Duchet, M. 1971. *Anthropologie et Histoire au Siecle des Lumières: Buffon, Voltaire, Rousscau, Helvetius, Diderot*. Paris: Maspero

76.* Dumont, L. 1970. *Homo Hierarchicus: The Caste System and Its Implications*. Univ. Chicago Press

77. Educational Encyclopedia (Hebrew) 1959-61. Thesaurus of Jewish and general education, ed. M. M. Buber, Vol. 1, 2. Jerusalem: Ministry of Education and Culture, and the Bialik Institute

78. Eisenberg, J. F., Dillon, W. S., Eds. 1971. *Man and Beast: Comparative Social Behavior*. Washington: Smithsonian Inst. Press

79.* Epstein, T. S. 1962. *Economic Development and Social Change in South India*. New York: Humanities Press

80. Erikson, E. H. 1969. *Gandhi's Truth: On the Origins of Militant Nonviolence*. New York: Norton

81. Firth, R. 1967. *Tikopia: Ritual and Behel* London: Allen & Unwin
82. Firth, R., Ed. 1967. *Themes in Economic Anthropology.* New York: Barnes & Noble
83. Foerster, H. von, Ed. 1950-1956. *Cybernetics.* New York: Macy Found. 5 vols.
84. Fortes, M. 1969. *Kinship and the Social Order.* Chicago: Aldine
85.* Fox, R. 1968. *Kinship and Marriage: An Anthropological Perspective.* New York: Penguin
86. Franken, H. J. et al 1960. *Bali: Studies in Life, Thought and Ritual.* The Hague: van Hoeve
87. Freilich, M., Ed. 1970. *Marginal Natives: Anthropologists at Work.* New York: Harper & Row
88. Freud, S. 1960. *Totem and Taboo.* Transl. A. A. Brill. New York: Random House (first publ. 1918)
89. Fried, M. H. 1966. On the concepts of 'Tribe' and 'Tribal Society.' *Trans. N.Y. Acad. Sci.* 28:527-40
90. Fried, M. H. 1972. *The Study of Anthropology.* New York: Crowell
91. Fried, M., Harris, M., Murphy, R. Eds. 1968. *War: The Anthropology of Armed Conflict and Aggression.* Garden City: Natural History Press
92. Fromm, E., Maccoby, M. 1970. *Social Character in a Mexican Village.* Englewood Cliffs: Prentice Hall
93. Gans, H. J. 1962. *Urban Villagers.* New York: Free Press
94. Gardner, R. 1964. *Dead Birds.* 16 mm color film, sound (83 min). Cambridge: Peabody Museum, Harvard Univ. Distributed by Contemporary Films, New York
95. Gardner, R., Heider, K. G. 1968. *Gardens of War.* New York: Random House
96. Geertz, C. 1959. Form and variation in Balinese village structure. *Am. Anthropol.* 61:991-1012
97. Geertz, C. 1963. *Agricultural Involution: the Process of Ecological Change in Indonesia.* Berkeley: Univ. California Press
98. Geertz, C. 1964. *The Religion of Java.* Glencoe: Free Press (first publ. 1960)
99. Geertz, C. 1968. *Islam Observed: Religious Development in Morocco and Indonesia.* New Haven: Yale Univ. Press
100. Geertz, C. 1972. Deep Play: Notes on the Balinese cockfight. *Daedalus* Winter: 1-37
101. Geertz, C., Ed. 1972. *Myth, Symbol and Culture.* New York: Norton
102. Geertz, H. 1961. *Javanese Family. Glencoe: Free Press*
103. Geertz, H., Geertz, C. 1964. Teknonymy in Bali: Parenthood, age grading and genealogical amnesia. *J. Roy. Anthropol. Inst. Gt. Brit. Ireland* 94: 94-108
104.* Gellner, E. A. 1969. *Saints of the Atlas. Univ. Chicago Press*
105. General Systems Yearbook of the Society for General Systems Research 1956 to date, ed. L. von Bertalanffy, A. Rapoport. Washington: Soc. Gen. Syst. Res.
106. Gilbert, C. 1968. *Margaret Mead's New Guinea Journal.* 16 mm color film, sound (90 min). New York: Nat. Educ. Telev.

107.* Gillespie, J. V., Nesvold, B. Eds. 1970. *Macro-Quantitative Analysis.* Beverly Hills: Sage Publ.

108. Gluckman, M. 1964. *Custom and Conflict in Africa.* New York: Barnes & Noble (first publ. 1955)

109. Gluckman, M., Ed. 1964. *Closed Systems and Open Minds: The Limits of Naivety in Social Anthropology.* Chicago: Aldine

110. Gluckman, M. 1965. *Politics, Law and Ritual in Tribal Society.* Chicago: Aldine

111. Golde, P., Ed. 1970. *Women in the Field.* Chicago: Aldine

112. Goldman, I. 1970. *Ancient Polynesian Society.* Univ. Chicago Press

113. Goldschmidt, W. 1971. *Exploring the Ways of Mankind.* New York: Holt Rinehart & Winston

114. Goldschmidt, W., et al 1965. Variation and adaptability of culture. *Am. Anthropol.* 67:400-47

115. Goodall, J. V. L. 1971. *In the Shadow of Man.* Boston: Houghton Mifflin

116.* Goodenough, W. H. 1970. *Description and Comparison in Cultural Anthropology.* Chicago: Aldine

117. Gorer, G. 1965. *Death, Grief and Mourning.* Garden City: Doubleday

118. Gorer, G. 1966. *The Danger of Equality.* London: Cressett

119. Gorer, G. 1966. Man has no killer instinct. *New Nov. 27:47ff.*

120. Gorer, G. 1971. *Sex and Marriage in England Today.* London: Nelson

121. Gould, R. A. 1969. *The Yiwara: Foragers of the Australian Desert.* New York: Scribner

122. Graubard, S. R., Ed. 1965. Science and culture. *Daedalus* Winter issue

123. Graubard, S. R., Ed. 1969. Ethical aspects of experimentation with human subjects. *Daedalus* Spring issue

124. Gwaltney, J. L. 1970. *Thrice Shy: Cultural Accommodations to Blindness and Other Disasters in a Mexican Community.* New York: Columbia Univ. Press

125. Hagen, E. E. 1962. *On the Theory of Social Change.* Homewood: Dorsey

126. Hall, E. T. 1961. *The Silent Language.* New York: Fawcett (first publ. 1959)

127. Hall, E. T. 1963. A system for the notation of proxemic behavior. *Am. Anthropol.* 65:1003-26

128. Hall, E. T. 1966. *The Hidden Dimension.* Garden City: Doubleday

129. Harris, M. 1964. *The Nature of Cultural Things.* New York: Random House

130.* Harris, M. 1968. *The Rise of Anthropological Theory: A History of Theories of Culture.* New York: Crowell

131. Heider, K. G. 1970. *Dugun Dani.* Chicago: Aldine

132. Henry, J. 1963. *Culture Against Man. New York: Random House*

133. Henry, J. 1972. *Pathways to Madness. New York: Random House*

134. Henry, N. B., Ed. 1959. *Community Education.* Nat. Soc. Study Educ. 58th f Yearb., part 1. Univ. Chicago Press

135. Herskovits, M. J. 1953. *Franz Boas.* New York: Scribner

136.* Heusch, L. de 1972. *Le Roi Ivre ou L'Origine de L 'Etat* (Les Essais CLXXIII). Paris: Gallimard

137. Hilger, M. I. 1954. An ethnographic field method. In *Method and Perspective in Anthropology,* ed. F. Spencer. Minneapolis: Univ. Minnesota Press

138. Hilger, M. I. 1966. *Huenun Namku: an Araucanian Indian of the Andes Remembers the Past.* Norman: Univ. Oklahoma Press
139. Hill, R. B. 1972. *The Strengths of Black Families.* New York: Emerson Hall
140.* Hodgen, M. T. 1964. *Early Anthropology in the Sixteenth and Seventeenth Centuries.* Philadelphia: Univ. Pennsylvania Press
141. Hogbin, I. 1970. *The Island of Menstruating Men.* Scranton: Chandler
142. Holt, C. 1967. *Art in Indonesia.* Ithaca: Cornell Univ. Press
143. Holt, C. 1972. *Culture and Politics in Indonesia.* Cornell Univ. Press
144. Romans, G. C., Schneider, D. M., 1955. *Marriage, Authority, and Final Causes.* Glencoe: Free Press
145.* Horton, R. 1960. A definition of religion and its uses. *J. Roy. Anthropol. Inst. at. Brit. Ireland* 90:201-26
146. Ianni, F. A. 1972. *A Family Business: Kinship and Social Control in Organized Crime.* New York: Sage Found.
147.* Jarvie, I. C. 1964. *The Revolution in Anthropology.* New York: Humanities Press
148. Jochelson, W. 1908. *Material Culture and Social Organization of the Koryak.* Mem. Am. Mus. Natur. Hist. 10, part 2. Leiden: Brill
149.* Kay, P., Ed. 1971. *Explorations in Mathematical Anthropology.* Cambridge: MIT Press
150. Kroeber, A. L., Ed. 1953. *Anthropology Today.* Univ. Chicago Press
151. Kroeber, T. 1970. *Alfred Kroeber.* Berkeley: Univ. California Press
152.* Kronenberg, A. 1972. *Logik und Leben.* Wiesbaden: Steiner Verlag
153. Kuhn, T. S. 1968. *The Structure of Scientific Revolution.* Univ. Chicago Press
154. Kunst, J. 1949. *The Cultural Background of Indonesian Music.* Amsterdam: Indish Inst.
155. Kunz, R. M., Fehr, H., Eds. 1972. *The Challenge of Life.* Basel, Stuttgart: Birkhauser Verlag
156. Lambert, W. M., Minturn, L. 1964. *Mothers of Six Cultures: Antecedence of Child Rearing.* New York, London: Wiley
157. Land, G. *Transformation.* New York: Random House.
158. Lawrence, P. 1964. *Road Belong Cargo.* New York: Humanities Press
159. Leach, E. R. 1965. *Political Systems of Highland Burma.* New York: Beacon (first publ. 1954)
160. Leach, E. R. 1970. *Claude Lévi-Strauss.* New York: Viking
161. Lee, R. B., De Vore, I., Eds. 1968. *Man the Hunter.* Chicago: Aldine
162. Leeds, A., von Foerster, H., Eds. 1965. *The Potentiality of Systems Theory for Anthropological Inquiry.* New York: Wenner-Gren Found. Anthropol. Res.
163. Lehman, F. K. 1959. *Some anthropological parameters of a civilization: The ecology and evolution of India's high culture.* PhD thesis. Columbia Univ., New York. 2 vols.
164.* Lenneberg, E. H. 1967. *The Biological Foundations of Language.* New York: Wiley
165. Lévi-Strauss, C.1961. *Tristes Tropiques: An Anthropological Study of Primitive Societies In Brazil.* New York: Atheneum (first publ. 1961 as *A World on the Wane*)

166. Lévi-Strauss, C. 1964-1971. *Mythologiques*. 4 vols. Paris: Plon.
     Vol.1: *Le Cru et le Cuit*
     Vol.2: *Du Miel aux Cendres*
     Vol.3: *L 'Origine des Manières de Table*
     Vol.4: *L'Homme Nu*
167. Lévi-Strauss, C. 1972. Structuralism and ecology. *Barnard Alumnae* Spring issue: 6-14
168. Lewis, O. 1960. *Tepoztlan: Village in Mexico*. New York: Holt, Rinehart & Winston
169. Lewis, O. 1961. *The Children of Sanchez:*. New York: Random House
170. Lewis, O. 1963. *Life In a Mexican Village: Tepoztlan Restudied*. Urbana: Univ. Illinois Press (first publ. 1951)
171. Lewis, O. 1966. *La Vida.*. New York: Random House
172. Lewis, O. 1966. The culture of poverty. *Sci. Am.* 215:19-25
173. Linton, A., Wagley, C. 1971. *Ralph Linton*. New York: Columbia Univ. Press
174. Lomax, A., Ed. 1968. *Folksong Style and Culture* (Symp. Vol. 88). Washington: Am. Assoc. Advan. Sci.
175. Lomax, A. 1972. The evolutionary taxonomy of culture. *Science* 177:228-39
176. Lorenz, K. 1971. *Studies in Animal and Human Behavior*, vol. 2. Cambridge: Harvard Univ. Press)
177. Luszki, M. B. 1958. *Interdisciplinary Team Research: Methods and Problems*. New York: University Press
178. McLuhan, M. 1962. *The Gutenberg Galaxy*. Univ. Toronto Press
179. McPhee, C. 1966. *Music in Bali*. New Haven, London: Yale Univ. Press
180. Malcolm, L. A. 1969. Growth and development of the New Guinea child. *Papua and New Guinea* J.: 6:23-32
181. Malinowski, B. 1967. *A Diary in the Strict Sense of the Tenn*. New York: Harcourt, Brace
182. Mandelbaum, D. G. 1970. *Society in India*. Berkeley: Univ. California Press. 2 vols.
183.* Marshack, A. 1972. *The Roots of Civilization*. New York: McGraw-Hill
184. Marshall, J., Gardner, R. 1958. *The Hunters*. 16 mm color film, sound (72 min). Cambridge: Film Study Center Peabody Mus., Harvard Univ.
185. Maybury-Lewis, D. 1968. *The Savage and the Innocent*. Boston: Beacon Press (first publ. 1965)
186. Mayer, P., Ed. 1970. *Socialization*. Scranton: Barnes & Noble
187. Mead, M.1937. A Twi relationship system: *J. Roy. Anthropol. Inst. Gt. Brit. Ireland* 67:297-304
188. Mead, M. 1950. The comparative study of cultures and the purposive cultivation of democratic values, 1941-1949. In *Perspectives on a Troubled Decade: Science, Philosophy, and Religion, 1939-1949*, ed. L. Bryson, L. Finkelstein, R. M. Mclver, 87-108. New York: Harper & Row
189. Mead, M. 1951. *Soviet Attitudes Toward Authority*. New York: McGraw-J Hill
190. Mead, M. 1954. Research on primitive children. In *Manual of Child Psychology*, ed. L. Carmichael, 735-80. New York: Wiley. 2nd ed.
191. Mead, M., Ed. 1955. *Cultural Patterns and Technical Change*. Mentor Books. New York: New Am. Libr. (first publ.1953)

192. Mead, M. 1959. *An Anthropologist at Work: Writings of Ruth Benedict.* Boston: Houghton Mifflin

193. Mead, M. 1961. Psychiatry and ethnology. In *Psychiatne der Gegenwart: Forschung und Praxis, III:Soziale und Angewandte Psychiatrie,* ed. H. W. Gruhle et al, 452-70. Berlin: Springer

194. Mead, M. 1963. Anthropology and the camera. In *The Encyclopedia of Photography,* ed. W. D. Morgan, 166-84. New York: Greystone

195. Mead, M. 1963. *Totem and Taboo* reconsidered with respect. *Bull. Menninger Clin.* 27:185-99

196. Mead, M. 1964. *Continuities in Cultural Evolution.* New Haven: Yale Univ. Press

197. Mead, M. 1964. Vicissitudes of the study of the total communication process. In *Approaches to Semiotics,* ed. T. A. Sebeok, A. S. Hayes, M. C. Bateson, 277-87. The Hague: Mouton

198. Mead, M. 1966. *The Changing Culture of an Indian Tribe.* Cap Giant 266, New York: Putnam (first publ.1932)

199. Mead, M. 1966. *New Lives for Old: Cultural Transformation-Manus 1928-1953,* with new preface. Apollo Editions. New York: Morrow (first publ. 1956)

200. Mead, M. 1968. Cybernetics of cybernetics. In *Purposive Systems: Processes of the First Annual Symposium of the American Society for Cybernetics,* ed. H. von Foerster et al, 1-11. New York, Washington: Spartan Books

201. Mead, M. 1968. Incest. In *International Encyclopedia of the Social Sciences,* ed. D. L. Sills, 7: 115-22. New York: Macmillan. 17 vols.

202. Mead, M. 1969. Crossing boundaries in social science communication. *Soc. Sci. Inform.* 8:7-15

203. Mead, M. 1969. From intuition to analysis in communication research. *Semiotica* 1:13-25

204. Mead, M. 1970. *Culture and Commitment: A Study of the Generation Gap.* Garden City: Natural History Press & Doubleday

205. Mead, M. 1970. *Ethnicity and Anthropology in America.* Wenner-Gren Conf. Ethnic-Identity, Burg Wartenstein Symp. 51.

206. Mead, M. 1972. *Blackberry Winter: My Earlier Years.* New York: Morrow

207. Mead, M. Systems analysis and metacommunication. In *The World System,* ed. E. Laszlo. New York: Braziller.

208. Mead, M., Byers, P. 1968. *The Small Conference: An Innovation in Communication.* Paris, The Hague: Mouton 209. Mead, M., Chapple, E. D., Brown, G. G. 1949. Report of the committee on ethics. *Hum. Org.* 8:20-21

210. Mead, M., Dobzhansky, T., Tobach, E., Light, R. E., Eds. 1968. *Science and the Concept of Race.* New York, London: Columbia Univ. Press

211. Mead, M., Heyman, K. 1965. *Family.* New York: Macmillan

212. Mead, M., Macgregor, F. C. 1951. *Growth and Culture: A Photographic Study of Balinese Childhood.* New York: Putnam

213. Mead, M., Metraux, R., Eds. 1953. *The Study of Culture at a Distance.* Univ. Chicago Press

214. Mead, M., Metraux, R. 1965. The anthropology of human conflict. In *The Nature of Human Conflict,* ed. E. B. McNeil, 116-38. Englewood Cliffs: Prentice Hall

215. Mead, M., Newton, N. 1967. Cultural patterning of perinatal behavior. In *Childbearing—Its Social and Psychological Aspects*, ed. S. A. Richardson, A. F. Guttmacher, 142-244. Baltimore: Williams & Wilkins

216. Mead, M., Schwartz, T. 1960. The cult as a condensed social process. In *Group Processes: Transactions of the Fifth Conference, October* 12-15, 1958, ed. Bertram Schatfner, 85-187. New York: Macy Found.

217. Meadows, D. et al 1972. *The Limits to Growth*. Washington: Potomac Assoc.

218. Murdock, G. P. 1949. *Social Structure. New York: Macmillan*

219. Murdock, G. P. 1967. *Ethnographic Atlas*. Univ. Pittsburgh Press

220. Murdock, G. P. 1972. Anthropology's mythology. *Proc. Roy. Anthropol. Inst. art. Brit. Ireland for* 1971, 17-24 221. Murphy, R. F. 1971. *The Dialectics of Social Life: Alarms and Excursions in Anthropological Theory*. New York: Basic Books

222. Murphy, R. F. 1972. *Robert Lowie.* --"= ,,~— New York: Columbia Univ. Press '

223.* Nader, L:, Ed. 1969. *Lawn Culture and Society*. Chicago: Aldme-Atherton.

224. Naroll, R. 1970. What we have learned from cross-cultural surveys. *Am. Anthropol.* 72:1227-88

225. Naroll, R., Cohen, R., Eds. 1970. *A Handbook of Method in Cultural Anthropology*. Garden City: Natural History Press

226. Norbeck, E. 1970. *Religion and Society in Modem Japan: Continuity and' /T Change*. Houston: Rice Univ.

227. Norbeck, E. 1971. Man at play. *Natur Hist. Mag.* 80:48-53

228. Norbeck, E., Walker, D. G., Cohen, M. 1962. The interpretation of Data: Puberty rites. *Am. Anthropol.* 64:463- 85

229. Norbeck, E. et al, Eds. 1968. *The Study of Personality*. New York: Holt, Rinehart & Winston

230.* Nurge, E., Ed. 1970. *Modem Sioux. Lincoln:* Univ. Nebraska Press

231. Oliver, D. L. 1955. *A Solomon Island Society*. Cambridge: Harvard Univ. Press

232.* Ortiz, A. 1969. *The Tewa World*. Univ. Chicago Press

233.* Otterbein, K. F. 1970. *The Evolution of War: A Cross-Cultural Study*. New Haven: Human Relations Area Files Press

234.* Owusu, M. 1970. *Uses and Abuses of Political Power*. Univ. Chicago Press

235. Payne, M. M. 1973. The Leakey tradition lives on. *Nat. Geogr. Mag.* 143: 143-44

236.* Peacock, J. L. 1968. *Rites of Modernization*. Univ. Chicago Press

237.* Pelto, P. J. 1970. *Anthropological Research: The Structure of Inquiry*. New York: Harper & Row

238. Pfeiffer, J. E. 1972. *The Emergence of Man*. New York: Harper & Row (first publ. 1969)

239. Pietsch, P., Schneider, C. W. 1969. Brain transplantation in salamanders: An approach to memory transfer. *Brain Res.* 14:707-15

240. Poggie, J., Lynch, R., Eds. *Modernization: Anthropological Approaches to Contemporary Socio-Cultural Change*. Westport: Greenwood.

241. Pribram, K. H. 1969. The neurophysiology of remembering. *Sci. Am.* 220: 73-86
242. Radcliffe-Brown, A. R. 1930. A system of notation for relationships. *Man* 30: 121-22
243. Rappaport, R. A. 1968. *Pigs for the Ancestors.* New Haven: Yale Univ. Press
244. Read, K. E. 1965. *The High Valley.* New York: Scribner
245. Redfield, R. 1930. *Tepoztlan: A Mexican Village.* Univ. Chicago Press
246. Redfield, R. 1962. *A Village that Chose Progress: Chan Kom Revisited.* Univ. Chicago Press (first publ. 1950)
247. Redfield, R., Villa Rojas, A. 1962. *Chan Kom: A Maya Village,* abr. ed. Univ. Chicago Press
248. Richardson, F. L. W., Ed. *Allegience and Hostility: Man's Mammalian Heritage.*
249.* Rigby, P. J. 1969. *Cattle and Kinship Among the Gogo.* Cornell Univ. Press
250.* Rivière, P. 1969. *Marriage Among the Trio.* London: Clarendon
251. Rohner, R. P., Ed. 1969. *The Ethnography of Franz Boas.* Univ. Chicago Press
252. Romanucci, L. *Violence, Morality and Conflict.* Palo Alto: National Press Books.
253.* Rosman, A., Rubel, P. G. 1971. *Feasting With Mine Enemy.* New York: Columbia Univ. Press
254.* Sahlins, M. 1972. *Stone Age Economics.* Chicago: Aldine-Atherton
255. Schaffner, B., Ed. 1955-1960. *Group Processes.* New York: Macy Found. 5 vols.
256.* Schlegel, A. 1972. *Male Dominance and Female Autonomy.* New Haven: Human Relations Area Files Press
257. Schneider, D. M. 1968. *The American Kinship.* Englewood Cliffs: Prentice Hall
258. Schwartz, T. 1962. *The Paliau Movement in the Admiralty Islands,* 1946-1954. Anthropol. Papers Am. Mus. Natur. Hist. 49, Part 2
259. Schwartz, T. 1963. Systems of aerial integration: Some considerations based on the Admiralty Islands of Northern Melanesia. *Anthropol Forum* 1:26- 97
260. Sebeok, T. A., Hayes, A. S., Bateson, M. C., Eds. 1964. *Approaches to Semiotics.* The Hague: Mouton
261. Segall, M. H., Campbell, D. T., Herskovits, M. J. 1966. *The Influence of Culture on Visual Perception.* Indianapolis, New York: Bobbs-Merrill
262.* Selby, H. A. 1970. Continuities and prospects in anthropological studies. In *Current Directions in Anthropology.* ed. A. Fischer. *Bull Am. Anthropol Assoc.* 3:35-53
263.* Silverman; M. G. 1971. *Disconcerting Issue.* Univ. Chicago Press
264.* Simons, E. L. .1972. *Primate Evolution: An Introduction to Man's Place In Nature.* New York: Macmillan
265.* Singer, M. B. 1972. *When a Great Tradition Modernizes: An Anthropological Approach to Indian Civilization.* New York: Praeger

266.* Sinha, S. 1970. *Science, Technology and Culture: A Study of the Cultural Traditions and Institutions of India and Ceylon in Relation to Science and Technology.* New Delhi: Res. Counc. Cult. Stud,, Munshiram Manoharlal

267. Soddy, K., Ed. 1961. *Identity: Mental Health and Value Systems.* London: Tavistock

268. Soddy, K., Ahrenfeldt, R. H. 1965. *Mental Health in a Changing World.* London: Tavistock

269. Spicer, E. H. 1952. *Human Problems in Technological Change: A Casebook.* New York: Sage Found.

270. Spindler, G. D., Ed. 1955. *Education and Anthropology.* Stanford Univ. Press

271. Spindler, G. D. 1970. *Being an Anthropologist: Fieldwork in Eleven Cultures.* New York: Holt, Rinehart & Winston

272. Steiner, S. 1968. *The New Indians.* New York: Harper & Row

273. Stocking, G. W. Jr. 1968. *Race, Culture and Evolution.* New York: Free Press

274.* Strathern, M. 1972. *Women in Between: Female Roles in a Male World, Mount Hagen, New Guinea.* New York: Seminar Press (Academic)

275.* Sturtevant, W. C. 1964. Studies in ethnoscience. *Am. Anthropol* 66:99-131

276.* Sudnow, D., Ed. 1972. *Studies in Social Interaction.* New York: Free Press

277. Swidler, W. W. 1972. Some demographic factors regulating the formation of flocks and camps among the Brahui of Baluchistan. In *Perspectives on Nomadism,* ed. W. Irons, N. Dyson- Hudson. Leiden: Brill

278. Tanner, J. M., Inhelder, B., Eds. 1956-1960. *Discussions on Child Development.* London: Tavistock. 4 vols.

279. Tax, S., Ed. 1960. *Evolution After Darwin.* Univ. Chicago Press. 3 vols.

280. Tax, S. et al, Eds. 1953. *An Appraisal of Anthropology Today.* Univ. Chicago Press

281. Texter, R. B., Ed. 1967. *Cross-Cultural Summary.* New Haven: Human Relations Area Files Press

282.* Thomas, K. 1971. *Religion and the Decline of Magic.* New York: Scribner

283.* Tiger, L., Fox, R. 1971. *The Imperial Animal.* New York: Holt, Rinehart & Winston

284. Tiselius, A., Nilsson, S., Eds. 1970. *The Place of Value in a World of Facts.* Nobel Symp. 14. .New York: Wiley

285. Tuden, A., Plotnicov, L. 1970. *Social Stratification in Africa.* New York: Free Press

286. Turnbull, C. M. 1961. *The Forest People.* New York: Simon & Schuster

287. Turnbull, C. M. 1972. *The Mountain People.* New York: Simon & Schuster

288. Turner, V. W. 1967. *Forest of Symbols: Aspects of Ndembu Ritual.* Cornell Univ. Press

289. Turner, V. W. 1969. *The Ritual Process: Structure and Anti-Structure.* Chicago: Aldine

290.* Tyler, S. A. 1969. *Cognitive Anthropology.* New York: Holt, Rinehart & Winston

291. Valentine, C. A. 1968. *Culture and Poverty: Critlque and Counter-Proposals.* Univ. Chicago Press

292. Valentine, C. A. 1972. *Black Studies and Anthropology: Scholarly and Political Interests in Afro-American Culture*. Reading, Mass.: Modular Publ.
293. Vayda, A. P. 1969. An ecologist in cultural anthropology. *Bucknell Rev.* March issue
294. Vincent, J. 1971. *African Elite*. New York: Columbia Univ. Press
295. Vizedom, M. B. 1963. *The concept of rites of passage in the light of data from fifteen cultures*. PhD thesis. Columbia Univ., New York
296. Vogt, E. 1961. *A model for the study of ceremonial organization in highland Chiapas*. Presented at 60th Ann. Meet. Am. Anthropol. Assoc., Philadelphia
297. Watson, J. B. 1963. A micro-evolution study in New Guinea. *J. Polynesian Soc 72:188–92*
298. Watson, J. B., Kimball, S. T., Eds. 1971. *Crossing Cultural Boundaries*. San Francisco: Chandler
299. Wax, M. L., Diamond, S., GearIng, F., Eds. 1971. *Anthropological Perspectives on Education*. New York, Lon- don: Basic Books
300. Westlake, P. Ro 1970. The possibilities of neural holographic processes within the brain. *Kybernetik 7:129-53*
301. White, L. A. 1959. *Evolution of Culture*. New York: McGraw Hill
302. White, Lo A. 1963. *The Ethnography and Ethnology of Franz Boas*. Austin: Memorial Mus. Univ. Texas
303. White, L. A. 19660 *The Science of Culture: A Study of Man and Civilization*. New York: Grove Press (first publ. 1949)
304. Whiting, B. B., Ed. 1963. *Six Cultures: Studies of Child Rearing*. New York, London: Wiley
305. Williams, R. R. 1967. *Field Methods in the Study of Culture*. New York: Holt, Rinehart & Winston
306. Williams, T. R. 1972. *Introduction to Socialization: Human Culture Transmitted*. St. Louis: Mosby
307. Wolfe, A. W. 1963. The African mineral industry: Evolution of a supranational level of integration. *Soc. Probl. 11:153-64*
308.* Young, M. W. 1972: *Fighting with Food*. Cambridge Univ. Press

Part Two

SOCIAL THEORY IN THE STUDY OF CONTEMPORARY CULTURE

THE METHODOLOGY OF RACIAL TESTING:
Its Significance for Sociology*

The unquestioning quotation of the results in one field of re-search by workers in another field carries with it at least tacit approval of the methodology which produced those results. The soci-ologist is, therefore, very much concerned with the methods em-ployed in experimental psychology, which furnishes him with so much of the raw material for generalization. Perhaps no results of experimental psychology have been utilized so widely and so uncrit-ically as the results of intelligence testing, and particularly of the intelligence testing of different racial and nationality groups. In the discussion of race problems, a controversy so encumbered by worn-out dogmas and hot partisanships, this quantitative type of material was particularly welcome.

The first research to be generally exploited was the army testing. But here so many opponents of the resulting generalizations came forward with destructive criticism, and so many defenders of the tests carefully tried to warn the layman against unjustified conclusions, that the mischief became too public to be dangerous. No discussions today which pretend to scientific caution quote the army tests with-out many explicit reservations. But the criticisms of the army tests were in great part devoted to the deficiencies of all intelligence tests, of verbal tests, or of group tests as such. Far less attention was devoted to the special problems inherent in racial and nationality testing. Thus, while the writer on general social problems has learned that the methodology of intelligence testing is still in swaddling clothes, he is not so conscious that a methodology adequate to deal with racial and nationality testing has not even been born. And, unwarned, he draws freely and uncritically upon the findings of special studies which appear from time to time in the scientific journals. Many of these studies appear to have avoided the pitfalls into which the army tests fell. They are often individual tests instead of group tests; the question

*Originally published in *The American Journal of Sociology*.

of inequalities of education is ruled out when school groups are used as subjects; the selection argument does not seem to be so readily applicable when the subjects are all taken from the same city and often from the same public school. So these results come to be utilized in far other ways than their authors intended. Paradoxically enough, one of the experiments most often quoted in heated discussions is by the author of "On the Need for Caution in Establishing Race Norms."[2] A discussion of the methodology of this particular province of intelligence testing, a province so pregnant with explosive results, would seem, therefore, to be both pertinent and necessary. I shall first review the experiments which have substantiated the need for one or another of these special methodological requirements—no published experiment has taken them all into consideration.

The special problems involved in this type of testing are three in number: (1) the practicability and validity of attempts to equate test score and amount of racial admixture; (2) the effect which social status has on the results of such tests—the problem here is threefold: Does social status influence test score? Is it particularly influential in the case of immigrant groups or groups which suffer from social discrimination because of their race? What methods are adequate to evaluate the social status of the children so tested? (3) What effect does linguistic disability have on the test results? These three aspects of the matter will be considered in turn.

RACIAL ADMIXTURE

On the face of it, no method of determining race differences in intelligence seems more promising than this attempt to equate test scores with the amount of Negro or Indian blood, as the case may be, when it is possible, as it often is in this country, to study such a mixed group. In such an instance it seems highly probable that language and social status might be controlled, and the effect of race as such isolated and studied. But here we are confronted with two difficulties: one technological, the other theoretical. Does a quantitative expression of degree of admixture have any qualitative significance and, if so, how may this quantitative expression be arrived at? Garth suggests: "If the genetic law works in mental traits as it does in physical traits, possibly we ought to get multimodal effects in one distribution of mixed bloods' performance in a mental test; particularly should we get at least bimodal effects in a distribution of performances of an F2 population." But this is not enough. We cannot use either degree of variability or a multimodal distribution first as hypothesis and then as proof. And while increased variability is generally recognized by physical anthropologists as an index of racial admixture, it is not so specifically developed a concept as to make possible exact equations between the expression of intelligence in a test and exact degree of intermixture involved.

If, however, we lay aside this theoretical objection as incapable of solution on the basis of our present knowledge of the laws of heredity, and an attempt is made to establish a purely empirical relationship between degrees of racial admixture and intelligence scores, what methods can be used? Garth[3] and Hunter[4] used the official records of the government schools. Subject to the accuracy of these genealogical records, this method is thorough and valid. But here Garth admits that his results are quite indeterminate because the social conditions for his various groups were probably extremely varied before the children entered the government schools. Methodologically however, the procedure is sound.

In his studies on the American Negro, Ferguson has made a less objective method the basis of his determination of amount of admixture. In 1916[5] he tested 907 school children in several Virginia cities, 421 of whom were colored. He made his estimate of amount of Negro blood on the basis of skin color graded by an eye judgment, and finds an increasingly high score with increased amount of white blood. From which result he generalizes as follows:

> Such considerations indicate that it is a native ability and not an acquired capacity that differentiates the mixed from the pure negroes, and that *skin color is its outward sign.* [Italics mine.] They also indicate that the tests used are primarily tests of native capacity, and the consequent differences found between whites and negroes as a whole are innate differences.... The average performance of the colored people of this country in such intelligence work as that represented by the tests of higher capacity appears to be only about three-fourths as efficient as the performance of the white with the same amount of training.

This is obviously reasoning in a circle; he divides his group according to skin color, finds differences between these divisions, then assumes that this proves skin color a valid index and that, therefore, the differences so found are innate. In 1919[6] Ferguson made a similar analysis of the results of the army testing of 5,425 Negroes at Camp Lee. Again on the basis of an eye judgment he divided 1,132 of these Negroes into a "darker" and a "lighter" group, and found that the median Alpha score for the "lighter" group was 51, for the "darker," 40; on the Stenquist combination test the group classified as "lighter" made a median score of 19; those called "darker," a median score of

17. Eight additional companies were classified by other observers and gave results comparable to these. Ferguson has severely criticized[7] a similar attempt, made by Morse and Strong,[8] as "rough," yet his own methods are open to the same criticism. There is no conclusive evidence that skin color, *accurately determined,* is a reliable index of racial admixture. Such a classification is even less admissible when unchecked by any such quantitative device as the color top. The methods of Garth and Hunter on one hand, and that of Ferguson and Strong on the other, are illustrations of a scientific and unscientific approach to this problem. If the genealogical method could be subjected to extensive verification and supplemented by some technique for holding the other factors constant it might be productive of valuable results.

SOCIAL STATUS

Several careful attempts have been made to ascertain the influence which social status has in this type of testing. Very often the conclusions of these experimenters have to be rejected because they have concentrated upon this one problem and neglected other complicating conditions, but they are none the less valuable as illustrations of the particular methodological point.

In 1912 Phillips[9] made an investigation of the intelligence of white and Negro children in the Philadelphia public schools, using the Binet scale. His treatment of the social status factor was a specific attempt to hold it constant. The homes of the children were visited and rated on a four-division scale. Only those children, twenty-nine from each race, whose homes were rated "good" were used in the final comparisons. This method of elimination of all cases of incomparable social status is open to two objections. In the first place, strict comparability is exceedingly difficult to determine, and the final use of only one status group prevents the utilization of other status groups as checks. And in the second place, it is enormously unpractical in that it pares down the number of cases, and the more exact the classification, the more cases there are which will have to be eliminated.

Miss Arlitt has studied the effect of social status upon race norms more carefully than any other investigator. In most reported work social status has been a side issue, a check upon the main body of the results, not the central problem. But Miss Arlitt undertook to study it specifically. She describes two investigations. The first one[10] was made on 304 children in the primary grades, 169 of native-born white parentage, 68 of Italian parentage, and 67 Negroes. They were divided according to social status and the following results were obtained when the total group was considered:

Median I. Q.

Very superior 126.9
Superior 118.7
Average 106.5
Inferior 87
Very inferior 83

Ninety per cent of the native-born whites came from families ranked as superior or very superior; 88.2 per cent of the Italians and Negroes came from families of inferior or very inferior social status. When the Italians were compared with native-born whites of the same social status, the difference in intelligence quotient was only 7.7 instead of 22.2, the difference when only nationality groups, without regard to status, were compared. In the case of the Negroes, consideration of the social status factor reduced the difference from 23.3 to 8.6 points.

In her second study[11] Miss Arlitt again studied native-born whites, Italians, and Negroes, making the social status ratings on the basis of Taussig's occupational grouping. She found a difference of 33.9 between the two extreme occupational groups in the same grade in school. When Italians and Negroes were compared with their own occupational group among the native-born whites of native white parentage a difference similar to the one quoted above was found.[12]

From which investigation Miss Arlitt concludes that: "Race norms which do not take the social status factor into account are apt to be to that extent invalid." Although many investigators, notably Terman and Yerkes, have endeavored to study the effect of social status upon tests scores, these are the only thorough attempts to analyze its influence when racial and nationality groups are being studied.

A less careful attempt along these same lines was made by Strong[13] in 1913 to correct the extreme differences found between the scores of Negro and white children by comparing the Negroes with the poor mill whites; they state that such a comparison was much less unfavorable to the Negro.

Another body of data on the question of social status is found in the army results where the effect of northern or southern residence is appreciably indicated in the Negro scores.[14] Fuckunda,[15] in a study of Japanese children, tried to equate occupation of parent and score of child. However, he found a correlation between social status and intelligence quotient of only .19. But he had only forty-three cases, and he fails to record the number in each of his three groups, for which his average I.Q.s are given as 103, 82 and 92, respectively.

These experiments are suggestive methodologically, although in almost every instance the results are vitiated by overemphasis of this one factor and a failure to deal with the other aspects of the case. Once the importance of the social status factor is established, it will be necessary to further refine the methods by which it is estimated. There will have to be experimental study of the adequacy of any such rough index as the Taussig occupational rating, which we know is unsatisfactory in at least one case, where rural children are involved. But these recorded studies represent a distinct advance over the type of investigation which tests a group, regardless of the social status factor, and draws unquestioning conclusions from the scores so obtained.

At this point might be mentioned a most interesting attempt to determine the relative influence of environment and race. A number of standardized tests were given to freshmen in three colleges in China and one in India; the results were then compared with American norms. Unfortunately, Waugh[16] does not give the number tested, but analysis of the results is extremely provocative. Comparing the scores of Americans and Indians, different environment but same race,[17] there was a difference of 2.34 points in favor of the American group; comparing the Chinese and Indians, more similar environment and different race, the difference in score was 2.5; comparing the Americans and the Chinese, different environment and different race, the difference was 7.8. This approach is highly suggestive.

LANGUAGE DISABILITY

Perhaps no complicating factor in appraising the results of this kind of intelligence testing has been so neglected as the question of language disability. With the exception of the work of two investigators, the whole matter has usually been dismissed with statements that the child was under no language handicap beyond the first grade if he had gone to an American kindergarten,[18] or that "all the Italians spoke English without difficulty,"[19] or that the children were selected by the principal of the school as having no language handicap.[20]

Rudolph Pintner[21] has emphasized the importance of this language factor: "The question of prognosis value for school purposes must not be confused with the question of absolute intelligence of different racial groups. It seems to the writer that non-verbal tests alone are adequate for this purpose. It is inconceivable that children living in an English-speaking environment, hearing, speaking, and reading nothing but English, should not have a distinct advantage in tests requiring the finding of opposites, the hunting for an analogy, the filling in of an uncompleted sentence, and the like as compared with children who hear a foreign language at home and, in many cases, are required to communicate in a foreign language to some people in their environment. Such contrasting groups are very far from having had equal previous practice on the elements which go to make up the usual verbal test." Pintner made two studies in which the performance of children speaking a foreign language is compared with that of American children, on the Binet[22] scale and the Non-Language test, and on the National and the Non-Language.[23] The English-speaking children gained six months in the Non-Language over their Binet mental age; the foreign-speaking gained sixteen months. From which Pintner concludes that ". ...when classified according to mental age, those children who hear a foreign language in their homes may suffer a serious handicap when tested only by the revision of the Binet scale." When the National tests were used, Pintner found that 50 per cent of the foreign-speaking children exceeded the median mental age for American children on the Non-Language scale, but only 37 per cent did so on the National tests.

Colvin and Allen[24] sought to isolate the effect of language on score by comparing the performance of fifty American and fifty Italian children of the same school grade and attainment on a group, the National, and an individual, the Binet, test. They found a difference of thirteen points when the written group test was used, and a difference of only one point when the oral individual test was used. Furthermore, in the group test, it was in Arithmetic alone, the section of the test requiring least verbal facility, that the Italians approached the American score. They conclude: "From the evidence now in our possession we can reasonably conclude that linguistic ability is an important factor in the score obtained by an individual in an intelligence test that is based largely on words and their uses." They further remark that the difference is greatest among younger children.

This last result is apparently directly contradicted by an experiment reported by Young,[25] wherein a group of children of "Latin" and North European descent were retested after a period of three years, and "the average change of the intelligence quotient downward was somewhat greater for the Latins than for the other groups." It does seem plausible that if the difference in score be primarily due to language disability, it should diminish, not increase, after three years further exposure to English. In this connection a study on "The Effect of Bilingualism on Intelligence," by Saer,[26] is pertinent. He tested some 1,400 Welsh children, bilinguals and monoglots (speaking only English) by the Stanford scale, with special dextrality tests and special composition tests. His results are careful and detailed, presented with full analysis and cautious checking up. He finds a distinct superiority of the monoglot children in rural districts, a superiority somewhat diminished in urban districts; he finds a superiority of monoglot university students over bilingual university students; the sense of dextrality is much more highly developed in the case of the monoglots, and the range of their vocabulary exceeds that of the bilinguals in either Welsh or English. He suggests that this difference seems permanent, persisting to adulthood. Similar results are reported by Smith,[27] also working with Welsh children over a period of three years of careful observation. He concludes: "Regarded as a whole, therefore, these tests indicate that the monoglot child has an advantage over the bilingual child, an advantage which increases during his school life."

We have here two distinct approaches, that of Pintner and Colvin and Allen, which is mainly concerned with the vitiation of test results due to language handicap,[28] and this more speculative suggestion of Saer and Smith that bilingualism may have a fundamental influence on intelligence itself, and not merely on its manifestation in verbal tests.

From these various attempts to elaborate a methodology of racial and nationality testing it is clearly evident that test scores are affected, to a degree not yet determined, by social status and by language disabilities. No attempt has yet been made to analyze the effects of that more subtle and less measurable aspect of environment which may determine the attitude of the subject toward the tests and profoundly affect his score. The method of equating test score and amount of racial admixture is subject to modification in terms of these other complicating factors, and also to the inherent weaknesses of the method in the present state of ignorance concerning the laws regulating the inheritance of mental traits.

All these considerations should suggest extreme caution in any attempt to draw conclusions concerning the relative intelligence of different racial or nationality groups on the basis of tests, unless a careful consideration is given the factors of language, education, and social status, and a further allowance is made for an unknown amount of influence which may be logically attributed to different attitudes and different habits of thought.

Notes

1. This article was submitted for publication in August, 1924.
1a. William McDougall, *Is the World Safe for Democracy* pp. 63-64. Lothrop Stoddard, *The Revolt against Civilization,* p. 63, quoting A. H. Arlitt, "Further Data on the Influence of Race and Social Status on the Intelligence Quotient," *Proc. Amer. Psych. Assoc.,* 1920.
2. A. H. Arlitt, *Jour. of Applied Psych.,* VI (1921), 378-80.
3. T. R. Garth, "Results of Some Tests on Full and Mixed Blood Indians," *Jour. of Appl. Psych.,* IV (1921), 359-72. "Comparison of the Mental Ability of Mixed and Full-Blood Indians on the Basis of Education," *Psych. Rev.,* XXIX (1922), 221-36. "Mental Fatigue of Mixed and Full-Blooded Indians," *Jour. of Appl. Psych.,* VI (1922), 333-41. "National Intelligence Tests Given to Mixed and Full-Blood Indians," *Science,* December I, 1922.
4. W. S. Hunter, "A Relation of Degree of Indian Blood to Score on Otis Intelligence Test," *Proc. Amer. Psych. Assoc.,* 1920
5. G. O. Ferguson Jr., "Psychology of the Negro," *Arch. of Psych"* Vol. XXIII, 1916.
6. G. O. Ferguson Jr., "Intelligence of the Negroes at Camp Lee," *School and Society,* IX (1919), 721-26.
7. Ferguson, 1916, *op. cit.*
8. A. M. Strong, "Three Hundred and Fifty White and Colored Children Measured by the Binet Scale," *Ped. Sem"* XX (1913), 485-515.
9. B. A. Phillips, "Binet Tests Applied to Colored School Children," *Psych. Clinic* (1914), 190-96.
10. A. H. Arlitt, "Further Data on the Influence of Race and Social Status on the Intelligence Quotient," *Proc. Amer. Psych. Assoc.,* 1920.
11. A. H. Arlitt, "On the Need for Caution in Establishing Race Norms," *Journal of Appl. Psych.,* V (1921), 179-83.
12. The difference between the Negroes and native-born whites without regard to social status was 23.1; when social status was considered it was only 8.6. For the Italians the corresponding differences were 21.5 and 7.
13. A. L. Strong, 1913, *op. cit.*
14. G.O. Ferguson, 1919, *op. cit.*
15. J. Fuckunda, "Some Data on the Intelligence of Japanese Children," *Amer. Jour. of Psych.,* October, 1923.
16. K. L. Waugh, "A Comparison of Oriental and American Students," *Proc. Amer. Psych. Assoc.,* 1920.
17. Race is here used in its widest sense.
18. K. Young, "Mental Differences in Certain Immigrant Groups," *Univ. Oregon Public. No.11,* 1922.
19. H. Arlitt, 1921, *op. cit.*
20. K. Murdock, "A Study of Race Differences in New York City," *School and Society,* XI (1920), 47-50.
21. R. Pintner, "Comparison of American and Foreign Children on Intelligence Test," *Jour. Educ. Psych.,* May, 1923.

22. R. Pintner and R. Keller, "Intelligence Test of Foreign Children," *Jour. Of Educ. Psych.* (1922), pp. 214-22. R. Pintner, 1923, *op. cit.*

24. S. S. Colvin and R. D. Allen, "Mental Tests and Linguistic Ability," *Jour. Of Educ. Psych.*, January, 1923.

25. K. Young, 1922, *op. cit.*

26. D. J. Saer, *Brit. Jour. of Psych.*, July, 1923.

27. F. Smith, "Bilingualism and Mental Development," *Brit. Jour .of Psych., XIII, 278.*

28. In this connection I would like to refer to an unpublished investigation of my own. I gave the Otis intelligence test to 276 Italian children and compared the scores with the amount of English spoken in the children's homes, *by their parents*. It is to be noted that all these children were above the fourth grade in school and all spoke English themselves. The comparison showed a steadily rising median from an index of brightness of 64.16 for the group whose parents spoke all Italian, 69.3 for those whose parents spoke some English, 74 for those of homes in which English was chiefly or entirely spoken.

THE STUDY OF NATIONAL CHARACTER*

The Evolution of Research into National Character[1]

Differences between the national or regional characters of peoples have long been a matter of concern to Europeans, as a key to literary criticism and in historical studies. Writers as far away in time and as varying as De Tocqueville[2] and Fouillée[3] have speculated about this question. The explanation of a particular historical or literary personality through the circumstance of his having an Italian grandmother or a German paternal grandfather, or even through his descent from one family line which stemmed from a part of a nation, as Brittany or Provence, has invoked interchangeability of concepts of cultural inheritance such as we are attempting to elaborate today, as we study in more systematic detail the way in which a Breton grandmother, through what her son learned from her, might in turn transmit something of the particular tradition of Brittany to a grandson whom she had never seen. When Madariaga was commissioned at the end of the First World War to make his study of Englishmen, Frenchmen, and Spaniards,[4] this was an articulate recognition that an understanding of the cultures of different peoples might be relevant to problems of world organization and peace.

In the United States, the study of national character as the application of anthropological and psychological methods to contemporary modern societies developed during World War II. It was the wartime situation—in which the United States was faced with the problem of waging a total war, including psychological warfare, against little-known and inaccessible enemies—which stimulated this special scientific development, but some of its roots may be traced to the particular nature of American society. Whereas modern European man is accustomed to place any contemporary development against the background of European history, within which the history of his own country provides a special framework, the attention of the American, living in a country whose population has been very recently

*Originally published in *The Policy Sciences: Recent Developments in Scope & Method.* Daniel Lerner and Harold D. Lasswell, Stanford University Press, 1951.

drawn from many other countries, is focused somewhat differently. In Europe, significant historical changes have been seen as the concomitants of the growth of new ideas, under such headings as the Enlightenment, the Reformation, and the rise of modern science and industry, with the men and women of each country as the medium through which the changing traditions of European culture have passed. Or emphasis has been placed upon the growth of national cultures, the attainment of a harmonious unity among a series of provincial local cultures each of which made a contribution, as men of the provinces participated in the life of Paris or Moscow or Geneva. Thus the child could be viewed as having spanned the period from one age to another, or from the special local style of a province to the wider style of the national capital. But in the United States attention has been focused upon another series of events—the process by which adults reared in one society emigrated and became participants in a very different society, and even more strikingly, the way in which their children entered into the new social heritage. In any historical change, of course, it is the people themselves who change, however much we may phrase the change as that of ideas or of institutions. But this circumstance is less abruptly forced upon the attention of the student of society in countries with a continuity of population than it is in the United States, where peoples from many European countries arrived who conspicuously altered their speech and their manners, their posture and their gesture, and became part of a new culture.

Within this historical situation, two scientific approaches to human behavior have developed: comparative ethnology, called in the United States *cultural anthropology;* and the study of child development within the general schema of Freudian psychology, with its emphasis on the dual importance of the regularities within human development and the ways in which the human child, through communication with other people, learns its particular social tradition.

American cultural anthropology has been based primarily on the intensive study of the American Indian groups sharing the continent of North America with the newcomers from Europe, sometimes successfully contesting the possession of a part of it, stubbornly maintaining their language and traditions against the encroachment of the invaders. Their history was unwritten and unknown, to a large extent unrecoverable; and the history of the America of the European colonist was inaugurated on the same land, under the same trees. The Indians, in fact, were not the mysterious inhabitants of a tropical or arctic land; not savages who could be read about and from whose strange beliefs and rituals theories of prelogicality could be built up, unchallenged by their physical presence; not a passive conquered people, slaving for a race of superior beings, about whom hypotheses of childlikeness could be comfortably constructed. Rather, they were groups of people who took over the horse and the gun of the white man and conspicuously adapted them to their own traditional purposes, different from and often antithetical to ours. Red Indians, furthermore, conspicuously were not our actual ancestors, and the temptation to consider their forms of culture as prototypes of our own was not so great to Americans as to a British nineteenth-century scholar seated in his study thinking about mankind. Under the influence of Franz Boas, given an earlier impetus by Morgan,[5] an American school of ethnology grew up in which the primary stress was upon the usefulness of comparing different cultures, ignoring (except when a particular problem required it) the question of their relative antiquity, the differences in specific racial composition, and the stages by which any given culture might have reached its present state. Emphasis was placed upon the spatial position of each group of people, and the continent was divided into regions technically called *culture areas*—divisions which were made on the basis of studies of the way Indian groups had utilized the stock of ideas available to them through interchange with their neighbors.

The dividing lines between culture areas were found where a group had used more from one area than from another, but emphasis was placed not so much upon the divisions as upon the centers where the particular style of the area was most highly developed. This approach provided methodological tools for describing any culture as a variant of a group of cultures, these groups in turn being seen as variants of the forms characteristic of the continent. Understanding of anyone of these variants was possible primarily because the others were known—shades of difference in the form of an artifact, the proportions in a design painted on leather, the steps in a ritual, or the way in which kinship relations were categorized, when studied carefully, made it possible to characterize the distinctive pattern of any given culture. With this emphasis upon variation, attention was also focused upon those categories of behavior which occurred in every culture—facts such as that one human group built with stone, a second with wood, and a third made dwellings of skins could all be subsumed under the heading of *shelter*—and this provided more workable categories than an emphasis upon the deep historical discontinuities implied by the presence, for example, of such inventions as the kerosene-burning lamp or the electric torch. By training, the American anthropologist looks at a one-room hut, a many-roomed pueblo, a stone castle, an American twelve-room suburban dwelling equipped with every modern invention of heating and lighting, and simply says: These are various forms of shelter; their construction involves certain problems; life within any one of them will take a form recognizably related to the design and the size of that particular shelter. Whereas the historian focuses upon differences within *time,* involving enormous and progressive changes (the growth of complexities in terms of significant discontinuities such as the invention of writing, or of steam, or of electricity), the anthropologist focuses upon differences within *space,* comparing coexisting cultures in such a way that, while the contemporary accessibility of human inventions is taken into account, each culture's position on the scale of historical development is allowed for but is treated as less significant than the particular nature of the pattern. Thus, from the anthropological point of view, it is possible to compare simple and complex cultures, high and low cultures, and to obtain illumination from the comparison.

The spatial approach also makes it possible to select the size of the universe which will be considered, so that it is possible to compare the aboriginal culture of Australia and the aboriginal culture of North America as continental patterns, or to compare two tribes, or two hunting bands within the same tribe, or the inhabitants of two hilltops who count themselves as one village. This spatial approach also enables the investigator to treat as a unit, for certain kinds of problems, all of Europe, or Western Europe, or the European Latin-speaking peoples, or the peoples speaking Latin languages, or to narrow the field so as to compare the culture of Normandy with the culture of Brittany. But as the referent is always the total way of life of the group of people who constitute the unit, anthropologists will not separate out the culture of a class (e.g. the working class, or the aristocracy) but will treat it as an organic part of a culture in the same fashion that they will treat the behavior of men as distinguished from women, of one occupational group as distinguished from another, or of children as distinguished from adults.

Whatever the size of the universe within which the anthropologist works, he works with the same type of unit—items of behavior, acts identified in time and place, and the social positions of those who perform them. It is not necessary that any two items be collected from the behavior of the same person—although in practice they usually are—since the anthropologist's aim is to build a set of abstractions which will describe a pattern of learned behavior characteristic of a group which shares a common tradition. Thus he may collect vocabulary from one person, record the gestures appropriate to ritual from the behavior of others, and describe the methods of cooking or carpentry or the steps of the dance by observing still other persons. He must always know enough about the person whom he is observing to know in what respects the person is representative of his culture, that he is not a stranger, and whether or not he is insane or ill, or physically or socially handicapped in some way which will make his behavior aberrant within the general pattern.

It is, of course, essential for this comparative method to assume that all human beings share in a basic humanity that varies from individual to individual but, for those aspects which are relevant, is in no way related to those physical differences upon which we base racial classifications.

While anthropology was developing along these lines, Freudian psychology made possible a new approach to problems of the development of individual personality. First based upon the retrospective accounts of the patient, from which the psychiatrist began to construct hypotheses about sequences of experience, later reinforced by the study of children themselves as they passed through the successive stages of growth which had been hypothesized, Freudian theory provided a way of describing the learning of a whole human being living within a social group. Attention was focused upon the series of stages by which the child learned to perceive and deal with the world through his realization of his own developing body. As Freudian theory was based upon the study of individual patients, emphasis was placed upon the response of the child rather than upon the behavior of the parent which evoked the response—upon the way in which each individual interpreted his experience of eating, sleeping, eliminating, learning to walk and to run, to speak and to read, on the basis of patterns laid down by previous experience. Because Freudian theory developed in the highly differentiated and individualized middle and upper classes of Western Europe, England, and the United States, those elements in the structure of the personality which were found to be shared among most patients were initially regarded as universals inherent in human nature, rather than as the systematic results of the responses of individuals with a common biological make-up to a particular shared culture.

During the last twenty-five years, there has been an increasing body of research which has attempted to combine the basic Freudian theories and the methods of cultural anthropology in an approach which was originally called the study of *personality and culture*.[6] The use of this term represented a stage in the assimilation of the theoretical framework of the two sciences to each other, before it was clearly stated that all study of personality involved the study of culture—since every human being embodies in an individual form the culture or cultures within which he has been reared and within which he lives. When the two methods are combined, a culture is studied

through the way in which children learn it, and individuals are studied to throw light upon this process of learning within a known cultural frame. It is no longer possible simply to collect items from any
one of a large number of individuals within the group being studied.
Instead, attention is focused upon making enough observations on
particular individuals, so that we have data on the way in which particular identified organisms have learned a particular cultural pattern.
The field worker collects autobiographies, long commentaries from
single individuals on events, art productions of individual children as
they develop, and responses of individuals to the series of projective
tests which have grown out of the Freudian psychology, such as the
Rorschach Test and the Thematic Apperception Test. With such materials, it is possible to identify the particular psychological dynamics
by which individuals learn and act in any culture and to relate this
dynamics to the customary behavioral sequences of child rearing in
such away that methods of feeding the child can be seen to be systematically related to the ways in which the child learns to respond to
people, to ideas, to events.

Uninformed critics of the method often misinterpret this as a
statement by the student of cultural character structure that the adult
personality of a member of a New Guinea tribe or a Plains Indian
tribe, of an American, an Italian, or a Turk, is *caused* by the way in
which the child is reared.[7] This is an error introduced by the necessities of therapy and the attempt to transfer the findings of therapy to
educational practice. Thus the therapist, finding in his individual
patient the record of an unhappy childhood, will regard that childhood experience as the antecedent cause of his patient's state, and
recommend that changes be made in the upbringing of all children to
obviate similar suffering in other individuals. But the student of cultural character recognizes rather a circular system[8] within which the
new-born child or the adult immigrant receives, perpetuates, and
stimulates behavior in others in terms of the entire cultural tradition,
so that the method of child rearing, the presence of a particular literary tradition, the nature of the domestic and public architecture, the
religious beliefs, the political system, are all conditions within which
a given kind of personality develops.[9] Attention is focused upon the
child's learning process[10] simply because this is a convenient place to
interrupt the circle for purposes of study when we use a system of psychology that describes dynamic processes in terms of the way in
which the individual has learned to experience his own body, his
own impulses, and the world around him.[11]

Up to 1940, this combined approach was used for purposes of
pure research. When this was the objective, particularly suitable cul-

tural milieus were selected—such as primitive societies, isolated caste groups, and special immigrant groups—in which the size of the group, its contact with other groups, and the complexity of the culture were all capable of delimitation and description as a whole. Alternatively, studies were made with a primarily therapeutic or educational emphasis, in which the culture was taken into account as background for the attempt to understand enough about some process in modern society so as to correct it—as, for example, studies of Negro-white relations, studies of juvenile delinquency and crime—or in the attempts to construct a new form of education. In these latter studies in complex modern societies, the theory gained from the study of primitive societies and isolated groups was applied rather than added to. It was recognized that modern societies with their complexity and heterogeneity provided very poor laboratories for the development of new hypotheses, but the exigencies of some situation demanding correction or reform impelled students impressed with the significance of theories of cultural character structure to make use of them.

It is in this latter category that the study of national character[12] (as this method has come to be called when applied to the peoples of modern nations) must be considered. When, during World War II, attention was focused on the need to understand and predict the behavior of a nation's enemies, its allies, and its own population, and their responses to bombing, to food scarcity, to wars of nerves, to invasion, to occupation, small groups of students who had been devoting themselves to research, either in primitive societies or with selected individual subjects, began to experiment with the application of these methods to contemporary peoples. Research, begun privately, was absorbed into governmental agencies; teams were developed to work on psychological warfare, techniques for relieving friction among the allies, methods for supporting friendly groups in countries occupied by the enemy, and methods for building morale, obtaining acceptance of wartime regulations, etc., within the United States. Within these teams, the "national character" approach was one of several methods used. Content analysis, polling, historical analyses, etc. were also used. The countries studied and the particular problems studied were all functions of the course of the war and the personnel of different agencies, accidents of application rather than the result of deliberate planning.

Thus, study of Japan was focused heavily upon problems of surrender, ranging from how to obtain the surrender of a handful of troops who had retreated to a cave on a Pacific island to the question of the relationship between preserving the Emperor and obtaining a simultaneous and complete surrender of all the Japanese armed forces—this last a problem to which the predictions based on the

study of the "national character" were perhaps the most notable contribution made by this method during the war.[13] Studies of Germany
were focused on problems of the occupation and postwar reconstruction of a people who had been subjected by the Nazis to a systematic
attempt to alter their national character.[14] Work on Burma and Siam[15]
involved predictions about the behavior of the native populations, in
terms of internal subversion, response to propaganda, behavior after
occupation, etc. In studies of the United States, attention was focused
upon behavior in relation to governmental regulation of food,[16] civilian defense organization, and the mobilization of attitudes toward
sending supplies abroad, and—to a slight extent—upon morale problems within the army.[17] Work on British national character was confined to questions of friction between American troops and the
British population,[18] of relationships between American and British
intelligence personnel in the East, and of American attitudes toward
help to Britain. Virtually no work was done on Russia, and only a
beginning was made in a study of France, Holland, Italy, Belgium,
Poland, and China. Rumania[19] was intensively studied at one point in
strategic planning. Since the war, research in this field has taken several forms. Government and foundation-aided projects have been set
up at various universities (notably Columbia, Harvard, and Johns
Hopkins) to explore particular cultures, and concomitantly to train
personnel and to test methods, so that the improvisations of wartime
may be systematized. Although these studies are currently occupying
the center of attention of most of the senior scientists in the field,
they remain an applied science, justified by the exceedingly critical
state of the entire world and the urgent need to devise better methods
of co-operation between national groups and within national groups
which are torn by regional, class, or ideological conflicts.

In the United States, almost all of the work, which has been done
on national character, has been done through the use of selected
informants from and on the countries studied. Therefore, although
the concepts involved are based upon fieldwork, the results are
inevitably colored by the circumstance of working at a distance. There
are a few exceptions: my own brief work in Britain; some of the special studies done in the United States;[20] Dr. and Mrs. Rodnick's forthcoming book on the Czechs, based on nine months of field work in
Czechoslovakia in 1948;[21] Erikson's discussions of American character
based on the psychoanalyses of selected patients;[22] Kardiner's discussion of American character[23] based on West's field work in the American Southwest;[24] and the studies of Schaffner, Levy, and Rodnick,[25]
and, Lipkind[26] in postwar Germany. My own book on the United
States[27] and Mr. Gorer's book on the United States[28] should be placed

in a special class in that they use an anthropological approach to a mass of direct observations, which were not systematically collected for the particular use, which we later made of them. The circumstance that the largest amount of work in this field is at present being done, again necessarily at a distance, on the Soviet Union[29] tends to perpetuate the type of work, which can be done through work with individual informants and documents rather than through fieldwork in the countries being studied.

DIVERSE APPROACHES

We may now turn to a more detailed discussion of the methods used. Data are collected whenever possible from living subjects, so that experienced anthropologists, accustomed to collecting their material from nonliterate peoples, and psychiatrists, accustomed to listening to patients, may utilize their developed skill in listening to and evaluating the total response of the informant, in which a gesture or a tone of voice may be as important as a word. Interviews recorded on the spot remain the principal method. When informants cannot be found, and to supplement material from informants, other sorts of data are used, including films,[30] books, cartoons, newspaper articles, propaganda, instructional manuals, and photographs. These are analyzed as the records of the behavior of living persons within anthropological and psychiatric categories. To obtain other identified angles of observation, considerable use is also made of interviews with members of other cultures who are familiar with the culture being studied and whose own "national character" is known. It is assumed throughout that anthropology and psychiatry,[31] by emphasizing those elements in human culture which appear in all cultures—because of the nature of human beings and their interrelationships—provide a framework within which scientists from anyone culture can make generalizations which have cross-cultural validity only as long as the individual and cultural position of the scientist himself is systematically allowed for. The astonishment that an American anthropologist[32] feels over a Zuñi Indian's acceptance of the way his emotional expression is patterned, must be placed side by side with the astonishment that a Chinese anthropologist,[33] looking at the Zuñi and the American, feels at the American's astonishment. Both are data, if treated systematically as such. If the observer is untrained, he gives more data about his own cultural position than about the other upon which he is reporting; but in a trained social scientist there will be a sharp difference in level in the abstractions which he finds relevant between the order of material he presents about another culture and that which he includes on his own.

Although the approach to the study of national character employs a common set of theoretical assumptions about the psychic unity of mankind, the regularities involved in human growth and learning, and the systematic interrelatedness of a culture pattern when items within it are referred to the whole, there is considerable variation in the methods, which different students have used. Geoffrey Gorer[34] and Erik Erikson[35] both work primarily from the clues provided by the way in which the growing child experiences, in his own body, his relations with other persons; the way in which the different zones of the body and the different modes of response-reception (e.g., incorporation, retention, elimination, intrusion) are handled; and the way in which the image of the self and the integration of the ego may be traced through his periods of growth. Geoffrey Gorer treats the total cultural character structure as an intricate pattern, which can be unraveled once one has found a single significant thread. One example of such patterns is the contrast between indulgent feeding and strict training of sphincter control among the Japanese,[36] with its reflections in a rigidly obedient type of behavior alternating with periods of formless excess. Another example is the importance of swaddling for the Russian character:[37] in which the firm outer binding of an infant that is conceived as strong and capable of doing itself harm provides a clue to the Russian's attitude toward authority as external, hateful, but necessary, and in which the exhausting rages of the swaddled, teething baby provide a pattern for understanding the later valuation of strong feeling—any type of feeling—as preferable to the feeling of lifelessness. Erikson,[38] Gorer, and Leites all emphasize the usefulness of thinking of changes in character structure, such as have occurred as some of the ideals of the old Russian intelligentsia—originally polarized to the main emphases in Great Russian culture—have become the models for the current Soviet generation, with the attempt to build a character with a spine of steel, to replace the externally supported diffuseness of the old Russian character. All three, as well as Wolfenstein,[39] use the conventional Freudian assumptions of stages of relationship to each parent and to siblings, systematically asking such questions as: How do individuals in this particular culture pass through the Oedipal phase? Kardiner's approach,[40] developed by applying his particular version of Freudian theory to field materials collected by others, emphasizes particularly the importance of the basic disciplines; he builds assumptions from the way in which the child is said to be treated in certain significant respects involving the bodily functions and impulses, and then traces connections between these assumed effects and other cultural manifestations. His approach is distinctive in that he assumes that human cultures are projections of the conflicts and sufferings of childhood, and their symbolic solutions, in such a way that childhood experience is assigned a definitely causal role in history. Those students who have worked with cultural as well as psychiatric material reject this approach in favor of one in which human society is seen as a self-perpetuating circular system within which specific causality cannot be assigned to any part.[41]

Ruth Benedict's distinctive approach was an outgrowth of her earlier work,[42] in which she demonstrated that, by regarding each culture as a series of selections and rejections from an available stock of cultural items common to a wide area, it was possible to describe the unique configuration which each culture represented just as one would describe the choices which an individual makes from among all the diverse ideas and customs offered him in a modern society. Where the individual's pattern of choice may be seen as an expression of his innate temperament and particular individual character structure, Benedict made the hypothesis that the selectivity of a culture was to be found embodied in a persistent preference for some human potentialities at the expense of others. Accordingly, the persistence of what might be called "Frenchness" or "Germanness" would be attributed to the favoring of individuals who at birth or by accidents of early upbringing found French values or German values most congenial. Thus, a mystical culture would be seen as favoring individuals with a capacity for mysticism, while a culture in which practical, matter-of-fact values were stressed would favor individuals who were temperamentally fitted for practical life. With her greater interest in temperament than in character (that is, in the innate rather than the learned aspects of personality), Dr. Benedict invoked data on child rearing mainly as a way of documenting the expression of the prevailing temperament, rather than as a dynamic explanation of how individuals within a given culture develop a particular character structure—the approach used by those of us who use Freudian theory and other material on the regularities in human growth. When she began her studies of national character, first on Rumanians,[43] then on Siamese,[44] then on the peoples of the Low Countries, then on Germans, and finally on Japanese,[45] she continued to use the way in which a given people differed from their neighbors in the handling of an event or a shared economic practice as a crucial element in her descriptions. For example, in her study of Rumanian national character she examined the way in which Rumanians viewed their own history, showing how consistently they conceived themselves as having held the initiative in situations where Germans, for instance, would have conceived themselves as the victims of attack. Or, looking at economic practices, she would consider the French emphasis upon maintaining a nest egg of property intact from generation to generation as contrasted with the Italian practice of spending money with an expectation that there would somehow be more. Her study of Japan set such practices as hara-kiri against a wider background of injuring oneself and one's own property as a way of asserting one's position. Throughout her work, she stressed the uniqueness of each culture and of each wider historical tradition within which several cultures developed, the importance of recognizing that man had many potentialities, which no known culture had ever used, and the value of using even very small and simple cultures as clues to possibilities, which might otherwise be missed. As she depended upon no theory of constitutional types nor any systematic theory of biological growth and development, hers was an open system, an approach, which depended entirely upon contrasts between cultures and within culture areas.

Gregory Bateson takes as his point of departure an analysis of the patterns of interaction between individuals or groups of individuals.[46] He calls a relationship symmetrical when individual A or group A is seen to be essentially similar in motivations, purpose, and strength to individual B or group B, as in the relationship between two young men of equal social position aspiring to a lady's hand or between two opposing football teams of approximately the same strength. When, however, the two individuals or groups contrast with each other, in that one is seen as dominant, the other submissive, one as initiating, the other responsive, one as weak and the other as strong, etc., their interaction is described as *complementary.* When two individuals or groups alternate in their roles of domination and submission, initiative and responsiveness, and the like, their interrelationship is described as *reciprocal.* These processes when they are seen as disruptive and cumulative are called processes of *schizmogenesis.* The behavior of any national group may be analyzed in respect to particular situations, such as its attitudes and behavior toward other national groups which are conceived as rivals, as stronger or weaker, as dependent or threatening, etc. It is then possible to predict the type of response, which will be made, as an aspect of the prevailing emphasis in the national character. People among whom a premium on symmetrical behavior is highly developed (as it is among the British, with their emphasis on "fair play" and "handicaps") will respond positively to an enemy conceived as stronger than they are; while a people who place a premium upon disparities in human relationship will be more prone to attack the weak and appease the strong. Problems of propagandic wars and of armament races can thus be placed in perspective.

These processes of schizmogenesis may be further studied by an analysis of the way in which parent-child relationships are culturally patterned in respect to a series of attitudes such as succoring and dependence, dominance and submission, exhibitionism and spectatorship. These interrelationships are systematic, so that exhibitionism is not only the part of the father vis-à-vis the son, in upper- and middle-class English culture, but is also the mode of behavior of all those placed in a dominant and responsible position; while in the United States, where the child-rearing behavior is so reversed that it is the child who is exhibitionist while the parent acts as spectator, a person in exhibitionist situations such as those of a speaker, teacher, writer, or even a man who talks in a public bar or holds the attention of an audience in a private drawing room, will have in his voice the assertiveness congruent with that of a small child claiming the attention of a parent.[47] This type of analysis, which Bateson has called *end-linkage*,[48] provides a key to unlock the regularities in a whole series of interpersonal relationships within a society, between teacher and pupil, employer and employee, speaker and audience, leader and led. Natalie Joffe[49] has recently used it to define the relationship of benefice and deference characteristic of Eastern European Jewish culture, in which the rich, the learned, the powerful, and the advantaged expect to give, teach, protect, and care for the poor, the ignorant, the disadvantaged, and the sick, and expect to receive formal deference in return. Among the Great Russians,[50] there seems to be a demand for symmetrical relationships, for a kind of mirroring between leader and led, as when Stalin applauds his own speech, the army marches past Stalin bearing pictures of Stalin, or a famous Russian actor describes acting as like a game of tennis: "You send the ball to the audience and they return it to you." These tendencies may be placed in the context of the Great Russian intolerance of ambiguities in human relationships—the demand for very clear super ordination and subordination, or for absolute, unqualified equality. The importance of tolerance of ambiguity has been emphasized by another set of studies, by Sanford and Frenkel-Brunswik,[51] in which ethnocentrism and ideological absolutism are seen to be associated with demands for extreme clarity and definition of role. This type of analysis of end-linkage becomes more useful when the question of origination of any interaction sequence is considered. A dominance-submission sequence, for instance, can be seen as originated either by a command or by a submissive action. Another anthropologist, Eliot Chapple,[52] has been interested in specifying the course of such sequences of originated action, and has devised a machine, the *interaction chronograph,* which records the formal aspects of the patterns of two or more persons as they react to each other by speech. His analysis has been used particularly in problems of relations between labor and management, and in specifying invariant elements in the personality of individuals being considered for training in aviation.

Bateson's type of analysis can also be related to the method by which Erikson has systematized Freudian theories of pregenital development, so that the *zones* of the body and the *modes* of behavior appropriate to the zones may be related to different types of complementary relationships, as suckling between mother and child, and copulation, as interpersonal modes; and intake and elimination of waste as forming a model of interpersonal behavior mediated by intervening objects—food, gifts, money.[53] Furthermore, to the extent to which an individual sees himself as a whole being among other whole beings, or retains a sense of his partially complementary relationship to another being (as parent, employer, leader, etc.), such forms of character structure can be related to political patterns such as the German emphasis on duty rather than on the content of action, the absolute obedience of the Japanese to the Emperor, or the type of full, autonomous assent requisite for political functioning in the citizens of Britain or Norway.[54] These three approaches, which may be combined and used to study particular problems, are: (1) a description of the configuration of a culture in comparison with other cultures which have drawn upon the same historical background or shared during the last two centuries in the same widespread trends (such as secularization and industrialization); (2) an analysis of the relationship between the basic learning of the child as a total individual and the other aspects of the culture; and (3) a systematic treatment of the patterns characteristic of parent-to-child, peer-to-peer, and other interpersonal relationships in the culture. Within a society, such a problem as military morale would include an examination of how the relationships of officers to men and private to private correspond to, or contrast with, the expected relationships for which individuals were reared. Such relationships may present a romantic contrast to the surrender to a dull conformity, as in Germany; may be an echoing restatement of family relationships, as in Japan; or may necessitate a premature weaning and a culturally unprepared-for separation from home, as in the United States.

Another possibility, used in the detailed studies of problems of effecting temporary or permanent changes in the food habits of Americans,[55] is to make specific investigations of how eating is integrated into the character structure. Within the United States, for example, there is a contrast between the Northern and Middle Western attitudes toward food and the attitudes found in the Southeast. There is a moralistic attitude toward food in the former regions, where the foods, which are good for one but not particularly enjoyable— such as milk, green vegetables, fruit juice, and calves' liver—are those, which the mother requires her child to eat. Here, too, the foods which are both good and good, for one are associated with the father—meat, butter, and fish, for instance; and those which are good but not wholesome—mainly sweets of all sorts—are given as rewards for eating the foods which are defined as good for one. In the Southeast, on the other hand, there is a personal relationship, mediated by mother or wife, between each individual and his food; and it can be said interchangeably, that the food likes or dislikes the individual, or that the individual likes or dislikes the food. When the process of changing nutrition and improving the very meager and unsatisfactory diet of the sharecropper of the Southeastern United States was entrusted to nutritionists born and trained in the North, very poor results were obtained. Studies of the character structure of those individuals who elected nutrition education—that is, the purposeful alteration of other people's eating habits—as their chosen vocation in life, showed that they possessed to an unusual degree a northern Puritanism, a desire to make people exercise their wills and discipline themselves. Whenever new practices of health or education are to be introduced, discrepancies between the characters of the executants of the change and the character of those whose living habits are to be altered must be allowed for if they are not to defeat the whole program. In this example of nutrition education in the United States, two aspects of the application of studies of national character arise: (1) the relationship of the character structure of a particular occupational group—in this case nutritionists—to the culture from which they derive; and (2) the impact of such a group upon people with a different culture who, because of the growth of a national unit, the acquisition of colonies, or the concerted efforts of international organizations, become subject to their persuasions and ministrations. Two other American studies have illuminated the problem of such interrelationships between differentiated groups sharing the same national character but in different ways. One of these is a study of American public school teachers by Warner, Havighurst, and Loeb.[56] The other study, by Ruesch and others,[57] considers the question of which groups in the population prolong their convalescence in the hospital.

The national character approach may also be applied to the relationships between two groups of allies, such as Anglo-American relationships during the war.[58] Such a method of analysis as that of end-linkage, discussed above, may be used to illuminate and reduce friction when British and Americans have to work together on commissions and committees and joint planning boards. The extent to which the differences in the permitted exhibitionism in childhood are linked with the note of paternal sureness combined with a gentle, protective underplaying of their own power in Englishmen can be illuminatingly contrasted with the assertiveness and overstatement of Americans when placed in comparable roles, congruently, with the American child's permitted and encouraged self-assertion to which his parents play audience.

Furthermore, particular situations within such an allied relationship may be studied. An example is the problem of the relations of American soldiers to British girls in Britain in wartime, when most of the British men were overseas.[59] Enormous misunderstanding and mutual ill-feeling resulted from the contrast in the ways of rearing British and American adolescents for dealing with sexual advances. In the United States, the boy is permitted great initiative, but the girl is trained to be able to exercise such a strong veto upon his importunities that he can trust her to impose an external check upon them. In Britain, on the other hand, the girl is reared to a certain protective shyness but has an expectation of yielding to the determined advances of a man, who will discipline his impulses in appropriate ways. The combination in wartime Britain of large numbers of American young men, accustomed to ask for a great many more favors than they expected to receive, and a group of girls trained to say yes when asked did not necessarily result in a greater number of illegitimate children than is usual when troops are quartered in any community; yet it produced great friction between British and Americans. Each American boy encountered in his advances to British girls some type of misunderstanding peculiar to the differences in national background. One would repulse him immediately with cold shyness, another, would collapse into his arms at his first verbal approach, and still another would permit his exuberant public courtship and then expect marriage on the basis of it. With analysis of the situation, educational and administrative measures to prevent such difficulties could be taken more easily.

The national character approach also provides for a special form of opinion sampling. In any large national state, programs in education, in health welfare, or in voluntary professional organizations, trade unions, and similar groups originate at the center. Such programs cannot take positive account of regional, class, and ethnic differences, except by leaving to local officers and executants certain areas of decision in the organizational structure. During World War II,

Rhoda Metraux 60 developed a method of qualitative attitude sampling by which, on the basis of an anthropological type of analysis of verbatim responses collected from many parts of the country, it was possible to delineate main patterns of attitudes toward government and toward particular programs. Such studies showed how a given situation, such as a food shortage, a rationing measure, or a request to conserve in order to send food abroad, evoked a definite pattern of responses, systematic within themselves, which could be placed and interpreted by our general knowledge of American character. Such responses could not be derived without study, since they were specific to and dependent upon a series of initially unrelated conditions. Among such conditions were the activities of other governments, publicized in the United States but over which the United States had no control—e.g., a change in governmental regulations in Canada, the diversion of some shiploads of rice from Egypt to relieve a famine in India, a rumor that the Russians were using butter to oil their boots. The method developed by Metraux highlights the possibility of combining a basic knowledge of the national character with historically fortuitous situations to which those who must take action are too close for any sort of long-time perspective. With the disturbed state of the world today and the need for rapid and often contradictory programs on the part of national states, the usefulness of a method, which is able to include the immediate concrete situation within a systematic scientific framework, is very great.

Another specialized field is that of medicine, specifically the approach known in the United States as *psychosomatic medicine*,[61] in which the distinctions between mind and body are replaced by a view of the total personality, within which changes may originate in a somatic lesion, a prolonged state of tension, a severe dietary deficiency, a depression resulting from the death of a parent, an allergic reaction to a specific agent, an activated fear of impregnation, etc. Any attempt to relate special disease manifestations to special types of character structure—as has been done for asthma, essential hypertension, diseases of the skin and the mucous membranes, gastrointestinal ailments, arthritis, and Parkinson's—involves placing such character structures within the larger national character in time and in space. Studies of asthma suggest that one point of vulnerability occurs in connection with feeding conflicts combined with a severe upper respiratory infection or whooping cough at a given early age in childhood. This obviously is directly connected in the United States with a character structure in which maternal anxiety about nutrition and the use of food, as reward and punishment are essential aspects of child-rearing, and in which problems of intersex dependency assume special forms in the context of boys reared by mothers and feminine teachers to be simultaneously peaceful, obedient, and able to stand up for themselves when attacked. It is possible to consider a whole set of pathological conditions, as was done by Wolff;[62] or a shift in incidence of a disease from one sex to another, as in Wolff's and Mittelmann's study of the shift of peptic ulcer from a female disease to a male disease in the last fifty years;[63] or the relationship between the expression of conflict in marked somatic form as compared with the use of neurotic symptoms, as studied by Booth.[64] National character studies make an obvious contribution to qualifying and interpreting results on given populations in terms of the actual cultural background of the patients and the culture of the particular milieu in which they live.

Finally, something may be said about the possible contribution of this approach to the construction of new political forms,[65] suitable for better international co-operation[66] and cross-national communication[67] in the modern world. Within each culture, attitudes toward the hearth, the soil, and the country, toward rulers and enemies, are very highly patterned and can be shown to fit into the coherent character structure of the people. Whether one's country is conceived as masculine, as in Germany, or feminine, as in France and Russia; whether men are more willing to fight to hold fast a boundary against invasion, or to maintain their right to sail the seas, or to uphold some abstract value like freedom threatened somewhere else in the world— these differences can all be shown to be systematic and explicable. Similarly, whether the government represents a grandparental generation; whether it is divided into the ideal and the mundane aspects of the father (as in Britain, where the King is the permanent representative of the ideal aspects of the father); or whether each higher governmental unit is regarded as in fraternal rivalrous competition with each smaller one (city with state, state with nation, as in the United States)—such matters can be stated in terms of national character. When it comes to devising international constitutions and methods of joint operation, forms must be invented which will take into account, and either use or successfully discount, the very different ways in which French and Swiss, Burmese and Great Russian, Argentinean and Nigerian and Javanese, American and Greek, are at present able to relate themselves to larger units of authority.[68] A problem which a small number of men of genius were able to grapple with in the French Revolution and in the development of the American Constitution has now assumed proportions such that more formal methods are required.[69] Just as the scientific laboratory in a modern munitions plant with the coordinated teamwork of a large number of trained specialists has replaced the age-old personal virtuosity of a sword maker, so in the political field also we need a set of abstractions within which material can first be gathered and later so organized that political forms, can be thought about, in the same way that the composition of a particular alloy is thought about today. This in no sense means that men and the affairs of men can be thought of as if men were things and their values of no moment. It means rather that an approach is needed which is built upon detailed attention to the significance of the touch of a mother's hand, the note in a father's voice, the lines of a window opening into a garden, or the particular aspect of the life of Christ or the Virgin Mary or of the Buddha which a given people represent most often. Such an approach is directly responsive to human values and can therefore, through appropriate abstractions, help to perpetuate the values which men have built, by devising new forms to keep human beings safe in a narrowing world.

NEW YORK, 1949

Notes

1. As this chapter is specifically about a particular development within the United States, I have had to omit for reasons of space all the interconnections between the European and English anthropological and psychological theory, and the American. It is important to remember the parallelism between Malinowski's work and much American work; the extent to which Sapir—whose teaching influenced Benedict, Dollard, and myself—drew upon Piaget and Jung; the lines of relationship from Durkheim, through Radcliffe-Brown, to Lloyd Warner; the quite independent development of a national character approach in Britain during the war, by Henry Dicks; and the number of Europeans and Englishmen who have played a conspicuous role in developing the present American approach, especially Gregory Bateson, Erik Erikson, Geoffrey Gorer, and Nathan Leites.
2. Alexis de Tocqueville, *De la démocratie en Amérique* (1835)
3. Alfred Fouillée, *Psychologie du Peuple Français* (1898)
4. Salvador de Madariaga, *Englishmen, Frenchmen, Spaniards: An Essay in Comparative Psychology* (1928).

5. Lewis H. Morgan, *Systems of Consanguinity and Affinity of the Human Family* ("Smithsonian Contributions to Knowledge," Vol. XVII, Art. 2, Publication 218 [1870]).

6. Gregory Bateson, "Some Systematic Approaches to the Study of Culture and Personality," *Character and Personality*, XL (1942), 76-84; Lawrence K. Frank, *Society as the Patient* (1948); Douglas Haring (ed.), *Personal Character and Cultural Milieu* (1948); Clyde Kluckhohn, "Personality in Culture," in his *Mirror for Man* (1949), chap. viii, pp. 196-227; Clyde Kluckhohn and Henry A. Murray (eds.), *Personality in Nature, Society, and Culture* 1948).

7. Harold Orlansky, "Infant Care and Personality," *Psychological Bulletin*, XLVI, No.1 (1949), 1-48.

8. Margaret Mead, "Social Anthropology and Its Relations to Psychiatry," in Franz Alexander (ed.), *Dynamic Psychiatry* (University of Chicago Press, in press).

9. Margaret Mead, *Male and Female: A Study of the Sexes in a Changing World* (1949).

10. Ruth Benedict, "Child Rearing in Certain European Cultures," *American Journal of Orthopsychiatry*, XIX, No.2 (1949), 342-50.

11. Margaret Mead, "Research on Primitive Children," in Leonard Carmichael (ed.), *Manual of Child Psychology* (1946), pp. 667-706.

12. Gregory Bateson, "Moral and National, Character," in Goodwin Watson (ed.), *Civilian Morale* (1942), pp. 71-91; Ruth Benedict, "The Study of Cultural Patterns in European Nations," *Transaction, New York Academy of Sciences*, Ser. 2, Vol. VIII, No.8 (1946), 274-79; and Otto Klineberg, " A Science of National Character," *Bulletin of the Society for the Psychological Study of Social Issues*, XIX (1944), 145-94.

13. Ruth Benedict, *The Chrysanthemum and the Sword* (1946), Geoffrey Gorer, "Themes in Japanese Culture," *Transactions, New York Academy of Sciences*, Ser. 2, Vol. V, No.5 (1943), 106-24; Douglas Raring, " Aspects of Personal Character in Japan," *Far Eastern Quarterly*, VI, No.1 (1946), 12-22; and Weston LaBarre, "Some Observations on Character Structure. In the Orient: The Japanese," *Psychiatry*, VIII, No.3 (1945), 319-42.

14. Richard Brickner, *Is Germany Incurable?* (1943); David M. Levy, "Anti-Nazis: Criteria of Differentiation," *Psychiatry*, XI, No.2 (1948), 125-67; R. R. Lowie, *The German People: A Social Portrait to* 1914 (1945); David Rodnick, *Post-war Germans* (1948); and Bertram Schaffner, *Father Land: A Study of Authoritarianism in the German Family* (1948). See also, "Germany After the War: Roundtable, 1945," *American Journal of Orthopsychiatry*, XV, No.3 (1945), 381-441.

15. Geoffrey Corer, *Burmese Personality* (1943), Ruth Benedict, *Thai Culture and Behavior* (1946). These are mimeographed, issued by the Institute for Intercultural Studies, New York.

16. National Research Council, *The Problem of Changing Food Habits: Report of the Committee on Food Habits*, 1941-43 (National Research Council, Bulletin 108 [1943]).

17. Irving Janis, "Psychodynamic Aspects of Adjustment to Army Life," *Psychiatry*, VIII, No.2 (1945), 159-76; David M. Schneider, "The Social

Dynamics of Physical Disability in Army Basic Training," *Psychiatry*, X, No.3 (1947), 323-34; G. Dearborn Spindler, "American Character as Revealed by the Military," *Psychiatry*, XI, No.3 (1948), 275-82.

18. cf. the following by Margaret Mead: *The American Troops and the British Community* (1944), "What Is a Date?" *Transatlantic*, X (1944), 54, 57-60; "The Application of Anthropological Techniques to Cross-National Communication," *Transactions, New York Academy of Sciences*, Ser. 2, Vol. IX, No.4 (1947), 133-52; and "A Case History in Cross-National Communications," in Lyman Bryson (ed.), *The Communication of Ideas* (1948), chap. xiii, pp. 209-29.

19. Ruth Benedict, *Rumanian Culture and Behavior* (1946), mimeographed, issued by the Institute for Intercultural Studies, New York.

20. John Dollard, *Caste and Class in a Southern Town* (1937).

21. David and Elizabeth Rodnick, "Czechs, Slovaks, and Communism" (in preparation).

22. Erik H. Erikson, "Ego Development and Historical Change," in Anna Freud et *al., The Psychoanalytic Study of the Child*, II (1948), 359-96.

23. Abram Kardiner *et al., The Psychological Frontiers of Society* (1945).

24. James West, *Plainville, U.S.A.* (1945).

25. Schaffner, Levy, and Rodnick, works cited in Footnote 14.

26. William Lipkind, "A Community Study of the Town and Kreis of Miesbach, Germany" (unpublished manuscript).

27. Margaret Mead, *And Keep Your Powder Dry* (1942).

28. Geoffrey Gorer, *The American People* (1948)

29. Research in Contemporary Cultures, Columbia University, 1947-1949, directed by Ruth Benedict during 1947-48 and by Margaret Mead during 1948-49. Russian Research Center, Harvard University, 1947-52, directed by Clyde Kluckhohn. Studies in Soviet Culture, American Museum of Natural History, 1948-50, directed by Margaret Mead.

30. Gregory Bateson, "Cultural and Thematic Analysis of Fictional Films," *Transactions, New York Academy of Sciences*, Ser. 2, Vol. V, No.4 (1943), 72-78; Nathan Leites and Martha Wolfenstein, *The Movies* (1950)

31. Clyde Kluckhohn and Henry A. Murray (eds.), *Personality in Nature, Society, and Culture* (1948); Margaret Mead, "Social Anthropology and Its Relations to Psychiatry," in Franz Alexander (ed.), *Dynamic Psychiatry* (University of Chicago Press, in press); Harry Stack Sullivan, "Towards a Psychiatry of Peoples," *Psychiatry*, XI, No.2 (1948), 105-16.

32. Ruth Benedict, *Patterns of Culture* (1934).

33. Li An-che, "Zuñi: Some Observations and Queries," *American Anthropologist*, XXXIX, No.1 (1937), 62-76.

34. "Themes in Japanese Culture," *Transactions, New York Academy of Sciences*, Ser. 2, Vol. V, No.5 (1943), 106-24.

35. "Problems of Infancy and Early Childhood," *Cyclopaedia of Medicine, Surgery, and Specialties* (1940); "Childhood and Tradition in Two American Indian Tribes," in Anna Freud *et al., The Psychoanalytic Study of the Child*, I, (1945), 319-50; and *Childhood and Society* (1950).

36. Geoffrey Corer, "Themes in Japanese Culture," *Transactions, New York Academy of Sciences*, Ser. 2, Vol. 5, No.5 (1943), 106-24.

37. Geoffrey Gorer, "Some Aspects of the Psychology of the People of Great Russia," *American Slavic and East European Review*, VIII, No.3 (1949), 155-66; Geoffrey Gorer and John Rickman, *The People of Great Russia* (1949).

38. Erikson, *Childhood and Society* (1950).

39. Nathan Leites and Martha Wolfenstein, *The Movies* (1950).

40. Abram Kardiner, *The Individual and His Society* (1939) and Abram Kardiner et al., *The Psychological Frontiers of Society* (1945).

41. Gregory Bateson, "Some Systematic Approaches to the Study of Culture and Personality," *Character and Personality*, XL (1942), 76-84; and "Morale and National Character," in Goodwin Watson (ed.), *Civilian Morale* (1942), pp. 71-91. See also Norbert Weiner, *Cybernetics* (1948).

42. *Patterns of Culture* (1934).

43. *Rumanian Culture and Behavior* (1946).

44. *Thai Culture and Behavior* (1946).

45. *The Chrysanthemum and the Sword* (1946).

46. Gregory Bateson, *Naven* (1936) and "Morale and National Character," in Goodwin Watson (ed.), *Civilian Morale* (1942), pp. 71-91.

47. Margaret Mead, *The American Troops and the British Community* (1944).

48. In "Morale and National Character," in Goodwin Watson (ed.), *Civilian Morale* (1942), pp. 71-91.

49. Natalie F. Joffe, "The Dynamics of Benefice Among East European Jews," *Social Forces, XXVII, No.3 (1949), 238-47.*

50. Geoffrey Gorer, "Some Aspects of the Psychology of the People of Great Russia," *American Slavic and East European Review*, VIII, No.3 (1949), 155-66; Geoffrey Gorer and John Rickman, *The People of Great Russia* (1949).

51. Else Frenkel-Brunswik and R. Nevitt Sanford, "Some Personality Factors in Anti-Semitism," *Journal of Psychology*, XX (1945), 271-91; Else Frenkel-Brunswik, " A Study of Prejudice in Children," *Human Relations*, I, No.3 (1948), 295-306.

52. Eliot D. Chapple and Carleton S. Coon, *Principles of Anthropology* (1942); Eliot D. Chapple and Conrad M. Arensberg, *Measuring Human Relations: An Introduction to the Study of the Interaction of Individuals* (Genetic Psychology Monographs, Vol. XXII, No.1 [1940])

53. Margaret Mead, *Male and Female* (1949).

54. Margaret Mead, "Collective Guilt," in *Proceedings of the International Conference in Medical Psychotherapy* (1948), pp. 57-65. The conference was a part of the International Congress on Mental Health, London, 1948, and the volume is the third of the four-volume series *International Congress on Mental Health, London*, 1948, edited by J. C. Flugel *et al.*

55. National Research Council, *The Problem of Changing Food Habits* (1943).

56. Lloyd Warner, Robert J. Havighurst, and Martin Loeb, *Who Shall Be Educated? The Challenge of Unequal Opportunities* (1944).

57. Jurgen Ruesch *et al., Chronic Disease and Psychological Invalidism* (Psychosomatic Medicine Monograph No.9 [1946]).

58. Margaret Mead, "The Application of Anthropological Techniques to, Cross-National Communication," *Transactions, New York Academy of Sciences,* Ser. 2, Vol. IX, No.4 (1947), 133-52; and " A Case History in Cross-National Communications," in Lyman Bryson (ed.), *The Communication of Ideas* (1948), chap. xiii, pp. 209-29.

59. Mead, *The American Troops and the British Community* (1944).

60. "Qualitative Attitude Analysis: A Technique for the Study of Verbal Behavior," in National Research Council, *The Problem of Changing Food Habits* (1943), pp. 86-94.

61. Margaret Mead, "The Concept of Culture and the Psychosomatic Approach," *Psychiatry,* X, No. 1 (1947), 57-76.

62. Harold G. Wolff, "Protective Reaction Patterns and Disease," *Annals of Internal Medicine, XXVII, No.6 (1947), 944-69.*

63. Bela Mittelmann, Harold G. Wolff, and M. P. Scharf, "Emotions and Gastroduodenal Functions: Experimental Studies on Patients with Gastritis, Duodenitis, and Peptic Ulcer," *Psychosomatic Medicine,* IV, No.2 (1942), 5-61.

64. Gotthard C. Booth, "Variety in Personality and Its Relation to Health," *The Review of Religion,* X, No.4 (1946), 385-412, and "Organ Function and Form Perception: Use of the Rorschach Method with Cases of Chronic Arthritis, Parkinsonism, and Arterial Hypertension," *Psychosomatic Medicine,* VIII, No.6 (1946), 367-85.

65. Gregory Bateson, "Atoms, Nations, and Culture," *The International House Quarterly,* XI, No.2 (1947), 47-50; Nathan Leites, "Psycho- cultural Hypotheses About Political Acts," *World Politics,* I, No.1 (1948), 102-19.

66. Gregory Bateson, "The Pattern of an Armament Race: I. An Anthropological Approach; II. An Analysis of Nationalism," *Bulletin of the Atomic Scientists,* 11, No; 5/6 (1946), 10-11, and No. 7/8, 26-28.

67. Margaret Mead, "The Application of Anthropological Techniques to Cross-national Communication," *Transactions, New York Academy of Sciences,* Ser. 2, Vol. IX, No.4 (1947), 133-52.

68. Gregory Bateson, "Atoms, Nations, and Culture," *The International House Quarterly,* XI, No. 2 (1947), 47-50.

69. Kurt Lewin, *Resolving Social Conflicts: Selected Papers on Group Dynamics, 1935-46* (1948), edited by Gertrud W, Lewin.

THE SWADDLING HYPOTHESIS:
Its Reception

In this paper[1] I propose to deal with some of the confusions which have arisen during the last four years regarding the study of cultural character and which have been given their most definite expression in misrepresentations of the swaddling hypothesis developed by Geoffrey Gorer.[2] It seems important to clear these up not only for the sake of the general development of theory, but also because they provide an unusually good opportunity to examine the cultural setting within which theoretical approaches flourish or wither, pass unchallenged or attain ready acceptance. It should be the responsibility of professional students of culture to take into account this question of the effect of cultural setting on ideas. Conspicuous examples of this relationship are the heated tones in which questions of Old World origin of New World traits were discussed in the period of American isolationism, and the atmosphere of disinterested academic controversy in which such discussions are conducted today. Even the dramatic popularization of *Kon-tiki* fails to stir the same excitement that much milder speculations aroused in academic circles in the early twenties.

The principal misunderstandings have clustered around two foci: the difference between the history of a culture and the history of an individual personality, and the difference between hypotheses which attribute high efficacy to single causes and hypotheses involving circularity and dynamic equilibriums. Stated briefly, Gorer's hypothesis is that an unusually long swaddling experience is a significant aspect of the educational process by which human infants, born to and reared by Russian parents, become Russians. By analyzing the way in which Russian swaddling differs from the swaddling in surrounding areas, the special features of Great Russian swaddling are identified and related to other aspects of Russian child rearing. Gorer then invokes developmental theory from another field, that of psychoanalytically oriented studies of character formation in children in our

*Originally published in *American Anthropologist,* New Series, vol. 56, issue 3 (Jun., 1954), p. 395-409.

own society, to provide a theoretical basis for hypothesizing the intrapsychic mechanisms involved in the process of the formation of Great Russian character, one expression of which can be found in the traditional attitudes of Great Russians toward external authority as being both hateful and essential.

Before discussing the assumptions involved in this hypothesis, it is important to dispose of the two principal misunderstandings. The first comes mainly from the fields of history and political science, where biology or psychology usually are not taken systematically into account. It is not, perhaps, surprising that some historians and political scientists have been unable to distinguish between statements about Russian culture or specific Russian institutions and statements about the Russian people. When Gorer discussed the way Russians— human individuals born in Russia—learned Russian culture, students in these fields, accustomed to subsume human behavior under phrases like "technological revolution," thought he was discussing the *origins* of Russian culture. However, this misconception should not, as it has done, confuse anthropologists and psychologists, the one having a fairly adequate theory of culture and the other having at least some working knowledge of child development. It is a working assumption of anthropology that human cultures develop from other human cultures through processes of diffusion, convergence, parallelism, and invention. We do not seek "origins" either in the events of early childhood, in the lives of single leaders, or in epidemics or famines; we may find in any one of these some of the conditions within which cultural change occurs. When there is an attempt to explain cultural change (such as "adoption of a sedentary way of life" or "shift from matrilineal to patrilineal inheritance under missionary pressure"), the cultural character formation existing among the representatives of the culture at the period being studied becomes one of the conditions within which change occurs. A different culture at the given moment of history would have meant a different character formation, since the abstraction "culture" and the abstraction "cultural character" are different ways of organizing material about the same human beings. In any detailed outlining of a change (such as, for instance, a revolution in which a different class with a different version of the national character is placed in power), the cultural character of those individuals who carry it out is taken into account—sometimes inexplicitly and unsystematically under clichés such as "peasant habits," sometimes by using cultural statements such as "the practice of bride price" to cover behavior which could also be described psychologically. Because anthropologists have, on the whole, continued to recognize biological man, the inclu-

sion of the character of a people in any historical statement has to a
degree been taken for granted, although often it is not spelled out.

But although one culture develops from another through
processes which, even though mediated by human beings, can be
described in general terms without specific reference to the given biological carriers (as we discuss "urbanization" or "militarization," for
example), individual human beings as biological organisms embody-
ing human culture do have a specific identifiable, beginning at conception, and an equally identifiable ending. Early learning precedes
later learning; certain types of events may preclude the possibility of
later learning altogether. The common anthropological assumption
of the psychic unity of mankind is that a child at birth is equally
capable of learning any natural language and of coming to embody
any human culture. No existing studies of racial differences or of the
proclivities of different constitutional types have provided us with
any evidence which would necessitate our abandoning this assumption. Therefore, if human infants at birth are capable of becoming
equally complete representatives of Eskimo, Mexican, Siamese,
French, or Russian culture (subject to the extent to which physical
type is socially identified with particular cultural forms), then the
process of becoming a member of one culture rather than of another
must be ascribed to learning. Because all human beings so far
observed go through a process of development which in all its broad
outlines has been found to be the same, it is possible to assume in discussing this process of learning, the same general type of implication
of the organism. Furthermore, whenever children have been
observed they have been found to display, within the limits of their
biological development, the types of learning characteristic of their
culture. The first ten words of French children are French, not
Siamese. Children habituated to a diet of chili pepper will be able
to eat hotter food than those who are not; children who have been
accustomed to being carried passively will relax in the arms, and children who have been taught to hang on will hang on; children who
have slept in cribs or been fed from bottles will respond to the sight
of the crib or the bottle differently from those who have not. These
points may and certainly should appear truistic to any educated
observer—with or without anthropological training—but since so
much of this controversy has focused around the inadmissibility of
suggesting that anything that happens in childhood could have any
effect in adulthood, it seems necessary to go over them. While the
origin of any cultural institution after many thousands of years of
human history is shrouded in a long historical past which can at best
be traced laboriously through antecedent institutions, the life of any

human being need not be so treated (see also Mead 1952, 1953; Mead and Metraux 1953).

In other words, the question *How did X or one hundred X's learn to be French?* is not the same question as *How did French culture arise for X or one hundred X's to learn?* In the synchronic study of national culture either in a country on which there is voluminous documentation or in any culture for which we have only speculative history, if our scientific concern is with the present population, the first question is a legitimate one. It does not, as has frequently been claimed, "ignore history." It merely, for purposes of a particular inquiry about a designated group of living individuals, holds history constant. By making certain that every individual being studied is actually representative of the culture of a given society which has a given history, we may then proceed to discuss how those individuals, who have identified beginnings, learn their culture. In such a discussion of how French or Russian children are handled, disciplined, and taught by other members of their societies, it is no more or less necessary to take into account the details of French or Russian history of two hundred years ago than to take into account the historical events of twenty thousand years ago. In the period under discussion, infants are being born into French society and learning to be French, or into Russian society and learning to be Russian. Before discussing how a French child learns to use a pencil, one may refer to the point at which man learned to make tools, discuss writing *per se,* or take up the standardization of the French language. All are historically relevant, but none is necessary in order to delineate the particular process through which living French children learn to write. *What* French children learn *about* the past, near or remote, is exceedingly relevant. Any synchronic statement (for example, about the present functioning of French political parties) has to take for granted the historical antecedents of present-day France, of present-day Europe, of Indo-European languages, of the invention of human social organization.

In discussing a segment of human society during a period of, let us say, twenty-five years, one is making an artificial cut through a living fabric of members of that society of all ages; in discussing the life histories of individual human beings, one is dealing with an isolatable event which has a beginning—when the infant is cultureless. So, in discussions with historians and political scientists, it is important to stress that in *synchronic* studies of national character, we are discussing not the origins of the culture or the society, but the process of learning of identifiable human beings living within that society at a given period. (I am fully aware that any extrapolation over a twenty-five year period in a modern society, even without revolutionary changes, involves new problems, and they will be dealt with below.) We are concerned with the regularities within these individuals' learned behavior which can be attributed to their membership in a society or, specifically, a subgroup within the society. We are concerned with Great Russians, with Frenchmen, with Thai—not with Russia, or the Soviet Union, or France, or Thailand.

The second misunderstanding is an assertion that when a student of national character attempts to delineate the way in which being swaddled by Russians communicates to an infant in specific ways which become part of his culturally regular character, this description is equivalent to saying that swaddling *per se* by members of any culture will have definite predictable effects of the same sort on all infants, regardless of their culture. This assertion derives principally from attempts to apply to whole cultures findings on the clinical study of individuals, and it takes two forms: one based on Kardiner's treatment (1939) of cultural forms as "projections" of individual fears and hopes which themselves originate in infantile experience; the other, the sort of statement made by Kenneth Little (1950)—that the way to find out whether swaddling was an important element in Great Russian character is to trace swaddling as a single trait through a variety of cultures to see if it always has the same effect. The direct extrapolation from individual infantile fears to developed cultural forms is one that is usually rejected by anthropologists; they rely instead on the comparative study of related cultural forms to provide clues to the function any given form may serve in a given society, realizing that any given culture trait has been modified many times as it becomes embodied in members of different cultures with different characters. Confusion in the mind of the reader between the use of psychoanalytically based psychodynamics and psychoanalysts' speculations about culture is responsible for this misconception. Stated concretely, the Russian institution of a strong leader, whether called Czar or Stalin, is not to be attributed to swaddling. But the forms of the acceptance of such a leader are grounded in the way children are reared to be members of Russian culture.

The second misunderstanding confuses the use of cultural material in the study of educational mechanisms with the invocation of an educational mechanism to describe the psychodynamics of a particular culture. If we wanted to know whether swaddling has any universal effects on child development and ultimately on adult character, then we would examine as many cultures as possible which used swaddling and finally come to a rigorous cross-cultural definition of swaddling, applicable to all instances where the infant body is tightly constrained by cloth or skin wrappings, which are wound around the child, constraining both arms and legs and not involving the use of a pillow, board, or cradle. Within these swaddling cultures, we would observe in great detail at just what point the swaddling was applied, how often the child was unswaddled, how long it was swaddled, etc. Then a proper sized sample of children for whom a constant type of swaddling had been established would be compared in those details which might be expected to be relevant, such as age of walking (established by actual observation and not by parental report), with a similar sample of children from cultures in which the child's body was left free and uncovered. If significant differences (for example, in the way the body was held in walking or the age at which the eyes focused) were found, then a further detailed study could be made among the different swaddling groups, possibly extended to users of cradle boards, swings, etc., to attempt to isolate just which features of the swaddling—even pressure on the whole body, comparable confinement of arms and legs, long periods without being changed, restraint of the hand-to-mouth gesture during teething, etc.—were determinative.

Not until such a complete study had been done could any statements be made about the effect that swaddling procedures had *per se*, regardless of the culture in which they occurred, that is, regardless of the configuration of cultural practices of which they were a part. It is important to stress that we have no such information on any single aspect of child rearing, and it is likely to be a very long time before the time and money are available to make such a study. Preliminary hypotheses which would repay investigation can be developed by the methods used by Whiting and Child (1953) if it is recognized that there is no possibility of proving anything by comparing such incomparable data on child care. It should be noted carefully that students of national character do not assert any universal effect of any single item of child care, such as swaddling, breast feeding, sudden weaning, etc., as may be suggested by advocates of particular regimens who attribute special characteristics to practices as world-wide as breast-feeding. Neither are studies which isolate one item of child care such as breast-feeding from the entire behavior of a group of mothers and then find no differences between the breast-fed and the non-breast-fed child (Peterson and Spano 1941; Sewall 1952) of a sort which students in the field of culture and personality need take seriously. We are attempting to understand the complex process by which a child with an innate biologically given potential, exposed to a certain very complex cultural configuration, develops a character structure with observable regularities which can be referred to the experience of being reared in that culture. To do this, we draw on whatever detailed clinical studies have been made of the functioning of specific bodily disciplines or learning sequences. We attempt not to generalize blindly from breast feeding in one set of circumstances to breast feeding in another, or constraint in one setting (Greenacre 1944) to constraint in another, but to increase our capacity to assay the part played by breast-feeding in any given historical pattern of mother-child relationships. Cross-cultural studies can be used to isolate universals, but such isolation is not the aim of studies of national character; they are more appropriately pursued under less complex conditions.

Suggestions like those of Little (1950) are therefore not relevant. We are not studying swaddling; we are studying Russians, using such data on character formation of individuals in our own culture and of members of other cultures as we have. This definition of aim immediately imposes another requirement; we do not focus upon those aspects of Russian education or of Russian child development which are, as far as we know, universal but specifically on those which are special to Russian culture. So it is expected (but irrelevant) that when Russians are asked why they swaddle infants they reply first that it is done for the protection of the child. All peoples who coat their children with clay or butter, wrap them in buffalo hide or tapa or silk, swaddle them or fasten them on cradle boards will give as the primary reason for so doing their desire to protect the child. If we found a people who gave as a first response, "We do it in the hope the child will catch cold and die," their statement would be a profoundly interesting one. The converse is not true. Nor are we primarily interested in those aspects of swaddling that Great Russians share with surrounding Slavic peoples and that were once shared by most if not all the peoples of Europe.

It is essentially the *differences* in this widely distributed practice (Benedict 1949), the special reasons which Russians spontaneously supply for swaddling, and the specific ways in which swaddling images appear in their literature and art[3] which are used by the student of national character to delineate Russian character by demonstrating the ways in which it differs from the culturally regular character of the Polish, Czech, or Eastern European Jewish peoples. In this particular case, it is the recurrent spontaneous emphasis on the child's strength, the extent to which it was thought the child could endanger *itself,* and the very long period of very tight swaddling which are significant and which provide a clue about the type of communication between adult and child which the swaddling mediates.

A further question is raised by those who ask why it is necessary to study child-rearing habits in order to understand the adult character of a given people. Granted that it is desirable to study the psychodynamics of any group of people if we are to understand the group, why is it necessary to go back to childhood? Is not the behavior of adults the best sample of the behavior of adults? The reasons for approaching the study of adult character via an account of child-rearing practices, interpreted by the knowledge we have of child development, are primarily functions of the present state of methodology. When we study the character formation of adults, we are dealing with a complex synchronic system or set of systems for which we need a spatial conceptual model. The mathematics (and therefore also the more rigorous forms of conceptualization) for dealing with space, except in the very much simplified of map-making, are still almost entirely lacking. If, however, we follow character as it is formed, introducing a sequential element by including the whole period from birth to maturation, we obtain a type of material which is manageable. Because of the complexity of the material, simpler states are preferable to more complex states as objects of study, and very often it is necessary to invoke an observed change between two states in order to define the states themselves. When it is a question of studying a culture at a distance because there is no possibility of studying the living society, the living growth processes of the members of that society have seemed the best available substitute.

Finally, it is important to consider the validity of using any particular item of child training as a clue to the dynamics of the whole system of child interaction. We assume that culture is systematic, however diverse the historical elements which form its content may be. The circumstance that the same individuals administer the laws, hoe the beans, and worship the gods is a regularizing factor. When analyzed, the kind of law enforcement, the way the beans are hoed, and the manner in which a set of gods (who may be shared with all the other peoples of a continent) are worshiped will be found to be parts of the same configuration. This does not mean that all parts of a culture are in harmony with each other. Some parts may be strikingly discrepant, but the way the discrepancies are handled can be referred to the whole. The assumption is that these regularities are imposed by regularities in the biological nature of man and the functioning of the human nervous system and are not merely designs read into a mass of material by a human being, himself capable perceiving pattern where no pattern is.[4] However, if it is recognized that all the behavior of any given people embodies their culture, then it is reasonable to object when any single item of child rearing is made to carry undue weight as terminant of cultural character. With this position the students of national character are in full agreement. Russian children undoubtedly learn about authority in a thousand different ways, simultaneously—from the fear that comes over the household when there is an unexpected knock at the door, from the tone of voice in which certain officials are mentioned, from the nervousness expressed by adults when infants cry, from the angry baby in the pantomine, from the legend of Prince Ivan and the witch baby born with iron teeth, from the position of the Red corner, from the stiffness with which adults sometimes hold themselves. Swaddling is not regarded as the only way or the most essential way in which infants may be educated to be Russians, but from a detailed analysis of swaddling practices, as described by adults, it was possible to analyze attitudes toward impulse and authority. The statement is not *swaddling makes Russians.* It is: *From an analysis of the way Russians swaddle infants, it is possible to build a model of Russian character formation which enables us to relate what we know about human behavior and what we know about Russian culture in such a way that Russian behavior becomes more understandable.*

Nor does such a detailed analysis of swaddling practice imply that infants could not be brought up to have the same character formation if they were not swaddled. It does involve the assertion that if the parents, even if they did not swaddle their babies, retained the same character formation themselves, other educational devices (Mead 1951b) having the same communicative effect to the child would in all probability replace swaddling. If, on the other hand, the discontinuance of swaddling reflected a change of attitude on the part of parents, or on the part of educators who expressed it through parents, the changed attitude would in time express itself in many other ways also. The discontinuance of swaddling as a result of a government decree which was effective (which the attempts of the Soviet government to eradicate swaddling have not been) would not be expected to have an appreciable effect on Russian character formation if it involved no change in attitude on the part of parents. But a willingness to abandon swaddling, the spread of a belief that swaddling was too confining, a feeling that infants needed freedom to kick, would be expected to occur in company with other changes in attitude which would be communicated to children somehow, even if swaddling were perpetuated by effective government decree. It is the combination of an unusually confining version of a widespread practice, the age of the child which is thus confined, and an adult insistence on the need to protect the child from itself—the duration and type of swaddling—which are assumed to have distinctive effects in the formation of Russian character.

A further theoretical argument may be raised against drawing upon such an early period in infancy. Evaluating this argument calls for weighing the existing material on early memories, on the persistence of early experiences, on the importance of early learning. The case for the great importance of the very earliest learnings and for the extent to which childhood learning must be regarded as different in kind from adult learning, which primarily involves transfer of previous learning, has been cogently stated by Hebb (1949). As a general rule, discussions of the relative importance of different age levels in the formation of cultural character have to rely on material from psychological or detailed culture-and-personality studies in which exact ages have been recorded. Furthermore, in the study of culture at a distance, when the *society* cannot be studied as a living model (Mead and Metraux 1953), the child development model is the only model available.

In summary, then, as a method of constructing a model of Great Russian character formation, descriptive accounts and expressed attitudes of Great Russians were studied, the latter through anthropological interviews, and the accounts of swaddling were coordinated with material from developmental studies to provide an explanatory account of how the infant learned to be a Great Russian. No attempt was made, or could be made, to explain the culture of Russia or the history of Russia in terms of a child-rearing practice. No claim was made that swaddling would have any specified effects in other contexts, or that swaddling was essential in the Russian pattern.

We may now turn to the second step, the application of the study of Great Russian character formation to an understanding of contemporary Soviet character. Our interest in attempting to delineate Great Russian character as it was at the time of the Revolution grew from the assumption that when we deal with cultural change the character structure of the individuals of which the society is composed at the period when the change takes place will be one factor in the nature of the change. Thus, we believed that whatever we knew or could hypothesize about the Great Russians of 1917 might be useful and relevant when we attempted to understand Soviet Russians in 1948. Such understanding would be an addition to the other types of understanding contributed by other disciplines—economics, jurisprudence, and so forth.

We were handicapped by poor data more in studying postrevolutionary Russia than in examining prerevolutionary Russia. For the earlier period we had living members of the old culture to interview and also publications about Russia which were less colored by ideological controversy than those since 1917 have been. The old czarist censorship of publications was negative rather than positive; for the later period, we have only officially approved publications. However, using the only methods available to us (just as specialists on Soviet economics have to go through unsatisfactory operations to arrive at their estimates), we set up a project which would combine work on the model of old Great Russian character, the stated purposes of the Soviet regime, and the manifest behavior of the Soviet regime as found in Party Congresses, Soviet publications, and so forth, and from this we attempted to derive a working model of contemporary Soviet character (Mead *1951a*).

There are various tests to which this model can be put: To what extent are subsequent Soviet public acts in accordance with the model? To what extent does it agree with detailed interviews, including projective tests, of Soviet displaced persons? To what extent does it agree with the observations of other disinterested students of the Soviet Union?

It is important to realize that the model of Soviet character has not been challenged from any of these sources. The intensive interviewing done by H. V. Dicks and his associates in the summer of 1950 (Dicks 1952), and the early reports on the interviewing done by the Harvard research group interviewing ex-Soviet citizens in Western Europe, coincide substantially with the model which was constructed by this less direct method. Russian specialists like Crankshaw, while taking occasion to deride the weighty Freudian apparatus used to arrive at the results, nevertheless have recognized the accuracy of the picture when tested against their experiences. It must be emphasized here that the usefulness of the swaddling hypothesis lies in its function in leading to a coherent theory of Russian personality, within which our existing information about Soviet behavior can be ordered and made intelligible.[5]

We may now turn for a moment to the question of the high amount of affect which the discussion of this approach to Russian character has generated, viewing the controversy itself as a manifestation of contemporary culture. The attack has been led and maintained by the *New Leader,* and particularly by Dallin (Dallin 1949; Shub1950; Wolfe *1951a, 1951b*). The *New Leader* is devoted to the thesis that the Russian people are a freedom-loving people, exactly like Americans, and that they are oppressed by a tyrannous government for which they are not to be held responsible. It finds exceedingly distasteful the contention that there are traits in contemporary Russian character structure which tend to support the present dictatorship, and it has systematically attacked and derided not only the work on the Soviet Union but all other work of the same sort as "racist," "diaperology," etc., including the propagation of pieces of folklore such as its statements that Gorer did not know that Stalin was not a Great Russian, that no one in the Columbia University Research in Contemporary Cultures team spoke Russian, etc. This politically motivated attack is politically intelligent, because Americans may be expected to be more eager to liberate a freedom-loving than all-authority-demanding people. Similar arguments were brought forward by those who objected to any attempt to localize Nazism in German culture and character rather than in the individual leadership of Hitler, who—like Stalin—came from outside the country.

A second set of attacks comes from the Soviet Union at the same time that attempts are being made there to alter the character structure of the present generation by prescribing types of infant training in the most minute detail and where attempts are even being made to substitute a motor-kinesthetic imagery for visual imagery. (Haimson Ms.) But Marxian theory, which has always insisted that there is a correspondence between institutions and character, has never achieved any coherent theory as to how such a relationship is brought about, and the Soviets, in practice placing tremendous emphasis on early education, continue to reject any theory that attempts to delineate the connection.[6]

A third set of attacks stems from various types of self-regarding sentiment of Slavs or new Americans, who feel either that their historic culture has been demeaned by being traced to the details of infancy (a sentiment based, of course, on a total misunderstanding of the theory, which does not trace the origins of the culture but describes the process of learning within the culture) or that the success of their recent acquisition of a second culture, that of America, is impugned by the emphasis given to early childhood experience, in their case in the culture which they have now left. This latter feeling has a deep ethical justification in our traditional emphasis on the possibility of becoming an American as an adult. Once some research has been done on the way an adult, who as a child learned both about culture (and so became a human being) and about a particular culture (and so became a Navaho, or a Frenchman, or a Russian) can learn another culture, part of this difficulty call be dealt with. The difference between childhood learning and adult learning is to be compared to the difference between learning to eat and later learning a new dietary, or learning to speak and later learning a second language. More explicit statements about the possibility of change in adulthood under a new set of social and political institutions are needed to deal with these aroused objections.[7] We are hampered here, however, by the paucity of usable research on the subject.[8] This type of cultural opposition may be usefully likened to the opposition to theories of the importance of early childhood training by persons whose children have reached adolescence and who feel that such counsels leave them helpless, subject to remorse but with no chance to make reparation. If it were possible to plan research complexly enough, the danger of encountering such opposition might be foreseen and allowed for.[9]

A fourth type of opposition appears to come from the resistance which the explicit juxtaposition of statements about conscious and unconscious attitudes calls forth from those who have not been exposed to psychoanalysis, either in personal analysis or by working in other ways with the "primary process" and with "unconscious" materials. There seems to be less resistance when these materials are presented separately. Projective test results, if isolated from the rest of the culture, are often accepted as "scientific." Gorer's description of character-forming mechanisms explicitly implicates "unconscious" processes, and the objections are very often of the same sort as those encountered by Freud. As Freud was accused of "tracing everything to sex," Gorer is accused of "tracing everything to infancy." In these paired accusations, the words *sex* and *infancy* can both be regarded as surrogates for those aspects of experience which cannot be recalled without special operations and against which most persons have well-organized defenses. This situation, which was apparent in the first responses to Gorer's hypothesis about the Japanese (1943) and in some of the reviews of *The American People* (Gorer 1948), has been exacerbated in the case of the swaddling hypothesis by two circumstances: (1) swaddling is more respectable and less embarrassing to discuss than toilet training or castration fears (and note the extent to which scatological implications are brought in again by such words as "diaperology") ; and (2) the idea of swaddling is peculiarly horrifying to Americans, one of whose major commitments is to freedom of movement.[10]

Notes

1. Paper presented at the annual meeting of the American Anthropological Association, December, 1952.
2. Gorer and Rickman (1949), especially Appendix I; Gorer (1949). See Golden (1952a, 1952b), Goldman (19SO), Grygier (1951). For reviewers who have understood the position taken by Gorer, see among others Bruun (1950), Mosely (1951).
3. See, for example, Tolstoy (1913): "Here are my first recollections which I cannot arrange, not knowing what was before, what after, and about some of them I don't know whether they were dreams or real. Here they

are: I am tied. I want to free my hands but I cannot do it, and I am crying, weeping, and my cry is unpleasant to me, but I cannot stop. Somebody is staying upon me. And it is all in half-darkness. But I remember
that they are two. My crying affects them. They worry because I am crying, but they don't unbind me as I want them to, and I cry louder. It
seems to them it is necessary [that I remain tied], while I know it is not
necessary, and I want to prove it to them, and I break out crying, which
is repugnant to me but irrepressible. I feel the injustice and the cruelty,
not of the people, because they are sorry for me, but of fate, and I pity
myself. I don't know and will never learn what it was, whether I was
swaddled when I was sucking and drew out my hand or was swaddled
when I was more than a year old, in order not to let me scratch a rash;
whether I collected in one memory many sensations, as one does in a
dream. But it is true that this was my first and strongest sensation. And I
don't remember so my cry, my suffering, but the complexity, the contra-
riety of the sensation. I want freedom, it doesn't hurt anybody, and I,
who need it so much, I am weak and they are strong. ..." See, also,
Bylinov (1951).

4. This assumption can be tested by analyzing material on one set of cul-
    tural institutions, abstracting the pattern, and testing this pattern against
    an independent analysis of another set of cultural institutions from the
    same culture. Provided that the materials have been collected in the same
    detail and with the same degree of objectivity and that comparative mate-
    rial is available to distinguish what is actually characteristic of the culture
    rather than the area, it should be expected that the two sets of material
    would show the same configuration, which could be articulately related
    to the known regularities of growth, development, and functioning of the
    human nervous system.

5. See Dicks (1952: 157): "Without entering deeply into the difficult ques-
    tion as to what might be the origins of this Russian Super-ego (concern-
    ing which no specific data were collected during my pilot study), it is
    possible to see in the general cultural ego-ideal the well-known features of
    Russian home discipline at the verbal level. This enjoins the virtues of
    truthful, meek behavior, and deplores rather than severely punishes
    rough and arrogant conduct and rewards goodness and obedience by
    maternal love. The same virtues are still stressed in recent educational
    publications in the Soviet Union. For the earliest level, only Geoffrey
    Gorer has, so far, evolved a coherent hypothesis. His critics have done the
    very thing he warned them against; mistaken the paradigm for the the-
    ory. Nothing in my observation has contradicted his views. Obviously
    'swaddling' may only be the expression (as he would say) and not the *rai-
    son-d'être* for the dynamics Gorer's hypothesis covers. I should like to sup-
    plement his views by adding that though the Russian tends to behave *as
    if* he had experienced the privation-gratification cycle Gorer pictures, and
    so tends to have the diffuse persecutory anxiety and hopeless apathy, he
    does also experience the close nurtural-libidinal relation with his Mother,
    however fitful and intermittent, as Gorer shows. He also *does* have much

warm and protective love and indulgence in his family, also mentioned by Gorer, however split and multiplied his object world becomes by later social conditions. The Russian thus *does* have opportunities for the internalization of good and loving objects, in relation to whom the severe depressive guilt of the second phase aroused in his still earlier and indubitable oral frustration rage becomes intelligible and, so to speak, theoretically inevitable."

6. See Vladimir Orlov in *Isvestia* (1952) : "...American parrots, in doctors' mantles, spread fascist racial ravings, the goal of which is to prove the superiority of the American 'highest' race ...Before American learned men was placed the problem: to prove the existence of a 'tense, destructive wrath' as an original trait of Russian character, and having proved it, to explain the origin of the 'anger and violence' of Great Russians. A large collective of workers of the American Museum of Natural History under the 'scientific' guidance of Margaret Mead were directed to the solution of the problem. By the curious admission of the *New Leader,* all the work of this group is conducted at the expense of the Navy Department. The solution of the problem turned out to be very difficult. 'Scientific' disagreements arose as to the stage of personality formation of the Soviet man at which 'limitless wrath and violence' originated to become the foundation 'of the particular characteristic of the Russian soul.' In Soviet man's mature years when he was engrossed in peaceful construction of factories and hydro-stations? Or in his young years, of a blue evening around the pioneer bonfire? Or possibly in childhood, in the crèches while playing with a doll or a teddy bear? The problem seemed insoluble. And the 'most learned' Margaret Mead was beginning to hint to her colleagues that they were getting money for nothing. As with many a great discovery, the discovery of the solution came simply. One staff member leafing through the 'Works of the New York Academy of Science,' came upon an article in No.5 for 1943 by the psychologist and anthropologist Geoffrey Gorer, the same Gorer who although he had never been to the Soviet Union and does not know the Russian language, was advertised as a 'brilliant specialist' on the question of interpretation of the Russian spirit and history... 'Babies thus squeezed are limited in their movements which has an extremely traumatic effect on their sensations and calls forth a tense destructive wrath.' ...Soon another article of Gorer's was discovered in a publication by Columbia University. ...And again swaddling was given as reason for all the misfortunes suffered by the American war-mongers from the Russian character. The discovery appeared so valuable that the learned businessmen without hesitation decided to steal it and place it at the basis of their research without reference to the author. This is how Margaret Mead expounds her ideas on her future book in the magazine *Natural History* in an article 'What Forms the Russian Character?' 'Russian babies are swaddled as are newly-born in Eastern countries and in the past in Western Europe, but Russian babies are swaddled much tighter and for a longer period. ... This early period leaves an imprint on the Russian character.' As asserted by Margaret Mead tight swaddling of Russian

babies had and continues to have a decisive influence on Russian history. 'Wrath, anger, violence, stemming from the swaddling period' is considered by the American ignoramuses who over-reach themselves, as the source of 'civil war,' 'rebellion,' and revolutions. Were it not for this source there would be no offers of disarmament and the prohibition of the atom bomb, so inconvenient to the State Department. ... What concerns the glimmers of sense, those are impossible to discover in Margaret Mead and her likes."

Columbia University Research in Contemporary Culture was a project directed by the late Professor Ruth Benedict under a contract with the Office of Naval Research, in which Geoffrey Gorer and Margaret Mead worked in the Russian section. The swaddling hypothesis was developed in 1947-1948. A series of successor projects on Soviet problems, under other governmental auspices, were located at the American Museum of Natural History between 1948 and 1952. For fuller details see Mead and Metraux (1953).

7. See Mead (1950) for this example of change from the interviews of a research worker: "In an interview with a woman we were discussing this question of guilt and guilt of everything one has ever thought. She said, 'You know, I remember the day I became an American.' This is a pre-Soviet Russian who had lived in Europe quite a long while. She said, 'You know, I was talking to a married woman friend of mine out on Long Island, and she was talking about having fallen in love with a man, and she said, "But nothing happened." And I said [said the Russian woman], "But didn't you enjoy him in your mind?" And she said, "Ye-e-e-s." And I said, "Then you *were* guilty." And she said, "But nothing happened." And I looked at her and I suddenly realized that in America you are not guilty for the things you don't do, and all my life was re-modulated. Everything that had once been so complicated became so simple. That was the day I stopped just being a Russian and started being an American'."

8. There have been a few speculative articles: Mead (1949); Ruesch, Jacobson, and Loeb (1948); Bram's provocative paper on the choice of a different nationality (1951); Allport, Bruner, and Jandorf's classical study on lack of change in personality under conditions of D.P. status, etc. (1941).

9. The best one can do is to channel one's research in this direction. My 1953 field trip to the Admiralty Islands was planned to study change within a single generation, in the persons of members of Peri village originally observed twenty-five years ago.

10. I have experimented with naive audiences by mentioning the practice of swaddling only in passing when lecturing on Russia, but it tends to be elaborated on exhaustively in the question period, in comments in the local press, etc. Cf. also the comment of Bruch (1952) on American mothers' responses to suggestions of restraining children.

Bibliography

ALLPORT, G., J. S. BRUNER and E. M. JANDORF
    1941   "Personality under social catastrophe: ninety life-
            histories of the Nazi revolution." *Character and
            Personality* 10: 1-22.
BENEDICT, R.
    1949   "Child rearing in certain European countries." *American
            Journal of Orthopsychiatry,* 19: 342-50.
BRAM, J.
    1951   *The elements of choice and fiction in ethnic self-
            identification.* Paper delivered at American
            Anthropological Association annual meeting.
BRUCH, H.
    1952   *Don't be afraid of your child.* New York.
BRUUN, G.
    1950   "How the bear ticks." *Saturday Review of Literature*
            (Nov. 11), p. 19.
BYLINOV, A.
    1951   "The metal workers." *Oktiabr* (Dec.). Moscow, published
            by Pravda.
DALLIN, D.
    1949   "Exterminate the Russians?" *New Leader* (Oct. 29), p. 2.
    1951   *The new Soviet empire.* New Haven.
DENNIS, W.
    1940   *The Hopi child.* New York.
DICKS, H. V.
    1952   "Observations on contemporary Russian behavior."
            Human Relations 5: 111-75.
DINERSTEIN, H.
    1953   *Leadership in Soviet agriculture.* Glencoe, Illinois.
GOLDEN, J.
    1952*a* Review of: "The people of Great Russia, by Gorer and
            Rickman." *American Anthropologist* 54: 415.
    1952*b* Review of: "Soviet attitudes toward authority," by Mead.
            American Anthropologist 54: 414.
GOLDMAN, I.
    1950   "Psychiatric interpretations of Russian history," a reply
            to Geoffrey Gorer. *American Slavic and East European
            Review* 9: 151-61.
GORER, G.
    1943   "Themes in Japanese culture." *Annals of the New York
            Academy of Sciences* 5.

1948   *The American people.* New York.
1949   "Some aspects of the psychology of the people of Great Russia." *American Slavic and East European Review* 8: 155-66.

GORER, G. and J. RICKMAN
1949   *The people of Great Russia,* a psychological study. London and New York.

GREENACRE, P.
1944   "Infant reactions to restraint: problems in the fate of infantile aggression." *American Journal of Orthopsychiatry* 14: 204—18.

GRYGIER, T.
1951   "The psychological problems of Soviet Russia." *British Journal of Psychology* (General Section) 42: 180-84.

HAIMSON, L.
Ms.   *The Soviet theory of action.*

HEBB, D. O.
1949   *Organization of behavior.* New York.

HSU, F. L. K.
1950   "Anthropology or psychiatry: some test data from Hawaii." Paper delivered at Viking Fund Supper-Conference for Anthropologists, Oct. 20.

KARDINER, A.
1939   *The individual and his society.* New York.

LEITES, N. and E. BERNAUT
1953   *The ritual of liquidation.* Glencoe, Illinois.

LEVY, D.
1938-39 "Maternal overprotection." *Psychiatry* 1: 561-91; 2: 99-109; 3: 563-97.

LITTLE, K.
1950   "Methodology in the study of adult personality and 'national character.'" *American Anthropologist* 52: 279-82.

MEAD, M.
1941   "Review of: The Hopi child," by Wayne Dennis. *American Anthropologist* 43: 95-97.
1947   "The implications of culture change for personality development." *American Journal of Orthopsychiatry* 17: 633-46.
1949   "Character formation and diachronic theory." *In Social Structure: Studies Presented to A. R. Radcliffe-Brown,* edited by M. Fortes. Oxford.

1950   "Russian character and Soviet politics" (RCC-PR 2). Columbia University Research in Contemporary Cultures, New York. (Dittoed.)

1951*a*   *Soviet attitudes toward authority.* New York.

1951*b*   "What makes the Soviet character?" *Natural History* 51: 296-303, 336.

1952   "Some relationships between social anthropology and psychiatry." In *Dynamic Psychiatry,* edited by F. Alexander and H. Ross. Chicago.

1953   "National character." In *Anthropology Today,* by A. L. Kroeber *et at.* Chicago.

MEAD, M. and R. METRAUX (eds.)

1953   *The study of culture at a distance.* Chicago.

MOSELY, P.

1951   "A pro-Russian, anti-Stalin policy: The new Soviet Empire" by David J. Dallin reviewed. *New Leader* (May 21), pp. 22-23.

ORLOV, V.

1952   "Slanderers and swaddling clothes." *Izvestia* (Feb. 19). Moscow.

PETERSON, C. H. and F. L. SPANO

1941   "Breast feeding, maternal rejection and child personality." *Character and Personality* 10: 62-66.

RUESCH, J., A. JACOBSON and M. LOEB

1948   "Acculturation and illness." *Psychological Monographs,* No.292. Washington.

SEWALL, W. H.

1952   "Infant training and the personality of the child." *American Journal of Orthopsychiatry* 22: 150-59.

SHUB, B.

1950   "Soviets expose American baby." *New Leader* (June 17), pp. 11-12.

TOLSTOY, L.

1913   "The first recollections." In *Collected Works* (Polnoye Sobraniya Sochinenii), Sytin edition. Moscow.

WHITING, J. and I. L. CHILD

1953   *Child training and personality.* New Haven.

WOLFE, B. D.

1951*a*   "The swaddled soul of the Great Russian." *New Leader* (Jan. 29), pp. 15-18.

1951*b*   "Reply to Mr. Gorer." *New Leader* (May 21), p. 20.

SOME CULTURAL APPROACHES TO COMMUNICATION PROBLEMS*

by Margaret Mead

The cultural approach to any problem is by definition so wide and all embracing that each separate discussion which invokes it must, of necessity, limit itself. In this paper, I shall, arbitrarily and for purposes of this discussion only, treat communication as those activities in which one or more persons purposefully communicate with a group of other persons. In this way all the simple interrelationships of every day life, as a mother calls her child, or a husband a wife, a dog is whistled to heel, or a horse urged on to a gallop, will be excluded. So also will the simple message, the notched stick or the knotted bit of bark which is sent from one individual New Guinea native or American Indian to another, or the drum beat in which a single household in Manus calls the father home from the lagoon fishing grounds. All of these are of course communication, and the whole mesh of human social life might logically, and perhaps, in other contexts, fruitfully, be treated as a system of human communications. But the considerations advanced in this article will be addressed to the problems which are facing us today, specifically in mass communications, when the words or images fashioned professionally by one group of people are sent out to influence, persuade, or merely inform many times the number of those responsible for creating the original communication. Within this expanding field of activity, we may distinguish three smaller questions (1) the way *in* which communication systems are related to given cultural values, (2) the particular ethical problems of responsibility raised by our current use of communication systems, and (3) problems of communication when cultural boundaries have to be transcended.

Some Primitive Contrasts

In any consideration of the way in which formal communications fit into the values of a given culture records of primitive societies provide useful contrasts. Our knowledge of these small societies, in which the

*Originally published in *The Communication of Ideas*. Edited by L. Bryson, Cooper Square, 1964.

whole culture must be carried in the memories and habits of a few hundred persons, is much more detailed and exact than our knowledge of our own or other great civilizations. Furthermore, the great civilizations of which we do have any first hand knowledge are becoming more and more part of one great world culture, where comparable techniques of communication are—to a degree—producing increasing uniformities. Primitive societies which for many centuries have been isolated by land and water barriers and by their own ignorance of transportation, developed sharper contrasts, each to each. They provide ready-made examples from which it is possible to glimpse the diversity of ways in which the communicator and his audience have been institutionalized.

I shall discuss here three cultures in which I have worked[1] where the attitudes are exceedingly different; all three, however, come from the same part of the world, the Southwest Pacific. Other orders of contrast could be developed by examining material from other great areas of the world, North and South America, or Africa.

Among the Arapesh[2] people of New Guinea, communication is seen primarily as a matter of arousing the emotions of the audience. This small group of two to three thousand mountain people, who do not even have a name for the whole group who speak their language, live in steeply mountainous country, with hamlets perched precariously on razor back ridges, and stiff climbs intervening between one man's garden and another. Food is scarce and land is poor, and the people spend a great deal of time moving about from garden to garden, sago patch to sago patch, or hunting in small groups in the deep bush. Any unexpected event is likely to find them widely scattered, and a system of calls, with linguistic peculiarities, and slit-gong beats are used to attract the attention of those at a distance, and to convey a little imperfect information. Among the Arapesh the clue to the relationship between any communicator and the group is given by the behavior of a man or woman with a headache, or some other slight ailment, a burn from a fire stick thrown by an exasperated husband or wife, a scratch got out hunting. Such suffering individuals wind their foreheads or other affected parts in bark or scarify them slightly or daub them with paint and then parade up and down the village, invoking sympathy. The situation in which the wound was obtained, or the headache contracted, is irrelevant, but each individual turns his own personal state into a matter for group emotional involvement. So ready is this response that even the narration of some hurt, a finger crushed long ago in an accident in some other land, brings out a chorus of expressive vocalizations from any group of listeners. The communicator indicates a state of feeling, the group responds with a state of feeling, and a minimum of information is conveyed.

When, among the Arapesh, some event of importance occurs, a birth or a death, a quarrel of proportions, the visit of a government patrol, or a recruiting European, or the passage through the village of a traveling party of strangers who bring trade and the possibility of sorcery into each community they visit, there are shouts and drum beats from hilltop to hilltop. But all that the signals convey is that something has happened about which the listeners had better become excited. A furious drumming on one hilltop starts off a series of shouted queries in a relay system from hilltops nearer to each other, or a child or a woman is dispatched to find out what has happened. The listeners immediately set about guessing what all the excitement can be about, speculating rapidly as to who may be dead, or traveling, whose wife may have been abducted, or whose wife sorcerized. A dozen explanations may be introduced and, according as they appear plausible, the movements of all the listeners will be altered or not. If no one can think of a plausible reason for the commotion, most of the listeners are likely to set off in the direction of the sounds.

There is some slight attempt to differentiate drum beats, but so contrary is specificity to the cultural emphasis of the Arapesh, that the distinctions are always getting blurred. The point of communication is to excite interest and bring together human beings who will then respond, on the spot, with emotion, to whatever event has occurred. They will also, once gathered, bury the dead, set out to find the sorcerer, or reluctantly line up to fulfill the requests of the visiting government official. But all specificity of information about the event, and of behavior appropriate to the event, follows after the emotional response has gathered them together.

So, when a group of people are working on a house, some individual, not necessarily the owner of the house to be, will come and shout out to a group that rattan is needed. His voice emphasizes the need for people to listen and the need for somebody to do something about it. Sooner or later, someone will go and get some rattan, but the initial request, in most cases, does not directly set such a purposeful series of acts in motion. Interestingly also, when people tell stories about past events, they tend to impute to the moment when the drum beat was heard from a distant hilltop, a full knowledge of what they learned only after they had responded to the drum beat. So, a narrator will say, "when he was returning from a journey inland and still far away he heard the gongs being beaten and he *knew* that his brother had taken his wife," although he finds out only after he has reached his own village, his steps quickened in response to the sound.

This treatment of communication in which a state of readiness of excitement, a mixture of fear, dread, anxiety and pleasant expectation, is aroused before any information is given or any action sought, is obviously always a possible theme in any complex communication system, and one which is sometimes involved in our culture. Walter Winchell's strong punctuation of his broadcast with the word *Flash,* any radio program in which a strong signal is used first to awaken the audience, has this element in it. Some of the possible implications of such a theme become evident when it is seen writ large in the culture of a people; such as the extraordinary lack of precision which characterizes Arapesh thinking, their short attention span, their tendency to substitute emotional congruity for any sort of logical construct when each communicator seeks to evoke first undifferentiated emotional response, and only then to sharpen and specify events and action sequences.

Among the lagoon dwelling Manus[3] people of the Southern Coast of the Admiralty Islands, there is a very different emphasis. The Manus are a hard headed, puritanical, trading people, interested in material things, in economic activity, in continuously purposive behavior. Where the Arapesh seldom count to a hundred and then with units of a low degree of abstraction, the Manus count into the hundred thousands. Where the Arapesh set a day for a ceremony, and as likely as not the ceremony takes place a day earlier, or a week later, the Manus announce their plans weeks in advance and carry them out. Where the Arapesh set up traps and snares in the bush and then wait until game falls into them, often even depending upon a dream to direct their footsteps back in the direction of the trap, the Manus make their principal catches of fish each month in a timed relationship to the tide. Action is stimulated in Manus, not by creating an atmosphere of warm interdependent responsiveness, but by setting up exact instigating situations—a prepayment, a loan, an advance— to which other individuals respond, under penalty of supernatural punishment from their own exacting ghostly guardians, and the potentially hostile ghostly guardians of other people. Exact, effective, properly timed action, which is physically and ethically appropriate, is what the Manus are interested in.

In such a culture, communications take a very different shape. There are a series of drum signals, which include formal openings which set the stage, not in terms of excitement but of content, so that a certain pattern of beats means: "I am about to announce the date at which I will give a feast." Then, an intellectual readiness to listen for a piece of relevant information being established, the drummer goes on to beat out the number of days before his feast, accurately, carefully, and the listeners count and take note. Each houseowner has a special pattern of beats which is his signature, the same beat that his household use to call him home. Between villages, careful tallies and other accurate mnemonic devices are used to convey the same sort of information.

The other characteristic form of communication in Manus is oratory, used in most cases angrily, as a stimulant to economic activity. Some of this is purely ceremonial hostility, the accompaniment of some large scale economic transaction of display and exchange, but some of it is argumentative and situational. Men inveigh against their debtors and battle bitterly over details in the calculations. This sort of behavior in which actual items of the number of dog's teeth or jars of coconut oil are at stake confuses the clarity with which the Manus habitually operate. And it is significant that as soon as my pencil and notebook entered the scene, people began to try to substitute my records for this angry, confusing welter of accusation and refutation, which they had lacked the techniques to prevent. The Manus prefer action in a well defined context, under the spur of past careful definition reinforced by guilt, with anger introduced as stimulus in ways which will not compromise the accuracy of the operations. This attempt to keep thought and action clear of immediate emotion, but reinforced by unpleasant emotions, of anger and fear of the reproaches of their own consciences and supernatural punishments from their ghosts, runs through the formal communications of the society.

Bali[4] which is not a primitive society because writing is known, but is a society with a culture exceedingly different from our own and perhaps comparable in political and economic organization to the early middle ages in Europe, presents a quite different picture. The Balinese live in closely knit village communities, in which the citizens are bound together by a very great number of shared tasks, both ceremonial and economic. Each such community has its own traditional law which was respected by the Balinese feudal rulers in the past, and by their Dutch successors in the colonial period. Citizens, whose names are arranged in a series of rotas, share in the work necessary to maintain the elaborate irrigation system, keep up the roads, repair the numerous temples, provide the materials for offerings and prepare them for the gods, maintain forces of watchmen, town criers, messengers between the village and extra village authorities.

An intricate calendar of several systems of weeks which turns on itself like the cogs in several different sized wheels, governs the recurring series of ceremonial events, and systems of trance and possession give the necessary slight pushes to the calendrical system to provide for emergencies, stimulate a sluggish community, or slow down an excessively active one. Residence in a given village, location in a given place in the status system, as to caste, age, sex, and marital status, the day of the week, position on a rota of citizens, and occasional formal instigation of action by a diviner or seer, provide the framework within which each individual acts. There is no oratory, no exhortation, no preaching. A day or so before the ceremony in a village like Bajoeng Gede, the man whose turn it is to be town crier will go through the streets, announcing the coming feast, and specifying what each household is to contribute, *e.g.*, "rice, a large measure, betel pepper leaves five, grated coconut, a level container full." He may further specify what those who are on duty that month will give, *e,g.*, "two woven square packets, eight bundles of white cooked rice meal, eight bundles of cooked black rice meal, five small containers of rice, eight items of red sugar meal, and one hundred units of pork." He will announce which groups in the population, as the full male citizens, full female citizens, the boys' group, the girls' group, are to appear at the temple at what time and for what services.

The people do not have the burden of remembering from day to day what is to be done, for remembering is the assigned duty of special officials, most of whom take turns over the years. It is assumed that all that is needed is information about the correct behavior which will then, in most cases, be forthcoming. For those who fail to make their appropriate contribution, in work or offering materials, or fail to accept their share when the offerings are redivided among the participants— for in Bali there is small distinction between obligation and privilege— there are small fines, well within the resources of every citizen. If the fine is not paid, it mounts, and if the citizen is seen as unwilling to pay the fine, it mounts at a tremendous rate and the individual is virtually cut off from the community until it is paid. But neither to the man who fails to perform a single duty, nor to the man who refuses to pay his fine, nor even to those who have violated some fundamental tenet of the caste or religious system, is anger shown. The system is impersonal, unyielding and unequivocal. Those who run up against the laws of one community may, in most cases, leave it, but their choice is between a no man's land of vagrancy, beggardom and thievery and casual labor, and again becoming members of another community that has and enforces a different but equally stringent set of laws.

In this system the communicator, whether he be rajah, Dutch official, or village council (which contains all the full citizens of the village), acts as if the audience were already in a state of suspended, unemotional attention, and only in need of a small precise triggering word to set them off into appropriate activity. The stimuli are as simple as red and green lights in a well regulated, traffic situation, where no policeman is needed to reinforce the effortless, uninvolved stopping and starting of groups of cars, driven by men who accept the traffic signals as part of the world. Communications, even from the gods, when, through the mouth of a possessed person, instructions are given to renovate a temple, repay some old village obligation, combine two clubs, or regularize an irregular marriage, have all the impersonality of the voice which tells the telephoning American, "When you hear the signal, the time will be ...," or "United States Weather Bureau report for New York and vicinity, eight o'clock temperature forty-two degrees, ..." The voice that tells the time does not include in its note an urgency about trains to catch or children to get off to school, roasts to come out of the oven, or cows to be milked. People dial the correct number to find out what time it is so that they may act appropriately. Such a system, carried to the lengths to which Balinese culture carry it, in which there is a very deep personal commitment to maintaining a continuity and a steady state, can be maintained with a lack of either expressed emotion or expressed effortfulness. The communicator states a position; the people, conditioned throughout their development to find safety and reassurance in following well established routines in company with others, respond.

Description of the cultural setting of communication, such as these three from Arapesh, Manus and Bali, could be multiplied to sharpen appreciation of the variety of themes and their implications which are involved in our own communications system. They serve to point up the very great number of ways in which communicator and communicator's intent, audience and audience's responses, may be institutionalized in different cultural systems, and also in different facets of the same cultural system. In our own society, it is possible to distinguish the communication methods which rely on arousing emotion first and slipping in suggestions for action only after the individual members of the audience are suffused with feeling, those which are concerned with giving accurate information which will lead to indicated action, those which are concerned merely with giving information upon which individuals may act.

The Problem of Responsibility in Communications

The great contemporary concern with communication problems must be laid not only to the enormous advance in technology and the resulting shrinking of the world into one potential communication system, with all the attendant difficulties of communication across cultural boundaries, but also to the increase in social awareness on the one hand, and the disintegration of the institutionalized centers of responsibility on the other. It is true that, through the centuries, expanding movements and nations have used various methods of propaganda[5] to advance their causes, to convert the unconverted, bring in line the recalcitrant, reconcile the conquered to their lot and the conquerors to their conquering role. It is also true that secular and religious hierarchies have consciously used these methods to advance their avowed and unavowed ends. But the addition of modern technological methods, by which the ownership of one radio station may decide the fate of a local revolution, and a single film or a single voice may reach the whole of the listening and watching world, has changed the order of magnitude of the whole problem.

At the same time development of social science is making it possible for communications to change their character. Instead of the inspired voice of a natural leader, whose zestful "We shall defend our Island, whatever the cost may be. We shall fight on the beaches, we shall fight on the landing ground, we shall fight in the fields and the streets, we shall fight in the hills; we shall never surrender. ..." galvanizing people to action, the appeals can be, to a degree, calculated and planned. Instead of the politician's hunch as to how some program is going over, polls and surveys can be used to bring back accurate information to the source of the propaganda and introduce a corrective. Theories of human nature which are no longer the inexplicit emphases of a coherent culture, but instead the partly rationalized, partly culturally limited formulations of psychological research, can be used as the basis of planned campaigns.[6]

The thinking peoples of the world have been made conscious, during the past quarter of a century, of the power of organized and controlled communication, glimpsing that power both from the point of view of the victim or "target" and of the victimizer, he who wields the powerful weapon. Dissection of the methods of the enemy, the conscious cultivation of an immunity against appeals to one's own emotion, desperate attempts to devise methods appropriate to a democracy, while we envied totalitarian propagandic controls, have all contributed to the growth of this consciousness in the United States.

But consciousness of the potential power of communication has peculiar implications in the United States, in a country where no institution, neither Church nor State, has any monopoly of the organs of communication. The American, during the past twenty-five years, has seen systems of propagandic control develop in other countries, and even when propagandic moves of extreme importance have actually been promoted within the United States, they have usually been phrased as inspired by Berlin or Tokyo, London or Moscow, rather than as the expression of American attitudes.

The local American emphasis has thus been on resisting high powered communication pressures, and this has been congruent, not only with the Americans' fear of playing the sucker role *vis-à-vis* other nations, more skilled in international necromancy, but also with the great importance of advertising in the United States. Those European peoples which have felt the impact of modern totalitarian communications had as a background for the experience a past in which Church and State traditionally controlled and manipulated the symbols which could move men to feel and to act. The American on the other hand has experienced instead the manipulation of the same sorts of symbols, of patriotism, religious belief and human strivings after perfection and happiness, by individuals and groups who occupied a very different and far less responsible place in the social hierarchy.

In our American system of communications, any interest, wishing to "sell" its products or message to the public, is able to use the full battery of available communication techniques, radio and film, press and poster. It is characteristic of this system that the symbols used to arouse emotion, evoke attention, and produce action, have come into the hands of those who feel no responsibility toward them. In a society like Bali there is simply no possibility that such a symbol as "The Village," also spoken of as "Mr. Village" and as "God Village," could be used by a casual vendor or rabble rouser. The symbols which evoke responses are used by those whose various positions in the society commit them to a responsible use. But in the United States, most of the value symbols of American tradition are ready to the hand of the manufacturer of the most trivial debased product or the public relations counsel of the most wildcat and subversive organizations.

The American is used to experiencing the whole symbolic system of his society, in a series of fragmented and contradictory contexts. These beget in him a continually heightened threshold to any sort of appeal (with a recurrent nostalgia for a lost innocence in which his tears could flow simply or his heart swell with uncomplicated emotion) and a casual, non-evaluative attitude toward the power wielded through any communication system. As he straightens his tie and decides not to buy the tie which is being recommended over the radio, or in the street card ad, he gets a sense of immunity which makes him overlook the extent to which he is continually absorbing the ad behind the ad, the deutero[7] contexts of the material which he feels he is resisting.

We may examine the types of learning which result from the various uses of symbols in the United States in terms of: Whose symbol is used? What is the order of relationship between the symbol-possessing group and the group which is using the symbol? What is the nature of the product or message for which the symbol is being used? Who benefits by its use? As examples of various types of symbol usage, let us consider the use of the symbol of Florence Nightingale, devoted ministrant to suffering and dying humanity. In the first position, a maker of white broadcloth might put out an advertisement which said, "In the great tradition of Florence Nightingale, American nurses are to be found ministering to the suffering. And, needing the very best, in order to fulfill their devoted mission, they use *Blank's* broadcloth for their uniforms, because it wears—through sickness and death." The reader of this advertisement learns that Florence Nightingale is a name to conjure with, that she was admired and respected, and that *Blank's* broadcloth are using her to enhance *their* prestige. To this degree the value of Florence Nightingale's name is increased. But at the same time the reader or listener may also add a footnote, "Trying to tie their old broadcloth on to Florence Nightingale's kite," and the sense of a synthetic, temporary quality of all symbol associations is strengthened in his mind.

In the second case, the advocates of a dishonest correspondence course in nursing might use the name of Florence Nightingale in a plea to individuals to rise and follow the lamp once carried aloft by the great Nurse, and prepare themselves, in only twenty lessons, money down in advance, to follow in her footsteps. Here, to the extent that the listener realized that the correspondence course was phony, Florence Nightingale's name would also be shrouded with some of the same feeling of the phoniness, bedraggled and depreciated.

In the third case, a nurses' association might decide to put themselves back of a public education program in chest x-rays for tuberculosis control, and develop a poster in which they placed their great symbol, Florence Nightingale, beside an appeal for support for the local anti-tuberculosis committee. The reader and listeners here recognize that Florence Nightingale is a great and valuable symbol, because those to whom she is a value symbol have themselves used her name to advance some newer and younger cause. This last type is of course characteristic of the historical use of symbols in society. Even when groups which represented religious or political subversion from the point of view of those in power have appropriated to themselves the sacred symbols of those against whom they were fighting, such moves have been made seriously and responsibly by those who believed that their subversion and their heresy were neither subversion nor heresy but political justice and religious truth. Symbols which change hands between orthodox and heterodox, between conservative and liberal, do not suffer by the change as long as each group of users acts responsibly. Instead such exchange is an invaluable ingredient of continuity and consistency within a changing society.

But the advertising agency, the public relations counsel, as institutionalized in our culture, has no responsibility of this sort. An advertising agency, whatever the personal sense of conscientious rectitude of its staff, has one set of functions to perform, to sell the product successfully while keeping within the law. With sufficient sophistication, a refusal to spoil the market, either for the same product in the future, or for other products, might be included within its functions. But our society has no higher jurisdiction to which such agencies owe allegiance. The regulations formulated by patriotic societies to protect the flag have to be respected, or you get into trouble. Religious symbols can be used only if you are sure the churches will not get in your hair. Claims must be muted to the sensitivities of the Pure Food and Drug Administration. If you expect to keep the contract a long time, do not overplay a line which may go sour. If you do not want trouble from your other clients, or other agencies, do not take too obvious a crack at other products or organizations or causes. It is upon such disjointed rules of thumb that the day by day manipulation of the responsiveness, the moral potential of the American people, depends.

The National Nutrition Program, administered under Federal auspices during the war, was one interesting attempt to deal with this contemporary situation. Agreements were worked out by which advertisers were permitted to use the name of the National Nutrition Program, if, and only if, they acceded to certain conditions, the final ethical sanction for which came from the best scientific knowledge of nutritionists. Advertisers were not permitted to misquote, quote in part, or add to, the gist of the Nutrition theme which had been agreed upon, nor could they use it in association with products of no nutritional value. In spite of the many small expediencies which clouded the issues, this was a genuine attempt to supply an ethical sanction, rooted in science and administered by government, to a whole mass of communications on the subject of food and its uses. On a very simple level, this program represented one possible direction in which a country like the United States might move to give ethical form to the almost wholly unregulated mass of communications which now serve the interests of such a variety of groups—one way in which control can be vested in those to whom the symbol belongs.

A continuation of the present state of irresponsibility is exceedingly dangerous because it provides a situation within which steps backward rather than steps forward are so likely to occur. One possible response to the confused state of our symbolic system and the dulling of our responsiveness is an artificial simplification, a demand for the return of control to central authorities who will see to it that there is no more of the haphazard and contradictory use of important symbols. If the only choice open to us appears to be this increasing

immunization against any appeal, this increasing apathy and cal-
lousness, so that photographs of a thousand murdered innocents no
longer have any power to move us, the temptation to swing back to
authoritarianism may become increasingly great. If, however, we can
go on and formulate a system of responsibility appropriate to the age
in which we live, a system which takes into account the state of technology[8], the type of mixed economy, the democratic aspirations, and
the present dulled sensibilities of the American people, we may prevent such a reaction and, instead, move forward.

Any theory of the way in which responsibility for communications must be developed must deal with the problem of intent, with
the beliefs that the communicator has about himself, and about his
audience, as well as with the particular constitution and situation of
that audience. This facet of the problem is particularly important in
America, where the average citizen still identifies his position as a
minority one, and so always thinks of power as wielded by THEM,
and not by himself or a group to which he belongs. All discussions of
the locations of responsibility for the communication stream, in any
positive or constructive sense, are likely to stumble over this feeling
that responsibility means power, and power is always in the hands of
someone else. A set of negative controls, such as the rule that a radio
station must discuss both sides of a situation, no matter how imperfectly and destructively each side is presented, is more congenial than
any set of positive controls. So also were the teachings of propaganda
analysis; the American felt safer in learning how not to respond to a
false appeal than in permitting any effective development of appeals
which would be so good that he would respond to them.

It therefore seems that it is important to arrive at a phrasing of
responsibility which will meet this fear of misused power and develop
an ethic of communications within a democracy such as ours. Once
a climate of opinion expressing such an ethic begins to develop,
appropriate institutional forms may be expected to emerge, either
slowly or under intensive cultivation.

Such an ethic might take the form of an insistence that the audience be seen as composed of *whole* individuals, not artificial cut outs
from crowd scenes, such as are represented on the dust jacket of a
recent book[9] on radio. It might take the form of insisting that the
audience be seen as composed of individuals who could not be
manipulated but could only be appealed to in terms of their systematic cultural strengths. It might include a taboo on seeing any individual as the puppet of the propagandist, and focusing instead on the
purposeful cultivation of directions of change. It would then be
regarded as ethical to try to persuade the American people to drink

orange juice, as a pleasant and nutritional drink, by establishing a style of breakfast, a visual preference for oranges, and a moral invest-ment in good nutrition, but not by frightening individual mothers into serving orange juice for fear that they would lose their children's love, or their standing in the community.

Probably the closest analogue for the development of such sanc-tions can be found in medical ethics, legal ethics, etc., in which a group of self-respecting practitioners constitute themselves as a final court of appeal upon their own behavior. To the extent that advertis-ing, public relations, market research, and the various communica-tion media experts come to hold themselves and be held by the public in greater respect, such internally self-corrective systems might be developed.

If the contention is justified that democratic institutions represent a more complex integration of society, in which greater or different possibilities are accorded to each individual, we must expect corre-sponding differences between the communication ethics of societies representative of different degrees of feudalism and capitalism in dif-ferent political combinations. The wholly feudal state may be said to have localized responsibility for communications within a hierarchical status system, and avoided the problem of power over individual trends by regarding that system as fixed and immutable. The totalitar-ian system which has lost the sanctions of feudalism and cannot depend upon the character structure of its citizens, develops monopo-listic communication systems which seek to establish a direction in the society, but which in the interval are seen as operating on identified individuals, playing upon their most vulnerable points to bring them in line with a dictated policy. Whether it is claimed that the availabil-ity of concentration camps influence the propagandist or merely makes the audience members vulnerable, the interrelationship is there.

Political democracies have, to date, by insisting on negative sanc-tions, maintained systems in which the individual was the target of any sorts of propagandic themes but in which he was protected by the existence of contradictions in the appeals made to him. Such negative sanctions are better than none, but the target of American advertising is not a dignified human figure.[10] The target of political campaigns in the United States is not a dignified human figure. The limitation on the sense of power of the advertising agency copy writer or the campaign manager has merely been the knowledge that there were opponents in the field, free to act just as irresponsibly as he and free to present an equally contradictory and destructive set of counter appeals.

This negative approach is challenged whenever the country goes to war and wishes to mobilize its citizens toward common goals. It is doubly challenged when branches of the United States Army or the United States Government are charged with the task of reeducating peoples who have lived under totalitarian regimes. The resistance of the Germans, for example, to the sort of protection of freedom which is implied in the cultivation of a two party system, challenges American culture to the development of a more positive ethic.

Note: It is the purpose of this paper to raise problems, not to offer ready-made solutions. I shall therefore, [in my essay *A Case History in Cross-National Communications*], present a case history of the application of anthropological methods to an even wider problem of communication. M, M.

NOTES

1. The sacrifice of the widest amount of available contrast by restricting illustration to one area of the world seems justified because, when an anthropologist attempts to organize field results around a new problem, this can be done much better against a background of intimate knowledge of the culture.

2. For accounts of this culture see:

   Margaret Mead, *Sex and Temperament in Three Primitive Societies,* William Morrow and Company, New York, 1935.

   Margaret Mead, editor, *Cooperation and Competition among Primitive Peoples,* McGraw-Hill, New

   York, 1937, Chapter I, "The Arapesh of New Guinea."

   Margaret Mead, "The Mountain Arapesh," Part I, "An Importing Culture," *Anthropological Papers of the American Museum of Natural History,* 36, 1938, pp. 141-349.

   Ibid., Part II, "Supernaturalism," 37, 1940, pp. 319-451.

   Ibid., Part III, "Socio-Economic Life," 40, 1947, pp. 171-231.

   Ibid., Part IV, "Diary of Events in Alitoa," 40, 1947, pp. 233-419.

   R. F. Fortune, " Arapesh," *Publications of the American Ethnological Society,* 19, 1942, J. J. Augustin, New York.

3. For accounts of this culture see:

   Margaret Mead. *Growing Up in New Guinea,* William Morrow and Company, New York.1930.

   Margaret Mead. *Cooperation and Competition among Primitive Peoples,* McGraw-Hill. New York,

   1937. Chapter VII. "The Manus of the Admiralty Islands," pp. 210-239.

Margaret Mead, "Kinship in the Admiralties," *Anthropological Papers of the American Museum of*
Natural History, 34, 1934. pp. 183-358.
R. F. Fortune. "Manus Religion," *American Philosophical Society.* Philadelphia, 1935.
4. Gregory Bateson, "Bali: A Value System of a Steady State." *Social Structure: Studies Presented to*
A. R. Radcliffe Brown. Clarendon Press, England, 1948.
J. Belo, "A Study of Customs Pertaining to Twins in Bali," *Tijdschrift voor Ind. Tall., Land., en*
Volkenkunde, 75, 1935, 4, pp. 483-549.
Margaret Mead, "Administrative Contributions to Democratic Character Formation at the
Adolescent Level," in *Personality in Nature, Society and Culture,* Henry A. Murray and Clyde
K. Kluckhohn, Chapter 37, Part III. Alfred A, Knopf, New York, 1948.
Gregory Bateson and Margaret Mead, "Balinese Character," *Special Publications II,* New York Academy of Sciences, 1942.
5. Margaret Mead, "Our Educational Emphasis in Primitive Perspective," in *Education and the Cultural Process,* editor, Charles S. Johnson. Papers presented at Symposium commemorating the 75th Anniversary of the founding of Fisk University, April- May, 1941. Reprinted from the *American Journal of Sociology,* 48, May, 1943, 6, pp. 5-12.
6. Ernest Kris, "Some Problems of War Propaganda," *Psychoanalytic Quarterly,* 12, 3, pp. 381-399 (for a discussion of the way in which Nazi propaganda methods drew upon Le Bon's psychology of the crowd).
7. For a discussion of the concept of deutero learning see: Gregory Bateson, "Social Planning and the Concept of 'Deutero-Learning,'," *Science, Philosophy and Religion, 2nd Symposium,* Conference on Science, Philosophy and Religion, New York, 1942, pp. 81 - 97.
8. Lyman Bryson, "Introductory Chapter," *The Communication of Ideas,* Cooper Square Publishers, New York, 1948, p. 7.
9. Paul F. Lazarsfeld and Harry Field, *The People Look at Radio,* University of North Carolina Press, Chapel Hill, 1946.
10. Constantin Fitz Gibbon, "The Man of Fear," *Atlantic Monthly,* January, 1947, pp, 78-81.
11. Bertlam Schaffner, *Father Land, A Study of Authoritarianism in the German Family.* Columbia University Press, New York, 1948.

A CASE HISTORY IN CROSS-NATIONAL COMMUNICATIONS*

During the war anthropologists addressed themselves to various ways in which their discipline could be put at the direct service of their society, attempting to short cut the normal lag which obtains between the development of abstractions based upon laboratory and field research and their application to contemporary problems. One part of this anthropological effort concerned itself with delineating significant aspects of the national character, or culture pattern, of enemy peoples or peoples of occupied countries about whom our knowledge was wholly inadequate.

A second use of anthropological techniques was the attempt to select salient aspects of our own cultures and describe them in such a way that they could be, used for various sorts of rapid training or morale building.[3] The use of anthropological knowledge in operations directed toward the enemy involved only a limited analysis of our own culture, except when a policy either had to be carried out by large numbers of Americans whom it was impossible to train in detail to act in any way antithetical to their usual behavior, or when, as in our formal treatment of the Japanese emperor, widespread public support of a national policy was necessary. The use of similar anthropological knowledge within the limits of our own culture raised all the problems we have been discussing, the ethical problems of the responsibility of leaders of a democratic society not to manipulate, but to appeal openly to existing and cherished strengths.

When an attempt is made to use anthropological methods to strengthen a relationship between peoples of two contemporary cultures, still different problems arise. Here the focus is not upon points of vulnerability, which may be breached, as with the enemy, or strengthened, as for members of occupied countries, nor upon traditional strengths and coherencies to be enhanced, and weaknesses and contradictions to be guarded against, as in work in own culture.

*Originally published in *The Communication of Ideas* - a series of addresses edited by Lymon Bryson. New York: Cooper Square Publishers, 1964.

Instead, our efforts have to be directed toward finding areas of agreement which can be used as a background for the acceptance of differences which are causing specific friction and tension. Research and resulting communications are focused upon a relationship, and the nodes selected for emphasis are defined in terms of that relationship, not in terms of the emphasis within the whole culture pattern of each society. For instance, if foreign policy is to be discussed and the foreign policy of one culture is most congruent with upper class values, while in the other it is most congruent with middle class values, this asymmetry would be consciously explored, perhaps to the neglect of any exploration of the exactly corresponding class in the other country, because of its lack of immediate relevance to the problem in hand.

As illustrative material for such an operation, I shall draw upon my own experience in working on Anglo-American relations, and particularly use data upon the areas of friction and misunderstanding between American troops and British civilians in Britain in 1943. My own case is unusual because I had the opportunity to participate in framing the hypotheses with which I went to Britain, to combine field work on these hypotheses with lecturing all over Britain, under the auspices of the Ministry of Information, and later through the United States Office of War Information in London to prepare various sorts of materials, both as background and as immediate communication, for circulation to Americans and Britons. Thus activities which would more usually be divided among a large number of individuals with different skills—research, field work, analysis, interpretation, preparation of directives, writing, rewriting, broadcasting presentations, etc.—and which would be subject to all the hazards which attend communication within such a diversified group, were embodied in the work that I did. This is an accident which we have no reason to believe will be repeated often, and analysis of such an experience bears the same relationship to thinking about cooperative operations that an analysis of the functions of the vanishing general practitioner bears to an attempt to construct modern medical services in which many disciplines participate. It also provided a unique opportunity to explore some of the problems involved and to test our hypotheses on the spot.

I plan to discuss examples of a variety of the procedures and problems which arose so as to give as broad a picture as possible of the way in which anthropological methods may be applied to relationships between any pair of peoples, for the analysis of such binary relationships is a necessary step toward an understanding of more complicated patterns of relationship on which a world order will have to be built.

I have used the term *cross-national* deliberately, to indicate that I am dealing not with relationships between *nations,* self-maximating competitive national units, but between the peoples of different nations, whose effective communication is compromised both by differences in culture and the circumstance of different nationality which gives a special competitive coloring and significance to those differences. To the extent that local allegiance is an important ingredient of the picture of the own group, the acceptance of differences in culture will vary enormously according to whether any sort of boundary, even a state or county line, intervenes. In wartime, uniforms, and all the paraphernalia of nationalistic warfare exacerbate the sensitivities of the populations involved.

Application of General Theoretical Formulations to a Particular Case.

In the initial steps I depended upon the formulations of symmetrical and complementary schismogenesis, developed by Gregory Bateson,[4] in which the United States and Britain were both diagnosed as relying upon the stimulus provided by a greater strength in the opponent, (symmetrical pattern) rather than the stimulus provided , by relative weakness (complementary pattern). With this approval of symmetrical relationships, shared by both the United States and Britain, was associated a common moral disapprobation of bullying, picking on someone who was smaller, throwing one's weight around, etc.

In addition to the original statement of this diagnosis, I had elaborated, before going to England, the American version of adequate provocation to attack, under the formulation of "the chip on the shoulder"[5] in which I stressed that the American boy, reared by women was given a deep doubt of his essential aggressiveness, combined with a lack of pattern for exercising it, in contrast to the British boy reared by older boys and men to combine a belief in his innate aggressiveness with an obligation never to use his full strength unless pushed into an extreme position in which he could turn at bay. The famous "backs to the wall" order of Haig in World War I to the British, and reported exhortations of General Patton to his men, emphasizing the difficulty of the task, but also the fact that the enemy was on the run and the United States Army had the best equipment the world, are conspicuous examples of the way in which military leaders have intuitively relied upon these different patterns of a basically symmetrical schismogenic attitude. Phrased colloquially, underlying similarity became, "Both British and Americans believe that the strong have an obligation not to abuse their strength. We both hate bullies, and conversely those who cringe to bullies."

The second theoretical formulation was the hypothesis of *end linkage,*[6] that the way in which parent-child relationships are patterned in respect to such behaviors as: succoring-dependence, dominance-submission and exhibitionism-spectatorship, provides a learning situation for the child which patterns his subsequent behavior in situations where these behaviors are involved. Specifically, in Anglo-American relationships, the exhibitionism is reversed, in Britain it is Father who exhibits to his children; he is the model for their future behavior. Father does the talking, provides the model, and before a very quiet and submissive audience, in accordance with the keen ethical disapproval of overuse of strength. Father underplays his strength, understates his position, speaks with a slight appearance of hesitation in his manner, but with the cool assurance of one who knows. In the United States this position is reversed, and at the American breakfast table, it is not Father, but Junior, who talks, exhibits his successes and skills, and demands parental spectatorship and applause, with an insistence that can be clamoring and assertive, because after all he is speaking from weakness to strength. The American background for this reversal was explored and in the spring of 1943 we tried using the contrast in a radio program, in which samples of parent-child behavior at the breakfast table were followed by excerpts from American and British public speeches.[8]

For lecturing in Britain, these two formulations, of symmetrical schismogenesis and end linkage provided both a theoretical background for understanding and material for interpreting one of the acute points of friction between British and Americans. This point was British repudiation of American "boasting" and American repudiation of British "arrogance." It lent itself particularly well to use on the lecture platform and over the radio, as tone of voice was the principal medium in the demonstration. By a little careful interviewing in each new area in Britain, I could get verbatim, and therefore acceptable statements of the British objections. "The trouble with the Americans is that when they are good at something they *say* so" : "The trouble with the Americans is that they talk so much about what they are going to do; we don't talk, we just *do* it" (from the Scots). I could then rely upon the lecture situation, itself one in which the exhibitionistic role of the lecturer and the spectatorship role of the audience was defined, to provide me with additional illustrative material. I could quote from the chairman who in presenting me, putatively in the parental role on a British stage, to a great tired audience who had come out in the blackout on a freezing Sunday night in Scotland, said; "Be as kind to the audience as you can, Dr. Mead"; or I could refer to the whole institution of the "vote of thanks," in which the British audience, after sitting, docile and respectful while the lecturer plays Father, reestablishes the balance by the paternalistic tone in which the proposer of the vote of thanks addresses the now seated lecturer.

Explanations of behavioral differences which stressed upbringing were easily acceptable to the British, because of the strong cultural emphasis upon "character" as something which is acquired in the course of the right education rather than an innate possession of any individual or class of individuals. It was possible to show that whenever an American spoke, he spoke as he had learned to speak when he was small and so would put that irritating overstatement into his voice which the British called "boasting." Whenever a Briton spoke, he spoke as he had heard his father and other elders speak, as the strong and assured, carefully pulling his punches with that irritating understatement in his voice, which the American, called "arrogance." It was possible to show how the words *understatement* applied to the British and *boasting* applied to the Americans, emphasized the virtues of British behavior and devalued American, while by using the parallel words *understatement* and *overstatement,* both British and American behavior could be put in a common frame, that of habits learned in childhood.

Exploration of a Friction Point

When I reached Britain, our troops were still pouring into the country, there were still many British troops in the country, and very few American girls had yet reached Britain. The relationships between American men and British girls were providing an acute point of misunderstanding among both nationalities. The friction took many forms, which required quite different types of treatment. It was necessary to explain to British authorities that an American boy would have difficulty in judging the age and degree of discretion of a girl who told him she had been out of school and working for two years, and to try to construct ways in which the Americans could spend their disproportionately large pay on British girls without using up goods or creating new social problems. But there was the much more basic problem of the way in which disturbed heterosexual relationships were festering beneath the surface of Anglo-American relationships in general.

The problem was not primarily a police problem involving the reduction of illegitimate births, which seemed to be following a pretty similar curve whichever troops and whichever nationalities were involved, but rather to reduce the disorientation which expressed itself in the British statement that the American men were "immoral" and the American insistence that the British girls had "no morals." Accusations of this sort might have been, of course, mere expressions of symmetrical friction, in which case it would have been necessary to look elsewhere for more basic areas of discrepancy, but there is always a good possibility that under identical accusations there will be expressed some profound and unrealized difference, become the more dangerous because it is so completely masked.[9]

I set about to explore the relationships between American men and British girls. A key to the misunderstanding lay in the differences in the location of responsibility for sex advances and sex refusals, in fact for the whole modulation of sex behavior. The American girl is trained to look after herself, unchaperoned and without any insistence upon rules of etiquette which will insure her person immunity from physical advances. She is taught that her behavior is in her own keeping, and the boy learns to make advances and rely upon the girl to repulse them whenever they are inappropriate to the state of feeling between the pair. In Britain the situation is reversed; the girl is reared to depend upon a slight barrier of chilliness and frostiness which the boys learn to respect, and for the rest to rely upon the men to approach or advance, as warranted by the situation.

Both systems give about the degree of satisfaction which can be expected in any pattern which locates initiative formally in one sex, without reference to temperament. But in wartime Britain, it meant that American boys, taught to ask with a full expectation of being refused effectively most of the time, were confronted by British girls, taught to accede to every forceful invitation. Several characteristic patterns of response developed. Some British girls became even chillier and, repelling even American optimism, succeeded in keeping the Americans at arms length and sending them away to complain about everything in Britain. Some girls responded to the first stylized wisecrack with an impassioned surrender which was thoroughly disconcerting to the American in its intensity and implications. Some succeeded in maneuvering a middle course for a few hours until the Americans who seemed to be "serious" could be presented at home as future sons-in-law which annoyed a great many Americans very much. The interpretation of this difference to the men themselves, and to those who were charged with youth and protection programs, gave a working basis for improved relationships, and a phrasing under which the mutual accusations of immorality could be reduced.

Problems of Phrasing and Translation

The problem of communication in a language which was theoretically mutually intelligible, supposed to be "one language," presented a number of difficulties which could be partially resolved by reference to cultural differences. In all probability the greater the difference between the languages of the pair of cultures with which one is attempting to work, the more automatic warnings are provided to the translator. But between English and American, and between other cultures similarly related through a common tradition and a still somewhat intelligible pair of languages, language confuses rather than clarifies, and other sorts of clues are necessary.

Two systematic observations made it possible to communicate better. The first was analysis of the difference between the American and British sense of a scale of values. Americans tend to arrange objects on a single scale of value, from best to worst, biggest to smallest, cheapest to most expensive, and are able to express a preference among very complex objects on such a single scale. The question, "What is your favorite color?" so intelligible to an American, is meaningless in Britain, and such a question is countered by: "Favorite color for what? A flower? A necktie?" Each object is thought of as having a most complex set of qualities and color is merely a quality of an object, not something from a color chart on which one can make a choice which is transferable to a large number of different sorts of objects.

The American reduction of complexities to single scales is entirely comprehensible in terms of the great diversity of value systems which different immigrant groups brought to the American scene; some common denominator among the incommensurables was very much needed and oversimplification was almost inevitable.[10] But as a result, Americans think in terms of qualities which have unidimensional scales, while the British, when they think of a complex object or event, even if they reduce it to parts, think of each part as retaining all of the complexities of the whole. Americans subdivide the scale, the British subdivide the object. Americans are able to describe a room in terms of its "color scheme," where the British eye would retain a sense of some fifty elements involved in the whole interior pattern, even when speaking of a square inch of the rug. From this British insistence on complexity flows naturally enough, an insistence upon uniqueness and an unwillingness to make comparisons.

Discussions as to the relative merits of cities, which Americans make happily in terms of size, wealth, or some other common denominator, seem to the British either meaningless or as irrelevant boasting. In turn, the British refusal to provide statistics on the size or wealth of a city seemed to the Americans to be either obscurantist or unfriendly. In Anglo-American contacts of all sorts, committee meetings, teaching situations, etc., it was important to watch the misunderstandings which arose along these lines, as the British voted the Americans oversimplifying when they harped on some exact statement of a position on a numerical scale, and the Americans voted the British inaccurate, if not engaged in deliberate falsification, when they quoted the population of Bengal with an error of ten million, with the statement that "it doesn't matter," because they were concerned with the relative, not the absolute size of one Indian province.

Another sort of misunderstanding which influenced communication was the difference between the British and the American sense of the real world. The British see the world as something to which man adapts, the American as man controlled, a vast malleable space on which one builds what one wishes, from blueprints one has drawn, and when dissatisfied simply tears the structure down and starts anew.

The great sense of mechanical control of the environment, product at least in part of an empty continent and the machine age, extends to American attitudes toward crops and animals, which are again something to be planned for, streamlined, increased or decreased at will, and even to a certain degree, to human beings, who can be, if not completely molded by man made devices, at least sorted mechanically into simply defined pigeonholes. In contrast, the British see the world as a natural world to which man adapts, in which he assumes no control over the future, but only the experienced foresight of the husbandman or the gardener, who plants the best seed and watches carefully over the first green blades. Man is seen as the junior partner of God, expressed either in conventional or more contemporary forms, but still the junior partner of forces to which he can adapt but which he cannot control. He can "only handle one link in the chain of destiny at a time."

The humility of this phrasing has its own forms of arrogance, as in Milton's: "God is decreeing to begin some new and great period ... what does He then but reveal Himself to His servants, and as His manner is, first to His English-men."

Vis-à-vis this state of mind, ordinary American figures of speech, implying control and mechanism, not only fail to communicate but actually establish barriers. It was necessary to drop the familiar figures of an America converting for full production, laying down blueprinted acres of factories, six months ahead of schedule, and streamlining labor-management relations, and use instead the figures of speech of horticulture, to speak of "planting the seed" in "carefully prepared ground," of an effort which even when skill and experience were used to their utmost, still depended in final outcome on forces with which man could cooperate but which he could not control.

Roads and buildings in Britain which have been there a long time, become part of the natural world, not something to be swept aside lightly for a new plan. This was difficult for Americans to understand, who often found that a badly bombed city, once the rubble had been cleared away, which was still a wounded landscape to the British, looked to them very much like any American city, in eternal process of rapid transformation, in which the old was torn down with hardly a sign of regret.

The very different sorts of self-consciousness about all social process had also to be analyzed and allowed for: the American's willingness to think about the immediate future and his unwillingness to think very far ahead; the British unwillingness to let too great a degree of self-consciousness interfere with the smooth flow of highly disciplined habitual behavior but their greater willingness to think ten years ahead; the sudden shift in British attention which permitted them to attribute to themselves, retrospectively, a degree of planfulness which they would have repudiated at the time as paralyzing. I was at first confused by these contradictions, by being told in one breath that to think about the next week's plan would be unthinkable, and that in some earlier operation of exactly the same nature "we were very clever," and infinitely cunning. Once the contrast was clear, it was possible to discuss the past, when any detailed dissection of motive and behavior was desired, and the far future if articulate goals came into question.

The Interpretation of British Behavior to Americans

My formal mandate in 1943 had included only the British side of the task and the work which I did in the United States was under various scattered auspices and not a part of the Office of War Information program. But during the next two years I did have occasion to lecture on Britain, to various types of professional and popular audiences, to write, and to teach selected groups of personnel destined for the Far East where they would come into frequent and friction laden contact with the British.

The problems of addressing members of one's own culture about their relations with members of another culture presented some distinct features, and led to formulations of significant differences which had not been pointed up during my British experience. These differences in insight are to be laid primarily, I think, to the inevitable shift in one's type of participation under the two circumstances. In Britain I was a friendly visitor, using my professional skill to facilitate relationships between two wartime allies. In the United States, particularly in my teaching role in the various out-post schools, I was concerned with the strengths and weaknesses of Americans for the tasks of cross-cultural understanding which they were going to face. I had to find, if possible, approaches which, in clarifying their own cultural attitudes, would make it possible for them, not merely to be more understanding, but to act, in cross-cultural situations. Furthermore one faces, in discussing one's own culture with fellow members, a different sort of cross-fire of criticism, and is likely, occasionally, to abandon sympathetic impartiality for a note of urgency, if not astringency. In closed classes, designed for war purposes, there were no members of other nationalities, and it was sometimes difficult to convince the students that I would have used the same words and made the same points had there been British in the audience. In all work of this sort, it is essential to speak in terms which envelop the two or more peoples being discussed, and which represent the differences in ways acceptable to both, but this necessity is more vividly demonstrated if actual human beings of each group are present in the flesh.

Rapport difficulties

An American addressing an American audience about Britain is speaking to a people who have strong and partly unconscious attitudes about Britain which go very deep, much deeper than any attitudes which the British as a group had about America in 1943. The American sense of national identity contains the earlier and severed relationship with Britain as an intrinsic part, while the British do not use the loss of America as a component of their sense of their national identity. Furthermore, the Anglophile position is traditionally associated in the United States with the position of the upper class, the conservative, the wealthy, and the more easterly part of our population, added to the circumstance that the bulk of American tourists before the war were women devoutly following the footsteps of one or another bard. The Anglophobe position contains a mass of assorted elements, Middle West against the East, European ancestry against the older Anglo-Saxon stock, the plain man against the would be aristocrat, etc. To discuss Britain dispassionately, it was necessary for the lecturer to face and deal with these strong currents of feeling, sometimes existing simultaneously in the same individual.

I finally solved this problem, satisfactorily for myself at least, by beginning a lecture with a caricature[11] of the pro-American British woman, who represents in a capsule form, a way of repudiating the snobbish note which over sweetened the voice of the Anglophile, and startling the Anglophobe into a provisionally British identification with the kind of Britons who would not like the type of Americanphile

whom I presented. This produced a loosening of traditional identifi-
cations which permitted the clarification material to get a hearing.

A second difficulty arose from the inveterate American habit of
asking about every piece of behavior, "Is it better or worse than ours?"
This contrast with the British insistence on complexity and so on
uniqueness has been discussed above, but it presented itself in a new
form as I lectured on British wartime arrangements for community
feeding, advising disoriented citizens through the Citizens' Advice
Bureaus, or caring for the children of working mothers. Invariably the
American audience wanted to know, "Is their system better or worse
than ours ?"

Behind this question were two unexpressed attitudes, one, the
hope that ours would be better, and second, the tacit acceptance of
the obligation to copy theirs if ours was worse. As most of the audience vigorously resented any suggestion that they copy Britain, these
presentations were always charged with rapport dangers. It was necessary to stress over and over again, that the British solution was
different, not better or worse. While this point might be got over temporarily in a lecture, it usually did not survive in the next day's newspaper headlines, and actually represents one of the most serious
hazards to any sort of comprehension of other peoples by Americans.
A simple sense of either inferiority or superiority would be easier to
deal with than this belief that all institutions can be placed on a single scale, and that it becomes the American's obligation to choose the
best. The pleasure derived from the study of foreign behaviors which
can be voted as inferior is alloyed by the discomfort of encountering
those which are superior.

Attitude Toward Compromise

American audiences raised a question whose counterpart I never met
in Britain and which illustrates how valuable each side of such a relationship is, in drawing attention to parts of the whole which the other
side might neglect. "Why is it the British always insist on their own
way in international affairs and we always lose?" "Why do the British
always pull the wool over American eyes?" These were frequent questions. In comments upon our international negotiations the term,
"the poor little United States," cropped up with amazing frequency.

In working out a clarification of these questions, of this American
belief that we always lost, I again sought for a common element in
the two cultures against which the differences would be highlighted.
Americans share with the British a common tradition in regard to the

appropriate behavior of the minorities that are minorities because they are in some way more right than the majority. Such minorities, best represented by the long line of dissident Protestant sects, but today also represented by the Roman Catholic minority in England, have been accorded, as part of our whole picture of our form of government, the right to differ and the duty to stand up for their positions. A virtuous minority in both countries is virtuous just because it does not compromise. But here the parallel ends because the British, speaking from strength, from the paternal position, do not identify governmental negotiations as made from a minority position. The government acts from strength and, being strong, can *include* some of the minorities' demands in any proposal. T o compromise is the act of the strong and the entrenched, an act of graciousness, expediency, and a recognition that the heresies of today become the orthodoxies of tomorrow.

So in Britain the word *compromise* is a good word, and one may speak approvingly of any arrangement which has been a compromise, including very often one in which the other side has gained more than fifty per cent of the points at issue.

In the United States, the minority position is still the position from which everyone speaks: the President *versus* Congress, Congress *versus* the President, the state government *versus* the metropolis, and the metropolis *versus* the state government. This is congruent, with the American doctrine of checks and balances, but it does not permit the word "compromise" to gain the same ethical halo which it has in Britain. Where in Britain to compromise means to work out a good solution, in America it usually means to work out a bad one, a solution in which all the points of importance, to both sides, are lost. Thus in negotiations between the United States and Britain, all of which had in the nature of the case to be compromises as two sovereignties were involved, the British could always speak approvingly and proudly of the result, the Americans had to emphasize their losses. Out of the same ethic, but a contrasting interpretation of one's own position, came these mutually reinforcing estimates of a document or treaty.

Closely related to this sense of being weak but on the side of the right, and therefore committed to demanding hundred per cent victories, is the American fear of being exploited by other groups, best summed up in the vernacular phrase, "Don't be a sucker." This is so deepseated and has been so heavily exploited in discussions of our relationship to other countries, both those who are believed to outwit us in the diplomatic game, and those who ask us for help, that it seemed important to analyze it.

First it was necessary to work out the interpersonal dynamics of the conception. In America, a "sucker," one who is not to be given an even break, is anyone who enters a game in which he does not have the skill or wit or strength to compete. Superficially, the American ethic that a sucker should be trimmed, seems discrepant with the ethic that it is wrong to bully. But seen against the way in which American boys are reared it becomes intelligible. Instead of the British father who supports the eldest son, as a surrogate of himself, against the competition of the younger sons, and at the same time exhorts the eldest to be gentle but firm, the American boy is reared by a mother who defends the younger against the elder, and continually uses the success of the younger to goad the elder toward achievement. The slightly younger brother, backed up by the mother, becomes a threat, especially to the boy whose games are continually subject to the intrusion of the younger.

This contemporary child-rearing tradition combines with the frontier tradition in which the tenderfoot is a threat to the whole community. Older frontiersmen, alert to the dangers which one careless act may precipitate, and older brothers alert to the way in which the younger may spoil their games, both find refuge in the ethic, "Never give a sucker an even break," an ethic which is also honored by the admission of the American who loses, "I was a sucker, I asked for it." The extent to which this treatment of the sucker may justifiably be classified as a deeply rooted ethical attitude is by the report in *Time,* for November 6, 1944, in which Olendorf is pictured with the slogan "never give a sucker an even break," and his adherence to the slogan is then described as accounting for the way in which a successful ambush of Japanese ships was conducted. Stated for American consumption, the havoc was justifiably wrought among the Japanese because they had "asked for it."

At the same time the word sucker is used in another, and positively toned sense, to describe the man who is generous, enthusiastic, willing to give of his time and energy, as when a physician remarks in a public speech, "you know doctors always head the sucker list." This is said with approval of the doctor's kind heart, and is tantamount to saying "We are admirably tenderhearted people." Or the student, cited in a psychological study as a normal, well adjusted young American, will remark on the offices which he has held in organizations and adds, "I'm a sucker for work."

This dual attitude toward the sucker position further complicates the American attitude toward other peoples, because it is just when Americans are behaving well that they are most likely to suspect that they are being made suckers against their will. Then the whole negative set of sanctions comes into play, and the ethic of never giving a sucker an even break is projected on to the other national group. The formula reads, "We are suckers in the international game, both when we compete and when we are generous. We aren't up to it, either way. We are playing a game we do not understand, therefore we will be trimmed." A perfect instance of this interpretation confronted by the British insistence on the assumption of an appearance of model, self-controlled parental behavior, was provided in an article by Senator Brewster:[12]

> A number of different diplomatic commercial, and financial moves will be necessary if we are to hold our rightful place in world commerce, but one of the most important is this: We must stop being out-traded by our good friends the British, the world's greatest experts in economic diplomacy.
>
> One day I was talking with Sir Gerald Campbell, Lord Halifax's right hand man in the British Embassy in Washington, and I told him I believed our statesmanship is so bad that in nearly every negotiation with the British we came out second best.
>
> Sir Gerald smiled. "Of course, we put it over on you," he said. "But not half as often as we could! ..."

This passage sums up the whole position, the American fear of being trimmed as suckers who do not know the game, the British failure to recognize the issue which is being raised, and their response first with a jocular acceptance of the stated inferiority, which from their point of view takes the sting out, coupled with a statement of the high ethical behavior which all fathers, governors and persons in authority are supposed to display. The unpalatability of the British reply to the ordinary American can best be stated by referring to the Fijian form of insult in which most enemies were eaten but those who were to be most insulted were cooked and left uneaten. The jocular, Olympian assumption of restraint in the British answer simply exacerbates the American feeling of being treated negligently and condescendingly.

Another pretty example occurred in an article in the *Washington Star,* in 1945,[13] under the heading, "Critics air U.S.-British Views," in which Sir John Wardlaw Milne writes: "In this country we are thankful and *indeed proud* of the great United States, but we heartily dislike the tendency to suggest that America's intervention is a kind of act of grace from some superior beings who need not have engaged in the war at all." (The italics are mine.) And Senator Burton Wheeler writes, in the other column, "America wants no more deceptive slogans such as 'Give us the tools, we'll finish the job.' We are not going to tolerate any condescending attitude on the part of anyone that implies or assigns us the status of 'poor relations.'" Here we see the British tone of speaking from established position and discouraging any upstart claims, the American tone 'of maintaining their rights against those who would put them down.'

The phrase *proud of,* so galling to American ears, was a British way of boasting on behalf of the Americans. The whole problem of how Americans should speak of British achievement and British of American was a particularly ticklish one all through the war. After repeated instances of the degree of misunderstanding which was generated by the way in which each ally spoke of its own allied efforts, Geoffrey Gorer and I worked out a phrasing in terms of the conceptions of partnership which provided a form of clarification suitable for lecturing and teaching.

All through the war the United States and Britain were spoken of as "partners," a word which is common to both languages. But the British associated the word when applied to international affairs, with a sports concept, with the tennis partner, who, for the duration of the game is treated as like oneself, whose successes one acclaims and whose failures one grieves over. It was possible to invoke from the memories of anyone who had played deck tennis with British partners the continuous, "Good shot, partner!" "Hard luck, partner!" which is an inseparable part of the verbal etiquette of the game.

The American, seeing international relationships primarily in a business context, associated the word "partner" with a business partnership, in which the relationship is conventionally asymmetrical; one partner putting up the funds, the other providing the brains or the entry, but neither committed to a social relationship with the other, with an expectation of the partnership lasting until it is disrupted by disagreement or death, and with no obligation on either to boast for or grieve for the other partner. So a careful British attempt to boast for their partners, as in the case of the great emphasis given to the American contribution to bringing down the buzz bombs, was met by the Americans, not by a little piece of symmetrical vicarious boasting, about, say the landing platforms, but instead by blowups in the American papers of what the British had said about the buzz bombs. This produced inevitable confusion, and even some abortive attempts on the part of the British to do their own boasting.

Conclusion

The methods described in this case history are anthropological methods, that is, they rely upon an understanding of the cultural patterns of the peoples involved, they invoke regularities for purposes of clarification. It is, however, important to recognize that clarification alone will not promote understanding, that it is still necessary to set some tone within which feeling may flow freely. In the presentations and teaching described in this case history, I relied on these methods which invoked feeling; first on emphasizing symmetries and when possible reducing what looked like complementary contrasts to symmetrical terms, second on giving a description of the other people's behavior in terms which made *identification* possible and third on arousing the kind of laughter which comes from the exactitude of the cultural statement.

Members of an audience invariably laughed hardest at the description of their own cultural behavior, not at that of the others. To obtain this effect, it is very important to avoid caricature, which is self-defeating. The device also fails if there are many expatriates in an audience, as expatriates already see their home culture with a degree of distortion which makes any exact description, which will invoke the laughter of recognition from others, seem to them a caricature, and usually a hostile caricature. The method failed, in other words, when it was used with those who were themselves very ambivalent about their own culture, and very overaccepting of the other culture. Significantly enough, attempts to give equally exact descriptions of German behavior have usually failed to evoke the same sort of recognition from Germans in this country, and it is possible that it is a method best suited to cultures and to situations in which ambivalence toward the own culture is least in evidence.

Undoubtedly, in other interpretative hands or in different media, other ways of evoking feeling would be more appropriate than the deliberate attempt to embody the clarifying statement in exact laughter producing verbatim vignettes. That the method is suitable for more than one culture is evidenced by the very similar response which I received from British and American audiences when I gave the same material, in the same way. But the evocation of pity, or eager purposive aspiration, may also be feeling states which might appropriately accompany the type of clarification which an initial objective anthropological analysis of cultural patterns provides: evoking either fear or anger runs, I believe, into the danger of stirring up m the audience feelings which interfere with acceptance of the clarification. Strong identification is possible with an evocation of fear or anger, but the identification tends to be so strong as to interfere with the degree of distance which is necessary both for laughter and for an understanding of difference.

If we are to build a world in which a variety of cultures are orchestrated together so as to produce a viable social order, we need controlled exploration of the types of clarification and types of presentation which will increase understanding between pairs of cultural groups and then among more complicated groupings.

NOTES

1. This research is part of the program of the Institute for Intercultural Studies. Large sections of this material were presented in a lecture before the New York Academy of Science, January, 1947, and are reprinted here through the courtesy of the New York Academy of Sciences, from their *Transactions,* Series 2, 9, February, 1947, 4.
2. The most significant work was done on Japan and Germany, and references may be made particularly to:
    Geoffrey Gorer, "Themes in Japanese Culture," *Transactions,* New York Academy of Sciences Series II, 5, March, 1943, 5, pp. 105-124.
    Ruth Benedict, *The Chrysanthemum and the Sword,* Houghton Mifflin Company, Boston, 1947.
    "Round Table on Germany after the War," *American Journal of Orthopsychiatry,* 15, July, 1946,3, pp. 381-441.
    Talcott Parsons, "The Problem of Controlled Institutional Change. An Essay in Applied Social Science," *Psychiatry,* 8, February, 1945, I, pp. 79-101.
    And to unpublished work by Gregory Bateson, Ruth Benedict, Geoffrey Gorer, Douglas Haring, Frederick Hulse, Clyde Kluckhohn, David Mandelbaum, Rhoda Metraux, Marian Smith, and others. Some of the general implications of this work are described in Margaret Mead, "Anthropological Techniques in War Psychology," *Bulletin of the Menninger Clinic,* 1943, 7, pp. 137-140.
    Ruth Benedict, "The Study of Cultural Patterns in European Nations," *Transactions,* 8, June, 1946, 8, pp. 274-279.
3. Gregory Bateson and Margaret Mead, "Principles of Morale Building," *Journal of Educational Society,* 15, December, 1941, 4, PP. 206-220.
    "The Problem of Changing Food Habits," Report of the Committee on Food Habits 1941-43, *National Research Council Bulletin,* 108, October, 1943.
    Rhoda Metraux, "Qualitative Attitude Analysis—A Technique for the Study of Verbal Behavior," *Bulletin of the National Research Council,* October, 1943, 108, pp, 86-95.
4. Gregory Bateson, "Some Systematic Approaches to the Study of Culture and Personality," *Character and Personality,* 11, September, 1942, I, pp. 76-84.
    Gregory Bateson, *Civilian Morale,* 2nd yearbook of the Society for the Psychological Study of Social Issues, Houghton Mifflin Company, Boston, 1942, "Morale and National Character," pp. 71-91.

5. Margaret Mead, *And Keep Your Powder Dry,* William Morrow and Company, New York, 1942, Chapter IX, "The Chip on the Shoulder," pp. 138-158.

6. Bateson, *op. cit.,* pp. 71—91.

7. Mead, *op. cit.*

8. This program was given as part of the series, "Science at Work" of the American School of the Air of the Columbia Broadcasting System, published in *Education,* 65, December, 1944,4, pp. 228-238. The two speeches ran as follows:

British Lecturer:

"Ladies and Gentlemen. ...I have been asked to talk to you tonight about British war production. We have, of course, improved. Our over-all figures for the past year show a definite increase. But it is, I think, in planes that the picture is most striking. Our largest bombers, which incidentally carry four times the bomb load of yours, are now coming quite satisfactorily into production."

American Lecturer:

"Well, ladies and gentlemen. ... I see I'm down on the program to talk to you tonight about Alaska. I can think of one good reason why I know something about that country. It's because I've had to make upwards of 20 to 30 trips there, Summer and Winter in the past fifteen years.

Two or three of these trips, I might add, were by dog sled, far off the beaten track. On at least one of them, I nearly lost my life. But the thing I want to tell you folks about tonight, is the change that's come over Alaska since our boys went in there. Yes sir...mass production methods and the Good Old American qualities of hard work and initiative are showing results up there these days. I predict that five years after this war finishes, we'll be spending Summer in Alaska the way we used to spend Winters down in Florida. That's a tip, folks."

9. Early in the war the British were frequently advised by American expatriates and Anglophiles to retaliate against American comments about India, by remarks about the treatment of Negro Americans in the United States. This *tu quoque* phrasing only increase the bitterness and intolerance on both sides, as the two cases were felt as basically dissimilar by the Americans, who equated Indian problems with American prerevolutionary problems as a country, and racial problems in the United States as equivalent to the slum problem inside Britain, a purely domestic matter.

10. Mead, *op. cit.,* chapter VII, "Brothers and Sisters and Success," pp. 54-70.

11. It should be noted that caricatures contain a strong hostile element, which has to be recognized whenever they are used.

12. Owen Brewster, "Let's not be suckers again," *American Magazine,* January, 1945. pp. 24-26, 93-98.

13. Burton K. Wheeler, "Critics air United States-British Views," *Washington Star,* January 14, 1945.

ADOLESCENCE IN PRIMITIVE AND MODERN SOCIETY: The New Generation*

To many thinkers (sic) the *primitive* as opposed to the civilized or sophisticated man is one who is close to nature, close to the raw materials of life. Such a *primitive* man is supposed to recognize the vital importance of birth, puberty, marriage, and death, and to surround these crises with a wealth of ceremonial beneficial to mankind. These points of sharp significance to the individual are believed to be beautifully muffled by elaborate forms which enable the individual as a member of the social group to make terms with life and death, in a way in which we, less socialized, less primitive, cannot do. Although it is true that from the mass of recorded practice of primitive peoples it is possible to find many illustrations of such rituals, a wider survey of primitive societies does not bear it out. Some primitive peoples are as arbitrary as ourselves in the construction of patterns, which ignore the more obvious facts of life and death, and superimpose man-made definitions of the life cycle. This applies not only to puberty but also to primitive attitudes towards paternity, towards birth, towards death. So among the Todas of India, where one woman is taken to wife by a group of brothers, paternity is established by a ceremony, performed usually by the oldest brother. This ceremony determines the paternity of all subsequent children until a new aspirant to social fatherhood performs the same ceremony in his turn. Children are sometimes considered as the offspring of a man who has been dead ten years, because before his death he ceremonially assumed fatherhood. A similar overlay of physical facts, which, though known, go socially unacknowledged, is found in many societies, which practice infanticide. The child is not regarded as a member of the social group, to be jealously defended against misfortune, simply because it is delivered from its mother's womb. Rather it must wait upon a social recognition of its existence; until that is given, to kill it is not murder. Among

*Originally published in *The New Generation: The Intimate Problems of Modern Parents and Children.* Edited by V.F. Calverton and Samuel D. Schmalhausen. Arno Press and The New York Times, 1971.

the Wotjobaluk tribe of southeast Australia a newborn child was often killed to give strength to an older brother or sister. In other words, the older child was a human being, a member of the group, the newborn baby material of which alternative disposition might be made. So definite was this kind of distinction among the tribes about Maryborough (in Queensland) that if one saw a newborn baby with its body rubbed with red ochre and the burned bark of the bloodwood tree, one knew it was safe. The absence of such marks meant that it would quietly disappear. At the other pole from such an attitude are the sea people of the Admiralty Islands who give an early miscarriage all the honors accorded an adult individual. The fetus is named, mourned, and an elaborate economic machinery is set in motion. A woman in telling over her dead makes no distinction between miscarriages and children who died at several years of age; all are mentioned as beings who lived, were known, and died.

As with birth, so with death. In Fiji an old chief whose death has been determined upon is spoken of as dead. His wives and concubines are strangled in his presence and as he sits by, awaiting interment, he concurs in this social acceptance of his decease.

Individuals suffering from a distension of the abdomen are buried alive in one island of British New Guinea, but this is not murder, for the lives of such sufferers are regarded as formally closed.

If social conventions can so distort the recognition of paternity, of birth, and of death, it is not surprising that the same distortion applies to the period of puberty. About the point of puberty it is possible to center a number of cultural ideas: attitudes of fear and dread towards menstruation, education either social or individual, practices for the attainment of beauty and charm, magical preparation for life, or mere acceptance into the tribal life. Some societies stress one at the expense of all the others; some stress none. In general, it may be said that when the social emphasis lies upon the fact of menstruation itself rather than upon such derivative points as the girl's entry into tribal society or her marriage, the correspondence between first menses and ceremonial observance is closest. But although the observance of a girl's first menstruation was the principal tribal event among many California Indians, even here we find tribes, like the Luiseno, where the event had become socialized to such an extent that a whole group of girls were treated at once; only one of these was at the actual physiological period. And this was in a culture where women were secluded at menstruation throughout their lives; so acute was the dread of this uncanny state.

Whenever the emphasis shifts from menstruation to the more general point of maturity, correspondence between ceremonies and puberty becomes greater or may vanish altogether. So we find peoples like the Dobuans of the D'Entrecasteaux, where the sex life of girls begins long before puberty; where there is no tribal life into which the girl needs to be initiated; where there is no cultural fear of menstruation. Among these people adolescence goes unmarked by any social observance whatsoever.

Among the peoples who do recognize puberty it is interesting to note the diversity of emphases. Northern California tribal attitudes stressed particularly the danger, which the girl could do to the community. Her glance could dry up a spring or banish the deer. But among the Yuki in North Central California, the whole focus of the ritual was to influence the food supply of the people for good. The word for adolescence contains an element meaning *to lie,* and the success of the ceremony depended upon the degree to which the girl lay still while the people danced the acorn-song dance. This was followed by a period of licentiousness. The quieter the girl lay, the better would the sun be pleased and the more plentiful would be the crops. Among the Shasta, a girl's dreams at this period were believed to be prophetic. In puberty ceremonials of this type the girl herself is important because of her potency for either good or evil. The society is gathering up all its resources for its own sake rather than to tide a weak new member over a crisis.

In strong contrast to this formalization is a type which was also found in California but was especially pronounced among the Thompson Indians of British Columbia. Here adolescence was regarded as a magical preparation for the girl's later life. The girl was separated from other people and lived by herself in a special hut of fir branches and bark. This isolation lasted four months. During this time she practiced a series of acts of magical potency. She ran long races that she might be fleet of foot; she split fir trees that she might be strong of body. She dug trenches to shorten the duration of her monthly periods. She let pebbles fall from beneath her dress that she might bear children easily. To ensure the purity of her body she stuck the needles of the yellow pine into her skin until it bled. She put pads of wild strawberry leaves under her armpits and prayed that her skin might be sweet smelling. She made moccasins of sunflowers and grass and prayed that her real moccasins, though they became as frail as these, might never fail her when traveling. "If a girl was short, and wanted to be taller, her lodge was made very high; she took hold of one of the lodge poles with both hands, at the same time standing up and addressing the Dawn. Then she put her palms together, with the tips of her middle fingers almost touching her mouth, and taking a mouthful of water, she blew it four times through her tube[1] over the tops of her fingers, each time beseeching the Dawn to make her taller.

... If a girl was afraid she might have large feet, she spat on them at break of day, and, rubbing the toes with her hands, prayed to the Dawn that her feet might be small or that they might not grow any larger." She made models of every article, which she would have to manufacture in later years that she might be industrious.

In these ceremonies the whole stress is upon the girl: she is at the threshold of her career, her observance of taboo and performance of symbolic acts will ensure her a happy and useful life.

Girls in the Gilbert Islands of the Western Pacific were also subjected to a long period of confinement, but the motivation was different. The actual arrival at puberty was an anxious time for parents for the Gilbertese believed that the girl was now especially sensitive to enemy magic. To protect her from this evil she was made to sit perfectly still facing the west, without moving more than was absolutely necessary, eating no cooked food. Afterwards she was usually confined in a special house called a *ko*, where she lived in an inner cubicle in a dense gloom. Here she lived sometimes for a year or eighteen months that her skin might be whitened and her beauty enhanced. She was attended by her grandmother, who massaged her skin and molded her breasts and arms. Unlike the Thompson Indian girl she lived in idleness, as it was too dark for handiwork. But her grandmother taught her all the spells that she knew.

These scattered examples are sufficient to show that physiological puberty, when it is socially recognized, may be recognized in many different ways. And although any ceremony of which the individual is the center will have some significance for her, the effect upon the Thompson Indian girl upon whom endless purposeful activity is enjoined, must be quite different from that upon the Gilbertese girl, who must sit idle, being made beautiful by the command of others. Recognizing that puberty is a physical fact which may be either ignored or patterned as the particular society decrees, we will now look more in detail at the adolescent girl in three quite different societies: Samoa, which stresses puberty neither by ceremony nor uninstitutionalized mental set; the Manus people of the Admiralty Islands, where a great bulk of ritual surrounds first menstruation, which does not, however, coincide with any expectation of a mental crisis in the girl's life; and last, by way of contrast, ourselves, who have no ritual except reiterated anxieties.

In Samoa there are no important taboos relating to menstruation. Women are neither segregated, avoided, nor forbidden to prepare food. The girl at her first menstruation shares in this general lack of interest. The public eye is not upon her. Nor must she hide her new state from her friends: boys and girls can tell accurately the stage of physiological development of every girl in the village. Her outdoor life and general good health ensure her against the severe pain which so often stresses menstruation among modern girls. As she has been familiar with all the facts of procreation and sex physiology since early childhood, no new revelations come at this time. There is no anxious, shamed, but dutiful mother embarrassedly telling her "about life." She is not regarded as immediately marriageable, or even as ready for an amorous career. The whole tradition of Samoa is against hurry, against forcing any aspect of life. This characteristic mental attitude is vividly illustrated by a folk tale in which a polygamous high chief has two wives who each give birth in the same week, competing with each other for the inheritance. The chief prefers, not the first-born, but the child born second, whose mother "was in no unseemly haste." So a Samoan girl is seen to have passed puberty, but no new way of life is thrust suddenly upon her. Sometime in the next two or three years will come her formal entrance into the group of girls who surround the high chief's daughter. This is celebrated by a small feast and means that now she will be among the girls who serve the older women at feasts or entertain visiting youths from other villages. She associates with girls whom she has known intimately all her life and she will continue as a member of this loose, hardly defined group, until the husband whom she will marry presently, assumes a title, when she becomes automatically a titled man's wife. This will not happen until she is many years older, if at all. Meanwhile, two or three years after puberty her casual unimportant love life begins. Her favors are distributed among so many youths, all adepts in amorous technique, that she seldom becomes deeply involved. Her promiscuity seems to ensure her against pregnancy: at least illegitimate children are rare and greeted kindly if they do appear. Heavier industrial tasks are assumed when warranted by a girl's growth: this may precede or follow the attainment of puberty. Her society faces her with no difficult decision, no hard problems, and no new and startling facts. Painlessly, quietly, she slips from childhood into womanhood, loitering by the way, doing her share of the family work, but guarding herself against a reputation for too great proficiency, which might lead to early marriage.

Adolescence becomes not the most difficult, most stressful period of life, but perhaps the pleasantest time the Samoan girl will ever know. In the Samoan household of some fifteen or twenty individuals small girls have much work and little leisure. They are responsible for the baby tending and for all the small routine tasks. They must obey every older member of their household. But the sixteen-year-old girl is near the center of pressure, with as many younger children to command as there are elders to command her. She is relieved of the duties of baby-tending and errand-running and instead performs definite longer tasks. By common consent the nights belong to the young for dancing and courting and love making; and there is time to sleep in the day. So the young girl has freedom but slight responsibility, assurance that she will marry but no pressure to marry quickly. Human nature within a different social form lacks the conflicts, which are so often characteristic of adolescence.

The sea-dwelling people of the Admiralties put puberty in quite a different setting. Here the whole interest of the society is centered about wealth, particularly the exchange of property. Children are often betrothed very young and from the time of the formal betrothal, which is marked by an exchange of property between the kin of the bride and the kin of the groom, they are regarded as married. The little girl is shrouded in a long mat or a length of trade cloth whenever she goes abroad where she is likely to meet either her future husband or any of his male relatives. The line of demarcation between the growing girls in the village is not between those who have passed puberty and those who have not attained it, but between the betrothed and the unbetrothed. The occasional unbetrothed girl past puberty goes about freely, with uncovered head and eyes, which have no need to be alert against forbidden encounters. But the ten-year-old in whose name large numbers of cooking pots and grass skirts, pigs, sacks of sago and jars of oil have been given away, sits demurely veiled and speaks of "we married women." The attitudes of all the adults towards girls is dependent upon this engaged state. Engaged girls should not run about too much with younger children, should not play with boys, should stay at home and make beadwork for their dowries.

The fact of physical puberty is fitted into this context. Every household must make some display when a girl child has her first menses; only if she is "married" is the burden onerous. When a father sees that his daughter is at the point of puberty he collects a large number of cocoanuts. The day that her menses appear these are all thrown into the sea and the neighbors' children dive in and rescue them. The whole village now knows that the girl has attained puberty. A little room is made for her in the center of the house, by hanging up two mats. Here she must sit for five days without washing. Meanwhile, if she is engaged, pots of sago and cocoanut milk are prepared and delivered steaming to her future husband's family. His relatives in their turn bring fish to her family. This goes on for five days. Every night most of the unmarried girls in the village over nine or ten years old go to sleep with the girl. They come after sunset and leave before breakfast, sleeping packed close together in the center of the long, thatched house. At the end of five days large pieces of raw sago are prepared and torches are made of thin bamboo. All the girls gather in the house, to which comes the girl's paternal aunt or her paternal grandmother. The torches are heaped in the fireplace until the house is ablaze with light, then the officiating older woman seizes a torch and chases the girl up and down the house. The chase ended, she pronounces an incantation over her, appealing to all the ancestral spirits of her father's line to bless her, give her strength, give her wealth to finance the marriages of many boys and many girls, and grant that she may become a substantial wealthy woman.

The incantation ended, all the visiting girls carry the torches and great lumps of sago out to a canoe and punt through the village shouting and waving the torches, to place a torch and a lump of sago on the veranda of every relative. After this ceremony the girl is free to move about the house but she may not leave it except to bathe in the sea after dark. Meanwhile her kin are busy working sago to make a big exchange with her betrothed's family. When at last the necessary ton or two of sago, the cook pots, the grass skirts, are all in readiness, and all her relatives from afar have come over the sea to bring their contributions, the final ceremonies are held.

First a great meal of specially prepared sago balls, about the size of grapefruit, is prepared. These are placed in shallow black wooden bowls on the platforms of the family canoes. Then the whole female population repairs to a shallow part of the lagoon. The girl is ceremonially ducked and splashed by all the smaller girls, after which they swim about and pass the sago refreshments to all the visitors. The paternal aunt then pours oil over the girl's head and again recites an incantation. After the food is all distributed, the canoes return to the girl's house where she is decked in strings of dogs' teeth and shell money. Her hair is dyed red; her cheeks are painted with orange. Heavy earrings distend her ears; a long pendant hangs from the pierced septum of her nose. About her waist are fastened two heavy aprons of shell money. All her slender charm is blotted out as she is made into a peg upon which to hang property. The shelves of the village are ransacked to clothe all the other girls in apart of this same kind of finery and so arrayed they board a large canoe and solemnly parade through the village. A few days later canoes laden with oil and pigs and sago are rowed proudly through the village and the bridegroom's family receive them with appropriate speeches. The procession passes a tiny island where the fish skeletons of all the fish the girl has eaten during her confinement are thrown away with an invocation to the family spirits.

The ceremonies (many details of which I have omitted) are at an end. Her relations to her fellows are unchanged. The tasks prescribed for her, bringing wood and water, a little fishing, a little beadwork, lending an occasional hand with the sago making—these are unchanged also.

But the girl has made one discovery; namely, that women menstruate every month and that she must exercise the most unfailing vigilance in concealing her condition at such times.

For through the great antagonism and lack of confidence between the sexes in Manus, coupled with shame and extreme prudery in regard to all the natural functions of the body, women conceal from men the truth about menstruation. Everyone knows of first menstruation; it is heralded through the village, but no man knows, nor will believe if told by an outsider, that a girl menstruates between puberty and marriage. The menstruation of married women is attributed to intercourse; conception is the result of the combination of menstrual blood and semen. This conspiracy of silence is only half-conscious. Unmarried girls presume that married men know the truth; married women are not very clear about the limits of their secret, but simply jealously guard all knowledge of menstruation and birth from all males, including their husbands. The girls themselves, already used to conforming to the demands of a prudish society, count this as one more item for shame and concealment. They are given no zest for the game by being admitted into a conscious conspiracy.

The little girl who is the center of all this ceremonial is shy and solemn and behaves very much as she does when she has her ears pierced, that is, with an air of self-importance tempered by embarrassment. Older girls when questioned about their puberty ceremonials invariably stress two points: how many of their friends came to sleep with them every night and how much property was given away at the final feast. A girl who reaches puberty before she has been betrothed is pitied by her friends: such a puberty ceremonial is a very small show indeed, a mere family affair. I have never heard a girl comment upon the aspect of menstruation or upon the confinement in the house or the magical incantations, which were recited over her. Smaller girls who have not yet reached puberty look forward to having the big house party, the splashing in the sea, and the dressing up centered about themselves.

So here we have elaborate puberty ceremonial involving taboo, confinement, magical incantations, ceremonial washing and anointing with oil, offerings and invocations to the family dead. Half of the village is involved in the feasts held. Immense amounts of property are displayed and exchanged. The ceremony for one engaged adolescent girl may occupy the entire community for weeks. This is equally true of the big economic ceremonies surrounding betrothal, marriage, and birth of the first child, a "silver" wedding, or death. The ceremonious financial arrangements of the culture being cast in the form of exchange between the two parties to a marriage, center about the natural events in the lives of the persons concerned. And it is upon these that the attention of actors and spectators is focused. There is a vague feeling that evil would befall the girl if she broke her taboo of confinement or if the fish spines were not kept, but no one knows what the evil would be.

But with all this stress and fuss and institutionalization of adolescence, it is of very little psychological importance to the girl herself. She does nothing to prepare herself for life; she is confronted with no dangers. She cannot seize this moment to realize her dreams of personal beauty. She is a pawn in an elaborate social scheme and is as much and as little interested as any pawn ever is. The real moments of crises and strain in her life are quite different. If she was engaged as a very small child, the pall of taboo and shamed avoidance of the very names of her husband's kin descends upon her gradually. She is already set apart from her freer age mates and as she grows older sees one of these after another join her state. But this hardly decreases her isolation, for often the girls who as unengaged girls could go fishing with her or join her at her beadwork, are now cut off from her because some of her kin belong to their future husbands' families. The growing up of the girls is marked by less and less fellowship between them. For besides this problem of taboo they have no happy secrets to share with one another. They are marrying boys they have never seen, whose very names they are not allowed to utter. And no romance hovers about the village meanwhile. The Manus language has no word for love, no word for affection or caress. The slightest bit of sex life outside legal marriage is punished by the spirits, by sickness and death, sometimes visited upon the culprit, sometimes visited upon a child or parent. The few young people who do become involved in a hasty, unromantic sex experiment, are reviled by their elders, shunned by their companions. All women fear the love magic of men, which may involve them in sin and misery. Moonlight falls whitely on the village but there is no sound of singing on the water; the daughters of the house are safely within doors.

The adolescent years, sometimes the early years of womanhood, sometimes all the years of childhood, are spoiled by the omnipresent demands of society upon the engaged girl, demands enforced by that subtlest instrument of torture, shame. Whatever age the veil descends upon her is the beginning of psychological maturity for the Manus girl, a grim, dogged, abashed kind of maturity which will not leave her until as the mother of children, the manager of financial transactions in the community, she becomes a person of importance and resumes some of her childhood freedom. Her married life is one of prudish respectability, and often outspoken hostility to her husband. Shame has ruled her life too long to be laid aside for one who also has been stung with the same merciless lash.

It is noteworthy that the strain in a Manus girl's life is distributed with so little reference to puberty—and this in a society, which gives puberty such thoroughgoing cultural recognition. The whole weighty ritual slips over the girl's head and leaves her far less moved than she is by the first occasion when she must go shrouded about the village where formerly she has run as free as a boy. Nor is the period of adolescence that of greatest rebellion in Manus. This comes rather in the early years of marriage, especially when there have been no children or the children have all died. The dreariness of a marriage in which there is neither love nor even any amorous technique, in which there is as yet no common enterprise but where the wife works for her kin and the husband for his, often goads her into rebellion and either elopement or periodic running away to her unenthusiastic relatives.

So we see that it is possible to leave puberty unstressed or to stress it; nor is the deciding factor whether or not the adolescent years will be the storm center in the girl's life. The pattern of social institutions alone is not sufficient to produce or eradicate conflict; it is rather in the far less tangible balancing of cultural forces that the seeds of conflict lie. In Samoa there is no conflict, because the adolescent girl is faced by neither revelation, restriction, nor choice, and because the society expects her to grow up slowly and quietly like a well-behaved flower. In Manus the insistence upon the shamefulness of sex, the repression of all freedom of action that the taboos of betrothal may be observed, the low standard of relations between the sexes, all serve to produce conflict irrespective of the period of adolescence or its elaborate ceremonial.

When we turn from primitive societies to our own, let us lay aside for a moment the many and vivid differences between a primitive and a civilized society and view our own solutions as just another attempt to meet the problems which the California Indians, the Gilbertese, the Samoans, the Manus solve in such different ways. First, take our attitudes towards the physical basis of puberty. We have kept a large enough amount of Victorian prudery so that menstruation seems salacious to men and shameful to girls. We still have many girls who do not know of menstruation until they attain puberty, thus suffering a cruel and utterly purposeless shock. A Manus native walking our streets would approve our practice, a Samoan would be amazed at our strange revulsion towards anything so simple and universal. But our attitude remains such that we could not seize upon first menstruation and institutionalize it even if we wished to do so. The physical facts have been relegated to the back-stairs and our girls are taught the need for lying and circumlocution to account for their backaches and headaches and refusals to play tennis. When we consider the great number, particularly among city girls, who suffer severe pain, we can see how shame and pain play into each other's hands to give an unpleasant feeling tone. But men-struation among ourselves is a problem of hygiene, not a focus for social ceremonial.

If we look at the picture of adolescence among ourselves, what do we find? There is a lack of any rites, any social recognition of the period. There is no segregation of girls who have passed puberty. There is no definite change of costume or method of doing the hair. Institutionally we ignore adolescence as completely as the California Indians recognize it, And yet as the minds of the elders of the tribe were then occupied with the clinking of rattles and the singing of songs to link up the attainment of puberty of one child with the wel-fare of the tribe, the minds of educators among ourselves are similarly, though not so formally, preoccupied. We confront the adolescent girl with a state of mind which demands a far more complex response from her than is demanded by a ritual of sitting still and scratching her head with a scratching stick and observing other similar taboos. The California Indians, the Thompson River Indians, the Gilbert Islanders, prescribed a ritual, a series of definite, easily comprehended acts, often exacting, often boring, but not baffling.

We prescribe no ritual; the girl continues on a round of school or work, but she is constantly confronted by a mysterious apprehen-siveness in her parents and guardians. Her society—if it be a self-con-scious one—has all the tensity of a roomful of people who expect the latest arrival to throw a bomb. This is our puberty ceremonial, unin-stitutionalized in its broader aspects, gaining some explicitness in girls' club work, social secretaries, personnel workers, etc. Our attitude is as mystical as that of the Indian who feels that the girl who has just reached puberty is potent to dry up a spring. Each year the Indian must organize his society to cope with this menace: so we hover about each new group of maturing children, our every gesture indi-cating: "They are certainly going to explode. Let's hope they won't damage anything very important." Such an attitude begets its own offspring—self-conscious nervous unrest in the adolescent.

Yet Samoa and Dobu both suggest that adolescence is not neces-sarily a period of stress and strain, that these familiar and unlovely symptoms are the result of culture rather than original nature. But our present attitude consists not so much in examining the cultural set, which produces these conditions as in regarding the result of these conditions as inevitable and rooted in human nature.

Turning to the kind of conflict which is found in the adolescent girl in our own society, we find that it centers about the problems of sex, the discipline and authority of the home, the assumption or rejection of social responsibility, religious and ethical conflicts. A consideration of primitive society will throw some light upon the degree to which culture may schematize these conflicts.

Despite the evidence from the psychiatrists on the one hand and from such societies as the Trobriands on the other, of prepubertal sexuality, the development of heterosexual interest and activity at puberty does serve to distinguish this period from the periods preceding it and from maturity, in which in most societies heterosexual patterns of behavior have been established.

The growing individual is presented with at least one new problem to solve. This is undoubtedly less of a problem if she has, like the Dobuan or Trobriand girl, engaged in sex play during childhood; it is less of a problem if she has learned something of the mechanism of her own body from manipulation and also has pretty full data about the activities of her elders, as in Samoa. It is even less of a problem for the country girl than for the city girl in our own culture: the country girl can hardly escape a minimum of physiological knowledge, which a city girl often lacks. But all these different educational factors simply vary the intensity with which the girl confronts the need for heterosexual adjustment. Culture can similarly artificially distort the age at which these problems must be met. The present plantation labor system in New Guinea often postpones the period of heterosexual activity for boys several years beyond sexual maturity. With girls who seem to require more definite stimulus to sex interest, segregation is effective in postponing the development of heterosexual interest. But despite the possibilities for alteration, for better or worse, of the intensity of sex adjustment, and the distortion and postponement which culture can produce artificially, there will still be a period at which adjustment must be made without cultural distortion. This period seems to fall in the years following physical puberty in both primitive and modern societies. Students who draw freely on primitive material are likely to assert either that primitive society seizes this period as the most impressionable in a girl's life or that it constructs a gracious *rite de passage* to tide her over a period pregnant with difficulty. These two interpretations of primitive material represent the approaches to the problem of adolescence in our society. The first group is most prominently represented by the churches and also those societies, which put forward social theories in a spirit of pious evangelism. Adolescence is chosen as the ideal moment to get points across, to make permanent recruits, to mold and form ideals. Human nature, young and malleable now, will shortly crystallize into rigid patterns. Let's be sure it crystallizes as we wish it to, say these apostles of special ways of life.

To the other school belong those who regard adolescence as *ipso facto* a period of stress and difficulty, many psychiatrists, social workers, educators. The young life is at its most critical stage; let us handle it delicately, apprehensively, and watchfully. Let us equip ourselves for an inevitable attack of mental and spiritual measles!

Yet primitive material does not support either point of view. The point at which society decides to stress a particular adjustment will be the point at which that adjustment becomes acute to the individual. This is true within the limits indicated above, even of sex. It is preeminently true of adjustment to cultural values less directly oriented to physiology. The period at which religious problems become acute to the individual is the period which social usage declares suitable. Among the Winnebago Indians, young children are sent out into the wilderness to fast and see visions. Whether the children see the visions or merely lie so that they may be taken home again does not alter the fact that religion is forcibly thrust upon their attention long before puberty. In societies like that of some of the Plains Indians, where all men are expected to see visions, religious experience becomes a far more pressing matter than among the California Indians where such experience is reserved for those who wish to become shamans. In Manus the only people who are expected to have any direct contact with the spiritual world are women who have lost male children. Only the mature woman with a dead child, who has paid an older medium to train her and still finds herself unable to understand the talk of the spirits, is faced by a definitely spiritual problem. So the society can define the age and range and sex to which religious experience is presented as a problem to be solved. (This does not of course ignore the presence in every society of a few culturally aberrant individuals.)

Even more subject to cultural definition is the question of the assumption of social responsibility. The Cheyenne treated the tiny bird caught by the child hunter as seriously as the buffalo shot by the grown man. Very young boys were permitted to join war parties and were tenderly guarded by the older men lest thoughtless youth should ridicule their presence. Here social participation was made so gradual and gentle a business that the irksomeness of a sudden accession of responsibility was lacking. In contrast to this is the Manus system by which young boys are free as birds, owing no obligations to their elders until marriage, which reduces them to an ignominious position of acute economic dependence and which makes large demands on their time and energy. Samoa follows a third system in pushing the period when real responsibility is assumed up into the thirties: until that time a man and woman, although married, are insignificant members of a larger household directed by someone else. Perhaps the most drastic deferring of responsibility yet reported is found in the island of Mentawei where some men do not publicly acknowledge their wives nor assume the responsibilities of the head of a household until their own children are half grown and old enough to work for them.

As it is possible to find societies, which can assign these problems to different ages or omit their solution entirely, it is not reasonable to regard them as inherently part of the adolescent period of development. If we are faced with adolescents trying to solve all these difficulties at once, this is an aspect of American civilization, not of human adolescence. Granting that theoretical point, just what do we demand of the adolescent girl?

The American girl does not grow up in a coherent society as does the Manus girl and the Samoan girl. Instead she must enter a world filled with conflicting standards, contrasting philosophies, angry propaganda. Her home is not her world in little, within whose sheltering walls she can learn to play her future part in society. Instead her home subscribes to only a tithe of the standards, only one of the many patterns of her society. Instead of preparing her for life, it often handicaps her by striving to limit and direct her choice in terms of filial devotion. In a primitive society, no matter how fantastic the cultural solutions, the young are forced to subscribe to them because no alternative is presented to them. But in our heterogeneous modern society, choices—of religion or doubt, of kind of work, of type of love—face the girl from the moment she reaches a thinking age. She can choose not only whom she will love, but whether she will love in or out of wedlock, one or many. She can choose love without marriage, marriage without children; she may be tempted occasionally to choose children without marriage. And every girl who consciously makes one of these choices sets small patterns for scores of weaker, less articulate comrades. The burden of painful thought from which even the most mature thinkers have been fain to flee in former ages, is now being thrust, willy-nilly, upon ill-educated inexperienced children. And in addition to this penalty of modern civilization the everyday conditions of American life are complex and difficult for the adolescent.

The average American girl is asked to leave school, become a wage-earner, meet the new demands of living, economically independent but socially dependent in the home where she was hitherto entirely dependent, and to subject her home and its religious and ethical standards to the ordeal of contrast with other standards. All of this is thrust upon her suddenly, in addition to the problem of sex adjustment. This is a pretty selection of puzzling situations to present to any young, untrained person. Certainly even those enthusiasts who feel that adolescence is the time for all things would hardly plan such a tangle. It is rather the combination of several factors: the development of modern education with its sharp dichotomy between school, home, and work; the entrance of women into industrial and office jobs; the tendency of American homes to use economic dependence as their only disciplinary weapon; the great number of discrepant standards and choices which are present in so heterogeneous and changing a culture as present-day America. A number of relatively unrelated forces have combined to make the adolescent stand at the point of highest pressure and difficulty, just as another set of forces place her at the lowest point of pressure in Samoa.

Realizing this, we find there are two possible approaches to the problem. One is to say: granted all this, granted the difficulties of adolescence are culturally determined, we will simply accept the fact that American adolescents are in difficulties because American conditions select this age as the battlefield. If a later age were selected the results would be similar; postponing all these complications would simply postpone the evil day. "Let them get it out of their systems." This would be a logical solution if it were not for the question of sex, the one problem that only the most drastic social settings permit the adolescent to shirk and then with very doubtful results. The problem is socially ruled out in Manus, at great cost to future happiness. It is reasonable then for social philosophers to ask instead: Why should a society demand that an age group with one problem set for it by nature, neglect that problem and solve instead problems which are not particularly germane to this age? Is it not socially wasteful to demand so much from children already preoccupied by sex?

If the answer be in the affirmative, the problem is only posed, not solved. Most of the factors which complicate the lives of the adolescent: changing sex mores, the present economic system, the heterogeneity of American society, are hardly subject to manipulation by the most earnest social legislator or purveyor of panaceas. We cannot make the choices of our adolescents easy, nor can we postpone them. Probably the most we can do is to devise a new ritual of expectation. Judge Lindsey has attempted to do this in trying to make people recognize the experiments of young people as natural, inevitable accompaniments of present-day society. An acceptance of his humane and reasoned viewpoint would have more influence upon relations between children and parents than it would, presumably, upon the number of irregular sex unions of young people in their teens. The attitudes of the adult world are by and large the more malleable material for manipulation. The Gilbert Islander kindles a fire on his son's shaven head and expects the boy to bear it without flinching. If he denied the presence of the fire on the one hand and with the other nervously grasped a pail of water to quench the flames if they spread too far, the ordeal would be far harder for the boy.

So it is with our youth. We cannot, if we would, vary the ordeal to any marked extent. Our hands are practically as tied as those of the Gilbertese condemned by tradition to torture young initiates.

But we have one great superiority over him, over all primitive peoples. To them their customs are immune from criticism—given, ordained, immutable. They move unselfconsciously within the pattern of their homogenous, self-contained societies. We, caught almost as completely in a far more complex pattern, have acquired the ability to think about it. Our young people pay the price of heterogeneity in the choices, which they must make, choices that never confront primitive youth. But it is possible for us to give them in some slight measure the benefit of that heterogeneity also. It is choice, which makes us culture-conscious, which makes it possible for us to see our society as a complex of possible courses. If we trained our children to meet this emergency of choice, this emergency which we cannot shirk for them if we would, we might go far to ameliorate the secondary difficulties of adolescents and leave them free to solve the sex problems proper to their ages. Those who admire the ordered rituals of primitive man would do well to devise a less explicit but even more compelling puberty ritual in which training is substituted for anxiety, confidence for apprehension, in our conscious dealings with the younger generation.

In comparing primitive and modern societies, one other marked contrast between their adolescence is most notable. If we lay aside the purely physical definition of physical maturity and consider adolescence as the period following childhood during which the individual becomes placed in his society, we are struck at once by the enormous difference in range. Our material on individual adjustment in primitive society is slight, but such as it is it suggests that the unplaced person who has as yet come to no terms with his society is comparatively rare. Even marked potentialities for maladjustment, such as definite inversion, are very frequently fitted into a social pattern. The invert assumes the dress and habits of the opposite sex and from a stable social position adapts to his or her culture. Less pronounced liability to maladjustment does not seem to be accentuated in isolated societies without a complex cultural tradition. The conditioning to maladjustment, given by a home with one standard and a community with another, or by a diversity of possible social values, is by definition less frequent. The primitive culture, being coherent, seizes upon every individual born within it. Some will be temperamentally fitted to seeing visions or bargaining over dogs' teeth or devising social ceremonial, or whatever career the culture regards as preeminently desirable: these will be the leaders; the others are less distinguished adherents of the values which home and friends and neighbors all uphold. Only the extreme aberrant is selected out.

Any complex modern society presents a contrast to this. Although a civilization like America may set a definite premium upon a career, which deals with things, either as an engineer or as a financier, there are groups, which regard the career of the artist, the writer, the evangelist as of far higher value. There are monasteries for those who wish to deny the world, soapboxes or the formal stage for those who wish to play to an audience. Whether or not any one girl can actually make her own the one of these many choices which is most congenial to her, it does not change the effect upon youth's adjustment. With a range of possibilities equal to the range of temperaments, though most unequally possible of achievement, adolescence as a period of adjustment is inevitably prolonged. Besides the great number of young people who accept or choose a way of life at eighteen and placidly live it for all their active years are the ever increasing number of self-conscious individuals who make many and costly experiments before they are finally placed. Such experiments are unthinkable in an isolated primitive society.

This aspect of complex societies has affected men for generations. It is just beginning to affect women in our society. Marriage or the convent, or even marriage or a decent, socially defined, restrained spinsterhood did not give the range of choice open to girls today. To her the choice of a sex pattern is more pressing than to her brother: she has now also the possibilities of choice among careers, among ways of life which answer needs not met by any pattern of personal relations or physiological function. Because sex complicates a woman's life more conspicuously than a man's, the adolescent unplaced woman is perhaps an even more frequent phenomenon in urban life than is the unplaced man.

The analogy between primitive and modern society vanishes when we consider adolescence, which is the growth period of personality as a function of complex society, not merely of the human life cycle. It is conceivable that in societies more complex than ours this type of adolescence will encroach even more on the years of maturity and that while the primitive girl or boy is ready to assume the burden of his or her tradition at twenty and carry it unquestioningly to the grave, many of our most potentially gifted individuals will die adolescent, unplaced, and without realizing any of the promise of their genius. Among the Thompson Indians the gifted and the ungifted pass through a definite ritual to take their ordained places in their societies. But for the adolescence of the spirit there is no puberty ceremonial.

NOTE

1. This was a drinking tube, since it was forbidden for her mouth to touch water directly. It was the hollowed leg bone of a crane, a swan or a goose.

REFERENCES

BENEDICT, RUTH FULTON, "The Concept of the Guardian Spirit in North America." *Memoirs of the American Anthropological Association,* No.29. Also "The Science of Custom," *The Century,* April 1929.

GRIMDLE, ARTHUR, "From Birth to Death in the Gilbert Islands." *Journal of the Royal Anthropological Institute.* 1921. Vol. 51, pp. 25-54.

GRINNEL, GEORGE BIRD, *The Cheyenne Indians: Their History and Ways of Life.* Yale University Press, New Haven, 1923.

HOWITT, A. W., *The Native Tribes of South East Australia.* Macmillan and Co. London, 1904.

KROEBER, A. L., *Handbook of the Indians of California.* Bureau of American Ethnology, Bulletin 78. Washington, Government Printing Office, 1925.

LOEB, E. M., "Mentawei Social Organization." *American Anthropologist.* July-September 1928. Pp. 408-433.

MALINOWSKI, B., *The Sexual Life of Savages*. G. K. Routledge and Co., London, 1928. Liveright; New York, 1929.

MEAD, M., *Coming of Age in Samoa*. William Morrow & Co. New York, 1928.

RADIN, PAUL, *Crashing Thunder: The Autobiography of an American Indian*. D. Appleton and Co. New York, 1926.

RIVERS, W. H. R., *The Todas*. The Macmillan Co. London, 1906.

TEIT, JAMES, "The Thompson Indians of British Columbia." XX. *Memoirs of the American Museum of Natural History*. Vol. 2, iv. 1898-1900.

WILLIAMS, THOMAS, AND CALVERT, JAMES, *Fiji and the Fijians*. New York, 1859.

OUR EDUCATIONAL EMPHASES IN
PRIMITIVE PERSPECTIVE[1]*

Modern conceptions of education are contrasted with the primitive emphasis upon the need to learn that which was fixed and traditional, based primarily on the child as the learner. Today, owing to the meeting and mingling of peoples among whom superiority was claimed by one as over against another, our concepts of education have been shaped by the will to teach, convert, colonize, or assimilate adults. From the observation of this process in the next generation we have come also to believe in the power of education to create something new, not merely perpetuate something old. But not until the dogma of superiority of race over race, nation over nation, class over class, is obliterated can we hope to combine the primitive idea of the need to learn something old and the modern idea of the possibility of making something new.

In its broadest sense, education is the cultural process, the way in which each newborn human infant, born with a potentiality for learning greater than that of any other mammal, is transformed into a full member of a specific human society, sharing with the other members a specific human culture. From this point of view we can place side by side the newborn child in a modern city and the savage infant born into some primitive South Sea Tribe. Both have everything to learn. Both depend for that learning upon the help and example, the care and tutelage, of the elders of their societies. Neither child has any guaranty of growing up to be a full human being should some accident, such as theft by a wolf, interfere with its human education. Despite the tremendous difference in what the New York infant and the New Guinea infant will learn, there is a striking similarity in the whole complicated process by which the child takes on and into itself the culture of those around it. And much profit can be gained by concentrating on these similarities and by setting the procedure of the South Sea mother side by side with the procedure of the New York mother, attempting to understand the common elements in cultural transmission. In such comparisons we can identify the

*Originally published in *From Child to Adult: Studies in the Anthropology of Education*. John Middleton, ed., 1970.

tremendous potentialities of human beings, who are able to learn not only to speak any one of a thousand languages but to adjust to as many different rhythms of maturation, ways of learning methods of organizing their emotions and of managing their relationships to other human beings.

In this paper, however, I propose to turn away from this order of comparison—which notes the differences between human cultures, primitive and civilized, only as means of exploring the processes which occur in both types of culture—and to stress instead the ways in which our present behavior, which we bracket under the abstraction "education," differs from the procedures characteristic of primitive homogeneous communities. I propose to ask, not what there is in common between America in 1941 and South Sea culture which displays in 1941 a Stone Age level of culture, but to ask instead: What are some of the conspicuous differences, and what light do these differences throw upon our understanding of our own conception of education? And, because this is too large and wide a subject, I want to limit myself still further and to ask a question which is appropriate to this symposium: What effects has the mingling of peoples—of different races, different religions, and different levels of cultural complexity—had upon our concept of education? When we place our present-day concept against a backdrop of primitive educational procedures and see it as influenced by intermingling of peoples, what do we find?

I once lectured to a group of women—all of them college graduates—alert enough to be taking a fairly advanced adult-education course on "Primitive Education" delivered from the first point of view. I described in detail the lagoon village of the Manus tribe, the ways in which the parents taught the children to master their environment, to swim, to climb, to handle fire, to paddle a canoe, to judge distances and calculate the strength of materials. I described the tiny canoes which were given to the three-year-olds, the miniature fish spears which they learned to spear minnows, the way in which small boys learned to calk their canoes with gum, and how small girls learned to thread shell money in aprons. Interwoven with a discussion of the more fundamental issues, such as the relationship between children and parents and the relationships between younger children and older children, I gave a fairly complete account of the type of adaptive craft behavior which was characteristic of the Manus and the way in which this was learned by each generation of children. At the end of the lecture one woman stood up and asked the first question: "Didn't they have any vocational training?" Many of the others laughed at the question, and I have often told myself as a

way of getting my audience into a mood which was less rigidly limited by our own phrasing of the "education." But that woman's question, naïve and crude as it was, epitomized a long series of changes
which stand between our idea of education and the processes by
which members of a homogeneous and relatively static primitive
society transmit their standardized habit patters to their children.

There are several striking differences between our concept of education today and that of any contemporary primitive society;[2] but perhaps the most important one is the shift from the need for an
individual to learn something which everyone agrees he would wish to
know, to the will of some individual to teach something which it is not
agreed that anyone has any desire to know. Such a shift in emphasis
could come only with the breakdown of self-contained and self-
respecting cultural homogeneity. The Manus or the Arapesh or the Iatmul adults taught their children all that they knew themselves.
Sometimes, it is true, there were rifts in the process. A man might die
without having communicated some particular piece of ritual knowledge; a good hunter might find no suitable apprentice among his available near kin, so that his skill perished with him. A girl might be so
clumsy and stupid that she never learned to weave a mosquito basket
that was fit to sell. Miscarriages in the smooth working of the transmission of available skills and knowledge did occur, but they were not
sufficient to focus the attention of the group upon the desirability of
teaching as over against the desirability of *learning*. Even with considerable divisions of labor and with a custom by which young men learned
a special skill not from a father or other specified relative but merely
from a master of the art, the master did not go seeking pupils; the
pupils and their parents went to seek the master and with proper gifts
of fish or octopus or dogs' teeth persuaded him to teach the neophyte.
And at this level of human culture even close contact with members of
other cultures did not alter the emphasis. Women who spoke another
language married into the tribe; it was, of course, very important that
they should learn to speak the language of their husbands' people and
so they learned that language as best they could—or failed to learn it.
People might compliment them on their facility or laugh at them for
their lack of it, but the idea of *assimilating* them was absent.

Similarly, the spread of the special cults of sects among South Sea
people, the desire to *join* the sect rather than the need to make con-
verts, was emphasized. New ceremonies did develop. It was necessary
that those who had formerly been ignorant of them should learn new
songs or new dance steps, but the onus was again upon the learner.
The greater self-centeredness of primitive homogeneous groups (often
so self-centered that they divided mankind into two groups—the

human beings, i.e., themselves, and the nonhuman beings, other people) preserved them also from the emphasis upon the greater value of one truth over another which is the condition of proselytizing. "*We* (human beings) do it this way and *they* (other people) do it that way." A lack of desire to teach *them* our ways guaranteed also that the *we* group had no fear of any proselytizing from the *they* groups. A custom might be imported, bought, obtained by killing the owner, or taken as part of a marriage payment. A custom might be exported for a price or a consideration. But the emphasis lay upon the desire of the importing group to obtain the new skill or song and upon the desire of the exporting group for profit in material terms by the transaction. The idea of conversion, or purposely attempting to alter the ideas and attitudes of other persons, did not occur. One might try to persuade one's brother-in-law to abandon his own group and come and hunt permanently with the tribe into which his sister had married; physical proselytizing there was, just as there was actual import and export of items of culture. But, once the brother-in-law had been persuaded to join a different cultural group, it was his job to learn how to live there; and you might, if you were still afraid he would go back or if you wanted his cooperation in working a two-man fish net, take considerable pains to teach him this or that skill as a bribe. But to bribe another by teaching him one's own skill is a long way from any practice of conversion, although it may be subsidiary to it.

We have no way of knowing how often in the course of human history the idea of Truth, as a revelation to or possession of some one group (which thereby gained the right to consider itself superior to all those who lacked this revelation), many have appeared. But certain it is that, wherever this notion of hierarchal arrangements of cultural views of experience appears, it has profound effects upon education; and it has enormously influenced our own attitudes toward education. As soon as there is any attitude that one set of cultural beliefs is definitely superior to another, the framework is present for active proselytizing, unless the idea of cultural superiority is joined with some idea of hereditary membership, as it is among the Hindus. (It would indeed be interesting to investigate whether any group which considered itself in possession of the most superior brand of religious or economic truth, and which did not regard its possession as limited by heredity, could preserve the belief in that superiority without proselytizing. It might be found that active proselytizing was the necessary condition for the preservation of the essential belief in one's own revelation.) Thus, with the appearance of religions which held this belief in their own infallible superiority, education becomes a concern of those who teach rather than those who learn. Attention is directed toward finding neophytes rather than toward finding masters, and adults and children become bracketed together as recipients of conscious missionary effort. This bracketing-together is of great importance; it increases the self-consciousness of the whole educational procedure, and it is quite possible that the whole question of methods and techniques of education is brought most sharply to the fore when it is a completely socialized adult who must be influenced instead of a plastic and receptive child.

With social stratification the possibility of using education as a way of changing status is introduced, and another new component of the educational idea develops. Here the emphasis is still upon the need to learn—on the one hand, in order to alter status and, on the other, to prevent the loss of status by failure to learn. But wherever this possibility enters in there is also a possibility of a new concept of education developing from the relationship between fixed caste and class lines and education. In a static society members of different caste or class groups may have been teaching their children different standards of behavior for many generations without any essential difference between their attitudes toward education and those of less complex societies. To effect a change it is necessary to focus the attention of the members of the society upon the problem, as conditions of cultural contact do focus it. Thus, in present-day Bali, the high castes are sending their daughters to the Dutch schools to be trained as schoolteachers because it is pre-eminently important that learning should be kept in the hand of the high castes and profoundly inappropriate that low-caste teacher should teach high-caste children. They feel this strongly enough to overcome their prejudices against the extent to which such a course takes high-caste women out into the market place.

As soon as the possibility of shift of class position by virtue of a different education experience becomes articulately recognized, so that individuals seek not only to better their children or to guard them against educational defect but also to see the extension of restriction of educational opportunity as relevant to the whole class structure, another element enters in—the relationship of education to social change. Education becomes a mechanism of change. Public attention, once focused upon this possibility, is easily turned to the converse position of emphasizing education as a means toward preserving the status quo. I argue here for no historical priority in the two positions. But I am inclined to believe that we do not have catechumens taught to say "to do my duty in that state of life into which it has pleased God to call me" until we have the beginning of movements of individuals away from their birth positions in society. In fact, the whole use of education to defend vested interests and entrenched privilege goes with the recognition that education can be a way of encroaching upon them. Just as the presence of proselytizing religions focuses attentions upon means of spreading the truth, upon pedagogy, so the educational implications of social stratification focus attention upon the content of education and lay the groundwork for an articulate interest in the curriculum.

Movements of peoples, colonization, and trade also bring education into a different focus. In New Guinea it is not uncommon to "hear" (i.e., understand without speaking) several languages besides one's own, and many people not only "hear" but also speak neighboring languages. A head-hunting people like the Mundugumor, who had the custom of giving child hostages to temporary allies among neighboring peoples, articulately recognized that it was an advantage to have members of the group be well acquainted with the roads, the customs, and the language of their neighbors, who would assuredly at some time in any given generation be enemies and objects of attack. Those who took the hostages regarded this increased facility of the Mundugumor as a disadvantage which had to be put up with. But the emphasis remained with the desirability of learning. Today, with the growth of pidgin English as a lingua franca, bush natives and young boys are most anxious to learn pidgin. Their neighbors, with whom they could trade and communicate more readily if they know pidgin are not interested in teaching them. But the European colonist is interested. He sees his position as an expanding, initiating, changing one; he wants to trade with the natives, to recruit and indenture them to work on plantations. He needs to have them speak language that he can understand. Accordingly, we have the shift from the native who needs to learn another language so that he, the colonist, may be understood. In the course of teaching natives to speak some lingua franca, to handle money, to work copra, etc., the whole focus is on teaching; not, however, on techniques of teaching, in the sense of pedagogy, but upon sanctions from making the native learn. Such usages develop rapidly into compulsory schooling in the language of the colonist or the conqueror, and they result in the school's being seen as an adjunct of the group in power rather than as a privilege for those who learn.

Just as conquest or colonization of already inhabited countries brings up the problems of assimilation, so as mass migrations may accentuate the same problem. This has been true particularly in the United States, where education has been enormously influenced by the articulate need to assimilate the masses of European immigrants, with the resulting phrasing of the public schools as a means for educating other peoples' children. The school ceased to be chiefly a device by which children were taught accumulated knowledge or skills and became a political device for arousing and maintaining national loyalty through inculcating a language and a system of ideas which the pupils did not share with their parents.

It is noteworthy that, in the whole series of educational emphases which I have discussed here as significant components of our present-day concept of "education," one common element which differentiates the ideas of conversion, assimilation, successful colonization, and the relationship between class-caste lines and education from attitudes found in primitive homogeneous societies is the acceptance of discontinuity between parents and children, even if the actual teacher was not a parent but a maternal uncle or a shaman. Modern education includes a heavy emphasis upon the function of education to create discontinuities—to turn the child of the peasant into a clerk, of the farmer into a lawyer, of the Italian immigrant into an American, of the illiterate into the literate. And parallel to this emphasis goes the attempt to use education as an extra, special prop for tottering continuities. Parents who are separated from their children by all the gaps in understanding which are a function of our rapidly changing world cling to the expedient of sending their children to the same schools and colleges they attended, counting upon the heavy traditionalism of slow-moving institutions to stem the tide of change. (Thus, while the father builds himself a new house and the mother furnishes it with modern furniture, they both rejoice that back at school, through the happy accident that the school is not well enough endowed, son will sit at the same desk at which his father sat.) The same attitude is reflected by the stock figure of the member of a rural school board who says, "What was good enough for me in school in good enough for my children. The three R's, that's enough."

Another common factor in these modern trends of education is the increasing emphasis upon change rather than upon growth, upon what is done to people rather than upon what people do. This emphasis comes, I believe, from the inclusion of adults as objects of the educational effort—whether the effort comes from missionaries, colonizers, conquerors, Old Americans, or employers of labor. When a child is learning to talk, the miracle of learning is so pressing and conspicuous that the achievement of the teachers is put in the shade. But the displacement, in an adult's speech habits, of his native tongue by the phonetics of some language which he is being bullied or cajoled into learning is often more a matter of triumph for the teacher than of pride for the learner. Changing people's habits, people's ideas, people's language, people's beliefs, people's emotional allegiances, involves a sort of deliberate violence to other people's developed personalities—a violence not to be found in the whole teacher-child relationship, which finds its prototype in the cherishing parent helping the young child to learn those things which are essential to his humanity.

We have been shocked in recent years by the outspoken brutality of the totalitarian states, which set out to inculcate into children's minds a series of new ideas which it was considered politically useful for them to learn. Under the conflicting currents of modern ideologies the idea of *indoctrination* has developed as a way of characterizing the conscious educational aims of any group with whom the speaker it out of sympathy. Attempts to teach children any set of ideas in which one believes have become tainted with suspicion of power and self-interest, until almost all education can be branded and dismissed as one sort of indoctrination or another. The attempt to assimilate, convert, or keep in their places other human beings conceived of as inferior to those who are making the plans has been a boomerang which has distorted our whole educational philosophy; it has shifted the emphasis from one of growth and seeking for knowledge to one of dictation and forced acceptance of clichés and points of view. Thus we see that the presence of one element within our culture—a spurious sense of superiority of one group of human beings over another, which gave the group in power the impetus to force their language, their beliefs, and their culture down the throats of the group which was numerically, or economically, or geographically handicapped— has corrupted and distorted the emphases of our free schools.

But there has been another emphasis developing side by side with those which I have been discussing, and that is a belief in the power of education to work miracles—a belief which springs from looking at the other side of the shield. As long as the transmission of culture is an orderly and continuous process, in a slowly changing society, the child speaks the language of his parents; and, although one may marvel that his small human being learns at all, one does not marvel that he learns French or English or Samoan, provided that this be the language of the parents. It took the discontinuity of educational systems, purposive shifts of language and beliefs between parents and children to catch our imagination and to fashion the great American faith in education as creation rather than transmission, conversion, suppression, assimilation, or indoctrination. Perhaps one of the most basic human ways of saying "new" is "something that my parents have never experienced" or, when we speak of our children, "something I have never experienced." The drama of discontinuity which has been such a startling feature of modern life, and for which formal education has been regarded in great measure as responsible, suggested to mean that perhaps education might be a device for creating a new kind of world by developing a new kind of human being.

Here it is necessary to distinguish sharply between the sort of idea which George Counts expressed in his speech, "Dare the Schools Build a New Social Order?" and the idea of education as creation of something new. Dr. Counts did not mean a new social order in the sense of an order that no man had dreamed of, so much as he meant a very concrete and definite type of society for which he and many others believed they had a blueprint. He was asking whether the teachers would use the schools to produce a different type of socioeconomic system. His question was still a power question and partook of all the power ideas which have developed in the long period during which men in power, men with dominating ideas, men with missions, have sought to put their ideas over upon other men. His question would have been phrased more accurately as "Dare the schools build a different social order?" The schools of America have these hundred years been training children to give allegiance to a way of life that was new to them, not because they were children to whom all ways were new, not because the way of life was itself one that no man had yet dreamed of, but because they were the children of their parents. Whenever one group succeeds in getting power over the schools and teaches within those schools a doctrine foreign to many of those who enter those doors, they are building up, from the standpoint of those students, a different social order. From the standpoint of those in power, they are defending or extending the old; and, from the moment that the teachers had seriously started to put Dr. Counts's suggestion into practice, they would have been attempting by every method available to them to extend, in the mind of other people's children, their own picture, already an "old" idea, of the sort of world they wanted to live in.

It is not this sort of newness of which I speak. But from those who watched learning, those who humbly observed miracles instead of claiming them as the fruits of their strategy or of their superior teaching (propaganda) techniques, there grew up in America a touching belief that it was possible by education to build a new world—a world that no man had yet dreamed and that no man, bred as we had been bred, could dream. They argued that if we can bring up our children to be freer than we have been—freer from anxiety, freer from guilt and fear, freer from economic constraint and the dictates of expedience—to be equipped as we never were equipped, trained to think and enjoy thinking, trained to feel and enjoy feeling, then we shall produce a new kind of human being, one not known upon the earth before. Instead of the single visionary, the depth of those whose vision has kept men's souls alive for centuries, we shall develop a whole people bred to the task of seeing with clear imaginative eyes into a future which is hidden from us behind the smoke screen of our defective and irremediable educational handicaps. This belief has often been branded as naïve and simple-minded. The American faith in education, which Clark Wissler lists as one of the dominant American culture traits, has been held up to ridicule many times. In many of its forms it is not only unjustified optimism but arrant nonsense. When small children are sent out by overzealous schoolteacher to engage in active social reforms—believed necessary by their teacher—the whole point of view becomes not only ridiculous but dangerous to the children themselves.

Phrased, however, without any of our blueprints, with an insistence that it is the children themselves who will some day, when they are grown, make blueprints on the basis of their upbringing, the idea is a bold and beautiful one, an essentially democratic and American idea. Instead of attempting to bind and limit the future and to compromise the inhabitants of the next century by a long process of indoctrination which will make them unable to follow any path but that which we have laid down, it suggests that we devise and practice a system of education which sets the future free. We must concentrate upon teaching our children to walk so steadily that we need not hew too straight and narrow paths for them but can trust them to make new paths through difficulties we never encountered to a future of which we have no inkling today.

When we look for the contributions which contacts of peoples, of peoples of different races and different religions, different levels of culture and different degrees of technological development, have made to education, we find two. On the one hand, the emphasis has shifted from learning to teaching, from the doing to the one who causes it to be done, from spontaneity to coercion, from freedom to power. With this shift has come the development of techniques of power, dry pedagogy, regimentation, indoctrination, manipulation, and propaganda. These are but sorry additions to man's armory, and they come from the insult to human life which is perpetuated whenever one human being is regarded as differentially less or more human than another. But, on the other hand, out of the discontinuities and rapid changes which have accompanied these minglings of people has come another invention, one which perhaps would not have been born in any other setting than this one—the belief in education as an instrument for the creation of new human values.

We stand today in a crowded place, where millions of men mill about seeking to go in different directions. It is most uncertain whether the educational invention made by those who emphasized teaching or the educational invention made by those who emphasized learning will survive. But the more rapidly we can erase from our society those discrepancies in position and privilege which tend to perpetuate and strengthen the power and manipulative aspects of education, the more hope we may have that that other invention—the use of education for unknown ends which shall exalt man above his present stature—may survive.

AMERICAN MUSEUM OF NATURAL HISTORY

NOTES

1. This paper is an expression of the approach of the Council of Inter-cultural Relations.
2. This discussion, unless otherwise indicated, is based upon South Sea people only.

EARLY CHILDHOOD EXPERIENCE AND LATER EDUCATION IN COMPLEX CULTURES*

Education in a complex society may be seen as merely an extension of the educational process found in simpler societies, but taking longer, requiring more specialized institutions, and involving progressive absorption into wider or narrower segments of the total society. Or it may be seen as involving, from the very start (from the moment that a rattle is put into an infant's hands, or a set of alphabet blocks is spilled on the floor) a set of assumptions that are different in kind from education in a primitive society. Both approaches have their uses. By taking the former, Hart (1955) and Yehudi Cohen (1964) have been able to point out striking correspondences between the treatment of the prepubertal and pubertal young, and the initiation ceremonies and educational experiences to which they are subjected. I have used the same approach in discussing such questions as the way in which children learn sex roles or control of impulse (Mead, 1930, 1931d, 1935). It may be said that where we are concerned with character formation—the process by which children learn to discipline impulses and structure their expectations of the behavior of others—this cross-cultural approach is very valuable. It provides insights into such subjects as conscience formation, the relative importance of different sanctioning systems, sin, shame and pride, and guilt, and into the relationships between independence training and achievement motivation.

It may be argued that the younger the child, the more we are concerned with educational processes that are universal and of fundamental importance throughout life, and least imbued with the specific cultural differences that distinguish a Frenchman from an Egyptian, or an Eskimo from a Bushman or from an American. All infants must be weaned, but only a certain number will ultimately be asked to master calculus or a dead language. All infants must learn to respond with enthusiasm or apathy to adult incentives, but only a

*Originally published in *Anthropological Perspectives on Education*, eds. M. Wax, S. Diamond, and F. Gearing. New York: Basic Books, 1971.

certain number, in identified countries and at particular periods, will come to care about the controversies between Stoics and Epicureans, or between fundamentalists and contextualists. So it has been fashionable in many areas in which the relationship between child development and later character has been studied, to concentrate on uniformly present experiences, and to ignore the subtler and more difficult problems of what as well as how the child is learning.

Take, for example, the question of reward and punishment. It is relatively easy to characterize systems of child-rearing as using either reward or punishment in certain distinguishable proportions. The reflections of this learning can be followed in later life, and differences can be demonstrated in the school performance of children who act out fear of being wrong, as compared with those who actively seek rewards for being right. Such reflections can also be recognized later in the conformist behavior of the civil servant—secure unless he makes a positive mistake—and in the freer behavior of the politician who must perform in some positive manner if he is to be rewarded by re-election. It is upon the recognition of identifiable sequences such as these that constructs such as David McClelland's (1953) achievement motivation are built.

LITERACY

But we may ask instead what happens if we stress what a modern society requires its new members to learn, rather than start with the relationship between early disciplines and later learning. For purposes of study, we would then juxtapose two societies—one that required that children learn to read and the other that did not. We would not consider learning to read in terms of motivation, of who taught the child his letters, or whether, while learning, the child had his hands smacked, or had honey put on his tongue. We would say, instead, that learning to read involves first the idea that such a thing as reading exists, that artificial marks that are small, regular, identifiable, and recurrent have meaning. We would note that when someone who can read looks at one book, he utters a particular series of words, while if he looks at another book, he utters a different series of words. Children often learn this elementary fact by associating sequences of words with pictures, and "read" by reciting a memorized sentence that goes with a particular picture. They may then move to the over-all "look" of the sentence—whether it is long or short or contains a certain number of capital letters. The child who does this is not learning to read, but is, in fact, learning an early form of reading badly. He is dependent upon past experience and upon the extraneous and irrelevant likeness between the contours of words but is skipping the stage of learning that is the essence of reading—the arbitrary correspondence between symbols and sounds.

So one child may learn, depending upon the kind of home in which he lives, that there are many, many books, that the pages of each yield different materials, and that if he can learn to decipher these pages he will have a new experience, as compared with another child who learns to repeat, from minor clues, a sentence that an adult has read to him. This fundamental piece of over-all learning is probably determinative of whether individuals will be literate or nonliterate, no matter how much schooling they are exposed to. The history of developing countries—in which education is imposed, often in a different language, on people who own no books and read no newspaper—has demonstrated how it is possible to make a people formally literate, able to read and write simple information, decipher signs, and keep lists and records, although they never read, in the sense that they pick up a written object of unknown content. Sometimes, children from nonreading homes may learn by accident, later in life, that reading is a way of opening a window to something new. These individuals experience a tremendous sense of freedom and enlightenment, comparable in freshness but often greater in intensity to the experience of a child who for the first time reads something new by himself. Elementary education geared to establishing literacy but not reading ability in people who are thought of as "the masses" or even "the people," carries with it a continuation of what the child has learned at home. It strengthens the concept that reading is simply saying what you know is there (for example, whether today is Monday or Tuesday, or if it is the first or the second of the month) instead of being a way of finding out things you don't know, or of reading a new story with an end you don't know.[1]

One of the familiar phenomena of the American scene in the post World War II years, is the terrible boredom that reading parents feel toward Dick and Jane, the reader based on the simple expectation that learning to read is learning to reproduce correctly only what is in the reader.

A terrible degeneration accompanies the shift from teachers who read to teachers who do not read. It is often found in developing countries, as missionaries are phased out in favor of native speakers who never read but can teach competently enough from a text. Teachers who read can teach children what reading is about; teachers who have not learned to read but have only learned to be literate, cannot do this.

So we may usefully compare the infant in a primitive preliterate home, the infant in a literate but nonreading home, and the infant in a reading home. The infant in the primitive home never sees any event that suggests that there is a substitute for the spoken and heard word. If his father wants to send a message to his brother-in-law in the next village, someone has to go and tell him. If it is important to know whether a debt consists of forty dog's teeth or only of thirty, there is a lengthy debate with supporting evidence, and the matter is likely to be clinched by the dictum of whichever participant is most respected or known to have the most accurate memory. There is no way to go back to the event in question except in memory, and people's memories differ. Whether the child will learn that an event actually did occur, and that different people give different versions, some more accurate than others, or simply that the world consists of claims and counterclaims that are designed to promote the purpose of one person rather than another, depends upon the particular culture. This may seem a very small point, but it is perhaps not an accident that those people whose interest in relating past events is simply to validate present purposes, may, when writing comes to them, use it for forgery rather than for records. In contrast, those people who have been deeply concerned over establishing the actuality of an event, take delightedly to the possibilities of script that can provide them with accurate records and cross-checks on the process. This difference between regarding script as accurate and reliable, and regarding it as something to be manipulated, reflecting as it does much earlier attitudes—recurs at many levels of the use of records. It is seen, for example, in the fundamentalist approach to the Scriptures, which is based on an excessive reverence for the written word among people who themselves could read but did not write. It is seen in other peculiar manifestations, such as the willingness of otherwise well-trained scientists to believe that a film, in which they are dependent on the experimenter to identify the subjects, nevertheless is convincing proof that something occurred.

So, in the primitive home, into which the idea of script will penetrate with conquest and community development programs, are already a series of underlying expectancies that will partly shape the ways in which reading and writing will be learned. One of these expectancies will be the amount of curiosity that is cultivated within the particular sociocultural setting. If there is a strong interest in the strange and the unknown, then the groundwork is laid for looking at pictures and later reading books about that which is not known. Or one may find the society in which there is strong genealogical interest. Where writing is done by individuals it is used primarily to preserve the history of the family, the only photographs in which people are interested are those of family members. The intermediate position in which pages of *Life* magazine are pasted sideways on the wall to cover a crack, or as meaningless decorations, are active preparations for the rejection of reading. Probably the single picture pasted sideways is more threatening to the future literacy of children in the family than the differences in abstract and concrete thinking being so heavily emphasized today. The picture pasted sideways means that the symbolic nature of position in space is ignored, and also very often that even the representational quality of the picture is ignored; it becomes a bright red splotch on a gray wall.[2]

The first introduction of a primitive people to script may come in a variety of ways. A government official may come into the village and try to take a census. As people repeat their names, he writes down their responses, often with only the most faulty approximations. But still, since people remember things such as the order in which they gave their names, they can recognize their names the next time the official comes. At this point, another essential piece of learning may occur. Writing is seen as a way in which people can get the better of you, know who you are, relate your past actions to the future, check on whom you married, how many children you have, and where you live. In New Guinea, natives almost invariably responded in this way to attempts at census-taking by the government. It became fashionable to have a "government name" that was used for no other purpose, and that people remembered only with the greatest difficulty from one governmental visit to the next. Instead of records being considered as away in which one becomes securely placed in the world, so that over a period of time one's identity becomes firmer and more unassailable, record-keeping is thus turned into a hostile act. This response of the illiterate to the record-keeping abilities of the powers that be is reflected at a higher level in current attitudes toward a central computer. Such concern is constantly expressed as a fear that knowledge of who you are will only be used to do you damage. In New Guinea, the response means that electoral rolls are almost impossible to compile, that savings bank accounts lie dormant because the depositor has not claimed them—in fact, has often forgotten the name under which they were deposited—and that individuals who need treatment for leprosy or tuberculosis may either go unidentified or receive double doses of treatment.[3]

On the other hand, a first experience with writing may be brought by missionaries. If the missionaries refer their power and superior wisdom not to lists of the natives' names, but to lists of other peoples' names and deeds, then the power of the book, as compared with the power of the handmade list or record, can become salient. The aspiring young native will also want to learn to read that book.

Indeed, his ability to read it aloud, to read different things from different pages, will give him prestige among his nonliterate fellows. He comes among them clothed in a mantle of external and higher authority, conferred by books that he can vocalize and they cannot. The prestige of all sacred texts, read by the elite, memorized by the humble, and in cases where religion is transplanted from one language group to another, often "read" in the sense of being pronounced without respect to meaning, can be referred to this experience in which the one who reads has power not shared by those who do not.[4]

The ease with which literacy can be spread, among the children of immigrants or within a class or group to which education was previously unavailable, is partly explained by the obvious power that educated children acquire over their uneducated parents. Any association of reading or writing with increased autonomy and authority can be made attractive. This was so even where the parents were themselves literate, like shtetel Jews. As soon as he was literate, a boy could argue with the elders and be treated with respect, and thus he was permitted the verbal release of aggression which physically had been restrained since childhood. "And the love of learning was born" (Zborowski, 1955).

If we shift from the consideration of a primitive people experiencing script for the first time to children learning from their immediate surroundings what script is about, we find that early learning may be equally determinative. What is a book? One of many, standing on shelves, one of many kinds—some read by Daddy, some by Mommy, some by older siblings, some recent presents, some heirlooms, and some read by Mommy when she was a little girl. What is a book? Something that Daddy is writing and you mustn't disturb him or he won't get that chapter finished. What are those long shiny pieces of paper with printing all over the back that Mommy gives you to draw pictures on, but she says are part of Daddy's book. Why did grandmother look so stern when you knocked that book off the table, and why did she start talking about the way your dead grandfather felt about books? How does writing your name in the front of a book make it your book? What does "dedicated" mean—so that this book, which is dedicated to you, is somehow more yours than any other book, but nobody reads it to you because you aren't old enough? What is the difference between books with pictures for children and books without pictures for grownups? Why don't grownups need pictures to tell them what Little Red Riding Hood looked like? What tells them? What is a dictionary, and why are Daddy and Mommy always having a kind of fight that ends with one of them going and getting a dictionary, and one looks pleased and one looks angry? What is an engagement book, and what is an address book, and what is the difference between the telephone book Mommy made, and the big one that is printed? And what is printing? How do they make so many copies of the newspaper that are all alike, and yet there is only one copy of each book in the house? Why, if someone gives you a second copy of *When We Were Very Young* does Mommy say, "Oh, we have that; we'll give it to Jimmy?"

For the child in the home of those who not only read but also write books, a book becomes something that is made by the kind of people you know. A book is something that you yourself might write. In fact, you can begin now, folding pieces of paper together in book form and covering them with imitation letters. Or if you are a little older, write the beginnings of a story, labeled "Susan Lane, her book." Children from such homes passionately enter into reading. If they have difficulties, it is because they have serious problems of eye coordination, or deep emotional difficulties, or occasionally because they have gotten so far ahead of themselves that the discrepancy between what they can read and what they can write is unbearably frustrating. Such children have no image of a house that does not contain books, of an adult who does not often have a book in his hand, or of an individuality of which books are not apart. The hazards here are hazards that come from the overevaluation of books. The child whose eyes coordinate more slowly may become frightened and his parents may share his fright. "Maybe he isn't going to read" is a statement almost equivalent to "Maybe he isn't going to be human." The child who wants to learn, but who is held back because his parents have been warned not to attempt to teach their children prematurely, may give up. The bright moment passes, never to be regained. But attitudes toward the importance of reading have been established for good or ill, long before the child goes to school.[5]

It will be by careful detailed ethnographical study of different kinds of homes, of which the two quoted represent extremes, that we should be able to chart, and correct for, children's earliest learnings about reading and writing. Inevitably, experience will be diverse and defective with respect to the goals held up by a society in which reading is absolutely essential. In addition to the kinds of broad learnings that have been sketched in here, there will be many idiosyncratic miscarriages: children to whom letters or numbers come to have a magical significance, children who learn to read secretly and so become unintelligible to those around them, and children who block completely on part of the symbolic process. But these individual early sequences can only be fully identified, allowed for and treated, if the broader cultural outlines associated with class and occupation, region and religion, are better known.

ABSTRACT THOUGHT

Much of the current discussion of the relationship between types of thinking displayed by school children in the United States, which distinguishes between abstract and concrete thinking, lacks comparative perspective, and so fails to take into account many significant dimensions. However, when the various explanatory schemes for the development of thought that have evolved within one culture, or that include material from other cultures taken out of context, are subjected to comparative scrutiny, the kind of links between early childhood experience and type of thinking that individuals will display as adults can be distinguished in outline, however lacking we may be in detailed research on their implications.

Whether one follows the classical outlines of Binet (1916), the original schemes of Piaget (1926)—with their inclusion of Levy-Bruhl's (1923) armchair use of primitive materials, modified in the late 1950s in confrontation with living cross-cultural material—(Piaget, 1950; Tanner and Inhelder)—or whether one follows the developmental schemes of Gesell and Ilg (1943), it seems clear that we must take into account when, from whom, and in what way children encounter such types of thinking, as, for example, the Binet interpretation of proverbs, the Piaget demand for a recognition of the conservation of matter, or the Gesell-Ilg recognition of mathematical pattern as a recurrent spiraling capacity. Every intellectual capacity that is later tested by achievement, test, or observation is intimately linked with early childhood experience, with the level of education of parent or nurse, with the structure and furnishing of the home, with the content with which the members of the family and the neighborhood are preoccupied, and with the availability of the apparatus and technology on which abstract thought is dependent.

The child who is cared for in infancy and early childhood by individuals of a lower level of education than the child will later be expected to reach, faces a different educational situation than one who is reared from infancy by parents who represent the same level of education to which the child is expected to aspire. Whether it is an explanation of time or space, money, or the telephone, or a recognition of the child's attempt to search for some generalization among dissimilar objects, the highly educated parent or surrogate will meet the child on a different level than will the educated nurse, child nurse, or peasant grandmother. Where the educational level is lower, crude, or folk, concrete explanations may be given that will coexist in the child's mind and interfere with his later learning required by the school. This situation is further complicated by the relative intelligence of nurse and parent, which need not be proportional to their educational level. If the nurse is actually more intelligent, but less literate and less widely experienced than the parent, the child may develop considerable confusion about modes of thought. If the nurse or grandparent is able to draw on a folk level of thinking, rich in imagery and metaphor, while the parent represents the first generation of schooling—arid, disassociated from his or her primary learning—this may lead to the kind of repudiation of the intellectual life in which poverty and immediate existential experience are opposed to the hypocrisy, or aridity of formal learning. The importance to the total character structure of the child, of the nurse who taps a different cultural level, has long been recognized, but the educational consequences for thought remain unexplored. But it surely accounts for the superior achievement of parent-reared children who come from families with several generations of high achievement. They are exposed to highly abstract thinking from earliest childhood as contrasted with (1) children reared by nurses with low levels of literacy; (2) those who grow up with a lower level of thought at home than that encountered in church and school; (3) those who grow up in homes where no abstraction is ever made, and who in many cases are taught by teachers who came from similar homes, and who have only attained a schoolroom acquaintance with educated thought.

High intelligence occurs in all social strata and every ethnic group. A few individuals from primitive tribes or severely disadvantaged groups have risen to great intellectual distinction. But emphasis on these conspicuous exceptions has obscured the equally significant fact that the absence of a nurturing environment stunts and stultifies the mind of a child so that in most cases high natural intelligence is never realized. Early contact between young children and highly intelligent, highly educated adults is the best means we have yet devised for giving children a chance to escape the limitations imposed by uneducated parents and limited homes. This was evidenced in the striking contrast between the style—as expressed in posture, gesture, expression, and responsiveness—of the infants reared in Anna Freud's (1943) special residential home for children during World War II, where the children were cared for and taught by highly educated refugees, and that of children of the same class who were cared for by lower-class adults with limited education.[7]

But the failure to make finer discriminations than rural and urban, educated and uneducated, colored and white, professional and nonprofessional, rich and poor, is likely to obscure the issue, especially in the United States. In some ethnic groups—notably Eastern European Jewish groups—parents in the poorest homes, with the simplest occupations and very little formal schooling, may still provide a premium on thinking and exegesis that supports the child in school. Even before he enters school, the child learns the rudiments of analytical thought. On the other hand there are homes in which the father's highly paid occupation and specialized education is never made manifest, or where the children are left to the care of unintelligent and uneducated nurses. In such homes the children are more handicapped than those in a very simple home, where the Bible is read with reverence, and the preacher is expected to discuss Scripture like an educated man. When we are dealing with large populations or with whole ethnic groups, in the midst of transition, or with large urban immigrant groups with a given background, it may often be possible to establish some regularities. Such regularities can be discerned in the contrast between the adaptation of Japanese and Chinese immigrant children in California, or between the intellectuality of Eastern European and Middle Eastern Jewish children on the East Coast of the United States. But any attempt to generalize without research into the specific group is dangerous. What we need is more basic research on the one hand, and more devices for assaying the quality of preschool experience on the other.

The consequences of the differences, in the intellectual tone and interest of those who are most in contact with a small child, involve a variety of factors, some cultural, some idiosyncratic, and some familial. On the cultural level it is possible to work out in some detail the consequences for later learning of living in houses constructed without benefit of any precise measurement, without clocks or calendars, or even toys that embody some of the principles on which education is postulated. The house built to specifications—the fine machine tool, the clock and calendar, the thermometer and barometer, the compass and the blender, the thermostat and the television set—all carry a set of messages that can be absorbed in early childhood and later transformed into an interest in mathematics and computers. This can be so even when there is no adult in the home capable of explicitly fostering a child's interest in abstraction. Similarly, the city child learns from plants that mother keeps for show, or father keeps to impress the neighbors, or from herbs growing in the window box, things about a part of the universe that he would not otherwise experience. The regularities in the homes of any group of children can be analyzed for these mute messages that equip them, long before they enter school, for receptivities far beyond the level of the background from which they come. All this learning will be enormously reinforced if at least one adult in the home understands and explains a short-circuit, or the principle upon which the thermostat operates. But the artifacts that are the products of science nevertheless carry their own teaching: the child who comes from housing built on the basis of explicit geometrical knowledge makes a different order of discovery of geometry than the child who comes from a circular thatched dwelling, or from a crazy, sagging hut made of broken pieces of tin. In turn, the child who comes from a squatter's town built partly of thatch and partly of fragments of tin that have been shaped to recognizable geometrical forms learns still something else about pattern as being independent of materials.

Conversely, it is possible for homes to so smother children in words and high-level generalizations that their ability to work from direct perception of shape and size and material may be permanently impaired. High levels of verbal precocity may accompany very rudimentary understanding of basic physical and physiological relationships (Newman and Krug 1964; Parens and Weech 1966; Weisbergand Springer 1961; Wieder 1966) .

It should be borne in mind that each of the situations with which I have dealt may occur on a cultural, society wide basis. They may be characteristic of particular families, and therefore, incongruent with the over-all cultural emphasis. They may even be attributes of one individual within a family who gives the young child some extraordinarily deviant and unorthodox intellectual exposure. When the familial or individual style deviates from the wider style, the educator has still another element to cope with—the unexpected language of particular children that render them incomprehensible, unpredictable, and maladjusted in the schoolroom with its standardized expectations.

LANGUAGE LEARNING BEFORE SCHOOL AGE

During the 1920s it was argued that whatever difficulties children had on entering school, because they came from homes where a foreign language was spoken, would be eliminated by the third grade. The most significant attempt to refute this argument was a study of bilingual and monolingual children, in which the effects of a type of bilingualism associated with different contexts such as home, school, and play, were shown to be reflected in later school achievement. The design of this study has since come under criticism; there are still no definitive studies on the subject (but see the studies summarized in this volume by Cazden-and-John). However, from related fields, there have come some suggestive observations that should be considered.[9]

Jakobson (1941) has assembled evidence to show that the way in which a language is learned by an initial dichotomizing of a large unstructured repertoire of sounds, which are then progressively elaborated into a structured system, can be found to be repeated in the loss of the mastery of speech that occurs in traumatic amnesia. This study suggests— and the suggestion is supported by observations in other fields—that children learn the phonemic structure of their language at a very early age. It may be hypothesized, although there is no evidence yet in support, that certain fundamental morphemic generalizations are also learned early, and that fundamental ways of viewing the world, with contrasts between durative and punctuated action and with an insistence upon sources of information and matters of this sort, are also learned within the first three or four years of life. At present, it seems probable that the ability of the child to learn other linguistic and thought patterns is not so much a question of the interference of the latter pattern by the earlier one, as it is of the conditions of learning the two patterns. If two or more languages are learned, either sequentially or simultaneously, but one is the language of play and the other the language of discipline; if one is taught within the intimate environment of the home and the other in the more demanding and impersonal environment of school; if one is a language that is spoken by all the members of the child's environment, and the other spoken only by servants, or only by parents, or only by teachers; then the learning of the two patterns will be affectively weighted, and the learning will be of a different sort.

When, for example, a Spanish-speaking child is taught English by a teacher whose mother tongue is Spanish and who has only a classroom mastery of English, the situation is profoundly different from the case in which a child is taught English by a native English speaker with a good idiomatic knowledge of Spanish, or by a teacher who speaks no Spanish at all. It seems likely, but it has never been properly studied, that if the mother tongue is a dialect in which literacy is never attained, rather than a literate language in which literacy is first obtained, the results for the child's subsequent use of language will be very different. The success of the Colonial Dutch in teaching literacy and languages in Indonesia was based upon teaching literacy in the mother tongue, followed by literacy in Malay (the Indonesia *lingua franca* in the Netherlands Indies), followed by Dutch taught by native speakers, followed by English, French, or German taught as another formally mastered European language, by Dutch native speakers. Here a sequence of teaching had been developed that was severely mutilated when the school system was revised, and the Dutch dropped out. English teaching deteriorated markedly when the Dutch step was removed and Indonesian teachers were asked to go directly from Indonesian—a second language related to their own mother tongue—to English, a language that they had learned as a second European language from Dutch native speakers.[8]

Experience of this sort suggests that it is most important to explore the relationship between different kinds of language learning and to identify breaks and continuities in the sequence within which different versions of the same language, or different languages, are learned. The most significant situations may well be those in which significant adults in the child's world do not share a knowledge of the different varieties of speech with which the young child has to cope; different degrees of identification of these versions may be most important. For example, children who speak a dialect, identified and labeled as a dialect, in a country such as France or Germany or Italy, may have parents who speak the dialect at home, but use the standard language in all formal and public situations. Such children may be far less handicapped than those who speak aversion of the language that is treated not as a dialect with an identifiable style of its own but simply as class-typed, or regionally- or ethnically-typed, as in lower-class urban English in the United Kingdom, "bad English" in the English-speaking Caribbean, or the typical Southern rural Negro Americans in the United States. If the mother tongue is treated as an inferior version of the standard language, rather than as a dialect, movement becomes much more difficult between the phonemic, morphemic, and cognitive structures of the two forms, the home language and the school language (compare the discussion of these points by Hymes in this volume).

When, as is so often the case, the teacher has an inadequate grasp of the standard language and can only operate within a formal school context, the children with class-typed or race-typed speech are deprived of any formal grasp of the differences between the two forms. On the other hand, the teacher who is a native speaker of the standard language cannot recognize that the prevalent "mistakes" in grammar or spelling or thought found among children whose home language is "poor English" or "bad English" are, in fact, intrusions into the standard speech from unrecognized dialect.[9]

Experience therefore suggests the importance of making as articulate as possible the varieties of a language or of different languages that a child learns as an infant, as a toddler, in nursery and preschool, in elementary school, college and university. Such articulacy would include a detailed study of the various types of mother tongues, recognized dialects, recognized dialects associated with illiteracy and low prestige, unrecognized versions of the standard speech, standard expectations among the nonstandard speech speakers of what the standard language is like, divisions of experience that are learned in each language, counting, body parts, names for bodily functions, recitation of dreams, fantasy, disciplined logical thinking, authoritarian moral dicta, sacred scriptures, and poetry. Complementary to such an analysis, we will need the language style of the standard language and such contrasts as the Dutch emphasis on learning to speak foreign languages rather than on learning to listen; the Chinese emphasis on learning to read a cross language script and to *hear* different languages while speaking them imperfectly, and the contrasts among ways of learning English, Spanish, Russian, and German spelling. Of particular interest would be the consequences of the older and later German experiences, in which a teacher was accustomed to correct for local dialects and still teach the children to spell as they spoke, and the postwar experience when (owing to the wartime dispersal of populations throughout Germany) this was no longer possible.[10]

Similar interesting comparisons could be made of the ways that children progress in learning a standard language that is not their mother tongue for example, between the Soviet Union where a Russian-speaking teacher may be faced with a group of children with a common foreign language, and the United States where, in cities like New York, the teacher may be faced with children speaking several mother tongues as well as unrecognized dialects of English.

Detailed analysis of some of these situations should yield a set of early childhood deutero-formulations of the order of: "Real speech is how we speak at home; THEY speak and insist that I learn to speak in another way that has less reality." "Different people of the same kind speak different languages; it will be necessary to learn them all." "Different people of different kinds, some of higher or lower status, or greater or lesser warmth, speak different languages, learning these languages must include, these extralinguistic differences." There are, of course, the much more extreme cases of children reared in foreign countries who learn to speak their nurses' language, but whose parents do not. When these children are removed to their country of origin, the original nurse-tongue may be completely suppressed, only appearing as grammatical or phonemic intrusions, or under conditions of extreme amnesic stress, while providing a background for unrecognized cognitive confusions. Even more extreme are the cases in which children, after I having learned to speak, are adopted across a complete linguistic, cultural, and racial border, and are required to learn the new language from foster parents who know nothing of their mother tongues—as with Chinese, Korean, or Vietnamese war orphans adopted at the age of two or three in the United States.

Such deutero learning may be very potent in determining children's later ability to learn, to think in the abstract terms that are presented in the second, standard language. Access to their unconscious creativity is also affected. On the other hand, if these deutero learnings can be identified and articulated so that the mother tongue or the nurse tongue is treated with dignity as having equal reality standing with the standard language, much of the damage of such weighted compartmentalization can probably be avoided.

It will be particularly important to explore the later effects on the thinking ability of the coexistence of two languages: an infant or child language that remains rudimentary and undeveloped, unused since childhood, and a standard language that is reinforced with literacy, literature, and disciplined thought. The state of teaching the deaf in the United States is a case in point. American teaching of the deaf has until very recently repudiated the use of sign language, and insisted that deaf children be taught lip reading. The sign language, a language that uses many condensations for morphemes in addition to a manual alphabet, has continued to be used as a disapproved subversive form of communication among deaf children. Since it is not taught by competent and self-conscious teachers, as it is, for example, in the Soviet Union, dialects grow up; the deaf can easily recognize the great variety of divergent forms characteristic of sign language in the United States. But as the children do not connect the sign language with literacy, and no attempt is made to relate it systematically to standard English, it remains essentially the language of preliterate nursery years. In the Soviet Union, the use of a manual language coexists on formal terms with lip reading, reading, and writing, and very small children demonstrate an impressive mastery of thought and language.[11]

But the situation of the deaf is only an extreme and dramatic example of what happens when any form of communication, including the modalities of touch, taste and smell, is developed in childhood and left unrecognized and undeveloped by later formal teaching. Many cultures, including the highly literate versions of our own, depend upon using such separations to dramatize the difference between intimate and informal and distant, impersonal, and formal relationships. As a result, the uncultivated, preliterate modes of early childhood become the modes of communication within marriage, often carrying with them as unrecognized baggage, the unbridled fears and hopes and fantasies of early childhood, so that records of the intimate life of highly cultivated people contrast astonishingly with their level of sophistication and humanization in less intimate contexts (Hall, 1959; Ruesch and Prestwood, 1950; Corer, 1963; Frank, 1956; Wiener, 1966; Birdwhistell, 1959, 1962) .

Remembrance of such earlier forms of once efficient and now disallowed communications has many repercussions in learning situations at the beginning of school. In establishing a nursery school in a Southeastern city in the early 1940s for White children who had had Black nurses, it was found necessary to bridge the gulf from home to school, by including in the nursery school staff, a warm Black woman who fed the children to counterbalance the young White teachers who stood to the children for a different affective style.

It is probably impossible to overestimate the extent to which languages are the carriers of different kinds of thought. Quite aside from the resolution of the adequacy of the Whorfian hypothesis about the relationship between language and thought, the simple fact that more or less cognitively disciplined, socially hierarchical, or emotionally toned kinds of speech are used by the same individual, puts a burden on the transfer of learning. In the extreme case, the multilingual individual who has "lost" his or her mother tongue through migration or adoption may experience extreme hiatuses in his thinking processes. Such an individual may be denied all access to poetry as a form, or be unable to move easily through different levels of consciousness, or through different kinds of imagery. The sorts of imagery associated with primary process thinking—the figures of speech of classical rhetoric—may become so disturbed that little or no congruence remains between image and word. This is the case of a great deal of American slang where the visual image is lost in favor of an inexplicit motor image.

SEX AND TEMPERAMENT

Another conspicuous area of significant early childhood learning comes in the way a child experiences within the familial group cues to styles of intellectual behavior that are sex typed. Sex identity is imposed on children from birth; different terminology, different tones of voice, and different expectations all reinforce and elaborate underlying biological differences. Ways in which the world is to be perceived or represented may be so deep that when given pencils or crayons, children who have never drawn will nevertheless be sharply differentiated by the time they are five or six. Boys, for example, may draw scenes of activity from real life; girls draw patterns for cakes or clothing. Both style and content are conveyed to children very early, together with permission or prohibition about experimenting with styles of behavior culturally assigned to the other sex.

There is also great divergence in such cultural styles. In one culture, the small girls may be permitted to behave like boys, even in their stance and posture, as in Manus, where significantly the girls have taken to schooling as readily as the boys before puberty; their capacity to learn interrupted only by different expectations at puberty. In contrast, among the Iatmul, early childhood experience places the boys with the girls, with mothers as the first models; only in late childhood is a male model super-imposed on a female model. But in Bali each child is firmly assured of his or her sex identity, reared from earliest childhood to differentiated behavior, and individual children are given permission to experiment with the behavior of the other sex.

As a child learns its sex identity, it learns its appropriate cognitive style, and arrives in school with deeply ingrained expectations of what learning will be about. When the cultural style is rigid and extremely incongruent with the realities of human abilities, disturbances in the ability to learn are inevitable. This is so because of the child's already fixed sex identification and belief, such as that mechanics or mathematics are masculine and art is feminine, and because the teachers, as part of the same culture, reflect the same sex-typed expectations. Children whose abilities deviate sharply from normal expectation experience great difficulty in learning. This is exacerbated if, within the family, a child's proclivities for some sex-typed form of intellectual or artistic behavior is not only deviant from the cultural norm but also reinforced by temperamental similarities with the parent of the opposite sex. If a boy is both musical beyond the expectation for his class and region for male behavior, and has a musical mother with whom he identified, the complications are doubled. The school can help break down these very early, obdurate learnings, particularly if the school system presents at every stage both male and female models in sufficient profusion so that the child's earlier arbitrary learnings will be questioned rather than perpetuated. But small sensitive responses in early childhood to the cognitive style of the parents of the same and opposite sex can provide one of the often seemingly inexplicable blocks to learning, or a pathway of unusual facilitation, as when a certain high school provided an unusual number of good science students, all of whom went to the university from which the science teacher—also a first-class athlete—had come. As other cases, knowledge of the cultural style, by class and region, can facilitate teaching in school. Where the learning capacities of a particular child are complicated by idiosyncratic learning, additional analysis is required.

Finally, it is important to recognize that preschool children may be learning ways of dealing with life that are radically opposed to the expectations on which the school system is built. The American school system is based upon the belief that children should and will accept more and better education than their parents had. (The parent who insists that what was good enough for him is good enough for his children has been treated as a gross reactionary.) Such institutions as the Parent-Teachers Association are postulated on the parents' enthusiastic support of this position, whether it is reflected in the pride with which the first report card is exhibited, or in the foresight with which the parents enroll a child at birth for a particular school or college. Each piece of infant learning, mastery of a new skill, learning to count, or reciting a nursery rhyme or the alphabet is greeted in this model American household as a precursor of achievement that will eventually outstrip that of the parent. The child's learning is never begrudged; the child who suffers is the child whose early achievements do not promise such later educational success.

This is the model—one based on the style set up by hopeful immigrants from older societies who emigrated of their own accord to find better opportunities for themselves, and particularly for their children. Our whole educational system has been postulated on this style (here, see the essays, in this volume by Green and Khleif). It was, therefore, with a terrible shock that Americans woke up, in the late 1950s, to a recognition that for some 30 million or more Americans there was no such expectation. The enthusiasm, bred of immigration to a wider and more open world, has died among those who failed generation after generation to make the grade. It had only a fitful life among those who had not been immigrants out of self-propelling hope, but who had been brought here as slaves, or pushed here by desperation and starvation within their own borders, or who were slowly reduced to despair as their traditional ways of life became less and less congruent with modern American life. In such families achievement is not rewarded. The child is not gazed upon as one who will go further than his father but instead is clutched or pitied, loved or rejected as part of the misery, poverty, deprivation, or grudgingly accepted low status that his parents, grandparents, and great grandparents have known, and from which they have no genuine hope of escape. This is the child who is a dropout from the first day of school. Deeper than the marks of a different intellectual style, of a failure to grasp the meaning of literacy as access to new experiences, and deeper than the learning that comes from the content of the home and from the cues given by sex and temperament, is the mark laid upon the small preschool child by his parents' expectations of his achievement. It is this cultural factor that we are just beginning to appreciate and allow for; it is this deep block to achievement with which programs such as Head Start are attempting to deal. Without seriously coming to grips with this discrepancy between a school system built for the first generation of aspiring immigrants and pupils who are the product of many generations of low expectation and despair, we will not be able to reconstruct our schools so as to provide the type of education that will be needed in the coming world. But the reconstruction will need to provide ways through which children from whom little is expected may learn to expect much. It will also need to rescue those children—equally the victims of our one-way convictions of progress—from whom too much is expected and who are therefore branded as failures. Instead of a single-track notion of education from which those with the "wrong" cultural backgrounds were automatically excluded, and within which those with the "right" social backgrounds were often severely punished, we need to construct a system in which all sorts of lateral movements are possible, as some of the children of rural migrants become poets and physicists, and some of the children of lawyers and physicians and bankers become first-rate automobile mechanics or hospital orderlies. To accomplish this, the school needs to be more explicitly geared to compensate and balance, to take advantage of and when appropriate undo, the enormous strength of preschool experience.

NEW YORK, 1966.

NOTES

1. Those who have not learned to read fiction as children may be dangerously uneducated, unable in later life to exercise the discipline that separates fact from fantasy in the practical world.
2. We may ask whether the present popularity of the kind of pop art in which pieces of newspaper are cut into decorative shapes is not a rebellion against the arbitrary nature of script.
3. It has been fashionable to discuss such attitudes toward one's name as "primitive magical thinking" and those who do would assimilate the fear of their written name to fears of what others can do to them through

waxen images. But it is perhaps more useful to simply consider whether first encounters with reading and writing are experienced as ones in which other people have power, or you have power (compare the essay by Thomas and Wahrhaftig in this volume). If the more salient is power in the hands of others, then protective measures may follow. This may also be reversed as when relief clients learn that an ability to produce long sets of dates and figures gives their claims an appearance of verisimilitude. The client who has learned to rattle off a set of dates without any concern as to their accuracy will in due course believe that his investigator saves time by fabricating his record.

4. One of the puzzles of the modern world is the failure of the African peoples south of the Sahara to adopt script, a failure that has severely compromised the speed with which they can avail themselves of civilization. But if one remembers that they were offered the memorizing type of learning of the Moslem world in which neither innovation nor imagination was encouraged and the record-keeping of the trader and slaver, when they themselves had highly trained and highly trusted memories, this failure becomes more explicable.

5. The importance of a library, either a very large private library, or a public library, is the sense it gives a child that there are more and more new and different books to be read. Ownership of a few books, and no use of libraries and no books in their parents' library, means that children learn that reading is essentially a self-limiting and terminable part of life summed up in the wry joke, "She has a book."

6. Sartre's analysis of his repudiation of his grandfather's pretentious and unscholarly intellectual life gives a detailed account of the effect on a child of exposure to a type of intellectuality that he feels cannot be respected and must be repudiated (Sartre, 1964)

7. This statement is based on visits to residential nurseries through the United Kingdom in 1943.

8. Based on exploratory fieldwork in 1957-1958, in Bali, under NIH Grant No. M-2218.

9. I am indebted to the fieldwork of Rhoda Metraux, in the Caribbean, for my understanding of the significance of the failure to identify Caribbean dialects as dialects, and to a brief visit to her field site in Montserrat, W. I., during the summer of 1966 for an opportunity to listen to the sliding relationships between standard English and an almost completely unintelligible dialect, indulged in by both native dialect speakers and native English speakers born on the island, with minimal consciousness of the way in which they handle equivalent utterances. (NSF Grant to AMNH, No. MH-O7675-04.)

Fieldwork in the village of Peri, among the Manus speaking people in 1964 and 1965 where an Australian teacher, without a knowledge of either Manus or the Neo- Melanesian *lingua franca* (pidgin) was teaching English, gave me a further opportunity to compare the children's progress in English and the problems they encountered, with the progress of Manus-speaking children on Balowan, in 1953, with a native English-

speaking teacher who also spoke fluent Neo-Melanesian. (1953, Admiralty Island expedition, grant from the Rockefeller Foundation to the AMNH; 1964 and 1965, NIH Grant No. MH-O7675-02-03 to the AMNH.)
10. This material was a by-product of the analysis by Rhoda Metraux (1955) of a large sample of Anderson Story Completion Forms written by German children.
11. Unpublished field work on teaching of the deaf in the United States, by Rhoda Metraux and Margaret Mead, and in the Soviet Union by Margaret Mead. NIH grant to AMNH Factor in Allopsychic Orientation in Mental Health. (NIH Grant No. M-3303.)

REFERENCES

Aries, Phillipe
    1962   Centuries of childhood: a social history of family life. New York: Alfred A. Knopf.
Bateson, Gregory
    1942   Social planning and the concept of deutero learning. In Science, philosophy, and religion, second symposium, Lyman Bryson and Louis Finkelstein, eds. New York: *Conference on Science, Philosophy, and Religion,* pp. 81-97.
    1955   A theory of play and fantasy. *Psychiatric Research Reports,* 2:39-51.
    1956   The message "this is play." *In* Group processes, Bertram Schaffner, ed. New York: Josiah Macy, Jr. Foundation, pp.145-242.
_____ and Margaret Mead
    1942   Balinese character: a photographic analysis. New York: New York Academy of Sciences; reissued 1962.
Berkowitz, Leonard, ed.
    1963   Advances in experimental social psychology, vol 1. *Influence of Culture on Cognitive Processes.* New York: Academic Press.
Bemstein, Basil
    1960   Language and social class. *British Journal of Sociology* II :271-276.
    1961   Social structure, language and learning. *Educational Research* 3: 136-176.

Binet, Alfred
    1916   The development of intelligence in children. Baltimore:
            Williams and Wilkins, Inc.
Birdwhistell, Ray L.
    1959   Contribution of linguistic-kinesic studies to the
            understanding of schizophrenia. In *Schizophrenia, an
            integrated approach,* Alfred Auerback, ed. New York:
            Ronald Press Company, pp. 99-123.
    1962   An approach to communication. *Family Process*
            1:194-201.
Bloom, Benjamin, et al.
    1964   Compensatory education for cultural deprivation. New
            York: Bolt, Rinehart and Winston, Inc.
Bruner, Jerome S.
    1965   Toward a theory of instruction. Cambridge: Harvard
            University Press.
Bryson, Lyman, Margaret Mead, Rudolf Aruheim, and Milton Nahm
    1960   Conditions for creativity. In *The creative mind and
            method,* Jack D. Summerfield and Lorlyn Thatcher, eds.
            Austin: University of Texas Press, pp. 105-111.
Cohen, Yehudi A.
    1963   The transition from childhood to adolescence.
            Chicago: Aldine Publishing Company.
Dart, Francis E., and Panna Lal Pradham
    1967   Cross-cultural teaching of science. *Science* 155:649-656.
Deutsch, Martin
    1965   The role of social class in language development and
            cognition. *American Journal of Orthopsychiatry*
            35:78-88.
Entwisle, Doris R.
    1966   Developmental sociolinguistics: a comparative study in
            four subcultural settings. *Sociometry* 29:67-84.
Erikson, Erik H.
    1958   The syndrome of identity diffusion in adolescents and
            young adults. In *Discussions on child development,* J. M.
            Tanner and Barbel Inhelder, eds. London: Tavistock
            Publications, Ltd., pp. 133-167.
Ferguson, Charles
    1965   Directions in sociolinguistics: report on an
            interdisciplinary seminar. *Social Science Research Council
            Items,* 19:1-4.

Frank, L. K.
1956 Tactile communication. *Genetic Psychology Monographs* 56:209-255.
Freud, Anna, and D. T. Burlingham
1943 War and children. New York: Medical War Books.
Fromm, Erich
1951 The forgotten language. New York: Holt, Rinehart and Winston, Inc., reprinted 1962, Evergreen E47, New York: Grove Press, Inc.
Gesell, Arnold, and Frances Ilg
1943 Infant and child in the culture of today. New York: Harper and Row Publishers, Inc.
Goldman-Eisler, Frieda.
1958 Speech analysis and mental processes. *Language and Speech* 1: 59-75.
Gorer, Geoffrey
1963 The life and ideas of the Marquis de Sade. N226, New York: W. W. Norton Company, Inc.
Hall, Edward T.
1959 The silent language. Garden City, New York: Doubleday Co., Inc., reprinted 1961, R204, New York: Fawcett Publications, Inc.
Hart, C. W. M.
1955 Contrasts between prepubertal and postpubertal education. In *Education and Anthropology,* George D. Spindler, ed. Stanford: Stanford University Press, pp. 127-145.
Hebb, D. O.
1949 The organization of behavior. New York: John Wiley & Sons, Inc.
Hymes, Dell H.
1962 The ethnography of speaking. In *Anthropology and human behavior,* Thomas Gladwin and William C. Sturtevant, eds. Washington: Anthropological Society of Washington, pp. 13-53.
Jakobson, Roman
1941 Kindersprache, Aphasie and allgemeine Lautgesetze. Uppsala, Sweden: Almqvist and Wiksells.
Kaplan, Bert, ed.
1961 Studying personality cross-culturally. New York: Harper & Row, Publishers, Inc.

Lesser, Gerald, et al.
1965 Mental abilities of children in different social and cultural groups. In *School children in the urban slum,* Joan I. Roberts, ed. New York: Hunter College (Project True), pp. 115-125.

Levinson, Boris M.
1960 Subcultural variations in verbal and performance ability at the elementary school level. *Journal of Genetic Psychology* 97:149-160.

Lévy-Bruhl, Lucien
1923 Primitive mentality. Authorized translation by Lilian A. Clare. New York: Crowell-Collier and Macmillan, Inc.

Luria, A. R., and F. I. Yudovich
1959 Speech and the development of mental processes in the child. New York: Humanities Press.

Lynd, Robert S., and Helen M. Lynd
1929 Middletown. New York: Harcourt Brace Jovanovich.
1937 Middletown in transition. New York: Harcourt Brace Jovanovich.

McClelland, David C.
1961 The achieving society. New York: Van Nostrand Reinhold Company.
_____, et al.
1953 The achievement motive. New York: Appleton-Century-Crofts.

Malinowski, Bronislaw
1948 The problem of meaning in primitive languages. In *Magic, science and religion and other essays.* Boston: The Beacon Press, pp. 228-276.

Mead, Margaret
1926 The methodology of racial testing: its significance for sociology. *American Journal of Sociology* 31:657-667.
1927a Group intelligence tests and linguistic disability among Italian children. *School and Society* 25:465-468.
1927b The need for teaching anthropology in normal schools and Teachers' Colleges. School and Society 26:466-469.
1928 A lapse of animism among a primitive people. *Psyche* 9:72-77.
1929 South Sea hints on bringing up children. *Parents' Magazine* 4:20-22, 49-52.
1930 Growing up in New Guinea: A comparative study of primitive education. New York: William Morrow & Co.,

Inc.: reprinted 1962, Apollo A58, New York: William
Morrow & Co., Inc.

1931a   Education, primitive. *In* V, *Encyclopedia of the Social
Sciences,* Edwin R. A. Seligman and Alvin Johnson, eds.
New York: Crowell-Collier and Macmillan, Inc., pp.
399-403.

1931b   The meaning of freedom in education. *Progressive
Education* 8:107-111.

1931c   The primitive child. In *A handbook of child psychology,*
Carl Murchison, ed. Worcester, Mass.: Clark University
Press, pp. 669-686.

1931d   Two south sea educational experiments and their
American implications. In *Eighteenth Annual
Schoolmen's Week Proceedings,* March 18-21, 1931.
University of Pennsylvania School of Education
Bulletin 31 :493-497.

1932a   The changing culture of an Indian tribe. New York:
Columbia University Press; reprinted 1966, Cap Giant
266, New York: G. P. Putnam's Sons, Inc.

1932b   Contrasts and comparisons from primitive society.
*Annals of the American Academy of Political and Social
Science* 160:23-28.

1932c   An investigation of the thought of primitive children,
children with special reference to animism. *Journal of
the Royal Anthropological Institute* 62: 173-190.

1935   Sex and temperament in three primitive societies. New
York: William Morrow & Co., Inc.; reprinted 1963,
Apollo *A-67,* New York: William Morrow & Co., Inc.

1937   Cooperation and competition among primitive
peoples. New York and London: McGraw-Hill Inc.;
reprinted 1961, BP123, Boston: The Beacon Press.

1940   The student of race problems can say... *Frontiers of
Democracy* 6:200-202.

1942a   And keep your powder dry. New York: William Morrow
& Co., Inc.; reprinted 1965, Apollo edition A105, New
York: William Morrow & Co., Inc.

1942b   Educative effects of social environment as disclosed by
studies of primitive societies. In *Environment and
education,* E. W. Burgess, ed. Chicago: University of
Chicago Press, pp. 48-61.

1946   Professional problems of education in dependent
countries. *Journal of Negro Education* 40:346-357.

1947a   Babies in primitive society. *Child Study* 24:71-72.

1947b The implications of culture change for personality development. *American Journal of Orthopsychiatry* 17:633-646.

1947c On the implication for anthropology of the Gesell-Ilg approach to maturation. *American Anthropologist* 49:69-77.

1949 Male and female. New York: William Morrow & Co., Inc.; reprinted 1955, NP369, New York: New American Library.

1951a The impact of culture on personality development in the United States today. *Understanding the child* 20:17-18.

1951c The school in American culture. Cambridge: Harvard University Press.

1952 Some relationships between social anthropology and psychiatry. In *Dynamic psychiatry,* Franz Alexander and Helen Ross, eds. Chicago: University of Chicago Press, pp. 401-448.

1953 Cultural patterns and technical change. Paris, Unesco; reprinted 1961, MT346, New York: New American Library.

1954a Cultural discontinuities and personality transformation. *Journal of Social Issues,* Supplement Series, No.8: 3-16.

1954b Research on primitive children. In *Manual of child psychology,* 2nd ed., Leonard Carmichael, ed. New York: John Wiley and Sons, Inc., pp. 735-780.

1956 New lives for old: cultural transformation, Manus 1928-1953. New York: William Morrow & Co., Inc.; reprinted with a new preface 1966, Apollo . *A124,* New York: William Morrow & Co., Inc.

1957 Toward more vivid utopias. *Science* 126:957-961.

1958a Changing teacher in a changing world. In *The education of teachers: new perspectives.* Washington: National Education Association of the United States, pp.121-134.

1958b Why is education obsolete? *Harvard Business Review* 36:164-170.

1959a Closing the gap between the scientists and the others. Daedalus, Winter: 139-46.

1959b Creativity in cross-cultural perspective. In *Creativity and its cultivation,* Harold H. Anderson, ed. New York: Harper & Row, Publishers, Inc., pp. 222-235.

1960a   Adaptation to change, Participant in panel discussion.
        The social environment. In *Man's contracting world
        in an expanding universe,* Ben H. Bagdikian, ed.
        Providence, Rhode Island: Brown University Press,
        pp. 90-101.

1960b   High school of the future. *California Journal of Secondary
        Education* 35: 360-369.

1960c   Participant in discussions on child development: a
        consideration of the biological, psychological, and
        cultural approaches to the understanding of human
        development and behavior: proceedings of the fourth
        meeting of the World Health Organization, 4 Study
        group on the psychobiological development of the
        child, Geneva, 1956, J. M. Tanner and Barbel Inhelder,
        eds. London: Tavistock Publications, Ltd.; New York:
        International Universities Press, 1960.

1961a   Gender in the honors program. *Superior Students* (JCSS)
        4:2-6.

1961b   Questions that need asking. New York (Columbia
        University): Teachers College Record 63:89-93.

1962   A creative life for your children. Washington:
        Department of Health, Education and Welfare,
        Children's Bureau Headliner Series No.1.

1963   Socialization and enculturation. *In* Papers in honor
        of Melville J. Herskovits, *Current Anthropology*
        4:184-188.

1964   Continuities in cultural evolution. New Haven: Yale
        University Press; reprinted 1966, Y154, New Haven:
        Yale University Press.

1965   The future as the basis for establishing a shared culture.
        Daedalus, Winter: 135-155.

_____, and Frances C. Macgregor

1951   Growth and culture: a photographic study of Balinese
        childhood. New York: Putnam's Sons, Inc.,

_____, and Martha Wolfenstein, eds.

1955   Childhood in contemporary cultures. Chicago:
        University of Chicago Press; reprinted 1963, P124,
        Chicago: University of Chicago Press.

_____, and Rhoda Metraux

1957   Image of the scientist among high-school students: a
        pilot study. *Science* 126: 384-390.

_____, and Elizabeth Steig
    1964   The city as the portal of the future. *Journal of Nursery Education* 19:146-153.

Metraux, Rhoda
1955   The consequences of wrongdoing: an analysis of story completions by German children. In *Childhood in contemporary cultures,* Margaret Mead and Martha Wolfenstein, eds. Chicago: University of Chicago Press; pp. 306-323; re- printed 1963, P124, Chicago: University of Chicago Press.

Miller, Daniel R., and Guy E. Swanson
    1965   Social class and motoric orientation. In *School children in the urban slum,* Joan I. Roberts, ed. New York: Hunter College (Project True), pp. 188-199.

Newman, C. Janet, and Othilda Krug
    1964   Problems in learning arithmetic in emotionally disabled children. *Journal of the American Academy of Child Psychiatry* 3 :413-429.

Neisser, Ulric
    1962   Cultural and cognitive discontinuity. In *Anthropology and human behavior,* Thomas Gladwin and William C. Sturtevant, eds. Washington : Anthropological Society of Washington, pp. 54-71.

Parens, Henri, and Alexander A. Weech
    1966   Accelerated learning responses in young patients with school problems. *Journal of the American Academy of Child Psychiatry* 5 :75-92.

Piaget, Jean
    1926   The language and thought of the child. New York: Harcourt Brace Jovanovich. reprinted 1960, Meridan M10, Cleveland: World Publishing Co., Inc.
    1950   Psychology of intelligence. London: Routledge and Kegan Paul, Ltd.; reprinted 1963, Patterson, N.J.: Littlefield, Adams & Co.

Ruesch, Jurgen, and Gregory Bateson
    1951   Communication: the social matrix of psychiatry. New York: W. W. Norton & Co., Inc.

_____, and Welden Kees
    1956   Nonverbal Communication. Berkeley: University of California Press.

_____, and Rodney Prestwood
    1950   Communication and bodily disease. In *Life stress and bodily disease,* Harold G. Wolff et al., eds. Baltimore: Williams and Wilkins, Inc.

Sarte, Jean Paul
    1964   The words. New York: George Braziller, Inc., reprinted
            1966, Crest T883, New York: Fawcett Publications, Inc.
Spindler, G. D., ed.
    1955   Education and anthropology. Stanford: Stanford
            University Press.
Swanson, Guy E.
    1960   The birth of the gods: the origin of primitive beliefs.
            Ann Arbor: University of Michigan Press.
Tanner, I. M., and Barbel Inhelder, eds.
    1957-1960   Discussions on child development, 4 vols. New
            York: International Universities Press.
Useem, John
    1963   Notes on the sociological study of language. *Social
            Science Research Council Items* 17:29-31.
Vygotskii, Lev S.
    1962   Thought and language. Cambridge: Massachusetts
            Institute of Technology Press.
Weisberg, Paul S., and Kayla J. Springer
    1961   Environmental factors in creative function: a study
            of gifted children. *Archives of General Psychiatry* 5:
            554-564.
Werner, Heinz
    1964   Comparative psychology of mental development, rev.
            ed. New York: International Universities Press.
Whiting, Beatrice
    1950   Paiute sorcery. New York: Viking Fund Publications in
            Anthropology, No. 15.
Whiting, John W. M.
    1961   Socialization process and personality. In *Psychological
            anthropology,* F. L. K. Hsu, ed. Homewood, Ill.: Dorsey
            Press.
_____, and Irvin Child
    1953   Child training and personality: a cross-cultural study.
            New Haven: Yale University Press.
Whorf, Benjamin L.
    1947   Science and linguistics. In *Readings in social psychology,*
            Theodore M. Newcomb and Eugene L. Hartley, eds.
            New York: Holt, Rinehart and Winston, Inc.
    1950   Time, space and language. In *Culture in crisis,* Laura
            Thompson, ed. New York: Harper & Row, Publishers,
            Inc., pp. 152-172.

Wieder, Herbert
   1966   Intellectuality: aspects of its development from the
           analysis of a precocious 41/2 year old boy.
           Psychoanalytic Study of the Child 21 :294-323.
Wiener, Harry
   1966   External chemical messengers. I. Emission and
           reception in man. *New York State Journal of Medicine,*
           66:3153-3170.
Williams, Thomas R.
   1966   Cultural structuring of tactile experience in a Borneo
           society. *American Anthropologist* 68:27-39.
Wissler, Clark
   1923   Man and culture. New York: Crowell Collier and
           Macmillan, Inc.
Zborowski, Mark
   1955   The place of book-learning in traditional Jewish
           culture. In *Childhood in contemporary cultures,* Margaret
           Mead and Martha Wolfenstein, eds. Chicago:
           University of Chicago Press, pp. 118-49; reprinted
           1963, Phoenix P124, Chicago: University of Chicago
           Press.

Part Three

PERSPECTIVES ON
CONTEMPORARY SOCIETY

FROM PLIGHT TO POWER:
Youth as a Political and Economic Force

At the White House Conference of 1960, Eli Ginzberg provided the principal organizing theme that the position of American youth was changing from a group which was talked about, analyzed, lectured to, lamented, and worried about to a state in which they were emerging as a possible political influence in the American scene. There had been a foretaste in the early 1930s with the abortive attempt to organize the American Youth Congress, an attempt blunted in Washington, when Mrs. Roosevelt listened to them, the press attacked them, and they went home. For the rest of the Depression years, the elders of the society talked about Youth, now spelling it with a capital Y (after attempting to deal with the problems of a collective plural, "seven youth boarded a bus"). Special studies were made for the Youth Authority, The Adolescent Study of the Progressive Education Association, and the NYA, which provided jobs for indigent young people in the same tone of voice that the WPA provided jobs for the unemployed older people.

The problems of youth were assimilated to: problems of unemployment (where they were grouped with other problems of unemployment); problems of education, with an emphasis on studies of their hopes, aspirations, and faults in the current education system. These were combined with attempts to deal with the large high school populations which had emerged after World War I, and with the emerging sense of democracy, a conscious element in the late 1930s and early 1940s which included a feeling that Youth, who were being talked about, legislated for, inveighed against, should have some voice of their own. In the period of coordination of Youth-serving agencies, long serious discussions were held at meetings, at which no single youth was present, on whether young people being serviced by the agencies could somehow be represented in the deliberations of the bodies devoted to their interests. But most of these efforts were made in the same tone of voice that had developed student councils in high schools and colleges; by adult fiat, bodies were brought into being in which limited expressions of opinion were permitted or even solicited from the young, but they were always within an adult framework of control and budget.

Young people were benevolently permitted to exercise such authority as was delegated to them only when it did not clash with the interests of the powers that had given it to them in the first place. Those familiar with the way in which English schools operated commented on the difference between American and English schools in this respect. In English schools, authority to discipline was given to a student group and could not be capriciously withdrawn. Possibly this was based on a medieval view of a community of self-governing scholars, which even secondary schools might mildly approximate.

But the American model of authority was specifically a matter of delegation by a higher level to a lower one. When dealing with dependent groups, whether students, the poor, women, or ethnic minorities, authority came down by fiat from above.

Significantly, in the period at the beginning of World War II, the principal diatribe directed against youth, at a period when they were joining their seniors in marching for peace, or reflecting teaching which had made them suspicious of all news, was that they lacked the moral fibre that would be necessary if they were to defend this country. In the early 1940s I wrote two responses to this attack (*Harpers,* 1941; *National Parent-Teacher,* 1941), pointing out that when young people asked such questions as, "Ought one to have a conscience?" they were still profoundly concerned with ethical issues. During World War II itself, young people were so enmeshed in the war effort that the sense of possible conflict between generations disappeared.

Meanwhile, new questions were raised, even as the United States began enthusiastically building for greatly extended free higher education, with California leading the way. A careful scrutiny of elementary school education revealed grave discrepancies between stated goals and actual achievements. The tremendous amount of illiteracy found in the United States, especially in the southeast and among black, Mexican, Puerto Rican, and Indian groups, all of whom nominally had schooling, revealed the weaknesses of educational systems where minority children were conceived as inherently incapable of learning the culture which their teachers made a half-hearted attempt to teach them, succeeding only in teaching them their inability to learn.

During and immediately after World War II, there was a rash of adolescent dissident movements, whose followers dressed extravagantly, practiced various forms of socially disapproved behavior, who were, in fact, the adolescent failures, the drop-outs and cop-outs before the words were invented, from a system that had never seriously tried to educate them. The zoot suiters, the *eidelweis,* the teddy boys, the weegies and bodgies of Australia, were distinguished not by ethnocentricity but merely by uneducated lower-class status, coupled with discrepant, unsuccessful education. Almost forgotten today, in the turmoil of much more determined demonstrations against the present system, these youth groups were an early sign that the system was not working. Apprenticeship was dying; in rural areas children had no time nor taste for the manual tasks their fathers performed. The great exodus to the cities accelerated; and the overloaded city schools groaned under the weight of young people who could never be absorbed into the labor market.

Meanwhile there were other warning voices. The most gifted children of the American intelligentsia began to drop out of universities, finding somehow that the universities failed to give them what they wanted—what a decade or so later began to be called "relevance." And the speed of technological change made it abundantly clear that if the bulk of our population were to continue to work remuneratively within the present type of industrial system, whether that was capitalist or socialist, it would be necessary to retrain, if not re-educate, vast numbers of people two or three times during their lifetimes. This estimate was still associated with remunerative work, that is, with the expectation, which had ruled our thinking since the industrial revolution, that those who could not find remunerative work would be denied full status as human beings.

This emphasis on expected need for re-education to counter technological change was accompanied by the recognition that in technological societies, to be human one had to be literate. The ability to read and write was added to the abilities to walk and talk, which for a hundred thousand years had been the major requirements for rudimentary humanity. We looked at the illiteracy in the world, at the waste of manpower in the United States, revealed in Ginzberg's studies of the draft, at the vast uneducated masses of India and China, and were aghast. We counted up the needs in the United States for engineers, physicians, physicists, and enormously increased the investment in graduate schools. A vast educational machine, deeply deficient at the base, eroded by faulty and unwilling extensions of diluted educational methods to the entire population, and top-heavy with institutions of higher education modeled upon the past education of a handful of elite, came into being.

California began to reflect not only the demand for free education for all, but also the new demands for education after childbearing for married women, an educational second chance for those who had failed at lower levels, a return for more higher education after several years out of school, and the delights of education purely for itself, for the retired but still curious. The movement toward more and more publicly supported colleges, accessible to all, was spreading, and is still spreading from state to state as New York, Florida, and Virginia join the procession, even as student revolts from Berkeley to Tokyo to France have challenged and threatened the entire system. The revolts are so widespread, the complaints so diverse but so ubiquitous, the opponents and proponents of change use such contradictory arguments that we may well suspect that the causes lie deeper than we have guessed.

We have had in fact a growing clash between those who conceived education as contributing to the individual, to human development and fulfillment on the one hand, and those who conceived of education as serving the needs of what has come to be called the Establishment, that is, of established institutions—the state, the school, the church, industry, those institutions which represent only a part of the community life. Where there was as yet no distinction between community and government, or community and church, and no industry in the modern sense, the education of children simply served to perpetuate the maintenance skills of the small society; boys learned to hunt and fish, and a few learned special esoteric skills like garden magic or divination; girls learned to prepare food, care for babies, gather roots, or later, plant and weed and harvest; or both sexes shared the care of herbs or domestic animals. The development of each individual to be a full member of that society, however limited its skills and its viewpoint, was coincident with the educational system. Such are the educational systems of those isolated primitive peoples who still live a primitive life today.

Educational systems as institutions only came into being when there was a higher degree of division of labor and special training was needed for the sons of the ruling class, for military officers, for clerks and scribes and accountants, for priests and seers and keepers of mysteries, for specialists in the knowledge of the past, and additionally when children needed to be educated differently from the way their parents had been, either because the specialist occupations needed more recruits or because the children of conquered, annexed populations or immigrants had to learn the language and customs of the dominant culture. But the overriding goals of education were still the training of specialists, including hereditary rulers and gentry, and the recruitment of more members for some special skill. It was primarily some change of status, as from the country to the city, from slavery to manumission, from subjects of one state to subjects of another, which triggered the need for schools for those who were to be the majority of undifferentiated workers for any society. Apprenticeship, either within or outside the family, the learning by the young of what the old knew, in a face-to-face, one-to-one, situation, remained a dominant mode for the children of the elite who were tutored, and the skilled, who learned from parents or master workmen.

Our present situation in which we separate children at a younger and younger age from any relationship to the work activities of their parents, sort them by age, ability, past social status, and future occupational designations, and keep them shut up together, learning at a snail's pace what each could learn individually much faster, may be seen as the product of industrialization at a period when technology had not yet made machines that could free men from both manual, and tedious mental labor, and synthesis had replaced the search for raw materials. The demand for the extension of education to females, to the poor, to the previously enslaved, to the colonial peoples, has been a combination of the rising demand for democratic participation in the activities of society, and the rising demand of industrialized states for suitably trained workers, disciplined, literate, accustomed to the rhythm of the clock and the machine.

As increased earning power and increased mobility outside the confines of the home neighborhood were associated with freedom—freedom for women from the dependence on male relatives, freedom for the poor from the dependency on share-cropping and agricultural serfdom, freedom of ethnic groups from stigmatized menial service tasks, freedom of colonial peoples from the hard labor associated with the production of primary crops—rubber, ore, cotton, sugar. First literacy, then higher education, then freedom to work at more remunerative tasks in a society with arising GNP, based upon the consumer power (or, in socialist society on the consumer share) of those; who had the more remunerative tasks—this was the ideal toward which the world has been moving. Because of the close association between access to education and access to work, which was assumed to give freedom, it has not been sufficiently remarked how deeply exploitative these demands for more and more education were. The very concept of manpower is a society-based, not an individual-based concept, however humanely it be interpreted by Eli Ginzberg in his exposition of the successes of educated women. The assumption has been that the society's need for educated manpower and the individual's need for education in order to acquire greater mobility and hence greater freedom within an economic system postulated on scarcity of men, skills, and resources, would produce benefits for the individual has been in many ways illusory.

One of the principal undesirable side effects of these demands for more widespread and ever higher education has been the increasing segregation of the young during their period of highest learning capacity, ages 5 to 10, from the productivity and creativity of their culture, and the infantilizing of adolescents and young adults as long as they are classified as students, a separate segment of society, unfit for full responsibility and full respect. This tendency toward infantilization of students resulted in the extension of dependency, and virtual political and economic disenfranchisement, and the withholding of full adult rights up into the '30s for those who were learning special skills like social work or psychiatry, where supervision continued almost indefinitely.

The whole process of the extension of pupil-status into adulthood has been based on the egalitarian belief in education and the fear that once education is interrupted society will withdraw the privileges, which it has reluctantly accorded further education. All the gains that have been made in universal education have been accomplished by extending a single schooling period, down into kindergarten, nursery school, and today into day care centers, up into high school, junior college, college, graduate school, and postdoctoral education. The concept that there is a schooling period, to which all human beings are entitled, paralleling the needs of an industrial society, has been the dynamic underlying the idealistic part of our changing educational system.

As long as the needs of the economy and this idealistic educational ethic coincided, this continuing extension of the schooling period was possible, and continued to be viewed, for the most part, as an advantage and a privilege. In the United States, in the 1930s and well into the 1940s, Negro sharecropper parents, and poor parents in Harlem, worked hard to send their children through high school and to college. First-generation European immigrants saved to put their children through high school, and second-generation parents saved to put their children through college, now regarded as a prerequisite to everything worth having in the society. Education was both a right and a privilege, and stood against the early exploitation of children in the cotton fields, among migratory laborers, and the later exploitation of young people in blind alley jobs.

In 1954 when I suggested to the National Conference of Parents and Teachers that we consider letting children leave school at the age of 14 and return at any period in the course of their lives if they felt they could use more education, I was denounced as an advocate of child labor. It took only a few more years however, for diatribes against child labor to give way to schemes for youth employment, as it became increasingly clear that our present school system was coming under fire. The long, long years of compulsory school, the need to stay in school under threat, first of legal penalties, later of no worthwhile jobs, later still of being drafted, have all contributed their share to changing attitudes toward the infinite desirability of an increasing single stretch of education. But this disillusionment with our present-day schooling has continued to be complemented with the belief that a better type of schooling was all that was needed, a belief that better science education, readers suited to different economic groups, better schools in ghettos, provision for the children of migrants, etc. would remedy the present defects. Meanwhile the need for more highly educated manpower continued—and campaigns, began to keep pupils in school who were capable of doing college level work—pupils whom we had never expected to keep in school before were now described as "drop-outs" and committees formed in every state to keep them in. Women were told that the life of homemaking to which society's arrangements had condemned them, living in isolated suburbs far from help of any kind, was not fulfilling, after all, and a nationwide campaign to get women back for more education and training for the cheap educated labor market was underway.

The state of California represented the highest achievement of these new ideals. A statewide system of free education made it possible for young people to move from job to college and back again. Women could pick up their discontinued education and "complete" it (the old idea of one lump of education to which every citizen was legally entitled, remained). Retired colonels could study philosophy side by side with sixteen-year-old girls; students who had done badly in high school had a second chance. Students worked, married, fathered children, and went on to college. There were community colleges for those who would be motor mechanics and those who would go on to be automobile salesmen. Parents who wanted to educate their children themselves were prosecuted. Attempts were made to see that the children of migrant laborers went to school while at the same time excluding from the country the low-paid migrant Mexican laborers. Automation of services was everywhere speeded up, and drive-ins of all sorts superseded both restaurants and waitresses.

And then, in the mid-1960s the whole California system, so carefully and imaginatively built, a system that other states were beginning to copy, came under attack—first at Berkeley, then at college after college. The very principle of free higher education was called in question and has now been rescinded. Students burn down college buildings. Students in the National Guard attack their fellow students who are demonstrating for peace. The police maim and kill. Higher education for all who can benefit by it is so disturbed and disliked by the majority of the less educated populace—and note that with a continual system of upgrading there will always be a less well-educated older generation—that they will vote to keep in power the declared enemy of education, and all other forms of enlightened community behavior.

Nor is this all. In England students barricade themselves in buildings and private eyes with police dogs are brought in to deal with them; in France a political regime was brought down by student revolt; in Japan the major universities were closed for over a year with no one studying for the professions that are essential to maintain the state. The Soviet Union made one abortive attempt to introduce work into the plan of continuous education, and has just begun to feel the pinch as youth begin leaving school and find themselves unemployed.

So we may well ask, what has happened to this structure, which appeared so desirable that it was only a matter of extending it all over the world to produce, in fact, a much more satisfactory world? Why are the school system and the colleges coming under attack today where a generation ago it was the industrial system, as it employed those with little or no schooling, that was the principal target of reform movement? One explanation may, of course, be that the attack is the same, that it is merely the battleground that has shifted, as Marxists or anarchists denounce "the system," or a new group of advocates of natural man or primitivism rebel against industry and the way in which modern industrialization exploits and despoils the whole living world. These are the answers that are given on all sides by student rebels and armchair dissidents, and revolutionaries suckled on an outworn creed. Whether they see the present system as one stage in an inevitable set of stages which will in the end set man free by subduing the forces of evil, capitalism, nature, and human intractability—or as a perversion of man's true destiny of freedom and beautiful accord with a nature which he neither violates nor exploits, as he pursues his individual, or small cult group, salvation— both theories are bound to old styles of thinking, where salvation could be found either in straight-line progress, in pendulum swings against abuses, or in straight-line regression to earlier periods of human history.

But I believe that the educational system is bearing the brunt of the present attack for other reasons. It is, of course, partly because of the unique generation gap that separates those born during and after World War II, everywhere in the world, from those born before. This meant a period in which the oldest members of the post-World War II generation—a generation who never knew the world without a bomb, the population explosion, transistor radio and TV, space exploration and the threat of environmental pollution—were all still within the educational establishment, classified as too young for power. So our campuses erupted when these eldest members of the new generation were in college, and they gave leadership, which extended down into secondary schools. Now the circle is beginning to round, as they become teachers, supporting the revolts of the young against the outworn and archaic systems of education, which they are now entering as the youngest members of the establishment. This is one of the mechanisms by which the attack is spreading.

There is also no doubt a reflection of the moment when the United States and to a lesser extent the other older industrialized countries are shifting from a producer society that needs all its labor, to a consumer society where the problems are those of equitable distribution of the products of an increasingly automated industry, and a fantastically productive mechanized, commercialized, and officially engineered agriculture. Training for jobs for the groups who have become unemployable, as no longer needed unskilled labor, is a thinly disguised way of turning them into consumers, under the heading of created employment. It is part of a desperate attempt to make an educational system which transforms a manageable agricultural and industrial proletariat into either higher-level employees or more contented consumers. And yet at the same time we are faced with the fact that it will be quite impossible under the present system to make every member of society into a happy consumer. The level of life which mass advertising has taught him to desire—and this is true in the center of New Guinea where a page of *Life* magazine advertising is pinned to the door, as it is in Harlem, rural Mississippi, or on an American Indian reservation—is unobtainable without irreversibly wrecking the natural environment upon which the future well-being of mankind depends.

Since World War II we have gone through a rapid series of versions of the "good life," shared in depth by the United States, the Soviet. Union and Peoples' Republic of China. The spread of heavy industry was expected to guarantee a healthy and contented populace, but the realization that heavy industry at the expense of agricultural development was spreading a malignant and premature growth of cities, as well as the recognition that countries that produced raw materials for industry could not both improve their standard of living and continue to sell their products which could be out priced by synthetic materials, led to the perception of the widening gap between the "rich" and "poor" countries. And beyond this there was the still more dismaying recognition that if any country of any size, and particularly the United States, where 6 percent of the population consumes half of the earth's irreplaceable natural resources, continued to develop and spread its present style of life, it would strangle in its own waste and destruction, and pull the rest of the world down with it. But as poorly diffused and poorly understood as these new findings are, they are having a profound effect on the young, on the one hand, and on the adult expectations and hopes for the young, and fear and hatred of the young on the other.

We are witnessing the breakdown of a system of belief that was essentially linear in nature: more inventions, more progress, higher demands, more education to produce those who could participate as producers and consumers in the results of this endless progression toward a growing GNP. The words that were used were borrowed from biology; we talked of economic "growth," "maturing" nations. But the true metaphor came from a mechanical and irreversible sequence in which a linear process of factory-like production took raw materials and turned them into products: cars and washing machines and fertilizer, in factories; educated citizens in schools. As our faith in such a continuingly improving system, more heavy industry, more automation, more objects of consumption, a higher standard of living, all hitched to what was conceived of as an inexhaustible supply of raw materials and synthetic possibilities, there comes a demand for recycling. Children are no longer to be seen as future manpower, just as water is no longer seen as inexhaustible and wasteable, and the earth as inexhaustibly life-supporting.

As respect for life and its limitations, of the planet and its limited resources, are forced upon us by the evidence of pollution and population explosion and the risks of an annihilating war, we now face a renewed challenge as to what is meant by education. No longer are children to be pushed through a system of education which sorted them into different tracks, finished them off at later and later stages, and after a brief period of productivity and consumership were thrown on a compost heap, to be reluctantly and minimally supported until death relieved society of the burden. No longer was education to be simply a required stage in the life cycle, enforced, sometimes under the guise of privilege, on all the young, so that they might participate in this never-ending expansion of GNP.

The California type of universal higher education available at all ages becomes, at once, the last gasp of a system and the precursor of a new one. So we have the peculiar spectacle of one group of people weeping with tenderness as they see the young and the not so young of the poor and deprived, dressed in caps, gowns, and newly designed hoods, graduating from community colleges—given a second chance and a new skill or a new enjoyment and understanding of life—while the students at our most venerable institutions refuse to wear caps and gowns or threaten to come naked beneath them and throw them off to disrupt the ceremonies.

The community colleges in which the linear process is in part disallowed and the old are permitted to learn, or relearn or simply learn to enjoy, suggest a new form of education, even as the angry taxpayers of an earlier concept of a pioneer society devoted to rewards for hard exploitive labor and mindless consumption, send police and National Guardsmen to attack the students in the parent universities. They anticipate the new kind of recycling of education that must follow our recognition that our relationship within the natural world must return to biological model, in which all of life—and death—are of one process where no part is unessential, no part final, and no part irreversibly exploitive. When the day care center and the nursery school are added to the community college, and the university is close by, and when everyone, at different periods of life, both learns and teaches, we will begin to have a system of education which will not be seen as part of a factory process of shaping the young, into dispensable parts of a linear process, but instead as an indispensable part of life for every age.

With this new emphasis there can be provided a new emphasis upon nonmaterial consumption, to take the pressure off the kind of material consumption, which is destroying our environment. This is one of the things that youth are stressing, in their delight in song, the least exploitive and the freest of all the arts, and in flowers renewable each spring. Granted that they have very little comprehension of the extraordinary changes that will need to be made in the whole structure of the industrialized and industrializing world, to stem the destruction of the planet's resources and save it as a habitat for future generations of men, they show, in the speed with which adaption, for example, is replacing the demand for enormous self-replication, a prevision of what the wisest and best-informed economic and social prophets realize must come.

If consumption must be simplified, if the standard of living can no longer be based on every home being like a power plant, and on an ever-rising GNP, education becomes in great part a preparation for new kinds of joy, of being, participating, rather than of producing. The skills necessary to a simplified but nevertheless highly automated artificial environment, can be developed as special norms of delight, labor made light enough so that no backs are broken, can become part of being. Education, or schools, or the teaching learning centers of the community—whatever we call them—can become a part of society instead of a form of compulsory segregation away from it, where teachers are wardens and children and youth are prisoners, as it is becoming today, in these last stages in which the older system is being called in question and the newer systems have not evolved.

And meanwhile, we have the clash of values, as those who have just emerged from deprivation clamor for a voice and a place, and see education as the focus of their desires. So the militant black groups demand that credentials no longer be the criterion for entering college, and poets demand that the soul-destroying routines of the overburdened, over routined, out-of-date city schools no longer determine the curriculum for Head Start. Older people, prematurely retired by a rapidly changing industrial system, demand that they be allowed to learn, and to teach what they have newly learned. And there is hope—an ingredient which Eli Ginzberg always manages to inject, if necessarily by rigorous selectivity, into what he writes—hope, that the changing values of youth represent the changing recognition of the adults who still control our outmoded and dangerous social and economic forms.

RELIGION IN THE MELTING POT: Religion and Our Racial Tensions*

In an English schoolroom, a small girl stood up to ask the American lecturer a question: "Please, Miss, how does the black American's religion differ from the white American's religion?" Religion and nationality were firmly blended together in her mind and the assumption that there must be a difference in religion between people who, her recent experience had shown her, did not seem to blend too easily, was inevitable.

It would be possible to discuss the relationship between religion and the melting pot from the standpoint of what sanctions for and against the melting-pot process the different religious groups had offered. It could be shown, for instance, how those religious groups, which frowned upon marriage outside their own communion had in some ways impeded the assimilation process, in others accelerated it by that very emphasis. When an immigrant community, which is both foreign and Catholic attempts to keep its young people separate from the community life in order to assure that they will marry Catholic spouses, it may also be isolating them from the main stream of American life. But conversely, when several different foreign groups come to stand together in feeling, because they are Catholic, even though their languages and customs differ, so that many cross-national marriages take place within the bond of a common faith, the type of assimilation and strengthening of American life that comes with such mixture is actually furthered. In the same way, though perhaps less conspicuously, the national divisions among people of Jewish faith have been overridden in favor of marriage within the religious tradition, even though it took place between spouses who came from groups of different national origin, different dates of immigration, and different degrees of wealth and prestige. When members of these same foreign groups were Protestant this has been a definite road to assimilation, as a kind of counterpoint to the common American expectation that everyone from a Latin country would

*Originally published in *Religion and our Racial Tensions*. Harvard University Press, 1945.

be Catholic. So Italian Presbyterians or French Episcopalians seem to deviate so markedly from the pattern of expected behavior as to become, almost automatically, more easily assimilable. Where any group has insisted upon marriage within the communion and interpreted the restriction narrowly enough, this requirement has become a kind of strangling force on the growth of the group itself, in a country where mobility through free marital choice is so highly regarded. Even in regard to those groups arbitrarily defined as belonging to a different race, as in the case of those classified as Negroes, or Mexicans, deviation from the expected religion immediately confuses the caste-like behavior of the other groups. Catholic or Episcopal or Quaker Negro Americans are likely to receive slightly different treatment from that accorded to Methodist and Baptist Negro Americans. Presbyterian Mexicans are less likely to be suspected of not appreciating American housing, and Christian Japanese Americans are regarded with less suspicion than Buddhists. White Americans who belong to the more conspicuously emotional sects which practice "shouting" and open manifestations of religious ecstasy are likely to feel a loss of white caste and to be categorized with the Negro practitioners of the same type of religious behavior.

So throughout American history the threads of religious affiliation have cut across other lines—racial, linguistic, national, class—now serving as a barrier, and now providing a path where several groups could mingle with a sense of safety and common cause. The coincidence of religious affiliations with other types of differentiated behavior, race, national, class, linguistic, is a periodic threat to the orderly process of assimilation, and in the history of any large city can be read the struggle between the manipulators of social behavior who try to handle people in blocs, and the forces of community democracy which work against such efforts. There are parts of New York in which the words Democrat and Catholic or Republican and Protestant may be substituted for each other with such bewildering speed that the listener overhears statements such as "All the Republicans are moving away from here, but the Catholics don't like to live in Republican apartments because they have too many children and you know Negroes don't find Republican apartments as good as Democratic apartments because some of them want to sleep in the day time and there aren't enough doors." If one analyzes the bewildering set of assumptions, which lie back of that remark, that Republicans are also Protestants with small families, that Democrats are Catholics who need more rooms in their apartments and that Negroes are forced to double up so that apartments which have open, wide doorways are inappropriate, and finally that neighborhoods at any period are likely to be occupied by a group which belong to the same political party, have the same religious affiliation, and are of the same national origin, one gets a vivid picture of the way in which one affiliation can be substituted for another in people's minds. In one northwestern city the more usual division of social agencies into Catholic, Protestant, and Jewish is replaced by a fourfold setup, Catholic, Protestant, Jewish, and *Lutheran,* the division of the Protestant group conforming to the nationality emphasis where the word Protestant as the usual synonym for assimilated non-Catholic, non-Jewish Americans didn't work out. I asked one of the community specialists what would be a fifth category if one were ever added, and he said, "Labor"! There is also a developing tendency to speak of Catholic, Protestant, Jewish, and Negro agencies. So the struggle goes on, and sometimes the religious affiliation reflects divisiveness, sometimes not.

II

Underlying it all is the perplexing relationship between the amorphous, diversified, ordinary American agencies and institutions which are all assumed to be Protestant or non-sectarian, with an implied assumption that these are virtual synonyms—which may account for recurrent Catholic lack of enthusiasm for close identification—as over against non-Protestant groups whose solidarity is due to a positive and religious and often national origin point, and not to a mere negation of other types of solidarity. The tendency to make "Protestant" simply a synonym for "not Catholic and non- Jewish" (to such an extent that a Mohammedan American is likely to be classified as "Protestant") rather than a positive affirmation of any type of religious faith has had certain definite effects when we compare it for instance with such a practice as a division of schools of social work for Catholics and Protestants, and a secular school, such as that found in the Netherlands. It has resulted in America's being a Protestant culture, though many cities and states actually have a majority of Catholic citizens. If active church memberships and persistent rejection of intermarriage with those whose affiliations was not as definite had characterized Protestant groups, as it has Catholic and Jewish groups, the whole picture of American life would have been very different. But because to be Protestant is automatically to be assumed to share in all the ordinary institutions of American life, while to be Catholic or Jewish assumes minority status, a very different picture is presented. Meetings will be called in which twenty organizations interested in youth, or education, or the family will be called together;

eighteen of these will be diversified by function, type of program, etc., the other two will represent groups who are labeled as Catholic and Jewish. The Catholic and Jewish groups will be expected to subsume under a single organizational head all of the aspects which are represented by the other eighteen organizations, and to speak, not primarily as specialists in the field of youth work or the family, but as Catholics. With their membership, their very presence, labeled in divisive and minority terms, it is not surprising that their most frequent contribution is dissent from the plans of the diversified majority, whose professional differences become blurred when the group labeled as different objects to any single item in the category.

This peculiar situation in which being a Protestant—nominally—makes an individual thereby more of an *American,* and being Catholic, makes him more of a *Catholic,* places the Catholic religious group in the eternal position of seeming to be against developing trends in American education, social work, etc. By definition, they are believed to be less in sympathy with what any non-Catholic group wants to do than would any group of Protestants, although very often fundamentalist Protestants, or any group of Protestants who regard Protestantism as a religious faith rather than a series of social and political attitudes, would actually take an even stronger negative position if they were asked. But because there are so many different Protestant sects, it is usually possible to ignore them in detail, never give their opposition a chance to show itself, carry a program along under such liberal aegis as the Y.W.C.A. and the Federal Council of Churches, and ignore the less well-articulated protests of individual groups. After all, there is no organized Baptist patriotic organization to match against the Knights of Columbus, no Protestant Conference on the Family or Protestant Conference on Rural Life, which must be conciliated. Public-relations programs, public-welfare agencies, drives, and movements set themselves up with special liaison relationships with Catholic groups and Jewish groups, and assume that anyone who does not belong to either of these can get along with the rest of the country.

This whole tendency has operated to make American education, welfare, associational life increasingly secular. Programs are constructed and plans scanned to see if there is anything in them, which will offend the Catholics or prevent Jewish cooperation, and criteria from religious groups become thus labeled as negative, obstructive, and even subversive. Failure to have a primary religious emphasis in planning means, in practice, that not only are the Catholic groups and the Jewish groups not called in to make the plan—because obviously they would insist on some point which the others do not wish insisted upon—but also that no religious leaders are called in to make the plan, and usually only Catholic and Jewish groups are called in to give their assent to its final form. In many parts of the European world, Protestantism drew its religious fervor not only from opposition to Catholicism but also by actively defending a positive way of life. In America the dialectic has come out differently; the presence of the Catholic minority, more organized and homogeneous than the Protestant religious groups, has increased not Protestant orthodoxy but secularization. The pressure against having religion in the schools becomes expressed in the belief that as long as we merely teach Americanism, flag symbolism, and other national religious rituals, we are on safer, more American ground.

Related phenomena may be found in Jewish assimilation. The Jewish group is disproportionately important in the religious picture because of its being the religious group which makes most demands upon our ideals of religious toleration with its refusal to accept the dominant religious conceptions of the culture as such an important tenet in its faith. Judaism presents eternally the same problem to both Protestant and Catholic that Protestantism presented to the Catholic Church of the Middle Ages. In each case the group, which took its stand on negation has inevitably incorporated negative elements; to a Jew it is of great importance not to be a Christian, to a Protestant, not to be a Catholic, but Catholicism does not include as much negative definition—even in situations where Catholics are in a great minority. This difference in positive and negative emphasis is transformed by Protestant folklore into an enormous emphasis upon Catholic solidarity, which takes on the appearance of a plot. Whenever, as in ordinary cross-racial deliberations, the Jewish group is represented—as a body— where the Protestants are merely present by implication, the same feeling toward the Jewish group is accentuated, and a feeling that "they all band together" may assume almost paranoid proportions.

But because being Protestant and being American have become so closely identified, not only has Protestantism been weakened because it is possible to achieve all the social rewards of Protestantism while actually professing no faith, following no religious rule, and contributing to no church, but also conflicts are set up with Catholicism and Judaism in which orthodoxy is opposed not to heterodoxy, or to heresy, or the active acceptance of another religious faith, but to Americanism. In many areas in Massachusetts the assimilated young move first from the confining walls of the Polish church or the Franco-American church into the Irish church, and here they reach the edge of safety, for once speaking English (learned it is true under unimpeachable auspices) the next step is likely to be mingling in the general American community, and participating in the American atmosphere of freedom of marital choice. Then comes the danger of mixed marriages to the occasional young Catholic who in the height of romanticism, combined with general approved American behavior, decides that he "will become a heathen for her sake"—not a Protestant, but a heathen. The bulk of the Protestant community will approve his behavior simply because it is American. Protestantism has won no convert, the wife will probably also give up any religious tie that she had. Another family has been secularized. In the same way orthodoxy among the Jewish group is old fashioned, foreign, practiced by grandparents. "Americans don't eat kosher." The paring down of religious observances to a minimum so as to pass uncommented upon in the secular American throng becomes a sign of Americanism.

In the South and in the Middle West, rural Protestant sects fight the same battle against the standards of modernity and urban life that Catholic and Jewish immigrant groups fight against "Americanization" which results, almost inevitably in the watering down of religious allegiances in the younger generation, if not in its total disappearance. Social contacts, which may lead to intermarriage, or eating food of the *goyim,* or smoking, dancing, and card-playing—these are the three foci of attack by the conservative religious groups, and in no case is it a choice between one religious belief or another, the substitution of a God known in spirit alone for ritual, or of an old ritual for a less formalized system of worship, of a personal savior for an institutional and sacramental religion—but always a choice between adherence to the foreign or provincial or old fashioned standards and modern urban American life.

In this unequal battle, in which the parents feel that the exponents of the secularized life have all the weapons on their side when it comes to contending for the enthusiasm of the young, there has disappeared the old dichotomy between Good and Evil, between God and Satan. Satan is after all a positive concept, polarized to God. But Americanization, secularization, urbanization cannot be polarized against adherence to the same orthodox religious belief. American standards cannot be branded as anti-Christ, except by the most fanatic preachers. The possibility that they may be is of course always present, informing the words of the fascist fanatics in all three religious sects with an extra threat and danger. By a process of simple substitution, if to become more democratic, more enthusiastic about the expression in real life of the ideals of the American Declaration of Independence is associated with becoming less religious and more secularized, it is no far cry for the religious to array themselves on anti-democratic platform repudiating the very social virtues which their own faiths have begotten and nourished. So we see the uncomfortable spectacle of alternatives such as socialism versus Catholicism in some parts of Europe, initially bred from contrast between rural and urban life, but turned into a false dialectic. Christian socialist parties, while eagerly seized upon by both sides as pawns, sometimes simply exacerbate the conflict.

III

In the United States, the last ten years have seen many sporadic outbursts of religious backing for various types of anti-democratic programs, especially those programs which are essential to the effective operation of assimilation, programs of better race relations, better housing and community living, better labor relations. The vivid imagination of the preacher, sometimes, even more insidiously, the phrases with which such a preacher would communicate successfully with a religious congregation are used as the vehicles of anti-democratic action. Nor has the other side of the picture been wanting, in which the liberal press makes one-sided attacks on religious groups, and perpetuates the idea that they represent plots against democracy because they exist as coherent minority structures in a diffuse Protestant country which is incoherent and halting in its support of democracy.

But the major adjustment of American culture has not been the formation of rival attitudes, each one of which could appropriately identify the other with the devil, but instead the substitution of a vague diffuse affirmation of religion, which, however, knows no creed, and worships at no altar. The expression, "It's nice to believe in something, I wish I did," will be heard frequently on the lips of those who never enter a church or temple, but who give generously to the Red Cross and the Community Chest, work as volunteers in some "non-sectarian" agency, belong to Rotary or Zonta, and begin at least one meeting a year with prayer, and speak enthusiastically about "better race relations," "community integration," and "the American way of life." The adherents of this diffuse set of attitudes associate religion with works rather than faith, and with a positive attitude toward one's neighbor rather than toward God. God is an implied but unimportant part of the whole scheme. A belief in "some sort of God in Nature," that "there is good in all religions," and that "there are as many good people outside of churches as in them" leaves no room for the devil and in fact makes a very indifferent devil for religious polemics. A people who have forgotten God and run after strange idols can be castigated in good style, but a people who just don't remember God much or often but who always give their share in any charitable enterprise are much harder to rouse from their religious lethargy. A devil who can make no more conspicuous use of his expertness at temptation than to keep people abed Sunday morning or reading the funnies falls, inevitably, into innocuous desuetude. So the devil has slipped in importance, even in the most orthodox and evangelistic sects; he has lost his hold on the imagination, become not the proper adversary of the Hound of Heaven but a word to be meaninglessly invoked in the politer forms of profanity.

Just as the old opposition between God and the devil has diminished and been replaced by a continuum on which some people are "interested in religion" and others are "uninterested in religion" so also heaven and hell and all that they stood for have lost much of their dynamic implication. A punishing God who loved man so much that he also chastened those whom he loved was more congruent with old-world styles of human experience than with the freedom of the new. The tendency to associate a threat of hellfire with indulgence in the ordinary stream of urban American life, rather than with the commission of sins which even the standards of that life condemned, undoubtedly helped in this process. Transcendental beliefs provide consolation and support for groups, which are separated from or wish to separate themselves from the mainstream of a culture. Those who by temperament or personal experience find themselves out of touch with the "world" make the reliable personnel of monastic institutions. America initially provided a geographical and political refuge for just such separatist groups whose interest in the next world was proportionate to their desire to live differently in this one. But under the overarching generosity of the American sky, where a secular land of promise lay ready to the zealot's hand, the emphasis shifted from the way of life necessary on earth if heaven, which had seemed so distant to the starving landless peasant or the disappointed society exquisite, were to be reached to the way of life itself, which yielded tenfold to the investment of every talent. In early America, God prospered the good man in cases where goodness and industry were synonymous, and the inevitable shift came to a belief that many of the goods hitherto located in paradise were obtainable on earth, including freedom from want and fear, and better relationships between men. While heaven continued to mean, for the specially religiously gifted, the place where God was, and hell, the banishment from the presence of God, both vanished from the consciousness of the average American who was finding his whole energies absorbed by the pursuit of what he believed to be an obtainable paradise on earth. Except when death comes there is less and less need to think of heaven.

IV

But even here religion is very slightly invoked because of the increasing denial of death, not by a religious insistence upon the resurrection of the body and the life everlasting, but indirectly by a gradual sidestepping of the whole problem. Bodily death has long been the means of focusing attention on the problems of the spirit; as the mourners of other ages have held in their arms the breathless body of a loved child, or closed the eyes and washed the limbs of some aged neighbor, all man's questioning about the soul has trembled on their lips. The question "Is this all? " recurs and recurs to be answered by beliefs in reincarnation, in transmigration and transformation, in eternal bliss and eternal punishment, in purgatories and sevenfold rings of heaven and hell, or by various reëmphases of the solidarity of the social groups which have lost a member, as a member of the enemy tribe is adopted to replace the slain. The question by the unphilosophically minded takes, the form, "What will I—or we—do without him, or her? " or the form, "What will happen to me when I die? " The near kin, the close friend asks the first question, the distant mourner who unwillingly partakes of the funeral meats, the second. But the corruptible body, lying on the bier, was bound to raise both questions, especially in the minds of those who actually laid their warm living hands upon the cold flesh.

Modern American institutions have found a way round the presentation of this dilemma. For him whose own soul is troubled by the fact of death, not because he loved the dead but because he thinks of his own end, death is made increasingly unreal and untroubling. The funeral parlor where special officials care for the dead, embalming in which the corpse is made to look "lifelike," glimpsed only for a moment in its satin bed, and an increasing tendency to have private funerals—all protect him. Children are no longer taken to any funeral from which they can be kept away; adults who go from unwilling requirement of courtesy may avoid seeing the body. Many Americans live and die without ever having touched a dead body of a human being. The advertisements of undertakers' establishments emphasize "air conditioning winter and summer; private staterooms, parking space," subtle ways of assuring those who must witness death that their souls will be left undisturbed, and the most frequent approving comment on modern funerals is that they are "beautiful" in contexts where "sentimentally and untroublingly pretty" can be readily substituted for the word beautiful. Meanwhile students of American personality find thoughts of death, associations with the color black, etc., all definitely "unhealthy."

For the bereaved there is a different solution, in the increasing sense that people are replaceable. In cultures with very strongly developed close family ties, where the growing child is taught to channel his emotions narrowly, attachments to one person can be so deep that separation by death can mar a whole life. But in America when a man loses his wife, or a woman her husband, in proportion as the marriage was a good one, people say: "I hope he—or she—will marry again soon. They're just made to make *someone* happy, you know." The concept of being "good at human relations" is substituted for "being in a deep and important unique human relationship." Young people, questing for mates, are questing for someone who will fit into a pattern, not a pattern, which is cut deep on their hearts, but a pattern, which is widely approved in their social worlds. They want to "be in love," to "be married," to "have friends." Although old custom prevents quite such flagrant statements to those bereaved by death, it is only necessary to read the columns of advice to the lovelorn and the divorced to find over and over again the implicit suggestion that "no person is absolutely essential," "find someone else," quite in the sense that an Indian tribe replaced a dead member by adopting the live body of a hostage, but definitely with the idea of having a complete life in this world, and forgetting those who were no longer possible partners. Two wars, in which deaths occurred far from our shores and in which the only tangible evidences of death were the same that accompany a complete break in a relationship, have no doubt contributed to this attitude. A last letter is a very different harbinger than a last gasping breath from a dying throat. To the extent that most Americans are haunted, they are haunted not by the dead but by the living, and the haunting does not differ as between separation and death.

How much this gradual withdrawal from death is to be attributed to one force rather than another in American culture, it is difficult to say. Urbanization as well as secularization leads to a feeling that individuals are replaceable, that the world holds many other possible spouses and friends, whereas in small rural communities, in small groups who cherish their common religious faith, there may often literally be no one else to choose as spouse or close friend. As in so many other areas where the senses are involved, rapid assimilation has necessitated a denial of the body and its senses, a substitution of scents and soaps for natural body odor, an artificial separation of food into its elements to be recombined by individuals into a pallid imitation of some ancestral tradition of real taste. The body as we make it is being increasingly substituted for the body we are born with, and with this increasing control—by which a few well-turned cosmetic touches can adjust faces of different ancestry to the current type—

goes an increasing unwillingness to face any intractable or inalienable quality of the flesh. If the body does not live forever at least the embalmer's art can make it seem that it will—for the short time one has to look at it. Pain itself, which in other cultures has been heralded as giving meaning to life, is an affront to the personality, to be avoided whenever possible, and when it cannot be avoided, to be ignored, not used in any constructive way.

Some at least of this shift from a body which conditioned one's response to life and was the receptacle of an immortal soul to a body which was simply a more or less tractable instrument of the will of the individual may be attributed to the very rapid intermixture of cultures, and the need in each new home to abandon many of the old body-involved practices because those of the husband's family and of the wife's were incompatible. However that may be, death of the body and the focus on the soul given by death have become increasingly minor notes in American life. There is not space to discuss here in detail the extent to which the tenets of Christian Science are a peculiarly close fit to many of these trends, for that would raise the complicated question of why a religion which is so close to a current cultural trend has nevertheless not grown more, and whether, in fact, one of the strong religious dynamics, at least for a young religion, may not be a countercurrent rather than a with-the-current emphasis. Otherworldliness, which fits this world's major emphases, provides slight counterpoint.

V

A third important shift has been the shift from an attitude toward children as begotten in original sin, to be trained and pruned in godliness, to an increasingly high valuation on children's "natural goodness." Faith in children, in children's power to choose, in children's ability to take responsibility, in children's ability to learn by acting without endangering a delicate pattern of tradition which depends on perfect execution for its perpetuation—all of these attitudes are congruent with a culture which has developed by taking the children of many different kinds of people and turning them—in one generation—into Americans. It bespoke an optimistic, positive attitude toward children, as immigrant parents sent their children out to learn a language they themselves would never speak without an accent, to learn, supported but untutored by their parents, the ways of the New World. With a relinquishment on the part of adults of the belief that their way of doing things was the one and only way, and an expectation that the children would live and act differently, there came an attitude toward children which was increasingly expectant and permissive, and decreasingly protective of adult values. While accompanying a form of life in which rigid conformity and harsh competitiveness often harassed the adult, childhood became more and more a golden age, to which adults looked back. Parental authority dims in this process, and among the available aspects of the Trinity which Christianity has recurrently emphasized, it is the child Christ—the Christ among the Elders of Hoffman—and the Christ the Good Shepherd, primarily interested in children, which have become the most diffuse religious pictorial symbols. The child who can say to his earthly parents, "Wist ye not that I must be about my Father's business," is an especially fitting symbol for the American emphasis on youth, on the newness of each age, on the progress that comes with modernity.

Thus we find in America a vague positive attitude towards a religious system characterized by a kindly God who stands for all good things but who, after all, will not punish you for what are mostly mild infractions of his will, who presides over a friendly and kindly world, in which generosity, charity, and good fellowship are important, and in which what you do is more important than what you feel or believe. Church membership in this country (which is very high proportionately, compared with membership in England where it is still more rigorously connected with active religious practice) is a form of social orientation, expressive of class position, social concern, and a general affirmation of the good life. Children should go to Sunday school – some—even if their elders never go to church. Attacking the church or the more widespread religious symbols is "un-American," but any very great concern with them is also a little strange. Invocation of a religious ethic to alter existing caste and class inequalities in American life, to change the position of the Negro or Mexican American, or the miner or the agricultural migrant laborer, is felt to be hardly fair by people who give contented lip service to religions but have never passed through any fires of conversion or ritual of religious initiation, which have really touched them. The advocate of better intercultural relations who invokes scripture is often regarded as having hit beneath the belt, a danger, which the spokesmen of minority groups should take care not to risk. Appeals to religious belief are apt to lose out, where appeals for religiously and Americanly approved actions of fair play and generosity may win. In a religion of works, it is safer not to mention faith.

The curious this-worldliness, optimistic, positive affirmation of our present way of life, in which sorrow, suffering, and soul searching have no place, was summed up by the clergyman of a small-town church who told me of the victory altar he was building in his church, and added, "I hope to get it finished before there are any casualties among our own boys. That would spoil it."

In so many ways we are living on the residue of an age of faith, drawing our spiritual energy from sources, which we have also diluted almost beyond recognition. It remains to be seen whether the sheer spiritual challenge of developing a culture in which the age-old distinctions between different racial and cultural groups can be orchestrated into a pattern where each is given dignity, combined with the task of developing our place in a world society, may give new impetus to religion in America.

THE CONTEMPORARY AMERICAN FAMILY
AS AN ANTHROPOLOGIST SEES IT*

ABSTRACT

Among the variety of patterns which the family has taken in other cultures, the American type of family has distinguishing features. In the small isolated family characteristic of American cities, the husband is insecure about his job and the wife about hers, with consequent special problems. Correctives in the form of community services and a new ethic of continuous joint responsibility for family life are emerging.

An anthropologist looks at the American family as one of the many forms which the family has taken throughout human history since human beings first invented ways in which adult males could become more or less permanently responsible for the care of females and their children.[1] With a few exceptions which are so curious and contrived that they only emphasize the ubiquitousness of the institution of the family, all human societies have patterned the relationship between sexually paired adults and dependent young. The tie between the father and child may not be recognized as biological. It may be conceived as fostering only or as a spiritual body. The children of other men may be accepted readily; children of several brothers may be regarded as having equivalent claims on the care of one of the brothers; brothers may be treated interchangeably in their access to each other's wives; or sisters may be regarded as potential wives of the same man. The primary fostering tie between parent and child may be extended to include a three-generation family with many collateral lines or shrunk to the tiny biological family of the modern three-room apartment dwellers who have no kin within a thousand miles. The authority of the father may last until death, or all social relations between father and son, even speech, may end at puberty. Women

*Originally published in *The American Journal of Sociology*, LIII, May, 1988, #6, pp. 453-459.

may become completely absorbed into the kin group of their husbands, taking their names and their burial places, or they may even retain control over their own dowries. The life of the next generation may be minutely described in terms of family relationships or family choices made by the parents, or each generation may construct its family life for itself. Marriages may be for life between one man and one woman, or serially monogamous, or between one man and several women, or, less usually, between one woman and two or more men.

But nowhere are these crucial relationships, within which women are protected and cared for during childbearing and little children nurtured and reared, left unpatterned and unregulated. During periods of very rapid social change, of migration, of war and epidemic, the carefully devised and delicate patterns, which rely far more for their preservation on the habituated bodies and vivid expectations of those who were reared within them than upon any external sanctions, may break down. Then, for a period, the primary unit tends to become what it is among the primates, females and young, with the males exercising a nonspecific dominative and protective function in regard to the whole group. During such periods or in certain sections of a population almost the whole support of the children may fall on the mother, as in certain lower economic groups in large cities, or among ethnic groups at the moment of cultural breakdown. Old forms of legal marriage may become so expensive and cumbersome that a large part of a population may be said, at some period, to be living out of wedlock, but the new, altered, or simplified form will in time again become the recognized form of the family for that group.

Traditionally, societies have depended upon reproducing their orderly form of family life by rearing children within families, who will regard that form of family life within which they were reared as normal, natural, and desirable. Children absorb during infancy and early childhood the whole pattern of family interrelationships which they then will be able to repeat, subject to the distortions introduced by hiatuses in their own experience, or idiosyncracies of their own constitution and personality. Even in a society which changes as rapidly as our own, a large proportion of our patterns of family life are attempts—often faulty attempts because circumstances are so changed or the other partner has learned such different patterns—to reproduce the family behavior learned in childhood. A large part of the disorganization of family life today, the frequency of divorce, the incidence of neurosis and disease, may be laid to the discrepancies and contradictions between the expectations learned in childhood and the actualites of the present time.

The American family pattern is an urban middle-class pattern, although upper-class patterns occur, and lower-class practice deviates sharply from middle-class standards, and rural family life still retains the stamp of an earlier historical period. Films, comic strips, radio, and magazines presuppose a middle-class family. This family is typically formed at marriage, when young people finally cease to speak of "my family" as referring to the parental family and begin to look toward a family of their own. It is expected to consist exclusively of husband, wife, and minor children, with the presence of in-laws to be prevented if possible and almost universally to be deplored, particularly by the unrelated spouse. Support from parents to married children is not expected, and, where married children have to give support to their parents, this is regarded as a handicap, a burden on the young marriage. Nor are married children expected to plan their lives on the expectation of ultimately inheriting from either set of parents-in-law; such inheritances when they come along are windfalls, good luck rather than something which may be properly looked forward to. While married children will acknowledge some responsibility for the support of aging parents, especially when widowed, almost no responsibility is taken for brothers and sisters and their children, except in cases of extreme emergency or disaster. Unmarried adult women are expected to support themselves and are often also expected to assume a larger share of the support of a parent than that which is shouldered by married sons and daughters.

The orientation of the new family is forward, and the young couple are normally expected to provide their own establishment. The parents may provide for a wedding or give them a house or a car, but these are works of supererogation, not expected parental behavior, such as is expected in countries in which the parents have to set the young couple up with full household equipment. The assumption is that the parents have given their children of both sexes a "good education" which equips them to choose a mate, earn a living, and manage their lives for themselves with a minimum of help, advice, or interference.

The new family is expected to be formed entirely on the choice of the young people, with the young man taking the formal initiative in making the actual proposal. In selecting a mate, the primary considerations are personal attractiveness in the girl and attractiveness and ability as a breadwinner in the boy; all other considerations, even health, are regarded as subsidiary to them. Common background is very often subsumed under personal attractiveness and congeniality, and the skills which may be necessary to homemaking and mating are regarded as appropriately learned after marriage by practicing them on and with the chosen partner. Here a convention of premarital chastity for the girl and a preference for minimal premarital experience for the boy combine with an equal expectation that the girl will know nothing about running a house or a man about budgeting his income and that during the early years of marriage romantic ardor must balance ignorance and lack of skill. Young people may, without criticism, marry without any accumulation of property of any sort, without any certainty of where they are going to live, and, provided they have a little cash in hand and the man has proved earning power, without his having a job at the moment. Very few human societies have encouraged young people to start a new family with such very small backing from parents, and the wider kin group. Actually a great deal of help, both formal and informal, is given to new marriages, but it is not only not something which may be legitimately expected but is actually something about which young people may feel considerable hesitation if not a real sense of inadequacy in accepting.

The American wife is expected to be educated, as well educated although not as highly trained as the husband, for there is more expectation that he will have a special money-bringing skill than that she will. Differences in education between men and women vary from couple to couple, and the only consistencies are a generally accepted delegation of earning to the husband and management of consumption to the wife. Which spouse prefers driving the car, listening to the radio, keeping up with the news, or participating in the community is a matter of individual adjustment subject to the rules of local groups or cliques but not a matter which is patterned by role for husband and wife. Until marriage the girl has been almost as free as her brother; if she has had a job, she has spent her money as she wished, giving her family something for her board where circumstances dictate such a course, and in recent years often leaving home to work and live in another city, with steadily decreasing protests from parents. For an unmarried son to leave home is still regarded as more usual than for an unmarried daughter. Until her decision to marry she is expected to be guided by the same considerations in the choice of a job which influence her brother—chance for advancement or security, interest, or money, or any combination of these. Once engaged, however, her life-orientation is expected to undergo a sharp change—ambition to shift from job to home.

The new home, so unsupported by parents or kin, is designed and planned by the young couple, very often an ill-assorted compromise between home memories and the new standards of contemporaries, of the department stores, and of women's magazines. Even the simplest middle-class home in the United States is a sort of stage set, constructed with thought, on which the family are going to enact their parts, against which the wife sees herself and the rest of the family. If the furniture is not new, it is at least newly bought second hand, and refurnished and rearranged with care. Within this home, the wife is expected to occupy herself, using it also as a platform from which she goes out into community life, of which, however, she has very little during the early years of her marriage. Where marriages have not taken place inside an existing youthful clique, it is expected that former friends of either spouse will prove trying and uncongenial and that new social groups will be formed based on neighborhood and community ties cultivated by the wife and on business ties cultivated by the husband. The claims of the wife for the local ties grow stronger when there are children and when their neighborhood companionships have to be considered. Husband and wife are expected to rely exclusively on each other as far as cross sex relationships are concerned and never to go out in mixed company without the other partner. On the whole, where men continue social relations with men after marriage, they are either labeled rather dubiously as "business" or frankly regarded as periods of relaxation— fishing, card-playing, yarning—antithetical to the more regulated home life. Women's relations with women outside the home are patterned either as parts of a local prestige game or as earnest endeavors to "do something worth while," and the grounds upon which men and women resent their spouses' outside interests tend to be very different.

A small family, with at least one child of each sex, for whom the parents can make adequate, educational allowance, is regarded as more commendable than a larger family of children in which the children have to forego an education. A large family, however, all of whom receive good educations through a combination of parental help and their own energies is a great credit to everyone. It is regarded as unfortunate when children are born within the first two years after marriage, as this ties the young couple down too soon. Parenthood is a responsible anxious matter, in which the mother must keep herself continually up to date with changing standards of child care. Having children, for a woman, is pretty close in feeling to having a job, for a man—a necessary proof of adequacy and wholeness as a human being, something which one does not so much enjoy but something which one would be unwilling not to have done. Unemployed married women without children are under some compulsion to explain their lack of occupation to themselves or to their neighbors; until recently women who had successfully reared even one child felt that they had made an appropriate and dignified social contribution for which they deserved recognition and support for the rest of their lives. When the children marry and leave the home, the American woman is faced with the same type of readjustment as that facing her husband perhaps two decades later when he retires. The discrepancy in the timing of the husband and wife's retirement periods presents one of the problems of American marriage, as it is motherhood rather than housewifeliness which is the source of pride and self-sacrifice in the urban married woman. The period between the children's leaving home and old age is the main source of voluntary civic and social activity in the United States, as the married woman, trained to years of responsible social behavior in the care of family, finds her task cut in half while her strength is still unimpaired.

Marriage is for life, and all breaks in marriage are treated as failures, and failures which involve some degree of moral turpitude—either sexual or economic irresponsibility. At the same time, the extremely wide prevalence of divorce means that the possibility of divorce, defined as failure and as a disaster, is included in the picture of marriage. Women learn that they must keep their husbands, not merely from casual adventures or time spent wastefully elsewhere, but as husbands; and men learn that it is their wives' duty to keep them and that the world is filled with other women, married or unmarried, who, having failed or decided not to keep their own husbands, will try to attract them away from their present wives. This question of a wife's maintaining her attractiveness, in the face of the domestic routines, the sick bay, the broken drain, the unwashed coffee cups after last night's party, is felt to be a test of her adequacy and her sense of responsibility. A wife is not expected to try to keep her husband's love simply because love is a warm and pleasant thing or simply because she loves him and wants him to love her. Rather she must be continually on the alert to be a successful wife who is making a good job of her marriage. The moral alternatives are whether a woman is regarded as selfish because she "is just interested in keeping her husband," or is "unselfishly working to make a success of her marriage," which includes a sense of responsibility: to her husband and children. With this burden of making the marriage relationship a continuous articulately happy experience in which each partner would choose the other over again each day— which puts a premium on never being unshaven or in curlers—there goes an explicit recognition that it is wrong to insist on the trappings of success where one has failed. The husband or wife who holds an unwilling partner—whatever the reason for the unwillingness—to a marriage from which he or she is trying to escape is regarded as behaving in an unsportsman-like manner. It is the wife's duty to make her husband want to stay and to shy away from taking too great risks with other women's efforts to impress him with their superior attractiveness. Similarly it is the husband's duty to provide for his wife and children so that she will want to stay with him. But, except within orthodox religious groups who still regard marriage as a sacrament, it is neither husband nor wife's duty to stay, once they are sure they want to leave, and, indeed, they may be regarded as doing harm to the other spouse and the children by bringing them up in a "home without love." The average American male's job insecurity, the fear that his maturity, which is based on his ability to earn his own living and provide completely for his family, may be taken from him by personal failure or by a depression, is matched by the average American wife's fear that she may fail at her job of home-making and end up without a husband and perhaps with children to support.

Within this family, children are given an extraordinary amount of attention when judged by the standards of most other societies. Their needs, their wishes, and their performances are regarded as central and worthy of adult attention. The mother is the principal disciplining and character-molding parent and must both give love, comfort, and care and stimulate and goad the child to achievement and outside contacts. Her inevitable oscillation between demanding achievement as a proof of the child's love and threatening to withhold her love if the child does not achieve produces some of the typical conflicts in American character which were especially apparent in young draftees in World War II. The mother also has to train the male child in assertiveness, bidding him at the same time to be peaceful and co-operative and to stand up for himself, which training is responsible for some of the characteristic American uncertainties about their own strength. The father's role is to provide at one time a more horizontal fraternal relationship, supporting the growing child, especially the son, in conflicts with his mother when her demands are excessive or she is too unwilling to let the child grow up, and occasionally introducing a sharp unpredictable bit of violent disapproval in reinforcement of the mother's discipline. While the relationship to the mother introduces into the American child's character the principal strains and conflicts in regard to ethical behavior and giving and receiving of love, the relationship to the father provides a fairly steady, although not very aggressive, support of the child's individuality and pressure toward maturity. Both parents offer the child an appreciative audience for his growing independence, achievement, and autonomy and thus establish firmly his habit of acting, while young, weak, and inexperienced, with the overemphasis which is not regarded as inappropriate because the child is so small that it is all right to show off.

In the training of the young child there is a strong emphasis upon habit training, his learning to eat and eliminate and to sleep at the right times, and an enormous interweaving of beliefs about health and hygiene with morality. Next in importance is the attainment of some degree of motor autonomy. Training of the emotions is a matter more of teaching a child that it should not feel disapproved emotions, like jealousy, hate, or envy, than of any great attending to manners or minutiae of interpersonal relationships, and an ethical insisting that the other person's feelings, rights, etc., must be taken into account. Children are expected to develop consciences modeled upon the admonitions and supported by the rewards and punishments administered by parents. Each child is given its own property; a room to itself is the ideal, and toys and books and tools are personal possessions, respect for which is enforced among brothers and sisters. The custom of paying children for small jobs in the home, and encouraging them to undertake small money-earning jobs outside the home as good for their characters, is widespread. Children are permitted to exert considerable pressure upon the family's choice of food, magazines, and radio programs, and American advertisers regularly exploit this willingness to take consumption cues from children. Weaning is a gradual matter, punctuated by new privileges granted on birthdays and culminating in the period when either son or daughter becomes self-supporting. Self-support is defined not as actual ability to support one's self outside the home but as having a fulltime paid job, all of which may actually go into clothes and pleasure, while the parents continue to provide most or all of the board. The tendency to overestimate and overstate an earning child's own money—so sharply contrasted with urban working-class practice in many European countries—has a later reflection in the tendency to treat a married woman's earnings as in some peculiar sense her own and not simply the resource of the whole family—which is the view held of the husband's earnings. The expectation is that children will press toward maturity and that parents will provide an admiring audience, practical help, and a certain check on their impetuosity, which, however, should actually serve as a further stimulus to make them take on more responsibilities.

The relationship between the character formation of the child and the life-history of its own immediate family, its financial ups and downs, accidents, illnesses, etc., is extraordinarily close, because of the isolation of each small family. Events which would be blurred or reinterpreted by the behavior of neighbors and relatives here become crucial in forming the personalities of the children. This extreme importance of the small, intimate family is to some degree compensated for by the great importance of the age group and by the extent to which group standards supersede family standards at adolescence.

The theme of American parenthood was well summarized by the head of a great high school, who turned to the group of assembled parents, many of them foreign born, many of them showing the marks of sacrifice which had made it possible for their children to attend high school, and said: "Let us rise to greet the children," and then added: "They offer you, their parents, the only thing they have to offer you—their success."

Two major readjustments are taking place in the American family pattern today. The first is the new ways of life which are becoming necessary as the isolated biological family becomes more and more usual, at a period when the demands made on the housewife as a result of new knowledge of nutrition, pediatrics, psychology , and home management in general have also greatly increased. Society is expecting more of the wife and mother at the very period when she, through isolation and lack of help and resources, is less able to meet these demands. Community services of all sorts—all-year-round school facilities, housekeeping services, twenty-four-hour boarding for children during illness in the home, prepared foods, expert advisory services to supplement the homemaker's traditional behavior, which is no longer adequate—are the results.

These innovations find cultural support in our American focus on the welfare of children and in the major contribution to future success which is given by careful education in childhood. Resistence to these changes and a continued insistence that, because families managed in the past to meet every emergency of illness, unemployment, insanity, accident, death, without formalized outside help, they should continue to do so now are rooted in the American cultural belief in the importance of autonomy, independence, and responsibility. Only by a widespread recognition that the family of today is being asked to do a much more difficult task of child-rearing, with much fewer resources than were available to the farm and small-town family, nested among relatives and neighbors and informed by a trusted tradition, can this resistance be shifted.

The second great readjustment which is occurring in the family pattern is the terminability of American marriage. As the old religious sanctions which enjoined fidelity until death, regardless of such ephemeral considerations as congeniality or "happiness" have faded for large sections of the population and have been powerless to save many more marriages from dissolution, new ways of holding marriages together are developing. The life of a family is coming to be seen as a ship which may be wrecked by any turn of the tide unless every member of the family, but especially the two parents, are actively and co-operatively engaged in sailing the boat, vigilantly tacking, trimming their sails, resetting their course, bailing in storms—all to save something which is worth their continuous care. This new ideal, in which all the members of a family work together to keep alive an ever changing relationship, may in time provide us with the necessary new ethical sanction within which to give our changing family dignity and safety.

AMERICAN MUSEUM OF NATURAL HISTORY

Note

1. Anthropological contributions to the study of the American family have taken the form of (1) detailed studies of American culture made by anthropologists trained as ethnologists, (2) detailed studies of American culture on the basis of some of the premises and methods which had been developed in ethnological research, (3) diagnostic studies of regularities in American culture against the background of research in several other cultures, and (4) use of anthropological concepts in the theoretical analysis of American problems. Among these various contributions the following studies may be mentioned: G. Bateson, "Morale and National Character," in *Civilian Morale, Second Yearbook of the Society for the Psychological Study of Social Issues,* ed. Goodwin Watson (New York: Houghton Mifflin Co., 1942), pp. 71-91; Allison Davis and Burleigh and Mary Gardner, *Deep South* (Chicago: University of Chicago Press, 1941) ; Allison Davis and John Dollard, *Children of Bondage* (Washington, D.C.: American Council on Education, 1940) ; John Dollard, *Caste and Class in a Southern Town* (New Haven: Yale University Press, 1937); E. H. Erikson, "Ego Development and Historical Change," in *The Psychoanalytic Study of the Child,* ed. Anna Freud, Heinz Hartmann, and Ernst Kris (New York: Interr national University Press, 1947), Vol. II; Geoffrey Gorer, *The American People* (New York: W. W. Norton & Co., 1948) ; Robert S. and Helen M. Lynd, *Middletown* (New York: Harcourt, Brace & Co., 1929); *Middletown in Transition* (New York: Harcourt, Brace & Co., 1937); Margaret Mead, *And Keep Your Powder Dry* (New York: William Morrow & Co., 1942) ; "On the Institutionalized Role of Women and Character Formation," *Zeitschrift für Sozialforschung,* V, No.1 (1936), 69-75; "Contracts and Comparisons from Primitive Society," *Annals of the American Academy of Political and Social Science,* CLX (March, 1932), 23-28; "Broken Homes," *Nation,*

CXXVIII (February, 1929), 253-55; "What Is Happening to the American Family ," *Journal of Social Case Work,* November, 1947, pp. 323-30; "Conflict of Cultures in America," *Proceedings of the 54th Annual Convention of the Middle States Association of Colleges and Secondary Schools and Affiliated Associations,* November, 1940; Talcott Parsons, "Certain Primary Sources and Patterns of Aggression in the Social Structure of the Western World," *Psychiatry,* Vol. X, NO.2 (May, 1947); "Age and Sex in the Social Structure of the United States," *American Sociological Review,* VII (October, 1942), ~ 604-16; "The Kinship System of the Contemporary United States," *American Anthropologist,* XLV, iNo. I (January-March, 1943), 22-38; Hortense Powdermaker, *After Freedom* (New York : Viking Press, 1939); W. Lloyd Warner and Paul Lunt, *The Social Life of a Modern Community* ("Yankee Town Series," Vol. I [New Haven: Yale University Press, 1941]); *The Status System of a Modern Community* ("Yankee City Series," Vol. II [New Haven: Yale University Press, 1942]); W. Lloyd Warner and Leo Strole, *The Social Systems of American Ethnic Groups* ("Yankee City Series," Vol. III [New Haven: Yale University Press, 1945]); James West, *Plainsville, U.S.A.* (New York: Columbia University Press, 1945).

SEX AND CENSORSHIP
IN CONTEMPORARY SOCIETY*

Every known human society exercises some explicit censorship over behavior relating to the human body, especially as that behavior involves or may involve sex. Where there is no written literature and no representational art, this censorship may be limited to the prohibition of the use of certain words, the substitution of words from another language, or the restriction of the use of these words between men and women or between the parent and the child generations. The presence of certain restrictions on bodily behavior is equally widespread. It may be leaving off an earring rather than leaving off corsets, or even putting on earrings after marriage, which is the focus of feeling and taste, but even the complete absence of clothing does not prevent the exercise of certain canons of modesty and shame.

The phenomenon of censorship, as we know it, occurs when certain constituted authorities (usually prodded by other self-constituted authorities) use the power of the State or the Church to forbid the manufacture and sale of certain kinds of publications or pictorial representations. Such censorship not only depends upon the existence of such an organized state or church; it is usually, also, a response to the presence within the society of heterogeneous groups of people with differing standards and aspirations. What is literature to one group may be merely provocation to another, and a medical textbook written coldly and carefully may nevertheless be salacious reading for the adolescent. It is easier for the purveyor of pornography to flourish within the framework of such differing standards than when he is up against a single standard of what should and should not be said, written and drawn. Because this is so, because censorship by one group or authority over another, instead of by all the responsible members of a group of people, is a special circumstance of large organized societies or the small religious enclave within a large society, light may be thrown on the whole question by looking broadly, first, at the ways human societies have tried to regulate the ways in which sex is experienced.

*Originally published in *New World Writing*. The New American Library, 1953.

So, for the moment I shall not discuss censorship itself except to state my general position: that I feel that censorship is always to be deplored in a free society. Those interested in freedom of thought must inevitably be interested in freedom of expression, in broadening the areas of exploration and understanding. Particularly is retrogressive censorship to be lamented. Men who have not known freedom are limited but not irretrievably damaged by its absence, but such studies of Nazi Germany as Erich Fromm's *Escape from Freedom* suggest that freedom once glimpsed and valued cannot be denied without severe mutilation of the human spirit. Only in those instances where freedom has been feared rather than valued, regarded as anarchical rather than responsible, can men ethically justify to themselves its increased restriction. As a test of whether such ethical justification is possible or not, one may consider the acts of those in power who are enforcing the new disciplines. If those in power are driven to excesses of cruelty, such as concentration camps and mass murders, which the bulk of the population under control have to repudiate, it is probable that the whole new order is causing a serious ethical strain on the society. The contrast is very striking between the small righteous German burgher who continued to deny the gas chambers of Belsen and the Soviet D.P. who demands that the United States treat all Communists as the Soviet Union treated all non-Communists. In the one case, Western European standards of humanity and justice, of treating each person as an individual, had been violated; in the other, the Soviet D.P. simply thinks the contemporary Soviet government is using right methods (methods of mass accusation and punishment, which have always been a part of the Russian police state) for wrong ends. Abandoning one's grandmother may be merely a lamented necessity among a nomadic people with insufficient food, but it becomes murder and remains murder, unless there occurs again a necessity as urgent as that which faced the nomads, as soon as one has some method—dog sled or boat or horse—to transport Grandmother without danger to the food supply or to the younger members of the group. Probably the exercise of freedom is in somewhat the same category. Those who have never been able to exercise it can lead dignified human lives within very narrow confines, but once a society has achieved the self-discipline—both in those who wield power and in those who obey laws—necessary to exercise freedom, then a return to more restrictive measures necessitates the payment of an ethical price, often a price that involves suppression of very valuable and formerly cultivated human sensitivities.

However, our present knowledge does not permit us to extend this statement to the question of sexual freedom. We have no grounds for asserting that in a society where there is less restriction on shared sexual knowledge or experience there is necessarily a better, or worse, set of human values. It can be demonstrated easily that most large societies fail to develop a standard of sex behavior, which suits all groups and so often penalize the members of one class in favor of another, just as most small societies penalize a few individuals in attempting to maintain a single standard for the many. From the existing facts we can also easily plead for more kinds of standards, and especially we can argue against permitting children to grow up unprepared for the kind of sex life they will have to live. We know this to be seriously stunting to the personality. To be reared in a Catholic country where celibacy in the service of God is regarded as a high vocation is a preparation for a life of celibacy; to be reared believing in a Protestant definition of human behavior that regards sex as regrettable but inevitable, a low craving that had better be soundly disposed of within the bonds of holy matrimony, mindful of the saying, "It is better to marry than to burn," is a very poor preparation for celibacy. To those so reared, celibacy is neither a privileged nor a tolerable state. The unmarried are suspected of unmentionable vices, or, at the least, of predictable neuroses, a suspicion the more likely to be true as the deprived bachelors and spinsters share the definition of human beings as creatures unfortunately addicted to sexual behavior as long as the human soul is caged, alas, in this low mortal body. The Catholic position that both celibacy and marriage are holy states, that the body is not inherently evil, but that man must fight against himself to use that body wisely and well, permits a different sort of celibate adulthood.

So we know that it is possible for a society to bring up its children either to be helped or hurt by the alternatives offered them, and hurt in different degrees in terms of their innate capacities. As we learn more about those innate capacities—to what extent, for example, individuals vary in their sexual endowment, and to what extent they vary in their capacity to channel their energies into other activities—our sexual standards can be revised to provide a variety of outlets for these so differently endowed persons. Most human societies struggle in some way with the problem of reaching a balance between the demands of an orderly society and the intense capacities for sexual expression of, for example, young adolescent males, soldiers long isolated from women, or sailors ashore. The greater the recognition of intractable physiological appetites, which can only be diverted at a price, the more successful social standards can be. Many societies demand that the more successful and energetic men support two wives instead of one, and conversely, in Victorian England a whole bevy of well-disciplined maiden aunts sometimes subsisted emotion-

ally on the marriage of one sister, spending all their warmth and
affection on one set of nephews and nieces.

If human societies were faced only with the problem of disciplining sex, of making sure that children were protected from damaging
sexual advances, that little girls did not become pregnant too early or
young boys have too heavy a burden placed upon their sexuality, and
that some orderly division of sexual favors was worked out so that competition for them would not impair the social functioning of the society, the whole problem would take a different shape. But the restrictive
side of sexual regulation is only half the story. True, each society has
the task of seeing to it that men and women do not have sex relations
in socially disapproved ways, the task of bringing up boys and girls in
such a manner that they will adopt the socially approved alternatives
to sex at any given time, so that in societies with a celibate priesthood
a certain number of properly gifted boys will want to become celibates,
and so that, in a socially mobile society like our own, many boys and
girls will be willing to delay marriage until their education is complete.
But in every society it is necessary also to bring up a sufficient portion
of the population in such away that they will want to marry and beget
children. In a caste or class society, it is necessary to train children to be
positively attracted by suitable rather than unsuitable people, which
means in the last analysis that human beings need to be sufficiently
interested in the kind of spouses that society approves for them so that
they will be continuingly attracted to each other. How attracted members of each sex have to be, what is considered the ideal number of children, how long marriage partners have to maintain sexual interest in
each other if the marriage is to be stable—these things vary from one
society to another. But the problem is always there. Stripping the body
nude, performing all bodily acts in public, divesting sex of all mystery
and privacy would not, as the moralists who see only one side of the
question fear, result in unbridled license, but might very soon lead to
unlimited boredom. Our records of the courts of kings and the seats of
tyrants and dictators, of jailers who could abuse their prisoners, and of
slave owners who had free access to their slaves give a consistent picture: unbridled freedom to do anything one likes with anyone one
chooses, without regard to his or her genuine assent or consent, leads
in the end to satiety, to an increasing unreliability of response, to a
search for more and more artificial expedients.

Society has two problems—how to keep sex activity out of forbidden channels that will endanger the bodies and souls of others or
the orderly co-operative processes of social life, and how to keep it
flowing reliably in those channels where it is a necessity if children are
to be conceived and reared in homes where father and mother are tied

together by the requisite amount of sexual interest. If half the members of a society are celibate (because of the religious system or because of a shortage of land, for example), then the other half, charged with producing the children, must maintain a steady sexual interest in their mates if they are to produce and rear properly the necessary number of children. If the social ideal includes the belief, as is increasingly the case in the United States, that people who are not happy together should not stay together but should seek someone else to be happy with, and if "being happy with" is defined either as having children or as enjoying a shared sex life, we see immediately the growth of sterility clinics and the flourishing of adoption, if children are the emphasis, and the growth of books on sex technique and an increasing amount of marriage counseling on sex problems, if sexual satisfaction is regarded as central. Stated briefly, every society has the task of bringing up children who will focus their capacities for sexual feeling on particular persons, with or without overt bodily expression, and who will not only refrain from large amounts of undirected, objectless sex behavior, but will be able to produce the proper intensity of feeling, expressed or unexpressed, for the proper objects.

Seen in this way, the multitude of small and large taboos we find to surround talking about the body, witnessing the bodily acts of others, writing or drawing pictures of bodily acts, can be put in context. These taboos are two-way taboos. They prevent the kind of sex behavior one doesn't want—keep children and adults apart, keep men out of their neighbors' houses when the husbands are away, keep a chance encounter during excretion from turning into a sexual adventure—and they provide the necessary stimuli to sex activity in the right places. Where young men grow up with the degree of shyness characteristic of contemporary lower-class English or Australians, with one kind of language and behavior appropriate for the company of men and another for the company of women, where girls belong to a mysterious world, the mere excitement of sitting next to a girl in the movies is sufficiently enchanting to make it expected or usual for a man to marry the first girl he takes out, and with minor and regrettable occasional aberrations (which, however, are usually impersonal, brief and essentially meaningless) to remain faithful to this one girl, as his wife, through life. In societies that depend upon chaperonage rather than shyness, it is the *situation* that becomes the determining factor. After a chaperoned courtship, the young couple are left alone together, a sufficiently entrancing experience to work a magic of its own. In societies like modern America, where young people, unchaperoned and far from shy, are permitted a great deal of both casual and sexually open companionship, the reliance for attraction permanent enough to ensure marriage has shifted to a much more specific sense of "clicking," which often arises from highly accidental factors, such as meeting under circumstances when the good girl of one's own class looks as if she might really be a bad girl, etc. Such an attraction is often hard put to maintain itself through the years of croup kettles and dishwashing.

The question of regulation also comes up in relation to pornography, which manifests itself in some form in every human society—if only in an insistence on a euphemism for the sex organs which, if abandoned, can immediately create sex excitement. The bawdy laughter explodes as often in a primitive society where people wear practically no clothes at all at some pictured juxtaposition, for example, of a canoe prow and a human body, as it does in a men's smoking room in a university town. The sets of taboos and the requirements of etiquette ensure that the unusual or the unexpected which in any way involves the human body will be stimulating and will evoke in a group an explosive bawdy vocal response, usually loud laughter, and a more specific bodily response when the individual is alone or with possible sexual partners. Every human society has room in it for the pornographer to operate.

Every society has, and has to have, standards as to what is private and what is shared behavior, what behavior can only be shared decently by those who are equally involved in it. All bodily acts, which temporarily blot out other considerations and focus attention on themselves can become to some degree repellent and disgusting to those who are themselves momentarily or completely detached from such desires or urgencies, and all societies prescribe to what degree eating, elimination, courtship, copulation, childbirth, menstruation, illness and death must be sheltered from or shared with spectators. In some societies childbirth is a casual matter until there is danger that mother or child may die, and then the chattering people gathered at the other end of the house become quiet, hurry away to seek protective magic, or flee from the house that may become a house of death rather than birth. In some societies, a sharp difference exists between the degree of excretory freedom permitted males and that permitted females, and females must seek greater privacy, because it is male, and not female, aggression against them that is feared. In some religious groups, men and women who are strangers to each other may kneel close together in a church without fear that the presence of a member of the opposite sex will arouse thoughts and feelings inappropriate to the sacred occasion, but Moslem men, whose women are rigorously guarded from the eyes of strange men, want no women in the mosque to endanger the carefully prepared ritual purity of their bodies. Western Europe has long made a custom of the family meal at which members of both sexes and of all generations may eat together with pleasure and without embarrassment, but there are still many taboos, disguised as etiquette or "consideration," operating against the intrusion of people who are not eating upon those who are ("We'll wait till you finish your dinner"), or against the intrusion of someone who is eating on those who have no food, as for example taking out a large and beautiful lunch in a crowded railway coach on a train without a diner—the situation so skillfully utilized by Maupassant in *Boule de Suif.*

Many societies, especially primitive ones where all human behavior can be more consistently ritualized, have been able to dignify group sexual behavior on certain ritual occasions—a great feast, a ceremony to encourage the crops to grow so that the people may be fed. But here again the question of participation is central. An orgy for all, which serves group goals, ceases to be an orgy, and so is dignified. Participation at the ceremonial defloration of a bride where all the guests participate, publicly, is an occasion regarded as essential for the well being of the group. There is nothing secret, nothing shameful. Participation can be quite as solemn as is the non-participation of the men of the Manus tribe, who stay scrupulously indoors and do not peek while a recent widow is walked by a group of wailing women, naked through the shallow sea. These same men describe with lascivious giggles their spying on similar ceremonies in the neighboring tribe. But the insistence on regulating this question of privacy and participation, and the insistence that where experiences of bodily involvement are shared they must be shared under strict rules, are found in every society. The framework erected is never perfect. There are always chinks behind which the exploiter of inexperience and prurience can beckon and through which the ignorant and the prurient can peek.

And the most available source of forbidden stimulation becomes naturally the behavior of people with different rules, the people of the next tribe: for the Russians, the Armenians; for the English, the French; in a complex society, the people of a different class, a different religious persuasion, a different habit of life. Even in a relatively static society contrasts among rules permit a continuous traffic in accounts and pictures of behavior, which is dignified and meaningful for one group and titillating for members of another. Paintings of nude figures, medical works that give detailed descriptions of the body, records of psychiatric interviews, literature that deals explicitly with matters which members of less educated groups are accustomed to refer to only in half-images, half-glimpsed muscular innuendo—these are historically recurrent examples of materials that have a serious meaning for one group and a pornographic meaning for another. The situation is more acute when societies are changing rapidly and when, through translation, the literature of one society is available to another.

As the outspokenness of earlier centuries gave way to the smothering pruderies of the nineteenth, it became apparent in both England and America that young people, especially those in secularized Protestant homes, were not being prepared to deal with sex and that a great many, far too many even in the kind of society that has been content to count its delinquents, its insane, its criminals and its suicides in the millions, were being unnecessarily penalized. City life had replaced country life, the cheerful bawdiness of earlier centuries had succumbed to a primness of speech, families were becoming smaller, stage and music hall provided a less ample verbal and visual education, we were moving toward a single standard and articulate disapproval of a way of life into which men—themselves initiated by "bad women"—initiated their innocent and ignorant wives. There was, and remains, an urgent need for new forms of serious preparation for sexual behavior, for new ways of satisfying the curiosities of the young during the period when they are either physically or socially too immature to experience sex at first hand, for new kinds of instruction for those who are no longer acquainted with childbirth by the first-hand simplicities of the farm, who no longer see a cow bred or a lamb born, who are so unacquainted with the facts of life and death that they may never perhaps even have watched a bird or a kitten die. We need something to replace the warm ties that bound the generations together in the large families where births were frequent and death came to young and old alike, where marriages were greeted with group roistering within prescribed rules that were broad enough to leave the youngsters who wished to know what it was all about in very little doubt that marriage was a state into which bride and groom entered with nervous expectations of delight. The problem of transition from the nineteenth century was and still is acute. How were those who had been reared within one set of taboos to break them without conveying a sense of shock and outrage even as they spoke courageously? How were they to deal simultaneously with their elders and their contemporaries and the children whose eyes they wished to open more felicitously? The whole battle is vividly portrayed in the passionate aesthetic and ethical statements of Havelock Ellis. Thanks to the shock he gave his contemporaries, and to the activities of pandering fly-by-night publishers, his work—so intensely ethical—is still sometimes read for a pornographic thrill by naive and ill-informed college students.

It is fascinating to take up today such a book as *Nature's Truths Told to a Little Maid* by Margaret Irving, published in 1912, with its cover of a little girl with her arms around the neck of her gentle, highly bred mother, and with Longfellow's "Maiden with the Meek Brown Eyes" on the first page. This book explains gently that "Father and Mother Flower sometimes live in the same flower mansion," and "when they do not live together, they have to send their little messages of love and devotion by the butterflies and the bees." Nowhere in the book is there really anything on which a child could build an understanding of the male's role in procreation, although that of the mother is a little more explicit: "She is smaller than the father ... gentle, patient and loving and ... watches over her dear babies, feeds them and warms them from her own delicate body." But the sense of danger that every word spoken, even words that seem to us today pallid, cowardly, sentimental and evasive, may be turned into an occasion for snickering pornography or neighborhood scandal shines through the passionate admonition: "*Never* ask a question of a *sacred* nature, such as we have been talking about, of your little companions, or mention *any* of *these* things to them; for you have entered, dear, into the Holy of Holies. The subject is too solemn to be talked about; and the people who do mention these things should be avoided, as their talk is a desecration." Behind that statement stands the kind of father, reared in the late nineteenth century, who would say in a grave rebuke to a younger man, "My boy, that is an awfully nice thing to do, and an awfully nasty thing to talk about."

Precariously balanced as we are at every moment on the razor edge between sex in its place and sex out of place, every change in the treatment of any act of the body—in speech, from the pulpit, in literature, in the theater, in the films, in painting and photography—is bound to encounter fear and opposition from the side of the angels and the side of the devils. Those who have successfully mastered their own wayward hearts cry out against being tempted in places where they had thought they were safe; men who had learned to avert their eyes from women's ankles were singularly defenseless against Annette Kellerman bathing suits, as a later generation, schooled to the frankness of the bathing suit, can be caught again by the witchery of brassieres padded with foam rubber. And those on the other side have an even deeper commitment to the preservation of "decency," to keeping the definition of obscenity wide and loose, so that they may advertise their books in paper jackets, charge immense prices at night clubs where nothing at all happens, sell their packets of postcards of "Great Art." Every shift threatens the safety of those who have learned how to be good—often at a great price, and the pocketbooks of those who have lived parasitically off breaches in the stylized morality of their contemporaries.

Within this situation, the judges who must pass rulings in our courts interpreting the unchanging intent of our society, as of every human society, to protect the inexperienced, the ignorant and the innocent, the weak and the faltering from exploitation and unwanted temptation, have no easy task, beset as they are from both sides by those who do not want standards to change with changing times. New problems arise when radio or television can be turned on downstairs in the living room by a childish hand while mother is upstairs with the new baby, when books that once had to be carried out under the watchful eye of the village librarian or bought for three or four dollars from a meager allowance can be bought quickly, surreptitiously, for a quarter in a drugstore or in a crowded railway station. *Buyer beware* has never applied to children, nor does it apply to adults in any field where we find them incompetent, as in the choice of drugs or preserved foods or the selection of meat or milk. Just because all treatment of sex has to deal with two necessities—the necessity to control it and the necessity to cherish it—and because the releasing stimulus is simply *novelty;* this is a problem as old as human society and one that is likely to be with us always. It will never be solved, as some enthusiasts think, by spreading a "sane, healthy attitude toward sex," summed up in such home truths as "Play, play with boys and girls all *together,* live in the sunshine."

The nudist cults illustrate this dilemma vividly. Their exponents, while fighting for the right to sell on the newsstands magazines containing pictures the rest of the world finds suggestive, will also assure one that life in a nudist camp is very moral—the boys and girls never even touch each other. So, where in contemporary life there are few taboos on a boy's putting his arm around a girl's waist on the dance floor or on running arm in arm into the surf, provided both of them are wearing appropriate bathing suits, the nudist cults would substitute a world in which one may see but be careful not to touch! Most peoples of the world, having found that the sense of touch is the sense most reliably related to vividness of feeling, would feel justly deprived by such an exchange; they may feel that those who would promote it (having become, by accident or the exploited pruriences of an earlier period, unduly interested in looking) are elevating nudity to a morality, and thus robbing those who can better balance sight and touch in what they feel to be their birthright: the chance to explore the final mysteries of another's body only in the strictest privacy, while being permitted to lay a hand lightly in public on a dancing partner's arm. Some patterning, some mystery is necessary. Different periods, different kinds of work and play, different relationships between the sexes will demand new patterns. Absence of pattern is unthinkable; without it human creatures, hardly to be called human beings, would vacillate between promiscuity and boredom, and society would be impossible to maintain.

But once we recognize that contrasts between the standards of one group and another—between age groups in a changing society, between neighboring countries, between class and occupational groups within a country—create a problem because one milieu will always permit speech, writing, and visual representation which will be regarded as salacious in another, what kind of solution can be suggested? If we grant that we do not want a static, closed society in which every detail of life is fixed and unchangeable (even if such a society were possible), and if we grant that the problem of patterning bodily behavior—treating some aspects as public, some as private—will always be with us, are there any insights which can be offered as background for the style of censorship appropriate to the present period?

One possible contribution to the whole question would be to separate out and get very clear the ways in which intrinsically pornographic material differs from material that the prurient *finds* pornographic and from that which the panderer can *make* pornographic by focusing attention on five pages out of five hundred.

We may define pornography, cross-culturally, as words or acts or representations that are calculated to stimulate sex feelings independent of the presence of another loved and chosen human being. If the original expression was not designed to so stimulate—if, for instance, a book on obstetrics has been written to instruct midwives, a book on biology to describe reproduction, the biography of a poet to throw light on his creativity, or if a pair of lovers have sought what they thought was complete privacy in a country lane—and if it does so stimulate, then the reader of the book or the person who spies secretly on the lovers, hoping to be aroused, contributes his pornographic intent to something which is not itself pornographic. Similarly, the little fly-by-night publishers who sell repackaged serious literary works or serious scientific books with lurid promises of the titillation contained within the covers are comparable to the innkeeper who, unbeknown to the lovers who seek shelter beneath his roof, also conducts a voyeuristic brothel.

The starved, unhappy adolescent, curious, ashamed, afraid to talk to anyone, restlessly lifting books off top library shelves, is a subject for compassion. But those commercial outfits which debase serious work belong in the same class as panderers, exploiting pitiful needs in a way that does not still the needs but makes them all the more insatiable. In addition to the reader or watcher who searches wherever he is able, who finds even the dictionary a source of secret excitement, the bibliographical panderer who includes Havelock Ellis' *Little Essays on Love and Virtue* and a reproduction of Giorgione's Family on his lists of publications that will be mailed in a plain cover, and the seeking adolescent—all of whom are using for one special purpose books and paintings designed to meet the needs of men for knowledge and beauty—there is, of course, the *creator* of pornographic art and literature, the writer or artist or photographer who sets out to write or reproduce that which will, by its unusualness, by being something that ordinarily is not pictured or verbalized or done, whet the appetite of those whose desire does not yet have, no longer has, or never had an object.

Consider, for example, this advertisement for *The Whip: A Novelette:*

Showing how a beautiful young woman is seized with the frenzy of her father's great whip so that she cannot love or be loved without it. She methodically sets out to seduce a young English clergyman who is madly in love with her. She torments him with torturing desires and suspense until she has worked him to a point of madness, which is her aim. Then: "She let him see her body. She made him aware of every part of her. She moved her breast toward him with a gentle caressing gesture. She ran her tapering fingers down the length of her body like fluttering birds. And then she froze, and he knew she had done it deliberately. And then his eyes fell on the whip and he saw nothing else." From there on the developments are sensational beyond hint or suggestion.[1]*

The question of intrinsic pornography—whether a book or work simply contains passages that might be regarded by many as pornographic or whether there is anything in the way such passages are handled that provides a clue to the intent of the book as a whole—is admittedly an exceedingly difficult problem. But difficult as it may be to establish in a particular case, in general a discussion of intent clarifies the subject. As one vigorous young American woman remarked of a rather famous literary production containing passages of which the pornographic or the nonpornographic character has been disputed: "It is pornographic. For why, because fat little old bald Mr. X is writing about a lot of things he never did."

And she might have added, for people who will never do them.

The character of the daydream as distinct from reality is an essential element in pornography. True, the adolescent may take a description of a real event and turn it into a daydream, the vendor of pornography may represent a medical book as full of daydream material, but the material of true pornography is compounded of daydreams themselves, composed without regard for any given reader or looker, to stimulate and titillate. It bears the signature of nonparticipation—of the dreaming adolescent, the frightened, the impotent, the bored and sated, the senile, desperately concentrating on unusualness, on drawing that which is not usually drawn, writing words on a plaster wall, shifting scenes and actors about, to evoke and feed an impulse that has no object: no object either because the adolescent is not yet old enough to seek sexual partners, or because the recipient of the pornography has lost the precious power of spontaneous sexual feeling. From daydreamer to daydreamer the material passes, always bearing the hallmark of a disproportionate concentration on unusual types of recording or representation or action, "in such quantity or of such nature," to quote a legal decision "as to flavor the whole," so that it becomes, in a more direct colloquial definition, "dirt per se."

But if we have defined pornography as that which will stimulate the senses in the absence of an object on the one hand, or the absence of adequate desire on the other, we must then ask whether it is something to be regarded as wholly evil. What about the burning passions of adolescents, the prisoner in his cell, the soldier with his pin-up girl? Aswell's *The Midsummer Fires* describes with convincing clarity the relationship, which exists between the haunted painter of the pin-up girl and the old banker who has lived in meager marital fidelity, haunted by visions of pin-up girls.

In a society where there are several religious groups and many millions with no religion at all, can any one religious group demand that the government representing the wider society protect its particular members from temptation? Is it not fair, rather, for the state to reply: Train your young people to be less vulnerable. Do not rely on a degree of ignorance or inexperience, which can only be maintained in a closed system. Does not freedom of religion carry with it the obligation of any religious group to educate its members so that they can live in the wider society? (Conversely, how is the secular society to be protected from the products of small self-contained sects—whose shy, innocent girls may safely read sadistic horrors called the lives of martyrs—when their members write and publish the murderous daydreams, which did little harm within the closed enclave of an isolated sect, to be read by millions who were reared in a different way?)

Or a different line of argument may be followed when people wish to make a distinction between children and adolescents on the one hand, and adults on the other, denying to youth that which is designed to corrupt youth, but permitting adults, grown weary and impotent, to make their own choices. Such arguments are reinforced when adults make use of pornographic devices as a way of keeping alive the flickering flame of middle-aged passion within marriage, where the pornographic daydreams become essential to the continuance of the prescribed relationship between husband and wife. Isn't there a difference between the inexperience and immaturity of youth and the conscious choice of adults? Don't we everywhere distinguish between those who are too young and those who are old enough to accomplish their own ruin—or in less extreme terms, to choose the perverse autoerotic daydream rather than a whole living relationship with a real person? If we attempt to preserve this distinction, then mass communications—movies, television, paper books[2]*—bring us up against the fact that in such media it is impossible to discriminate between children and adults. We can keep children under sixteen out of theaters or movie houses, keep their allowances so low that they cannot afford to buy expensive books, and train librarians to hide books that are regarded as unfit for children. But where the child, with a turn of the dial or an easily earned quarter, can listen or look or read, with no adult present to censor, this becomes impossible. Either, in order to protect youth, one must protect everybody, even perhaps to the point of banning serious novels because a class of four-teen-year-olds, quite unable to comprehend the whole, will pass the book around the school room with a greasy little note, "See page 440," until page 440 becomes greasy and ragged, or of destroying the beauty of statues from other lands by adding little false sarongs. We have to choose between bowdlerizing everything and devising some better method. For today youth and age share in the same world; the mass media that have wiped out the difference between rich and poor, so that both may buy *Life* or *Look* for twenty cents, and both may enjoy Rita Hayworth even if one pays $1.50 at the Radio City Music Hall and the other thirty-five cents at a neighborhood movie, have also wiped out the possibility of discriminating between adult and adolescent.

But there are other remedies, and a page might be taken from the practice of the Catholic Church and its Index.[3]+ In the days when, and in the countries where, everyone was Catholic, it was possible to ban books altogether. No substantial proportion of the population would defend them, and unsuitable books could be impounded or burned. If the forbidden flourished, as it always does to some extent, it flourished in alleys, precariously, not on bookstalls in a railway sta-tion next to a church. But in the modern world where many different religious groups and those who acknowledge allegiance to none must live side by side, it is impossible to ban and burn books as can be done in a state where only one religion flourishes. The Church has devel-oped the Index, a list of books, which good Catholics are admonished not to read, except with special permission for scholarly or clerical reasons. This does not mean that some Catholics do not read such books; it is quite possible that in some cases unscrupulous publishers are as pleased when a book is put on the Index as they are when it is attacked by the Watch and Ward Society of Boston, for both insure a certain kind of sale, to those who read in hope of finding the forbidden. The Index performs a very important function: it makes Catholic readers aware of the kind of books they are reading. They may read them, but as they read, a persistent sense of alertness to sin defines the situation and to a degree protects them from a loss of values. In fact, it may even sharpen their sense of values, in the sense that Russian Christians used to claim that those who had sinned and repented had a more highly developed ethical sensitivity than those who had never sinned. When I was a child my mother forbade me to read the books of Horatio Alger because they were "bad literature." Of course this stimulated me to read them, but as I read, I searched diligently for some clue as to how the style, the choice of words and themes, constituted something that could be defined as "bad" as opposed to "good" literature. In a world where we are surrounded by bad literature, experience with what is labeled cheap, clichéd, dull, with bathos and synthetic daydream, may be a good insurance against a debased taste—a better insurance, perhaps, than steeping a child's mind only in great and beautiful literature.

The same course of reasoning can be followed in the case of pornography. But legislative decrees on the subject of decency are only half the answer. These will, it is true, ensure that the genuinely pornographic will be sold surreptitiously, and the whispered word, the leer of the vendor or of the schoolmate serves, like the Index, to put the new consumer on guard: "This is pornographic, forbidden." But this is not enough. It is likewise important that the guns of those who embody organized values, those who care about religion, those who care about literature and art, about science and medicine, and about protecting the young, should be trained against labeling anything pornographic when it is *not* pornographic.

Actually, it is as important at present to legislate against false labeling as against the content of a particular book. Every time a publisher puts a cover on a twenty-five-cent edition of a serious and important book promising illicit delights to the prurient, the issue between pornography on the one hand and literature, art, science and ethics on the other is obscured.

The Roman Catholic Church has long recognized the danger of "indifferentism" in religion, a lazy tolerance that casually accepts all religions without feeling any strong sense of the differences among them. Today we face the danger of indifferentism in literature dealing with sex. The serious and the cheap are not adequately differentiated;

the great novel of experience in which for the first time a writer tries to deal with some subject which has hitherto been taboo is placed side by side with a book in which the reader is guaranteed a story of rape in a church pew or a set of pictures of nudes in long black stockings. Serious manuals on sex behavior, which are needed in a world where individuals grow up in extreme isolation from the diverse ongoing processes of human life, are placed side by side with primers of exotic forms of eroticism. If every publisher who issued a serious work in a pornographic wrapper was subject to indictment similar—although paradoxically in reverse—to prosecution under the pure Food and Drug Act, we might begin to steer our way through this maze in which we find ourselves as we obliterate, hastily, without due consideration, the distinctions between the masses and the classes, adults and children, the pure and the impure. To the old abused adage, "To the pure all things are pure," should be added, "To the inexperienced, great confusion is possible."

It is, also, useful to distinguish between the pornographic, condemned in every society, and the bawdy, the ribald, the shared vulgarities and jokes, which are the safety valves of most social systems. Pornography is a most doubtful safety valve. In extreme cases it may feed the perverted imagination of the doomed man who starts by pulling a little girl's braid and ends by cutting off a little girl's head, as each increasing stimulus loses its effectiveness and must be replaced by a more extreme one. This is particularly true of the pornography primarily designed to be brooded over in secret. But it is quite otherwise with the music hall jokes, the folk ribaldry at a wedding, the innocent smut of the smoking room, where men who are perennially faithful to their wives exchange stories which release explosive laughter. Pornography does not lead to laughter; it leads to deadly serious pursuit of sexual satisfaction divorced from personality and from every other meaning. The uproarious laugh of the group who recognize a common dilemma—the laughter of a group of women at the story of the intractable unborn who refused to budge and merely shivered under the effects of the quart of ice cream hopefully eaten by its poor mother, the laughter of a group of men at the story of the bride who asked to be "frightened" a fourth time—is the laughter of human beings who are making the best of the imperfect social arrangements within which their life here on earth is conducted, colonizers of heaven working with recognizable, imperfect equipment for the development of the human soul.

Such laughter is the counterpoint of the good life. Shared, consecrated by usage and tradition, it is an underwriting of virtue rather than an incitement to vice. Like every other kind of material which deals with the body, and especially with sex, these jokes can be mis-used, or labeled pornography when they are not, but the criteria of happy sharing and of laughter holds. The difference between the music hall in which a feeble carrot waves above a bowl of cauliflower while roars of laughter shake the audience of husband and wives on their weekly outing, and the strip tease, where lonely men, driven and haunted, go alone, is the difference between the paths to heaven and hell, a difference which any society obscures to its peril.

Notes

1* From an advertisement for Number Seven of *American Aphrodite: A Quarterly for the Fancy-Free* (The Only Privately Published Periodical in the World).

2* For an excellent general comment on paper books see Freeman Lewis, *Paper-bound Books in America,* 16th of the R. R. Bowker Memorial Lectures, the New York Public Library, 1952.

3+ See Redmond A. Burke, *What is the Index?* Milwaukee: The Bruce Publishing Company. 1952.

SEXUAL BEHAVIOR: An Anthropologist Looks at the [Kinsey] Report[1]*

When an anthropologist is asked to look at material like the Kinsey report, there are several ways in which it can be done. I could try to infer something about the culture of the United States from this material, and then compare it with our material from other societies, because that is one of the contributions which an anthropologist is usually expected to make—placing behavior in our own society in the context of behavior in other human societies. But that is a congenial thing to do only when one is dealing with data that is arranged culturally.

Dr. Kinsey's report is not. Dr. Kinsey's report has taken a large amount of individual data about identified individuals, but then those identified individuals have been de-identified, the data has been scattered, and separate correlations have been worked out. So, we know something about persons who spent their adolescent years in high school, for instance, but that isn't the way in which the anthropologist puts his data together.

So, the anthropological comments that I can make best on this material are, I think, based on treating the Kinsey report as a cultural phenomenon, just as if I were to go to a South Sea island and attend a cremation ceremony, or a cannibal feast, or a puberty rite. I regard such phenomenon as cultural, study them, and find out what I can learn about the culture by examining events and data of this sort.

The principle things that make the Kinsey report a cultural phenomenon of sorts are two: its scale and the amount of publicity it has received, not its findings.

Last year there was a modest little article by Hohman and Schaffner, "The Sex Lives of Unmarried Men," published in the *American Journal of Sociology*. There were about 4,600 cases. They were gotten in the normal course of psychiatric interviews in the Army—quite a satisfactory mode of sampling. The results in the report that these

*Originally published in *Problems of Sexual Behavior: Research ... Education ... Community Action*. American Social Hygiene Association, Inc. 1948.

men give on when their first sexual experience had been, and with whom, don't differ substantially from the Kinsey report.

And it shows in that report too, that people that didn't go to high school started life younger. Nobody got in the least excited or in the least interested. *The New Yorker* didn't cartoon it, high school girls weren't reading it, and men and women weren't worrying about it. And it was, in a sense, not a cultural phenomenon at all, but a simple piece of sociological research, which gives us a little wider evidence on something that those who have studied the sex mores of the United States knew, but on which data was needed.

Now, contrast with that little article the Kinsey report, the role it has played, the fact that this Association is spending two days talking about it. I very much regret Dr. Kinsey's absence. If I had realized that this discussion was being held in his absence, I never would have consented to take part in the discussion. However, the discussion is being taken down stenographically, and I'm sure he'll read it. But I think it's unfortunate and out of keeping with our generally democratic traditions, to hold a two-day meeting to discuss the work of a living man who is not here.

This report is, because of its scale, and because of the enormous publicity it has been given, of importance in our society today, and this importance is of a very different sort than the mere importance of its findings. Some people may have found out something new out of the Kinsey report. But I doubt if any serious student of sex mores in America has been either surprised in any respect, or learned anything different from what he has known for a long while. So there is no surprise for us in the material. What is striking is its scale, its magnitude, the amount of money spent on it, the size of the book, and the amount of publicity it has received. In every society sex patterns depend on a careful and meticulous balance between ignorance and knowledge, sophistication and naiveté. The Eskimo who lends his wife to a visitor has very careful rules about wife lending—under what circumstances it occurs, and what remarks the lender should make afterwards. If those rules are upset, then instead of having comfortable and happy wife lending, you might instead have murder.

Now take a more elaborately organized society. We have found that almost every great society depends upon areas of ignorance and areas of knowledge. Prewar France depended upon her "jeune fille" tradition, and a young girl cast down her eyes up to the day she married, and the day afterwards, she could lift them. But the social order was threatened if she lifted them up the day before.

There are many societies that lie to children about where babies come from, as in parts of Africa. There are the most hair-raising tales of children, sitting around for the baby to come out of their father's bow, because the children have been taught that the babies drop out of the drawn bows. We have myths about cabbages and storks and department stores. Any set of lies that children are told about sex, are an important part of the character structure of adults in that society.

The most significant thing from this point of view is that the Kinsey report, by the publicity that has been given to this series of facts about extra-marital and abnormal and unusual forms of sex satisfaction, has upset the balance in our society between ignorance and knowledge, between the things we don't mention, and the things we do. And it may be expected to have considerable effect in our society for that reason. Quite a good deal of our virtue has depended upon people not knowing what other people were doing—if they had known, they would have gone and done likewise; and when they weren't quite sure, sometimes they didn't.

This balance has been upset, and it's bound to be not only worrying and troublesome to professional moralists, but worrying and troublesome to those people who are trying to work out their own code of ethics in our society today, because they have been led to believe that they would be protected from the knowledge that other people were doing these things that they wanted to do, but had been told they shouldn't. That protection they have been guaranteed in every lie they have ever been told.

There are probably very few children in America who haven't been lied to magnificently about birth and sex.

And now this guaranteed ignorance has been violated by their society. They no longer have the protection given by ignorance of what other people do. Individuals with a character structure that has been built up by relying upon ignorance will not have to act ethically without this ignorance.

Another aspect of the Kinsey report that must be viewed as a cultural phenomenon, is the extent to which it atomizes human behavior. Atomizing human behavior is a characteristic of American culture. It's nothing that we need to be especially deprecatory about, because it was inevitable that when there came to this continent people from 20 or 30 complex multi-dimensional cultures, set them down, and said, "You have got to get on with each other, and communicate with each other, and get on with each other's children", this would involve an enormous simplification, in the breaking down of values by dealing in such very simple units as dollars and grades, sizes and headlines, and so forth, so that Mrs. Jones could compare her Jimmy with Mrs. Smith's Billy.

But as a result, we have atomized life, and we have these little quiz bits, these "believe it or nots", this taking of every fact out of context, and regarding it as interesting in itself.

In the same manner, Dr. Kinsey has taken sex behavior out of its inter-personal context, and out of its biological significance, because we don't have physiological data to back up his observations any more than we have inter-personal data. His treatment of sex reduced it to the category of a simple act of elimination. This is perfectly congruent with the American tendency to treat knowledge atomistically, but all of those concerned with inter-personal relations know that this atomistic treatment of human behavior conflicts with the development of good inter-personal relations.

So long as young people don't go out with an "identified person", but have a date, dates are going to be less personal, than if one were going out with Mary Jane,—"I've got a date tonight". All one knows about the date is that it's with someone of the opposite sex, and one doesn't always know that. It's something to do on a Saturday night with an "unidentified" person of the opposite sex.

So that tendency to atomize, to break down, to take out of context, to discuss discretely—this general tendency of our culture is enormously exemplified in Dr. Kinsey's report.

Then, of course, there is this tendency in the United States to build our ethics out of what other people are doing this week. That again is not surprising. The Rumanian mother, the Italian mother, the Scottish mother and the Japanese mother who came to this country and sent their children to school, didn't know the mores. The mother didn't know what time a child should come in. She didn't know when a girl should go out with a boy. In some of their home countries kissing anybody under any circumstances was taboo, so when a daughter started kissing somebody on the doorstep, the only thing the mother could do was ask what do the other girls do. And our adolescent ethics are built on what the other girls and boys do.

This is perfectly explicable. We as a people have been dealing with this aspect of our culture. We have to deal with it because it's there, and because almost everybody in this country now, instead of operating on an absolutely moral code, bases his ethics on what the other people are doing and this even applies to religious groups. We have only got 66 million church members in this country, and of that number not half, probably, pay much attention. And the rest of the country doesn't even claim to be church members. So, the great proportion of the country refer their behavior to what the other people do.

We have been very badly handicapped about the matter of sex. We have measured the baby's gains in motor skills by the Gesell norm but we couldn't tell about norms of the sex behavior of other people. Whether one should have more sex expression, or less sex longer, or more sex shorter, or more or less frequent sex—this was something one just couldn't find the answer to. It has been making a great many Americans miserable for a very long time because they didn't know whether they were happy or not.

I think it is putting it lightly to say that Dr. Kinsey's book is going to have some of the effect that *Lady Chatterley's Lover* had, and you remember how many women that made unhappy back in the twenties. At least I suppose that some people here remember that D. H. Lawrence fantasy of what life could be like. It had a bad effect on a great many homes.

So that Dr. Kinsey's book, by purporting to give norms and ranges laid down for sex behavior of the male, does what the Gesell book does for babies, what Emily Post does for manners and quiz books do for one's education, giving a way of placing oneself and feeling more comfortable. Therefore, again, all this is going to be exceedingly important, the whole paraphernalia, tables and norms and graphs. One can find out where oneself or one's spouse really is. The fact is that a lot of people may be disappointed. This whole paraphernalia of statistics is something we approve of, something that we are used to, and something that gives us security.

There are in American culture, as an anthropologist looks at it, two tendencies. One is to say that whatever is done by the majority is right, is the norm, should be done. On the other hand, we have a Puritan tradition of very high ideals, which nobody is expected to live up to. From this point of view the tension between what you want to do and what you can do is what makes the world go round, and get better.

There is an eternal vacillation between these two positions, between having unobtainable ideals and just conforming to the norm. If the adolescent gets too disillusioned, then tension is too great. So some will argue that we ought to revise our society, we ought to stop holding up these high unobtainable ideals, and say whatever is done by the majority in the United States of America, is the best possible behavior that can be indicated. There has been quite a little talk about the fact that we ought to revise our laws because of the Kinsey report. Some of that talk has been most astonishing, I think, because nobody thought that people were obeying the laws. I mean, if all of them had been, we wouldn't have had these laws. We have laws to encourage people to do less of the things we don't want them to do. We don't have laws to tell them to eat ice-cream sodas. And why it should be said that we ought to reform our laws because it is now demonstrated more publicly that more people break them is very much open to question. But this is the sort of discussion that is going to come up because of the way in which the Kinsey report fits into our American mores.

The next point which seems significant, perhaps more deeply significant than any of these others, is the perpetuation in the Kinsey report of our traditional attitudes toward sex. The Kinsey report is not, from any point of view, a daring piece of work. Some people here may remember a short story that was published in *The American Mercury* in about 1922, called "Hatrack". That was a daring piece of work—it has some emotion in it. It is not daring in the United States to talk about copulation; it has been done for a long time. The thing that is daring in the United States is to discuss the fact that sex has emotional connotations and meaning to people.

Whenever you start talking about the meaning of sex, you get into trouble. Dr. Kinsey doesn't. Dr. Kinsey has limited himself to the description of a non-inter-personal and meaningless act. There is no suggestion of emotional content, of spiritual significance, of non-spiritual significance, of ethical significance, of rich fantasy. One of the most striking omissions of a book based on verbal data is the omission of any discussion of fantasy.

He is simply perpetuating an American tradition, that the best way to think about sex is in the same way we think about any other unfortunately necessary bodily act. And furthermore, he is perpetuating, to an extreme degree the tendency to confuse sex with excretion—excremental rather than sacramental. The very word "outlet" of course is an eliminatory word. The whole discussion in the book, and the whole handling of the subject, is the handling of a biologically necessary excretion. And the argument goes to prove that people will excrete—where, with whom, and under what circumstances is of course very carefully categorized, but is essentially irrelevant, except as a statement of frequencies and class typed, age typed, etc., behavior.

There has been a steady trend in the United States towards looking at the body in terms of health, and justifying any attention to the body in terms of health. Out of our old Puritan tradition we had the general picture of course that the body was completely evil. You just had to live in it until you got to heaven. Then we built up an increased respect or interest in the body, but this too has been camouflaged under the heading of "health". If you eat enough food, that's good for you—and not good; you can eat a little food, that's good—and not good for you. Sleep—you don't sleep because it's fun to sleep; you sleep because it makes you more efficient, more healthy. And you eat the right food to keep your bowels open, and your skin clear. With all this endless emphasis on health there has been a steady trend in this country to assimilate sex activity for both men and women to the same sort of thing—necessary for health and a hygienic activity, just like that advertisement in the subways last year: "A change of laxative is good for you."

Now this attitude is extraordinarily destructive of both intra-psychic and inter-personal relations, perpetuates a lack of sensuousness, a lack of happy familiarity with one's own body, a lack of happy relationship to one's own bodily functions, a lack of capacity of women to breast-feed their children, a lack of capacity of obstetricians to let women breast-feed.

The major abstraction which I think any anthropologist from Mars would get out of the Kinsey report as to what are the beliefs about sex in the United States is that it is an impersonal, meaningless act which men have to perform fairly often—but oftener if they haven't been to school much. So it sums up pretty adequately some very marked trends in the United States.

The next question might be what is the responsibility of a group like this to the effects that the report may be expected to have? Some people think that what one should say is, "Well, this is truth. All truth is good, all science is splendid. You can't criticize a man in any way for having found some truth and published it." We live in a world that depends upon the propagation of truth. But in the science of human relations, what problems you study, how you study them, how you present your results, these are all matters of social responsibility, from which the social scientist cannot escape.

You cannot exonerate a social scientist for the purposive cultivation of publicity for the report, so that instead of its being presented like Hohman and Schaffner's paper, in ordinary scientific channels, available to the people who could use such results responsibly, it has become a wide-spread best seller, become a part of our culture. When this happens, the educators and leaders of the culture then become in turn responsible for its effects.

Now, a great many people have welcomed it because, they say, it has lifted a veil from something that has been dark for many years. I'm inclined to think that it hasn't, but then, to the extent that people think it has, it will have. If therefore, a lot of words have been published in the public prints this time that haven't been published before, that may be an advance. I remember that in a review of a book on the behavior of apes, only four years back, that appeared in one of our leading book review sections in New York, they had refused to publish the word *present*. So we have made progress since then. And it is quite possible that the Kinsey report may be used constructively by those who feel that the present relationships between ignorance and behavior in our society are completely out of line, that the kind of behavior that is based on ignorance, a stereotype of what other people are doing and what in time you will do yourself, is no longer appropriate in our society today, with its diverse, shifting, changing mores.

We do have to work out a new set of sex patterns. And the Kinsey report could be used—if these things that I have said are held in mind, but I personally think, only if they are held in mind—constructively to underline our need to think more about human sex behavior. But I would like really to think about sex, rather than excretory, eliminative outlets.

We need to think about inter-personal relations, we need to give our young people a new code of inter-personal relations, which they haven't got, and then freedom to speak frankly about sex behavior will increase. I think that most of the people here undoubtedly believe that freedom to discuss freely, without taboos, is a necessary condition for the development of such a new ethic, even though the process may be expensive and confusing while it goes on. And I think the Kinsey report can undoubtedly be used in that way.

However, there is also the danger that the report—because it is so unpatterned, so atomistic, dealing with one single item of behavior, totally out of the relevant context—may promote the idea that we don't need patterns of sex behavior, that what we need is freedom, or common sense, or getting rid of taboos. Now, we know of no people in the world, primitive or civilized, who don't have an elaborate code of sex behavior to protect the young from the old, to protect members of the family from each other, to protect sons from the competition of fathers and fathers from the competition of sons, to provide the necessary rewards for men to stay at home, for which there seems to be no biological basis. Human society has been based on developing a code of behavior, of beliefs and manners sufficiently complex to bring up children inside a family in such a way that they can form a new family, and have children who leave home to form new families.

We have no indication from any of our cross-cultural anthropological material that we can get on without such a code today. We are going to need patterns of behavior, and this sort of material, because it is itself so unpatterned, so unrelated to meaning, is likely to create a sense of patternlessness, because there is nothing here to build with. And the most serious possible effects of the Kinsey report lie in its being so completely representative of these particular trends in American culture, of this quantification, justification by numbers, atomization, this tendency to handle sex non-inter-personally—and in its Puritanism. This is one of the most Puritanical documents I ever read in my life. Nowhere have I been able to find a single suggestion that sex is any fun, not anywhere in the book, not a suggestion. Sex is treated as a biological necessity, but the book rigorously eschews any recognition of the fact of the pleasure that men and women take in each other's company, take in their own bodies—that sex relationships have been the cement that has held all the world together for a very long time.

So it is, in its format, in its premises, in its implications also, representative of the very Puritanical trends, which have been so striking in our culture throughout. This same trend appears in our attempts to teach children the "facts of life" in which the only vital "fact of life" remaining now is copulation. Life and death have been removed, and the only thing we teach children as to the facts of life is copulation. A woman, a very prominent child psychologist and psychiatrist, told me recently that she had not seen a single instance of a mother who has successfully told her children *both* the anatomical facts of procreation, *and* the fact that there was pleasure in it! That's a striking example of the Puritanism, which has always split the two.

This is the thing that most sex educators are warning against, the sort of condition that produces the kind of sex behavior that we regard as social pathology, whether it is a question of frigidity or impotence or prostitution, whether it be social or individual forms of pathology. Yet this attitude is embodied and perpetuated in the Kinsey report.

So we have here a document of great size, validated by the expenditure of a great lot of money, which is very important in America. And, of course, every time there is a meeting like this, it is being validated more, because the more meetings there are, the greater its social reality. So it has every single requirement of importance—size, numbers, money, meetings, publicity and sales, all to reinforce the major basic trends in our society that have made sex behavior disassociated, sinful and meaningless, because it has not been placed in an inter-personal context, it is not attached to the most important values of the relations between people.

In the past, it was said, "It is better to marry than to burn." Now we translate "it is better to marry than to burn" to "it is better to have an outlet of some sort, because you've got to have an outlet of some sort."

You see, one of the curious things from the Kinsey report is that this emphasis is on the fact that there will be outlets and then you tell somebody that there is going to be an outlet anyway, so it's just a question of which outlet and the book suggests no way of choosing between a woman and a sheep.

The Kinsey report should reinforce, therefore, because it is so representative of them, all these trends. And it may, conceivably increase, to some extent, the number of young people who will feel less guilty while they are, possibly, indulging in a few more outlets with a sense of hygienic self-righteousness.

Note

1. This address was reported by stenotype.

JEALOUSY: Primitave and Civilised*

Il y a dans la jalousie plus d'amour propre que d'amour.
La Rouchefocauld. MAXIMES

At the very start I wish to register a protest against the title of this article and against its inclusion in this symposium. The coincidence of article and symposium suggests, first, that there is some special connection, some essential relevancy, between jealousy and women – which I deny; and second, that there is such a thing as "civilised" jealousy – although there is no doubt much jealousy among the inhabitants of civilized countries. With these initial demurrers, we can attack the problem.

SOME THINKERS have included under the term jealousy all those defensive attitudes of fear, anger, and humiliation, which centre about the loss of some object, be that object lands or flocks, spouse or title, position or reputation. Some theorists, like Müller-Lyer, have, erroneously, I think, insisted that primitive man does not know sexual jealousy because he often submits with the best grace in the world to situations, which would injure the ego of a present-day German citizen. Ernest Jones, claiming that the key to the meaning of sexual jealousy hangs side by side with all the other keys on the key ring of psychoanalysis, attributes sexual jealousy to a suppressed homosexuality which projects upon the suspected mate impulses of which the suspicious one is really guilty. The romantics have claimed that jealousy is the inevitable shadow cast by the perfect contours of real love. Here are contrasts enough: theories which would make jealousy any reaction to threatened self-esteem, set it down as special pathology, or justify it and even endear it to the world by tacking it on like a tail to the kite of romantic love. In this paper I shall adhere to the more catholic and less special view foreshadowed by Shand:
"If it is difficult to define jealousy by its feeling, which sometimes inclines more to fear, sorrow and shame, at others to anger, suspicion and humiliation,—we can still define it by its end or function.

*Originally published in *Woman's Coming of Age: A Symposiium*. Edited by Samuel D. Schmalhausen and V. F. Calverton. Horace Liveright, Inc., 1931.

It is that egoistic side of the system of love which has as its special end the exclusive possession of the loved object, whether this object be a woman, or other person, or power, reputation, or property." I would only amend his definition to expunge the word "exclusive," for many people are jealous of a privilege which they share with others but which they maintain against outsiders.

Perhaps nothing illustrates more vividly the essentially egoistic and selfish nature of sexual jealousy than a comparison of the different cultural conditions under which one man may have first access to another man's wife. There is no evidence for claiming that an intensely proprietary attitude towards one's wife is characteristic of simpler or more complex cultures, for the most uncompromising exclusiveness has been found in all levels of society. Let us then investigate the contrasting attitudes of the French peasantry before the Revolution and the present-day Banaro of the Sepik River region in New Guinea.[1] The French peasant resented fiercely the exercise of the *jus primœ noctis* by his seigneur. The proponent of jealousy as the inalienable ornament of the lover's spirit would say that it was outraged love which resented this intrusion of another male—that any man subjected to such a trial would be filled with the keenest and most righteous jealousy. But is it not equally plausible that it was outraged dignity, which tortured the peasant? He was no party to the scheme; his set of ideas did not include any soothing philosophy that he thought his bride was dignified by the lord's embrace. The exercise of the noble's power simply underscored in the most vigorous way possible the peasant's social impotence.

For legal arrangements under which another man has first access to a man's bride do not necessarily give rise to feelings of jealousy. Where the custom is merely that the chief's daughter should be deflowered by another, the eloping young chief will not approach his bride during the elopement, but, if he intends to marry her, bring her still a virgin to his father's house, where he knows she will submit to the cruel public defloration ceremony. He is more concerned with his reputation for having married a virgin than for the intimate ordeal to which he is subjecting the girl. And among the Banaro it is not only the defloration but a year's enjoyment of his bride, which the young bridegroom must yield to another man. Banaro society is divided into two exogamic moieties. Each of these moieties is subdivided into two divisions, making four divisions in all. In the other division of his own moiety, each man has a ceremonial friend, and it is the duty of this friend to initiate his friend's son's future wife into sex. This is done most formally in the "Goblin House" in front of the hidden sacred pipes upon which no woman may look, and the girl is then returned to her father-in-law's care. The ceremonial friend has access to her, always ritually, until a child is born, which is known as the "goblin child." Only then may the young man take his wife. Meanwhile he himself has been initiated by the wife of his father's ceremonial friend, whom he has been sent to seek out in the forest, carrying a charmed liana as invitation. Later on, on ceremonial occasions, the young bridegroom and *his* ceremonial friend of the other division will exchange wives, and their wives may even bear children to their husbands' friends, instead of to their husbands. So, in a lifetime, every individual has three goblin spouses in addition to a regular spouse.

Analysis will show that this social situation is simply packed with occasions, which among us would give rise to jealousy: an old man's jealousy because his wife takes a young lover, an older woman's jealousy of her husband's interest in a fresh young girl, a young man's thwarted desire for his young wife—for he has to accept the embraces of a woman of his mother's age while another enjoys his pledged bride's virginity. Yet we have peculiar testimony of the peaceful and satisfactory way in which this apparent set for jealousy really operates. All over New Guinea and the adjoining islands, wherever the white man has gone, recruiting offers an escape to those who are permanently or temporarily at odds with their society. Working for the white man provides a refuge, unknown in the old days, to the disinherited son, the betrayed husband, the discredited magician, the deposed leader. The eagerness with which men come forward to meet the recruiter's tempting offers is a measure of the peace and content within their respective cultures. And among the Banaro the recruiter has little luck; everyone is too contentedly involved in the fantastic intricacies of Banaro social life.

Or let us consider another familiar situation, which may give rise to the most intense jealousy or to which jealousy may be entirely irrelevant. If a guest seduces his host's wife among us, or indeed in any society where the crowd is ready to cry, "cuckold," the husband betrays the most furious resentment and jealousy. But let us go instead to a society where wife lending is the rule, as among the Eskimo, a society, which cries, not "cuckold" but "stingy," "inhospitable," "mean," to a husband who does not give his wife to his guest. Here the husband will upbraid the wife who is slow to respond to his guest, rather than resent the guest's demands. The most casual survey of primitive literature betrays the numerous ways in which exclusive sexual possession of the spouse is modified and contravened, and demonstrates how the self-interest of husband and wife is identified, not with the exclusive possession of each other, but with the appropriate carrying out, whether it be through wife lending, wife exchange, ceremonial license, or religious ceremony, of these very contraventions.

A conspicuous example of this is the attitude of women towards secondary wives in a culture where polygamy is the rule for the rich and influential. There is a case on record of a woman who actually haled her husband into court on the charge that she had been married to him three years and borne him two children, and he had not yet taken another wife. The native court allowed the husband six months in which to take unto himself without fail a second wife. Women urge their husbands to take other wives, which will add to their own prestige by conferring upon them the rank of first wife and also for the practical point of providing labourers and child bearers in the household. The self-esteem of the chief wife is enhanced by their entrance into the ménage and there is no occasion for jealousy— *unless* one of them tends to become the favourite and flexible custom permits usurpation of the first wife's dignities. In a society where there is emphasis upon virginity, a father will be jealous of his daughter's honour. In dissimilar case is the Maori father who has offered his daughter to an honoured guest, only to have her churlishly refuse the guest her favours. The guest is then entitled by custom to fasten a log by a long vine, and, naming the log after the ungracious girl, to drag it about his host's village, heaping the most definite and vigourous abuse upon this dummy. Such a father, although his daughter's virginity may be preserved, will bow his head in shame.

However varied the social setting, it will be seen to be the threatened self-esteem, the threatened ego which reacts jealously. Situations involving this self-esteem will, however, take widely different forms. One's reputation may be concerned with acquisition of wealth, display of wealth, distribution of wealth, or merely with having exchanged much wealth for value received. A man's personal reputation may be based upon the number of women he has purchased or the number of women he has captured, or, as among the Manus, upon the number of temptations, which he has resisted—or again in certain parts of Micronesia, he may boast of the honourable scars which he has received from the shark tooth knives of belligerent and unwilling women. A woman's reputation may be tied up with absolute chastity, or with the type of pre-marital prodigality of favours, which was so much admired among the ancient Natchez Indians that they pictured a spirit world entered by means of a bridge, which was treacherously slippery beneath the feet of the over-virtuous maiden. There is hardly any limit of performance or apparent deprivation to which the individual may not be pushed by his society's standards. Whatever the social set, however, it will inspire him to zeal for his socially defined position. And if he feels, his self-esteem is threatened, if his reputation as a gracious wife lender or as a successful ruler of a harem is in danger, jealousy will be the result.

The line between zeal and jealousy is a fine one; a line which the apologists for jealousy usually neglect to draw. An attentive interest in the attainment or the preservation of social or personal status is zeal, a positive attitude; a frightened, angry defense of such status is jealousy, a negative attitude, always unpleasant in feeling tone. This can be seen clearly in a polygamous society. A zealous man anxious to enhance his own prestige will buy many wives. But the South African king, who, impotent himself, tries to draw a fast line of police about his two hundred wives, instead of winking at their amours as was the custom of over-married monarchs, is no longer merely zealous in carrying out the dictates of social usage, he is simply jealous.

The same distinction can be observed between the behaviour of the zealous suitor and the jealous one. He who is zealous studies his mistress's face to learn her pleasure, seeks out special gifts to please her, tries to arouse her interest and fulfill her slightest wish; all of his behaviour is positive, constructive, directed towards a goal. But the jealous suitor looks into her face only to read there his own dismissal or signs of his rival's triumph; he is far too busy worrying about his fate to be an acceptable tennis partner or dinner companion. Turned in upon himself, his whole duty is not to please the lady but to pity himself and to blame her or his rival for the humiliation, which he is suffering. Although his goal is avowedly the same as his rival's, his whole behaviour serves to prevent his attaining it.

Compare also the behaviour of the woman, secure in herself, but anxious to please her lover, with the behaviour of her who fears to lose husband or lover. Aldous Huxley has drawn a vivid picture of the tears and tantrums of poor Margery, everyone of which served to precipitate her impatient lover into the arms of her rival. The jealous man or woman seldom comes bearing flowers, and if one does so, it is with such a look in the eye as warns the recipient that conquest of the rival and rehabilitation of the injured self-esteem was the prime motive when the bouquet was selected.

So often, conduct which is zeal in one age or in one society, because it is motivated by an eager and lively appreciation of the social pattern or the customary values in personal relationships, is motivated in another society by feelings of insecurity which lead to fear, doubt, and suspicion. The medieval crusader who cared so little for his chatelaine that he neglected to lock the metal girdle about her loins, would have been lacking in zeal and his wife might have felt just grounds for resentment, but the fifteenth century husband who kept up this practice would have been branded as a jealous monster.

The confusion between the two attitudes is increased by the inclusion in the romantic love pattern of certain conventional manifestations of jealousy. A failure to display a suitable amount of flatter-ing anxiety, to greet a broken engagement with alarm, or a smile to another with glowering hostilities, if a man, with tearful pouts, if a woman, is written down as lack of zeal. But a closer scrutiny will always reveal the point at which the lover no longer acts to reassure his beloved but to reassure himself, from fear of loss or hurt to his self-esteem. Hence the ridiculous comment, which is so often heard, "She likes him to be jealous of her." No one, not in some way pathological, likes to see another in an acute state of misery and humiliation. What such a commentator really means is: "She likes him to act in a way to which others are only impelled by self-love because she knows he is moved to it by love of her." The husband who dances close atten-dance from jealousy, the wife who goes meticulously over the events of an absence, from jealousy, is not appreciated.

In similar confusion was a woman who remarked to me recently: "Most men expect you to be jealous, and if you're wise you will be." What she meant was simply that most men were flattered by an amount of flutter, which simulated jealousy.

If, then, jealousy be not a matter of a normal man defending his natural rights, but of a frightened man defending himself against the infringement of rights not natural but merely guaranteed to him by his society, we can admit frankly that it is an unfortunate phenome-non with nothing to be said in its favour. Jealousy is not a barometer by which depth of love can be read, it merely records the degree of the lover's insecurity. And jealousy is notably an attitude, which arouses no sympathy in others. Yet if its display is really so strongly associated with true love, why should the world, having taken the lover to its bosom, evict the jealous lover? Is it not because jealousy, like all other forms of extreme egoism, is repellent, is necessarily of a sort with which others cannot identify themselves? Moreover jeal-ousy defeats its own ends, renders many a lover *hors de combat* from the start. It is a negative, miserable state of feeling, having its origin in a sense of insecurity and inferiority.

In turning to a consideration of the causes of jealousy, as an occa-sional or chronic state of mind of large numbers of the human race, it is necessary to consider two types of causation, one social, one per-sonal. Any society, which places groups of individuals at a disadvan-tage because of racial, religious, or class distinctions, will be laying the groundwork for many jealous citizens. Furthermore, any society, which arranges social or family life so as to provide inevitable clashes of interest of the sort, which cannot be avoided, will be opening the way to jealousy. Examples of this type of clash are those, which arise from primogeniture, emphasis on the blood kin at the expense of the marriage tie, or such social rules as that, which decrees that the eldest daughter must marry first. In this sense jealousy is directly dependent upon social causes; and in proof of it, some primitive peoples are far more jealous than others. Although every homogeneous culture inures those born within its confining walls to an unquestioning acceptance of its most difficult dictates, still some cultures force situations, which produce less pleasant emotions than others.

An example of a culture in which jealousy is a conspicuous characteristic of the normal individual, is the Dobuan culture of the D'Entrecastreaux Islands,[1a] east of New Guinea. Here the stage is set for jealousy and its expression in continual broils and dissension. The people are sorcery ridden and each maternal kin group of some half dozen families live to themselves in little villages where all others—even those married into the group,—are regarded as strangers, and probable witches and sorcerers. There is complete pre-marital freedom, a freedom the exercise of which the old people insist upon by turning all the boys over twelve or thirteen out of the family huts at night. The boy is then forced to wander about among the various villages of his locality—for the girls of his own village are his "sisters"—until he finds some girl who will reply affirmatively to his plaintive jews-harp which he sounds hopefully from house to house. Several years' amorous vagabondage assures a youth's having slept with practically every girl in the locality except those of his own village.[2]

Into this habit of amorous and undiscriminating vagabondage, betrothal intrudes rudely, and not always by mutual consent. It is a fast rule that the boys must be up and away to their own villages by dawn. If a boy oversleeps and the mother of his partner of a night's intrigue, who sleeps in the same hut, considers him a suitable husband for her daughter, she can rise before him and sit in the house door. The villagers, early astir, knowing the significance of a woman's being so seated in her doorway, cluster about to gape rudely at the unfortunate youth who must finally emerge. He is now engaged. He and his fiancée must rigorously avoid each other during the day and meet only clandestinely, as before, at night. But meanwhile the engagement sets up a round of economic exchanges for which the boy and his relatives must work hard. He is away for days, fishing and hunting. And no longer may he even speak to the girls who last week were his careless partners in love. The most strict fidelity is enjoined upon the engaged couple, as upon the married couple, in Dobu. And each partner is tortured by the suspicion that the other is returning to the so recently abandoned amorous adventures.

After marriage a new impetus is given to jealousy. In keeping with the general spirit of jealousy, the young couple are not permitted to settle down either in his village or in hers but are required by custom to live alternate seasons in each of the two villages. Here the one who does not belong to the village is treated as a stranger, must walk humbly, avoiding the names of all the "owners of the village." Meanwhile the vigilance of each spouse has been unflagging. A Dobuan husband follows his wife about everywhere, sits idly by while she does woman's work in the garden, counts her footsteps if she leaves the verandah for the bush. She is never allowed to go to another village alone. Such jealous surveillance, coupled with the strain of a marriage where one spouse is always resident among alien and suspicious kin, combined with the pre-marital habits of license, all combine to produce rather than to prevent infidelity. And here, the man or woman, depending upon which one is resident in their own village, turns to village incest for intrigue—a type of intrigue not tasted before marriage. But where there is such close espionage, inter-village intrigues are hard to manage. Furthermore, a man who has been discovered as the seducer of another man's wife is liable to have a spear thrust in his back. But against his wife's intrigue with one of her village "brothers" a man has no such redress. If he protests, his wife's relatives simply throw him out of the village. Should he slay a member of his wife's village, it would become a "place of blood" to him and he might never enter it again. In desperate case indeed is the man whose wife has betrayed him with a village "brother" and in such case also is the wife of the latter who also is only an in-law and a stranger in the village. In such cases the betrayed spouse has only one resource, a sort of pseudo-suicide in which fish poison, which may or may not be fatal, is taken. The kin of the unfaithful spouse, alarmed lest death will follow which will involve them in a blood feud, may then exercise pressure and reunite the pair. But marriages maintained by attempted suicides against odds such as these, do not make for security and happiness, but rather for suspicion and jealousy.

It is worth noting that this jealous attitude, which the Dobuan displays, bred from intolerable social arrangements, also characterizes his attitudes towards property and trade. He stays up half the night uttering incantations to protect his own yams and to seduce the yams of his neighbour's gardens into his own. If he attains a sudden supply of tobacco as a work boy returning from work for the white man, he will distribute it all, fearful of the jealousy and envy of others should he keep any for himself. He spends his life pitting his magic against the inimical magic of his neighbours, in a state of morbid anxiety and insecurity. Into this house divided against itself, the recruiter steps, perhaps acquiring in one trip a divorced husband who is leaving in furious chagrin and the brother of the former wife who wants to escape the extra work of helping with his divorced sister's garden.

Samoa is keyed to a very different note. Here instead of the tiny hostile kin groups of Dobu, are large villages the members of which are united in formal ceremonial and allegiance to a chief. Instead of the limited and unfruitful garden lands of Dobu, where no amount of spells and hard work will produce a really fine crop, there is fertile land, and enough for all. Although there is freedom before marriage, marriage itself is not viewed primarily as sexual, but as a social contract between individuals who are old enough to turn their attention to more serious matters. Residence is within that household where the young couple fit most perfectly, in terms of temperament or carefully laid plans. Rank is so arranged that there are titles for all of those capable of holding them. And jealousy, as a widespread social phenomenon, is very rare in Samoa. Where it does occur it centres about those points in the system of rank, which result in clashes of interest. So, occasionally, a Samoan wife is violently jealous of another woman who wishes to marry her husband, because as a divorced woman her rank is reduced and she has to sit among the young girls and the wives of untitled men. And in Samoa divorce is far less frequent than in Dobu, where intolerable circumstances breed jealousy, which breeds infidelity and divorce.

When my husband was leaving the Dobuans, the attitude they displayed was characteristic. All other emotions on the part of the men who had been his sailing and living companions for months were obscured by their jealous rage that he should actually choose to leave them. Sullenness, wounded self-esteem, was written on every face. But in Manus, of the Admiralties, where we had both lived for months, the people gathered in the thatched pile house which we were deserting and stood there silent, huddled together, possessing no customary phrase for so drastic a leave taking. But as our canoe was poled, solemnly, by the elders of the village, outside the last row of houses, the people we had left behind beat out upon the great slit drum first the call, which we had used to call our house boys and, second, the death beat. The dignified gesture was not marred by any injured self-esteem. And this perhaps is one of the chief reasons why sophisticated people should wish to ban jealousy from their lives, because it tends to blur the important issues, to obscure the fundamentals of personal relations, to muffle hurt in sullenness, and to deck separations in rags of bitterness and abuse.

But aside from the social causes of jealousy, the sets which decree that a whole people, or a whole class will be ridden by a morbid doubt of keeping their winnings or winning their chosen prizes, there are the special reasons, which predispose a given individual to react jealously to one situation after another. Some of these are purely culturally determined also. On the east coast of Africa, where marriageable girls are kept for months in the "Fatting House" and given a daily massage with butter to improve their physical attractiveness, the girl who refuses to put any weight upon her bones is at a social disadvantage, which may well give her a haunting fear of failure and desertion. Among the Bush Negroes of Dutch Guiana the man who does not know how to carve, who has unfortunately no gift for handiwork will be scorned by the maidens who are in a position to scorn, and be accepted grudgingly by the others. Whatever the mode of beauty or bravery, the style of accepted loverly address or premium upon ability, there will be some individuals who deviate strongly from the desirable type. And these, with rare exceptions, jealousy has marked down for her own.

Consider the historic cases of jealous obsession, and one finds the two causes for insecurity, cultural discrimination against groups and narrow cultural standards of beauty and achievement, as the motivating elements. Othello is perhaps the best example in literature of insecurity born of belonging to a racial group judged inferior by the group from whom he won his wife. Keats is as outstanding an example of the other type of jealousy, as he remarks in the revealing phrase in a letter in which he discusses, the local maidens: "But much they care for Mr. John Keats, five feet and a quarter." I do not claim that matter of race or social status on the one hand, of physique or natural aptitudes on the other are the only causes of the insecurity, which has its expression in morbid jealousy, but they are perhaps the strongest contributory causes to its chronic existence. It does not dignify Othello's jealous emotion to have to read it in terms of racial inferiority rather than the fair letters of true love, and the admirers of Keats could suffer more wholeheartedly with him under Fanny's cruelty were it not for the suspicion that he would have suffered with equal violence over others, because his jealousy was not relevant to Fanny but to himself and his self-doubts.

The only type of jealousy, which can be regarded as strictly relevant to the personality of the lover and which cannot, in final analysis, be reduced to any sort of cultural causes, is the result of bad luck. The individual, who has loved unhappily once, then twice, or perhaps oftener, develops a haunting fear of loss, which is a comment neither upon an accident of birth nor upon his use of his own endowment, but rather upon forces, which are completely out of human control. This same observation applies also to the artist, the scientist, or the businessman, who, starting without any fundamental attitude of insecurity, is beaten into it by ill fortune. With pathetic violence, the unlucky cling to any good fortune, which must of necessity appear to them as one lonely and unreliable spar salvaged from shipwreck. It is to be presumed that there will always be those who through a grain of unfortunate circumstances become chronically unsure and pitifully anxious to hold that which they have. In deprecating jealousy, one must include them, for jealous adds to rather than mitigates their misery, but the revision of social or personal attitudes which give rise to jealousy can do nothing for these unfortunates for whose sake it is necessary to indict, not culture, but the nature of the universe.

It is also revealing to re-examine the terms upon which women have been indicted as "the jealous sex." Throughout history, with a few rare exceptions, women have been the *insecure* sex. Their status, their freedom of action, their very economic existence, their right over their own children, has been dependent upon their preservation of their personal relations with men. Into the field of personal relations have been thrust all these other considerations not germane to it. The wife threatened with the loss of her husband's affection, fidelity, interest, or loyalty, whichever point her society has defined as the pivot of wifely tenure, sees the very roots of her social existence being cut from beneath her. She has been in the position in which a man would be if he had to read in his wife's averted shoulder the depreciation of all his stocks, a loss of his business reputation, eviction from whatever position he holds, both social and political, as well as the loss of his home and possibly of all control over his children. If women's superior morbid anxiety concerning their relations with the all-necessary male purveyors of economic and social goods be read in these terms, it becomes a truism that women probably always have been "the jealous sex." It is also possible that the inescapable fact that women age earlier than men, and are more handicapped by child bearing and child care, will always render them relatively more insecure than men, and therefore relatively more anxious to keep their lovers and husbands. But the disassociation of social, economic, and legal security from the field of personal relations should go a long way towards giving women a security which is as great as that which their culture permits to the men born within it.

Granting that jealousy is undesirable, a festering spot in every personality so afflicted, an ineffective negativistic attitude which is more likely to lose than gain any goal, what are the possibilities if not of eliminating it, at least of excluding it more and more from human life? Samoa has taken one road, by eliminating strong emotion, high stakes, emphasis upon personality, interest in competition. Such a cultural attitude eliminates many of the attitudes, which have afflicted mankind, and perhaps jealousy most importantly of all, but it also pays too high a forfeit for its pleasant serenity. High passion, intensity which produces great mystics and great artists, clash from which is born leadership and enterprise, all these are lacking also. And only the congenitally timid and the chronically disillusioned would want to pay so high a price for peace.

There is, however, another possibility latent in the very trends, which different modern societies are pursuing at the present time. Russia perhaps exemplifies the strongest effort to create social conditions in which no inevitable sting will lie in any accident of race, or economic status.[3] Russia's prophecy of eventual racial and social tolerance, however, holds no promise of relief from the less explicit and more insidious results, which flow from the standards of a homogeneous culture. There is always the possibility of strong selective mating, for instance, upon the basis of physical type or, perhaps, upon the basis of standard temperament. So, for example, Communism does not carry within its inclusive social program any promise of personal security to a short man where height is considered the standard of manly beauty, or to the dreaming, introspective man, where activity and social participation happen to be the standards of temperamental fitness. By offering a coherent, exacting social program which, if it succeeds, will tend to produce a strong homogeneity of attitude, Communism may increase rather than decrease the factors which doom the individual, not by virtue of class or race affiliations, but because of physical or temperamental factors, to a life of morbid anxiety and jealousy.

The other trend, which offers a guarantee of more immunity from accidents, which predispose to jealousy the individual who is short or fat, tongue-tied or undersexed, or deficient in mechanical ability, as the case may be, is the trend towards heterogeneity of culture, such as, is found in great cities. The voluptuous prima donna type of beauty has a chance to compete favourably with the boyish form, the slight, small-featured youth with he of prize fighting build. And as in matters of physical beauty, so in other matters of personal endowment. A variety of reputable professions and acceptable points of view make it possible for many discrepant types to grow up, live and die, without the cankering sense of insecurity, which is at the base of jealousy. Furthermore, because of the variety of national and sectional points of view represented, and because of the possibility of escape into one of these many different groups with sharply contrasting standards, an individual is less handicapped than he or she would be in any smaller or more homogenous group. Matters like height, or relative blondness, or excitability or instability of temperament, can be adjusted by crossing from one group, which draws on Northern European stock, to another of Jewish or Southern European, or vice versa. The girl who revolts against the warm and exacting intimacy of some types of Jewish home need no longer shrink into herself under a stigma of being cold and unresponsive; she can instead carry her fierce reticences among those who make a virtue of meagreness of response. A cosmopolitan city even offers those peculiar groups who welcome any aberrations as original, and so offer soothing refuges to the most bizarre personality types. Even such characteristic sets for jealousy as being undersexed or old may be salved by association with groups who eschew or despise the emphasis upon sexual adjustment and emphasize instead pure intellect or religious ecstasy. In short, the least stratified society, the one which has the fewest social, racial, or religious classes, which has the strongest tendency to stress only humanity, *sui generis,* offers the greatest refuge for those whose jealousy is like that of Othello. But the type of muddling, heterogeneous, multiple standard, many goaled society of a modern, cosmopolitan city, like Paris or New York, offers the best hope of eliminating those types of jealousy, which result from individual differences.

Notes

1. Thurnwald, R., Banaro Society. *Memoirs of the American Anthropological Association.*
1a. Based upon R. F. Fortune's *Sorcerers of Dobu.* Now in press.
2. With the additional provision that those with ringworm mate only with others similarly infected.
3. I say "effort to create" advisedly, for of course under present conditions the old securities are merely the new insecurities and the son of the despised Nepman is being given the type of background suitable to point the role of an Othello.

www.ingramcontent.com/pod-product-compliance
Lightning Source LLC
Chambersburg PA
CBHW060027030426
42334CB00019B/2207